THOMAS HARDY

THOMAS HARDY

*A STUDY OF THE WESSEX NOVELS,
THE POEMS, AND THE DYNASTS*

BY

H. C. DUFFIN

MANCHESTER
UNIVERSITY PRESS

© H. C. Duffin
Published by the University of Manchester at
THE UNIVERSITY PRESS
316–324 Oxford Road, Manchester 13

First published, 1916
Second edition, revised and enlarged, 1921
Third edition, with further revisions and additions, 1937
Reprinted 1962, 1964, 1967

Printed in Great Britain by Butler & Tanner Ltd, Frome and London

PREFATORY NOTE TO THE FIRST EDITION

THE addition of another study of Thomas Hardy to those in existence, including as these do books so forcible and so illuminating as the well-known essays of Lionel Johnson and Mr. Lascelles Abercrombie, seems to call for a word of explanation, perhaps of apology. It might be enough to say that every writer of Hardy's rank offers more stuff for critical apprehension than any one critical intelligence, however supple and penetrating, is likely to exhaust. But, in fact, Mr. Hardy is conspicuous, even among writers of his rank, for complexity of critical appeal—for the wealth of original perception, of challenging thought, of strange and elusive beauty, that lurks under the familiar, almost homely, semblance of his art. He comes before us, decidedly, in " a questionable shape ". There is irony in his kindly openness ; he has thus much, at least, in common with Shakspere (to the author of this volume he seems of yet closer kin) that in the very process of complying with our critical formulas he forces us to revise and expand them. Of such an artist and such a man, a young writer, who has lived for years in intimate companionship with his works, who has served a fairly long apprenticeship in comparative literature study, and who gives his impressions with absolute, even perhaps unchastened, sincerity, may well have something fresh and stimulating to say. These qualities I believe Mr. Duffin's book to possess quite as signally as some other literary studies more completely mature; and as such I venture to commend it to the student of Hardy, to those who love him, and to those, not least, whom he repels.

C. H. HERFORD.

THE UNIVERSITY,
MANCHESTER, *January*, 1916.

NOTE TO THE SECOND EDITION

FROM the reviews of the first edition of this book there stood out two very generally felt opinions—that the chapter called " Development " was a mistake, and that notice should have been taken of Hardy's poetical work. The offending chapter has, in this edition, been removed, and an Appendix on the Poems and *The Dynasts* has been added. I have made the addition in the form of an appendix, among other reasons, because I think Hardy's poetical work—certainly *The Dynasts*—is best considered separately from his prose writings : and this book remains essentially a study of the Novels. Apart from these two features, the book has not been seriously altered, but the text has been revised, and numerous infelicities and im-maturities of expression have been amended. I have left the Introduction unmodified, but if I were writing it now I should probably not consign all the other " modern novelists " besides Hardy and Meredith quite so com-prehensively to the limbo of a speedy oblivion—Stevenson, Butler, Henry James, Conrad, and H. G. Wells might be admitted to have claims upon posterity ; and I fancy the relative estimate of Hardy and Meredith, there stated to be generally held, has been reversed of late years.

Acknowledgment (which was culpably omitted from the first edition) is due to Messrs. Macmillan & Co. for permission to quote illustrative extracts from Hardy's prose and verse throughout, and in particular to include the following complete poems : *At a Lunar Eclipse* and

An August Midnight, from " Poems of the Past and the Present " ; *The Ballad Singer* and *The Division*, from " Time's Laughing Stocks " ; and *In the Room of the Bride-Elect*, from " Satires of Circumstance ".

H. C. D.

DORKING, 1921.

NOTE TO THE THIRD EDITION

SAVE for the addition of the " Appendix on the Poems ",
the second edition of this book did not differ materially
from the first published in 1916. The third edition is
almost a new book. It is much larger. The " running
commentary " is now for the first time here, and I hope
will be found of interest and value. The chapters of the
two sections on the " art " and " philosophy " of the novels
have all been enlarged by the accretion of fresh illustrative
material and by the consideration of sub-aspects formerly
unregarded. And the poetry has been treated more com-
prehensively, so that the section devoted to it has been
allowed to shake off the stigmatic title of " appendix ".

But there is a further change, possibly more important than one of size. The book no longer merits
the description of " the impressions of a young writer "
given to it in the kindly introduction written for it twenty
years ago by the late Professor Herford (to whose green
memory and growing reputation I desire to pay my sincere
tribute). For the purpose of this new edition I have
re-read the novels and the poems, and the estimates and
opinions now offered are those of middle age, not those
of the middle twenties. Not that I am claiming any
superiority—any nearer approximation to truth, any higher
critical wisdom—for these later views. If we did not know
it before, Dr. Ernest de Selincourt's publication of the
Prelude of 1805 showed us that the process of the years
may dull the spiritual faculties even while it brightens the

art that gives them a voice. Naturally some of the views expressed in the earlier editions of this study seem to me now stupid or extravagant, and I am glad to have the opportunity of expressing others ; but when I was twenty-five I should have thought these others flat where I did not think them preposterous. Neither view-point commands the whole country.

At the same time, I feel tolerably sure that experience in life *is* an advantage, even an essential, for the full under-standing of Hardy. And though I am prepared to let most of what I said such a long time ago stand on the same footing with what I say now, there is just one thing that I would wish blotted out from those earlier editions— the position there taken up with regard to Tess's " sin ", which reached its nadir in the cold assertion that " if that is so, all that ' the woman pays ' is justified ". Of that monstrous and perverted judgment I am heartily ashamed ; and I have done what I could in the way of atonement here.

In addition to the poems quoted by permission in the second edition, two further poems, *A Broken Appointment* and *By the Barrows*, are now reprinted from " The Collected Poems of Thomas Hardy," by permission of the author's Executors and Messrs. Macmillan & Co., Ltd. I have to thank Mrs. Hardy for her kind permission to make references to, and a limited number of quotations from, her two invaluable biographical volumes. I have not always mentioned Mrs. Hardy's volumes at the moment of quoting, but all quotations and references will be found collected in the Index under the heading, *The Early Life* and *The Later Years*.

H. C. D.

HOVE, 1937.

CONTENTS

CONTENTS

CHRONOLOGY AND CLASSIFICATIONS

FOLLOWING are the dates of publication of the Wessex Novels :—

Desperate Remedies	1871
Under the Greenwood Tree	1872
A Pair of Blue Eyes	1873
Far from the Madding Crowd	1874
The Hand of Ethelberta	1876
The Return of the Native	1878
The Trumpet-Major	1880
A Laodicean	1881
Two on a Tower	1882
The Mayor of Casterbridge	1886
The Woodlanders	1887
Tess of the D'Urbervilles	1891
The Well-Beloved	1892
Jude the Obscure	1895

Hardy classified the novels as under :—

I. *Novels of Character and Environment*—
Under the Greenwood Tree, Far from the Madding Crowd, The Return of the Native, The Mayor of Casterbridge, The Woodlanders, Tess of the D'Urbervilles, Jude the Obscure.

II. *Romances and Fantasies*—
A Pair of Blue Eyes, The Trumpet-Major, Two on a Tower, The Well-Beloved.

III. *Novels of Ingenuity and Experiment*—
Desperate Remedies, The Hand of Ethelberta, A Laodicean.

Another grouping might be :—

Tragedies—

> Jude the Obscure, Tess of the D'Urbervilles, The Return of the Native, The Mayor of Casterbridge.

Tragi-comedies—

> Desperate Remedies, A Pair of Blue Eyes, Far from the Madding Crowd, Two on a Tower, The Woodlanders.

Comedies—

> Under the Greenwood Tree, The Hand of Ethelberta, The Trumpet-Major (or does this belong to the tragi-comedies ?), A Laodicean, The Well-Beloved.

The four volumes of short stories were published :—

Wessex Tales	1888
A Group of Noble Dames	1891
Life's Little Ironies	1894
A Changed Man, etc.	1913

The dates of the poetry volumes are as follows :—

Wessex Poems	1898
Poems of the Past and the Present	1902
Time's Laughing Stocks	1909
Satires of Circumstance	1914
Moments of Vision	1917
Late Lyrics and Earlier	1922
Human Shows, Far Phantasies	1925
Winter Words	1928

The Dynasts was published :—

Part I	1903
Part II	1906
Part III	1908

and *The Famous Tragedy of the Queen of Cornwall* in 1923.

THE NOVELS

I. A RUNNING COMMENTARY
ON THE NOVELS IN CHRONOLOGICAL ORDER

§ I

APPRENTICESHIP

*Desperate Remedies ; Under the Greenwood Tree ; A Pair
of Blue Eyes*

To call any of Hardy's novels except *Desperate Remedies* the work
of an apprentice seems presumptuous. For *Under the Greenwood
Tree* is, though a slight book, a perfect one, and *A Pair of Blue
Eyes*, if imperfect, is a great novel. Nevertheless, Hardy's business was the production of masterpieces, and his first masterpiece
was *Far from the Madding Crowd ;* which fact justifies us in
regarding the three novels that preceded as in some sense preparatory.

There is something of Hardy's own irony in the fact that out
of the advice given by George Meredith to Thomas Hardy should
have come the novel *Desperate Remedies.* The first, lost, novel,
The Poor Man and the Lady, appears to have been a revolutionary
satire. *Desperate Remedies*, if sent to a publisher to-day, would
be marked by the reader as a likely Crime Club ' Book of the
Month '. The crime and mystery elements are rich and satisfying, and the amateur detective activities of Springrove and Owen
Gray would require but a moderate degree of further development to bring them up to modern standards. The defect that
the two principal problems are not sufficiently obscured could be
very easily rectified. These problems are the nature of the
connection between Manston and Miss Aldclyffe, and the reason

for Manston's pretence that his wife is still alive, though this prevents him from marrying Cytherea, whom he desperately loves. Writing for the uninstructed 'seventies, Hardy thought it necessary to furnish clues, slight enough to be missed by all but the brightest of the Victorians but staringly obvious to our crime-trained intelligences ; and the present-day publisher's reader would suggest the darkening or complete removal of these hints. It is astonishing that Hardy, the writer of the thirteen ' Wessex Novels ' that followed, should have made this particular kind of false start, but the important thing is that he realised at once not only that novels of this kind gave scope for little but ' ingenuity ', but that certain parts of the book stood out like oases in a desert. These were some half-dozen passages of rustic dialogue, so exquisitely easy and unforced as to read like dicta-phone records of actual conversations, yet artistically so perfect, and so vital in substance, that they could have come from the mouths of none but Olympian rustics. Here at least was a vein worth working. The novel that succeeded *Desperate Remedies* consists largely of such rustic scenes, strung on a slender story of Arcadian passion ; and Hardy kept the genre going with unfailing power almost to the end (it is missing from *Jude the Obscure*, for a variety of reasons). In respect of this kind of writing, he had little to learn : his mastery was complete from the beginning, and at least two of the rustic scenes in *Desperate Remedies* (those in VII. 3 and XIII. 2) are as good as almost anything in the later novels.

The only other way in which *Desperate Remedies* is recognis-ably Hardian is in the pinning together of the plot by coincidences and accidental happenings. Cytherea advertises for a situation, and the one reply comes from a woman who presently turns out to have been the lost love of Cytherea's father. When Manston consults a time-table with the object of meeting his wife's train he overlooks a ' shunting ' sign and meets the wrong train—with enormously complicated results. All Cytherea's efforts to avoid being married on a Friday are in vain : the inevitability with which the fatal day bears down upon her is quite in Hardy's manner. Springrove, whose long-standing and apparently in-violable engagement to Adelaide Hinton has drawn Cytherea into the arms of Manston, is set free (unknown to Cytherea) the day before her marriage ; he arrives at the church (by reason of the Friday contretemps just mentioned) as the married couple leave the vestry ; and the information that Manston's first wife is still living comes to hand a few hours after the honeymoon departure. But there is little evidence of the master hand that was so soon to be Hardy's. The machinery of the intricate plot is not too well oiled, and there is crudity in the method of discovering some of the necessary facts—as of those given by Manston in XIII. 3 to the woman masquerading as his wife. The chief characters have originality of conception and are carefully studied, but they seldom come alive : Cytherea's force of character and Manston's ungovernable passion are well shown, and provide the germ of later successes. The style begins by being clumsy and inexact, and though it improves later it never achieves more than a straightforward pedestrianism. Nature, that presently grew to almost Wordsworthian proportions in the Hardian scheme, is a thing of incidental mention here : but we must notice that water-butt, into which Manston gazed, with its myriads of happily sporting creatures—a forerunner of the heath-pool observed by Mrs. Yeobright ; and the analysis of rain-sounds at night, reminiscent of the classical passage, also in *The Return of the Native*, about wind-voices on Egdon.

> The rain now came down heavily, but they pursued their path with alacrity, the produce of the several fields between which the lane wound its way being indicated by the peculiar character of the sound emitted by the falling drops. Sometimes a soaking hiss proclaimed that they were passing by a pasture, then a patter would show that the rain fell upon some large-leafed root-crop, then a paddling plash announced the naked arable.

The deliberateness with which Hardy took hold of the rustic theme with the intention of making it characteristically his own is shown by the opening of *Under the Greenwood Tree*, with its careful nature observation (including those tree-voices that interested him right through to *The Woodlanders*), its conscientious description of the Mellstock villages, and its minute study of those of the inhabitants who are to form the staple of the book's interest. Much of the writing has a Georgic-like closeness to earth : or it reminds one again of those lovingly faithful drawings

that Hardy made for the *Wessex Poems*. Gradually the perfection
of the thing grows upon you : line by line the rustic group is being
built up ; and presently you are listening to the first of its many
colloquies.

The rustic group of *Under the Greenwood Tree* is the Mellstock
choir : old Grandfather William Dewy, his son Reuben, the
tranter, and Dick Dewy, Reuben's son ; Michael Mail, Robert
Penny, Elias Spink, and Joseph Bowman, with a merely musical
appendage, not otherwise important, in poor lath-like Thomas
Leaf. There are similar groups in most of the other novels, the
most notable being those of *Far from the Madding Crowd*, *The
Return of the Native*, and *The Mayor of Casterbridge*. They are
differently constituted—farm-labourers, malt-worms, town-idlers
—and apart from some tendency to repetition among the peasants
of *The Return of the Native* and those of *Far from the Madding
Crowd*, each group is strongly differentiated, the one indispensable
common quality being a mellow crustedness. These men and
women—there is an occasional woman, like Mother Cuxsom in
The Mayor of Casterbridge, but they are chiefly old and middle-
aged men—know life as a housewife knows her kitchen. They
have their daily work, but their business, their preoccupation, is
with life and human nature, which they see through the clear
country air with a humorous and not seldom a cynical eye. To
their humour we shall return, but it is their function as critics
that gives these rustic groups an almost unique importance.
They play no part in the action ; they stand aloof, interested yet
detached, and offer their humorous, cynical commentary on the
principal actors and their doings. Even if one of them, like
John Smith in *A Pair of Blue Eyes*, is the father of the hero, he
preserves the same impersonal attitude. The group has a sort of
collective mind, each member contributing his angle of observation ; and the collective judgment affords a tolerably shrewd
summation of objective truth. Occasionally a group is used to
give us information of certain things that are going on, things
that would be naturally known to these onlookers : it is thus that
we hear of the preparation for the ' skimmity ride ' in *The Mayor
of Casterbridge ;* or of things that are past, as of Grace's dead
mother in *The Woodlanders*.

The function of these rustic groups is closely parallel to that of the Greek chorus, the main difference being that the humorous detachment of the Hardian chorus-group generally precludes the sympathy with the fortunes of the active characters so frequently shown by the Hellenic prototype.

In *Under the Greenwood Tree*, where the new theme is being given a more extended treatment than it afterwards received, the choir becomes a collective entity, one of the actors in the village drama ; and their struggle to retain the time-honoured orchestra and keep out the intruding organ interests us far more than the love story which is the book's other subject : the interview with the Vicar has an epic quality, and is as thrilling as the knight's fight with the dragon to save the princess. But even here the group has more of a reflective than an active character : its action consists in the presentation of a point of view, and the choir is content with having presented it ; fate is not diverted, only a little postponed. For the rest, they make music, which is another kind of meditation ; and the first carol-singing chapter is a classic piece as faultless as one of those Dutch paintings to which the title-page refers us.

Upon this vivid, strongly-painted background the pale little love story of Dick Dewy and Fancy Day appears almost as an intrusion (like the ' human-interest ' the film-producers wanted to put into Wells's *Outline of History*—' a boy and girl wandering down the ages '). Nevertheless there is much cunning in the way in which the heroine is introduced, *via* a dainty boot in the pocket of Penny the shoemaker, the candle flame approaching the window-blind, and a vision of beauty that makes an anti-climax of the minx-like character of the young woman as it presently develops.

The limited aim of *Under the Greenwood Tree* prevents it from taking a place among the ' great ' novels, but within its limits it has a perfection achieved by none of the masterpieces. Its position is rather like that of *Youth*, though it does not represent Hardy's many-sidedness so fully as that other short but perfect tale stands for the genius of Conrad.

If in writing *Under the Greenwood Tree* Hardy learnt to use his rural background and his rustic chorus, he showed for the first time in *A Pair of Blue Eyes* that he could handle character on a large scale. Here, too, we first meet that prose style that presently became characteristic of Hardy in his tragic mood. It appears in the second half of the book, after the cliff-adventure, and might almost seem to have been acquired in the process of writing that magnificent scene. The earlier part of the book is often naïve and ineffective in its descriptions (though narrative and dialogue have a confident strength). The book is, on the whole, a ' society ' novel, and Hardy, whose native genius ran on other lines, was not yet at his ease with this kind—things were different by the time he reached the next ' society ' novel, *The Hand of Ethelberta*.

We see Elfride, the butterfly, full of sparkling shallow life, born for happiness, but destined to be broken on the wheel of a man's egotism. And we see Stephen Smith, her counterpart in everything except birth, the man she could have been happy with. The mystery of his parentage is more effective on a second reading, as the mystery is not intended for the reader but for Mr. Swancourt and his daughter. The accumulation of his ignorances, partial or complete—of chess, Latin quantities, riding, sauces, wine—is full of interest, and afterwards inspires the Vicar's angry epigram : " An unedified palate is the irrepressible cloven hoof of the upstart ".

Stephen's love-making is trivial and passionless, but not unreal in view of his youth and inexperience. Not for the last time we must beware of measuring the loves of Hardy's young people against those of the moderns, with their behaviour and their feelings artificially stimulated by the cinema and the post-war convention of unrestrained passion. In the same way, Elfride's prim reception of his modest advances seems annoyingly unnecessary, but after all, she is the daughter of a country clergyman, and mid-Victorian at that, so that it is second nature with her to check Stephen even while she wants him to go on. The artificiality vanishes at a touch of alarm, turning into charming simplicity and eventuating in ' Elfride's first kiss ' :—

And so awkward and unused was she ; full of striving—no relenting. There was none of those apparent struggles to get out of the trap which only result in getting further in : no final attitude of receptivity : no easy close of shoulder to shoulder, hand upon hand, face upon face, and, in spite of coyness, the lips in the right place at the supreme moment. That graceful though apparently accidental falling into position, which many have noticed as precipitating the end and making sweethearts the sweeter, was not here. Why? Because experience was absent. A woman must have had many kisses before she kisses well.

The same thought as to the difference between the Victorian and the modern novel comes again when Elfride and Stephen talk of the probability that they will be torn apart. In a modern novel, in these circumstances, if the young people managed to prevent their emotions culminating in physical union, it would only be at the expense of obvious agonies of repression : in ' pornographic ' Hardy the idea that they ought to be burning with frustrated desire never enters the heads of the lovers. And presently, when they make their ineffective attempt to get married (the first sounding of the ' secret marriage ' motif), Hardy knows that it is not passion but impulse and emotion, accident and circumstance, that control life at these as at other moments.

We have a glimpse of Hardy's terrifying powers of ironic situation in the scene where Stephen extracts, word by word, from Elfride the confession that she had a previous lover, who was now dead, and who lay buried under the very gravestone on which they were sitting. Narrative and dialogue are pared to the bone. The scene, like earlier ones, is darkened by the persistent and intriguing shadow of Henry Knight, and presently fate draws to a point, where, in the Row, Lord Luxellian looks at Elfride with frank admiration, and Knight, in the crowd, observes her with quiet and critical interest. Knight comes into Elfride's life, and with the " inevitability of gradualness " acquires complete dominance over her mind and feelings. Two of the stages are achieved in a way very characteristic of Hardy. Hardy makes a number of his men use some special device for inducing emotion in the heart of the women they want. Manston in *Desperate Remedies* used the piano, Troy in *Far from the Madding Crowd* uses the less commonplace broadsword, and we shall note others. Here Knight employs his ruthless superiority in chess to make the first breach in Elfride's defences. The second stage, which brings Knight and Elfride passionately together, is rather a device of fate than of human choosing—the adventure on the cliff.

The scene is marvellously written, in the deliberate manner.

Hardy is rather obviously out to make us see and feel every moment of the intensely dramatic episode, and he succeeds terrifyingly. He adopts a short and sudden style for the first part—Knight's fall, up to the point where Elfride is struck by her brilliant idea and vanishes from his sight, leaving him " in the presence of impersonalised loneliness ", after which the narrative proceeds with cruel deliberation. Elfride, too, was cruel, again because of her Victorian prudery. A modern girl would have eased Knight's mind by telling him what she was going to do— to tear up her underclothing and make a rope of it : on the other hand only a Victorian girl would have been wearing enough underclothing to make a rope ! After the rescue, and the embrace in which the tension breaks, the narrative moves swiftly again.

The relation between Elfride and Knight presently becomes a preliminary sketch of the story of Tess and Angel Clare. Elfride's lapse has, of course, been less serious than Tess's ; but then Knight's life has been, as he says, so " absurdly " unspotted that he, unlike Clare, has some right to expect his fancy for an in-experienced wife to be realised. Tess, the greater woman, confesses her fault ; Elfride obstinately keeps her smaller one to herself : the result is precisely the same in both cases. The series of scenes in which Knight slowly discovers the truth for himself are done with power and perfection. The first is full of dramatic irony, as Knight calmly insists that Elfride is even more in-experienced than himself. The last, in which the full ' truth ' of her association with Smith is at last forced from her, is as cruel as anything in the novels earlier than Tess. Perhaps the note of high tragedy is lacking because of the slightness of Elfride's character, and, above all, the preposterousness of Knight's wooden intolerance.

> It is a melancholy thought, says Hardy, that men who at first will not allow the verdict of perfection they pronounce upon their sweethearts or wives to be disturbed by God's own testimony to the contrary, will, once suspecting their purity, morally hang them upon evidence they would be ashamed to admit in judging a dog.

Elfride's fatal secretiveness—" I dared not tell you : I loved you too well "—is easily understandable in view of her youth and her timid, sensitive personality. Again, knowing what actually happened, we feel that Elfride was silly to leave unmodified the simple yes and no of the conclusion of the miserable catechism :—

" Elfride . . . tell me truly one thing more. Were you alone with him ? "
" Yes."
" Did you return home the same day on which you left it ? "
" No."

The laconic replies are not dictated, as they might well have been, by indignant pride, but by " utter despair of being able to explain matters ". A granddaughter of Elfride's would have cleared up the point in two words, but Elfride simply doesn't know what Knight is thinking, and wouldn't have known how to put him right if she had. Knight, too, is afflicted with the narrowest Victorian prejudice : what finally prevents him from relenting is the thought that " the proprieties " are a dead letter with Elfride.

Tess of the D'Urbervilles ends in appalling tragedy, *A Pair of Blue Eyes* in stark Hardian comedy—the quarrel of the two suitors, Knight and Smith, once friends, and their discovery that Elfride is dead, and has died Lady Luxellian.

§ 2

THE FIRST MASTERPIECE ; A REST ; AND ANOTHER MASTERPIECE

*Far from the Madding Crowd ; The Hand of Ethelberta ;
The Return of the Native*

It was Hardy's practice—not perhaps deliberate, but it worked out that way—to intersperse his major novels with novels of a lighter kind (those belonging to his second and third categories), using these as recreative exercises preparatory to the greater achievements. In this group we have a brilliant but facile story between two novels whose creation would have put a severe strain on any writer's imaginative and intellectual resources.

Far from the Madding Crowd is Hardy's first masterpiece ; and it went near to being his greatest. Only *Tess* surpasses it, and for sheer Hardian quality I doubt whether even *The Mayor*, even *Jude*, quite reaches the wonderful heights of this first wonder of all. The opening chapter is memorable for a picture as ever-lastingly beautiful as a Constable landscape—of Bathsheba on the halted wagon, with Gabriel Oak unseen but critically observant, the whole scene steeped in colour and sunlight. Our heroine is introduced to us by means of an act of charming vanity ; Gabriel, the hero, by a particularly bold piece of description : after giving an almost absurdly comic account of his face and his prehistoric watch, Hardy triumphantly wipes out the effect by a quiet insistence on spiritual factors of a high order, and a reminder that a somewhat uncouth exterior " may be said to be a defect in an individual if he depends for his valuation more upon his appearance than upon his capacity to wear well, which Oak did not ". The chapter, with its fresh, clear atmosphere, is followed by the classic ' Norcombe Hill by Night ', which passes from pure description to a moving picture of lambing operations—one glows as one reads : this is epic, this is earth, this is eternal ; and all is done with quiet deliberate beauty. After it comes the equally famous and perfect ' pastoral tragedy ', our first full sight of Hardy, the animal lover.

Meanwhile there have been some further preliminary encounters between Gabriel and Bathsheba, all on a pointedly comic level. There seems little promise of romance here : if this is Arden, these two are almost Touchstone and Audrey—only we remember what stature these rustic figures are ultimately to attain. Indeed, once these light preliminaries are over (and who would regret them ?)—once Gabriel has crashed, owing to the disastrous joking of the dog George, we start again in serious mood, the position of Gabriel and Bathsheba reversed, and both the man and the girl dignified by the reversal.

We see something of Gabriel in action, at the hiring fair, where attention is drawn to his basic quality, " indifference to fate ", and at the fire in Bathsheba's rick-yard (prophetic of the even greater storm episode of a later chapter), as a result of which he enters Bathsheba's service as a shepherd. About the same time we have our first sight of Farmer Boldwood, one of Oak's rivals for the love of Bathsheba. Unlike Oak he is of impressive appearance, and attracts Bathsheba by his superiority and his aloofness

—very much as Knight scored over Stephen Smith with Elfride. But whereas Knight was a cold intellectual, Boldwood is a man of overmastering passion, and the ' valentine ' which Bathsheba, in a fit of spring folly, sends him, lights a flame that eventually burns him up. There is a flippancy about the manner in which Boldwood's tragic fate is set, but Hardy, contriver of fate, speaks with majestic pity and understanding : " So very idly and un-reflectingly was this deed done. Of love as a spectacle Bathsheba had a fair knowledge : but of love subjectively she knew nothing." Troy, too, the third of Bathsheba's suitors, makes his appearance, waiting for the bride who arrived too late, and by his proud quiet bearing arousing a sympathy he does not deserve and does not long retain. Fanny Robin, the missing bride (who ought not to have mistaken the church on such an occasion !) is a flowery figure, and an earlier glimpse of her has already sealed her for deep pathos. Gabriel had met her, a stranger, creeping penniless into Weatherbury, and as he gives her a shilling there comes one of those earth-touches that exalt this book : " Gabriel's fingers alighted on the young woman's wrist. It was beating with a throb of tragic intensity. He had frequently felt the same quick, hard beat in the femoral artery of his lambs when overdriven."

For some time now Boldwood's strong personality holds the field. Hardy devotes a whole chapter to an analysis of his character : I believe he does this for no one else except for Eustacia Vye, the only woman—indeed the only character—in Hardy whose passionate nature can be paralleled with Boldwood's. Boldwood has a simplicity of nature that ennobles him far beyond Eustacia, and which colours the finely handled scene that presently takes place between him and Bathsheba :—

" I feel—almost too much—to think," he said, with a solemn simplicity. " I have come to speak to you without preface. My life is not my own since I have beheld you clearly, Miss Everdene—I come to make you an offer of marriage."

And then, as if to set these two great men side by side, Hardy gives us an equally fine scene between Bathsheba and Gabriel Oak, in which Oak's superb calm and moral integrity result in his angry dismissal from Bathsheba's service.

Now into Bathsheba's life, one would have supposed sufficiently enriched by Boldwood's passionate and Oak's patient

devotion, there comes the trumpery Troy and his lady-killing
attractiveness, heralded, in Hardy's fashion, by her singing of the
ballad, " For his bride a soldier sought her ".   For all his gallant
array of heroines more than half-divine, Hardy is something of a
cynic where women's behaviour is concerned, and this, I suppose,
accounts for Bathsheba's instant succumbing to Troy, when she
is almost pledged to Boldwood and knows Oak's unchanging love.
Of course it is our inside knowledge of Troy that makes him
appear one of the meanest of Hardy's figures, yet Bathsheba was,
at bottom, a great woman, and she had a standard of comparison
in Oak and Boldwood, and Troy ought to have rung false.
Nevertheless, the scene in the plantation, unpleasant as it is, has
a certain veracity.   It is probably nothing but convention that
makes one feel that a woman ought to resent being told by a
stranger that she is beautiful, and the fact that Troy's methods
are crude need not trouble us since Bathsheba is no ' lady '.
Later, as the monstrous wooing proceeds, one understands her
state of mind better.   Oak, as a candidate for her hand, has passed
out of her mind ; Boldwood's persistence is a nightmare.   Yet her
young life is full of thoughts of love, and Troy has caught her at
the crisis.   And having fascinated her by a dare-devilry which
to a woman of breeding would have been offensive, he completes
his conquest with his broadsword, in one of those passages of
natural magic to which reference has been made.   After many
distracted fears which show that her instinct is sounder than her
wishes, she marries Troy secretly.

  Meanwhile Boldwood's huge passionate nature looms ever
more darkly over the story, for his brooding and his desperate
desire have fostered an element of madness in his mind.   Oak,
on the other hand, continues to deserve the phrase, " the faithful
man ", which attaches to him as " *pius Aeneas* " to the Trojan.
In the great scene of the storm that threatens to destroy
Bathsheba's farm his steady work on the stacks is worth more
than some wild emotional " I would die for you ", as Bathsheba
realises.   After the two have worked together to save the stacks,
only time and opportunity are needed to make them husband and
wife.   The storm is magnificently done, and though at one point
it is said that " love, life, everything human, seemed small and
trifling in such close juxtaposition with an infuriated universe ",

the figure of Oak rises grander than the storm, like that of the little captain in *Typhoon*. And when heaven opens in " a perfect dance of death ", before the stupefying crash comes Gabriel notices " how strangely the red feather of Bathsheba's hat shines in this light ".

Fanny Robin comes back into the story, to die. Bathsheba's arrangements for her funeral breathe the smell of that older, lovelier England. Immediately afterwards she discovers that with Fanny in the coffin is a baby, her child by Troy. There follows a marvellous scene, first of Bathsheba and then of Troy and his wife, by the body of the dead girl. Troy shows a trace of finer sentiment—but it is the (perhaps sincere) posturing of a man who had no pity for the one woman and has none for the other now. His mood is continued into the remarkable chapter called " Troy's Romanticism ", where he lovingly plants Fanny's grave with flowers. But nature will not have this facile and belated repentance, and washes out the whole of Troy's labour. One cannot imagine this chapter of " The Gurgoyle " being done better : the cruel desecration advances upon the mind, as upon the grave, with an awful certainty. Troy himself presently goes swimming in the sea and is carried off by a current : this is not pure fortuitousness ; it is nature again intervening, as it does at so many critical moments in Hardy.

Bathsheba has been through the fire, and now at length begins to show the metal she is made of. The woman who restores Fanny's grave is a noble development from the girl who preened herself in the mirror and sent Farmer Boldwood the valentine. Oak, too, has risen—slowly as a growth of nature ; but his change has been mainly an expansion with widening fortunes : Oak, the bailiff of two farms, riding his cob over two thousand acres, is clearly the same man who stood to be hired at Casterbridge Fair. He has achieved, and is to achieve further, by waiting— again in nature's way. Even when he is almost invited by Bathsheba to speak again of love he makes no move, knowing the time is not yet : and there is enough of the old Bathsheba left to feel an " insect sting " at his cool unresponsiveness. Bold- wood, on the other hand, restored to hope by the disappearance of Troy, will not remain passive, and his wringing from Bathsheba of a conditional promise is a dangerous forcing of fate. The reappearance of Troy a few minutes after Boldwood, having placed a ring on Bathsheba's unwilling finger, has said, " I am happy now. God bless you," has a look of mechanism ; but, being aware of this, Hardy prepares the coincidence with minute care, so that the event when it happens is tremendously effective. Certainly the shooting of Troy is a most satisfying solution to that problem, although it leaves, as a painful consequence, an exceedingly ragged end in the fact that Boldwood, a fine and sympathetic character, must be, not indeed hanged, but " confined during his Majesty's pleasure ".

Once again Bathsheba draws strength from affliction. While all the others huddle back from the spectacle of sudden death, she takes command, and Gabriel accepts her orders, only remembering afterwards that he ought to have given some himself. But it is in character, not in understanding, that Bathsheba is great. Troy had been utterly worthless, and she knew it, and his death altered nothing of that : yet from her actions now it appears that she loved him.

The last chapters, where Gabriel and Bathsheba find beauty in loneliness by breaking it in two, have a sunset peace in which we see the loveliest side of Hardy's outlook on life : his faith in that *camaraderie*, the product of experience endured side by side, which alone can make love strong as death. It is also the logical and long-foreseen end of the story : this is where fate, character and the fitness of things have been leading.

The book is one of those few among the Wessex Novels in which beauty is commensurate with greatness. The action passes against a rich background of pasture and byre, sheep-fair and sheep-farm. And when we add to all this the constant and expert use of one of the grandest of the chorus groups—Smallbury, the aged maltster, with Jacob and William his son and grandson, Joseph Poorgrass of the saintly profile (of whom it was told that he once said ' sir ' to an owl), Jan Coggan, ' Henery ' Fray, Mark Clark and Matthew Moon—we find we have a pattern woven so cunningly of love, courage and death, beauty, humour and the basic meaning of life, that the annals of creative fiction will not often provide its equal.

Two years elapsed between the publication of *Far from the Madding Crowd* and that of *The Hand of Ethelberta*. It is certainly desirable that something like this period should interpose between the reading of the two books. To read *The Hand of Ethelberta* immediately after *Far from the Madding Crowd* is to find the surroundings irritating and the story nauseatingly dull. Not that the story is really uninteresting, but it must be admitted that even the third-rate moderns do this kind of thing better, with a liveliness that goes some way to justify poverty of content. However, it is the sudden contrast with the strong deep lines of its great predecessor that makes the intrigue and the petty motives of the book seem without significance : taken by itself the story is seen to be contrived with great skill. Its chief character-interest lies with the family of the heroine—her butler-father, her artisan brothers, and her younger sister Picotee. Ethelberta herself is powerfully drawn, and there is subtlety in the figure of old Lord Mountclere, the Marquis of Steyne of this later *Vanity Fair*. The story-interest is divided between Ethelberta's man-œuvres to get into high society and keep there ; and the race for her hand run by Julian, Neigh and Ladywell (at this time Hardy liked a triple male grouping : we have seen it twice before, and it appears again in *The Trumpet Major* amd *A Laodicean*, but not afterwards). Julian, who is perhaps the ' hero ' of the story, eventually marries Ethelberta's sister Picotee. Hardy had a tenderness for ' younger sisters '—it comes out again in 'Liza-'Lu Durbeyfield—and Picotee is made a very charming character, a much fitter mate for Julian than her terrifying sister. Ethelberta herself is snatched from under the eyes of the three by Lord Mountclere, who comes late into the story and revives its flagging interest. He is very much what Ethelberta deserves : rich, cultured, amenable—but given to dithering over fashion-plates. Before the marriage we have the familiar converging lines of a lesser Hardian situation, meeting in the church with the signatures of the married pair drying on the page.

The low key of the book is due to the habitual repression of emotion required by social tone : however impatient, these people do not stamp lest they disturb the floor below ; when inclined to smash the furniture, a lifted eyebrow serves their need. This sublimation is ' a Good Thing ', and a rock on which civilisation is built. But, except with great natures, emotions constantly repressed become atrophied ; and one ceases to believe that these characters have any real feelings at all. Hardy indeed denies this, and makes Ethelberta discover " a truth which she had been in danger of forgetting ", namely that " the town gentleman was not half so far removed from Sol and Dan, and the hard-handed order in general, in his passions as in his philosophy. He still continued to be the male of his species, and when the heart was hot with a dream Pall Mall had much the same aspect as Wessex." However, as in this case the " passion " and the " hot dream " have led to nothing more than that Neigh has " pressed Ethelberta's fingers more warmly than she thought she had given him warrant for ", it need not disturb the general thesis, which is of course part of the satiric picture of society that gives the novel its background.

Perhaps the most remarkable passage in the book is that in which Ethelberta coolly weighs her chances and her motives in deciding to marry Lord Mountclere rather than Julian, Neigh or Ladywell—" to commit her sin thoroughly if she committed it at all ". She seeks assistance from a book of Utilitarian ethics and an old treatise on Casuistry, and the intellectual process involved is not unworthy to be set side by side with the more inspired psychology of the ' country ' novels.

However, the final impression left by *The Hand of Ethelberta* is that it would make a first-rate film story. It is surprising that the producers, who tried one or two others of the Hardy novels, and had to leave out everything that mattered, should have missed this one, where all is on the surface, all is good screen incident, and there is a magnificent ' gold-digger's ' part for the star !

With *The Return of the Native* we are back on true Wessex ground : and this in a special sense. *The Return of the Native* is the book of Egdon Heath ; without Egdon it would not hold together. With most of the other novels the scene could be transposed to some other part of Wessex without vitally affecting the story : this story could not run its course anywhere other than amid the solitudes of Egdon. Egdon influences all the human characters, moving them to love or to hate, to despair or to the philosophic mind. Even pretty Tamsie, to whom it is just " a ridiculous old place ", confesses she could live nowhere else. And as if he had put so much life into Egdon that he had less to expend on the human figures, Hardy has given us here a set of characters not quite so high in the scale of being as those of *Far from the Madding Crowd*. If we place Yeobright, Venn and Wildeve over against Oak, Boldwood and Troy, the difference will be apparent ; and Eustacia, for all her splendour, is shoddy stuff to Bathsheba. Bathsheba stooped to Troy—she would never have sunk to Wildeve.

When Egdon has been set before us with all Hardy's unmatched powers of description, humanity is introduced in such a way as to leave the spell unbroken : the fantastic reddleman and his unexplained preoccupation ; the anomalous old naval officer ; mysterious figures on the barrow ; the woman momentarily queen of the solitude, then vanishing into Egdon's shade. Nevertheless, the opening of this novel is not so miraculous as that of *Far from the Madding Crowd* : it is conscious, deliberate, not a " growth of the soil ". So the marvellous description of Eustacia that comes presently is the product of an art less exquisite than that by which Bathsheba was shown in one bright flash. Eustacia herself is an otherwise unexampled type in Hardy : a woman who lives to love, and to love in a hot, blind, lustful way—not necessarily an animal way, but a way that leads to ' anything in trousers ', even to Wildeve. For Wildeve is really pitiful, and Eustacia's intrigues with him are painfully squalid. Troy, at least, had some glamour of tinsel and swordsmanship about him, but this man keeps a public-house called " The Quiet Woman ". Troy was (however inexplicably) fascinating ; Wildeve makes even Eustacia yawn. He provokes the simile of " a dancing master ", but is more like a tailor's dummy, in his " elegant new summer suit and light hat ". In a sense she uses him only as an instrument, but she is throughout attracted, and the fact robs her of some interest.

Eustacia is a strange enough personality to demand something of the bizarre in her story, and this element is provided by Diggory Venn, the Reddleman, a blood-red figure, isolated and aloof. He has his own hand to play, for the winning of Tamsie, but intervenes at a number of critical points in the larger action. Like Oak he is still and deep ; like him he is passive and unselfish, though more purposefully, less patiently so.

The second stage of the story begins with the return of Clym Yeobright from Paris. He has been a diamond merchant's

2

manager, and towards the end of the book he evolves an educational ideal which in practice means the opening of " a good private school for the sons of farmers " : two facts which perhaps do not necessarily rule him out from among the class of the heroic in fiction. To Eustacia the first occupation smells of heaven, though she is not attracted by the other more than she need be. In class, Clym is a little away from the Wessex norm, his mother having been a curate's daughter, and Eustacia begins at once to think and dream about him—goes to look at his house before he arrives, and reads into his passing good-night " all emotional things possible ". Perhaps seclusion on Egdon produces an artificial stimulation of the feelings as great as that caused by incarceration in office, school or nunnery, except to those who, like Clym, find the hills " friendly and congenial ". Clym is a true " native ", desiring to combine the intellectual life with the plainest of bucolic living. He is one of Hardy's pure intellectuals, and less suitable as a mate for the Eustacia we know than Knight for Elfride or Clare for Tess—for Eustacia's dissimilarity amounts to positive and violent antagonism. As their contacts progress— first at the mumming, then by the well, and swiftly to the first love scene, all handled by Hardy with beautiful care and restraint —the impossibility of their ever living and working side by side grows more and more evident. It is not only that their outlooks differ—that might have been modified by education : but she is essence of woman, he of man ; and to link those two essences in a bond can succeed only if no differences arise—if differences do arise they are irreconcilable.

By this time Clym's mother has come into the story and we have before us Hardy's own study of that mother-son relation which has since been luridly illuminated by the psychoanalysts and by the life and writings of D. H. Lawrence. Hardy is not much concerned with parents. Only in the cases of Clym Yeobright's mother and Grace Melbury's father is parental influence perceptibly exercised—in both cases with disastrous results. There are parents appertaining to Elfride, Stephen Smith, Ethelberta, and Anne Garland, but they are of a sensible easy-going, accommodating kind, and attempt no decisive part in directing or obstructing the lives of their children. Elizabeth-Jane has two dubious fathers, one of them that rumbustious character the Mayor of Casterbridge, but even he lets Elizabeth-Jane go her own gait—indeed, the dependence is rather the other way. Mrs. Durbeyfield's effect upon the life of Tess is bad enough, but only by reason of its negative quality. In all these cases the actual relation of parent and child is matter-of-fact, unemotional. When Hardy wishes his characters to be completely free to dree their own weird, he carefully deprives them of immediate ancestry. Bathsheba has an aunt who lasts only for a few chapters ; Swithin St. Cleeve is an orphan ; Jude and Sue have nothing but distant relatives (their fate is just as tragic as that of Tess and Clare, who are fully equipped with parents) ; and Eustacia has an eccentric but otherwise negligible grandfather.

The relation between Clym and his mother is stated to be a relation of love. Indeed, in one passage Hardy suggests that the love between them is of an exceptionally exalted kind, "indestructible", "profound". It is singularly unhappy in its conduct and its consequences for a love capable of this description. Mrs. Yeobright's opposition to her son's desire to give up the jewellery trade and take up work of real service to his fellows is partly due to her obvious inability to follow the reasons which Clym lucidly sets forth to her, and partly to her unwillingness to see him risk his livelihood. This second motive is doubtless akin to love, but a little sympathy with his vision would have brought it a good deal closer still. Not that there is anything wrong with the picture ; every line is ruthless in its veracity. Take a small section of the picture (Clym is walking with his mother on the heath) :—

" In that case I'll branch off here, mother. I am going to Mistover."

Mrs. Yeobright turned to him inquiringly.

" I am going to help get the bucket out of the captain's well," he continued. " As it is so very deep I may be useful. And I should like to see this Miss Vye—not so much for her good looks as for another reason."

" Must you go ? " his mother asked.

" I thought to."

And they parted. " There is no help for it," murmured Clym's mother gloomily as he withdrew. " They are sure to see each other. I wish Sam would carry his news to other houses than mine."

Clym's retreating figure got smaller and smaller as it rose and fell over the hillocks on his way. " He is tender-hearted," said Mrs. Yeobright to herself while she watched him ; " otherwise it would matter little. How he's going on ! "

He was, indeed, walking with a will over the furze, as straight as a line, as if his life depended upon it. His mother drew a long breath, and turned to go back by the way she had come.

The dialogue, the mode of contact, are different from anything else in the novels, because the relation is unique. " He was ", says Hardy, " a part of her ". That is the weakness, as it is the strength, of the parental attitude.

A second opportunity for loving sympathy, turned instead into a cause for acrimonious hostility, arises when Clym's feeling for Eustacia begins to develop. Parental opposition to a son's choice of a wife is age-old, and is not excused by the fact that quite often the parents are, as Mrs. Yeobright is here, right. It is simply the woodenness of the man with a set purpose that makes Clym think that Eustacia " would make a good matron in a boarding-school ", and we have seen that their dissimilarity of type was so fundamental as to render a successful marriage unlikely. Nevertheless, apart from the fact that Clym was an adult individual (not merely " a part of her "), his mother's opposition did nothing but make things worse : in its absence there was a possibility that Clym and Eustacia might have learnt enough from each other to have achieved some happiness ; as it was it was inevitable that Clym's divided loyalty should embitter the misunderstanding over Wildeve to a point where fate could thrust in and turn all to tragedy. But these are the materials out of which life makes tragedy.

After Clym's admission that he is engaged to Eustacia his mother's opposition reaches such an intensity that it becomes necessary for him to leave home. He goes, and she lets him go. The trouble with these two is that they are too strong. One touch of emotional weakness (call it softness, call it kindness) on either side would have brought the whole black structure of misery tumbling down. Mrs. Yeobright's weakness comes only afterwards, in talking to Thomasin, and then in a pathetically blind way : " Oh Thomasin, he was so good as a little boy— so tender and kind. . . . I did not think one whom I called mine would grow up to treat me like this. . . . This is maternity—to give one's best years and best love to ensure the fate of being despised." Things are not improved by the bitter ' Rencounter by the Pool ' of Clym's mother and Eustacia—an indictment of the incredible unreasonableness women can exhibit when occasion offers.

The genuine yielding—weakness that rises from strength—comes later on both sides, after Clym has married and turned furze-cutter owing to his failing sight. Clym tells Eustacia he must seek reconciliation with his mother, and about the same time Mrs. Yeobright is telling the reddleman she too has determined to make some effort to heal the sorry breach. It is an indication of the central position assigned to the mother-motive that the chapters describing Mrs. Yeobright's journey across the heath to Clym's cottage and back again stand as a climax to the novel. The later and perhaps more exact climax, the scene where Clym charges Eustacia with infidelity and his mother's death, is a consequence of the other one. The heath journey is marvellously done, and is punctuated, as it were, with the living creatures which Mrs. Yeobright, a noticing woman and a lover of animals, observes by the way : those maggoty things wriggling in the muddy pond, the sleeping cat, the drunken wasps on the fallen fruit, the ants' nest, the heron flying into the sun. And there was another she did not see until it was too late—the adder that bit her in the foot. But before this the well-intended visit has been tragically frustrated, and the stricken woman's creep back across Egdon is shown to us (and later to Clym) through the eyes of one of Hardy's rare but marvellous children, Johnny Nonsuch. It is by an extraordinary process of investigation and questioning, of Christian Cantle, Diggory Venn, and finally little Johnny, that Clym tracks down the truth of what had happened on that grievous afternoon. And yet not quite the whole truth : the missing witness is Eustacia herself. Her he does not question, except in such a way as to make reply impossible or valueless. His love for his mother has taken complete possession of him now : had it been balanced by an equal love for his wife (but that, in the nature of the case, was impossible) he would have been saved much raving despair. In the end he loses wife as well as mother, and he feels he has caused the death of both. The

self-accusation is not altogether just : yet Clym's egoism has
been dangerously ruthless. His point of view has been ' right ' in
both cases, but to follow right in scorn of consequence is stupid,
and to override other less ' right ' points of view is the mark of
simple strength but not of that more complicated thing, greatness.
The book closes with Clym thinking of his mother as a sublime
saint, and preaching his first sermon on Rainbarrow on the text,
" Ask on, my mother : for I will not say thee nay ".

It is a grim story, this first of Hardy's tragedies, with a single,
relentless drive to disaster. A striking difference between
Shakespeare and Hardy is that in every one of his tragedies
Shakespeare kills both hero and heroine. This may be due to
his sense of artistic finish, or to his tenderness for the children of
his hand. Hardy, more cruel, leaves, as life generally does, one
alive but maimed. Yeobright is among those few who are left
not only sadder but wiser for their experience and their loss.

§ 3

A Long Rest before a Giant Effort

The Trumpet-Major ; A Laodicean ; Two on a Tower

The ' rest ' principle enunciated in the foregoing section works
out differently in this group, which consists of three novels all
of the lighter kind. As they were followed by three masterpieces, we may regard the present trio as providing an adequate
recreative period preparatory to the abnormal activity that was to
come.

The Trumpet-Major is the lightest-hearted novel Hardy ever
wrote. If in John Loveday himself there are elements of pathos
not to be found in *Under the Greenwood Tree*, these are outweighed
by the comedy of Festus Derriman, the only rollicking figure of
fun in the Wessex novels. His swagger and funk, in the Bob
Acres tradition, are emphasised to caricature. Touch him on his
inferiority complex and he reacts in exactly the same way every
time. The scene in which he induces his man Cripplestraw to
persuade him, an officer in the yeomanry, that to go into hiding
on the news of Boney's landing is a more courageous thing than

to go to the front, is hugely funny in a farcical sense quite foreign to Hardy. His relations with his uncle, the old Squire, another but more restrainedly comic character, are highly diverting, Festus bullying, Uncle Benjy cringing but watchfully outwitting the simple-minded blusterer all the time. Festus is a comic opera figure, at times almost Dickensian.

The book is a return to the idyllic, and opens with a bright impression of the double ménage at the mill. Hardy is splendid at parties, and soon has a grand one going, given by Miller Loveday for the homecoming of his son John. This, however, is nothing to the Olympian feast that, at a later day, is prepared for the wedding of sailor Bob. A bare record of the fare makes the waistband feel tight. Four chickens and a little curly-tailed barrow pig; a cold chine, stuffed veal, and two pigeon pies; thirty rings of black-pot, a dozen of white-pot, and ten knots of tender and well-washed chitterlings, cooked plain, " in case the bride should like a change " ; sweetbreads, and " five milts, sewed up at one side in the form of a chrysalis, and stuffed with thyme, sage, parsley, mint, groats, rice, milk, chopped egg, and other ingredients ; roasted before a slow fire, and eaten hot ". Then there were apple pies—all windfalls and maggot-cored codlins being carefully excluded ; and puddings stirred up in the milking-pail and boiled in a three-legged bell-metal crock, of great weight and antiquity. In the liquor line the miller had laid in an ample barrel of Casterbridge strong beer—of the most beautiful colour, full in body yet brisk as a volcano, piquant yet without a twang, luminous as an autumn sunset, free from streakiness of taste, and rather heady ; and broached a hogshead of fine cider that had been mellowing in the house for several months.

It had been pressed from fruit judiciously chosen by an old hand—Horner and Cleeves apple for the body, a few Tom-Puts for colour, and just a dash of Old Five-corners for sparkle—a selection originally made to please the palate of a well-known temperate earl who was a regular cider-drinker, and lived to be eighty-eight.

And indeed the sweetness of the mill-house entourage—the miller and his two sons, Mrs. Garland and Anne, and all their simple-hearted goings-on—is a lovely thing to contemplate.

Hardy's sly skill at a middle-aged woman, seen in Parson Swancourt's second lady, is shown again in his picture of Mrs. Garland. Daughter Anne, our heroine, is a mild but charming young person who appears a little uncomprehending and stupid for most of the novel, until we find she really has a very clear notion of what is going on behind the manly bosoms of her three lovers. For there are three suitors again in this novel, and the triangle they form would fit inside that made by the three men of *Far from the Madding Crowd*. Festus Derriman is the Troy of this story, suitably lowered in tone : one touch of his absurd adventures—such as when Anne tips him into the stream, where he falls flat on his stomach and comes out bellowing fearful imprecations—would have ruined *Far from the Madding Crowd*. One cannot believe that Anne will regard his pretensions seriously —but one did not believe that about Bathsheba and Troy ! Boldwood's angle is occupied by Bob Loveday, a very different type of man, but with a sailor-like ardent affection to correspond with Boldwood's passionate desire. He is treated with some facetiousness by Hardy, and is little but a grown-up child ; but in spite of his philandering he is, like all the mill-folk, as honest as the day. The relations between him and his brother John are full of beauty.

John Loveday, the trumpet-major, approximates more closely to Gabriel Oak. Oak is a much more complex character, and has not John's simple self-sacrificing nature : patient though he is, he sticks grimly to his desire for Bathsheba, as Bathsheba well knows. John's instinct is to withdraw in favour of his beloved brother, whose need, he feels, is greater than his own. There are depths of feeling—the only ones in the book—in his still nature, but he shows them by instant service in the cause of Bob and Anne at Anne's expression of a wish. He is all honesty, honour, manliness, modesty : until he knows her well he keeps a distance of a yard when walking with Anne, of fifteen paces when conversing with her in the garden. He is a stronger man than Oak, equally enduring and with more initiative : the non-commissioned officer, of the finest type, against the shepherd. He is treated very seriously by Hardy, sometimes with a tender humour. His end, as he marches out into the night, leaving the others to their happiness, is swift and appropriate.

Most of the book is conceived in the spirit of the highest comedy, with many touches of a gayer humour and gentler satire than are usual with Hardy. There are some admirable war-pictures, again of an entirely cheerful sort, like that of the drilling of the ' incapables ' who were to meet the Grand Army, and especially the one of the passing of the *Victory*, seen through the eyes of Anne and the old sailor. But three times we are reminded that the cobbler is still within reach of his last. A piece of treachery with a bite in it stabs the idyll when Festus puts the press-gang on Bob's track. However, this is not as bad as it looks, for Bob doesn't mind going back to sea, and having escaped from the clutches of the Lieutenant and his marines pays a call on Captain Hardy and gets accepted for service on board the *Victory*. Closer to type is the moment when, after the battle of Trafalgar, a sailor brings to Anne, now desperately in love with Bob, the eagerly awaited news of his safety, and innocently throws in the additional information that Bob is courting a baker's daughter down in Portsmouth. Cruellest of all is the last blow that John is called upon to bear : just as Anne has begun to turn to him and recognise that he alone loves her and is worthy of her love, he receives a letter from Bob saying that he is coming back to .claim Anne, whereupon John stoically stamps underfoot his budding joy and leaves the field open again to his brother. Self-abnegation of this order is not a much admired virtue at the present time, but in a novel of the 'seventies it rings nobly, like the sound of John Loveday's smart step dying away upon the road as he goes to join his companions in arms and to die on a battle-field of Spain.

The ' rest ' theory does, as a matter of fact, hold with this group in the former as well as in the latter sense given to it. Though *The Trumpet-Major* and *Two on a Tower* are not among the great novels, they have very high merits of their own, and were not written without æsthetic pains ; the novel which comes between them, *A Laodicean*, should have cost hardly any effort at all, if quality were the measure of effort. It has fewer excellences, less interest, more faults, than any other of the Wessex novels, but is perhaps sufficiently accounted for by Hardy's own apology, to the effect that he dictated the book during a period of illness, and intended it as nothing more than an idle afternoon's entertainment.

The opening situation, of the young lady refusing baptism by immersion, is competently done, and, though verging on the ridiculous, affords us at once the desiderated explanation of the title. The Laodicean type of mind has never been thought attractive, and the young lady in question, Paula Power, who certainly maintains this character throughout, is the least attractive of Hardy's heroines, which is not to say that she is altogether devoid of charm. After this glimpse she is cleverly kept out of sight, though mentioned intriguingly several times, until Chapter VII, when she appears before the hero to thank him for a well-timed rescue, which was however nothing more heroic than the defeat of an aged Baptist minister in an argument on the subject of infant or adult baptism.

George Somerset, the hero aforesaid, has already been shown to us in what I feel to be the best and most original part of the book. In characteristic Hardy fashion, he is led to the girl he is ultimately to marry by a series of fascinating accidents. Wandering over the countryside in search of architectural interest, he becomes a spectator, through the chapel window, of the baptismal fiasco already mentioned ; and as he walks away from the scene he hears the humming of an overhead wire ; he follows the wire, for a whim, and finds it at length entering the wall of a feudal castle. It is a private telegraph wire, and Somerset meditates on the unexpected linking of the modern invention, symbolising a feverish cosmopolitanism, with the monument of an age which was hard, narrow and brutal, but was enviably rich in leisure, freedom from care, and architectural genius. Next day he gets permission to view the castle, and discovers it to be the home of the Laodicean lady of the previous afternoon's adventure.

This telegraph wire, which was evidently intended to be a kind of early telephone, is employed with much success in the novel as an instrument of romance. Hardy was one of the first to see possibilities that have since been exploited with an almost sickening thoroughness.

Somerset has a rival (only one this time) in the person of Captain De Stancy, representative of the family from whom Paula's father had bought Stancy Castle. At the moment when Somerset calls, Paula is away, and he is entertained by her companion, Charlotte De Stancy, sister of the Captain. Charlotte is a charming and pathetic figure, for she presently falls victim to a hopeless passion for Somerset. But it is De Stancy who, with a certain ' boy-man ' called Dare, constitutes the fatal weakness of this novel. Dare is a film-like, gangster sort of person, with a flashy pushful-ness and self-confidence based on a total absence of feeling. There are mysterious relations between him and De Stancy, which are explained when we learn that he is the latter's illegi-timate son.[1]

De Stancy is a very unsatisfactory figure. Hardy tries to arouse an interest in him which the reader finds it impossible to retain. He is weak, but not bad, and not unpleasant. When Dare is urging him to try to get Paula (and her castle) from Somerset, he replies, " If I care for anything on earth, I do care for that old fortress of my fathers. I respect so little among the living that all my reverence is for my own dead. But manœu-vring, even for my own, as you call it, is not in my line. It is distasteful—it is positively hateful to me." And Hardy's de-scription of him at the beginning of the section called " De Stancy " endeavours to present him as a figure of high romance. But the picture, reduced to commonplace terms, is that of a sen-timental artillery officer of forty who drinks nothing but aerated waters, and having landed himself with a sprig of illegitimacy eighteen years ago has sworn off women ever since ; and who now, because he has been tempted by the said sprig to watch through a crack a girl, clad in " pink flannel ", disporting herself in a gymnasium, ceremoniously pours his aerated waters out of the window and, exclaiming, " A man again after eighteen years ! " drinks a glass of " ruby liquor ", also conveniently provided by the sprig, to the name of " Paula Power ".

However, in spite of a strong flavour of the Gilbertian, De Stancy is, when Dare permits him, very decent and honourable. So much cannot be said for Paula, whose carryings-on with Somerset and De Stancy are more than questionable. She, too, comes under an evil influence, that of an uncle who suddenly

---

[1] Until De Stancy admits this relationship to Paula near the end of the book it is, I think, never explicitly stated. We have to deduce it from general evidence, and from the fact that Dare *once* calls de Stancy ' dad '. I am reminded of the surmise that Horatio was Hamlet's father, based on a variant reading of the line, " And smelt so, pa ? "

turns up from Australia. This is " the phlegmatic and obstinate Abner Power ", one of the best realised characters in the story. We see little of him, but he speaks a new voice, rich and vital against the general woodenness of the dialogue. And so, in spite of many turnings and twistings, we are quite cleverly led up to Paula's acceptance of De Stancy. By this time, however, old Abner Power has changed his mind, and is trying to stop the wedding, for he has discovered the secret of Dare's relationship to De Stancy. Dare, too, has not been idle, and has dug up certain incriminating passages in Abner Power's history. The scene in which the wicked uncle is outwitted by the wickeder bastard, the young man and the old one sitting one at each end of a vestry table, with the noses of their revolvers showing coyly over the edge, is much too good fun for anything outside Hollywood. But it is pleasant to find the interfering old Abner sent about his business, even by Dare, and even though he is interfering now on the right side. As usual, Hardy runs things very fine, and it is only a few hours before her wedding that Paula discovers the truth about Dare, through De Stancy's own disclosure, in a finely handled scene. Then, filled with repentance and love, she begins a pursuit of Somerset that can only not be condemned as farcical if we are definitely not intended to take this book seriously. Outwardly, at all events, she keeps up her Laodicean habit, for when at last she finds him she says, " I have been looking for you. I want some architect to continue the restoration." And Somerset, meek creature, is content.

In turning to our next book, we pass from the least important of Hardy's novels (*Desperate Remedies* always excepted) to what is perhaps the best of all the lesser ones. It has not the perfection of form of *Under the Greenwood Tree*, but it has the full Hardy quality in much greater variety, and an artistic excellence that is a constant delight.

To some extent the degree of a book's sheer inspiration can be judged from its opening, and certainly in the way of writing that comes lovingly off the pen we have had no opening chapter like the first chapter of *Two on a Tower* since *Far from the Madding Crowd*. The bare economy of the narrative in the first two pages is a joy to contemplate. There follows a description, expert and leisured, of the hill and the tower, with its sighing Hardian trees below. An impression is built up of the isolation and loneliness of the tower, after which comes the sudden but quiet disclosure, to the reader as to the woman who has ascended the tower, of the youth at the summit, a beautiful youth of twenty, with fair curly hair and early-Christian face, in contrast with the black hair and eyes of the woman, whom we know to be about twenty-nine, and who presently proves to be Lady Constantine, " wife of the absent Sir Blount Constantine ". The young man, Swithin St. Cleeve, is a student of astronomy, and the astronomical dialogue that ensues is in Hardy's best vein, leading up to the youth's naïve but dignified ambition to become Astronomer Royal. To crown all, the chapter concludes with a page of purest Hardian rustic (how one missed anything of the sort in *A Laodicean* !) in Haymoss Fry's account of Swithin and his origins. As so frequently, there are thrilling Shakespearean echoes in the old man's tale, as he tells how Swithin's father, the curate, had married Farmer Martin's daughter—" Giles Martin, a limberish man, who used to go rather bad upon his lags, if you can mind. I knowed the man well enough ; who should know 'en better ! The maid was a poor windling thing, and though a playward piece of flesh when he married her, 'a socked and sighed, and went out like a snoff."

The promise of the overture is not withheld. Here is the rustic-chorus again, a choir-group not so good as the Mellstock choir, of course, but very good indeed. There is plenty of easy, confident humour. We are given all the rather complicated facts about Sir Blount, and about the difficulties in his wife's position, in a completely natural way, partly by the chorus and partly in conversations between Lady Constantine, Parson Torkingham, and Swithin. Lady Constantine is a very feminine sort of woman : she persuades Swithin to leave a critical series of nightly star-watchings on which he is engaged, in order to do some business for her in London, and then calls him selfish and un-gallant because he asks her to carry on the watchings and record-ings for him. Much of their conversation necessarily goes on at night, and night in the country always stirs Hardy to a certain splendour of writing, and the astronomical theme suits well with his cosmic outlook. The wonderful conception, expressed in his purpose to set two souls against the universe, is finely realised. Swithin's disquisitions on the stars are full of personal feeling about the " ghastliness " of space and of stellar distances ; and a sense of the insignificance of human troubles broods over these pages. But it is not long before the young astronomer discovers that his gracious friend has interests more pressing than " the universe ".

We are left, from the outset, in no doubt about Viviette Constantine's character. She is repeatedly called voluptuous, perfervid, and she soon finds herself getting " foolishly interested " in Swithin, her feelings being described as maternal, sisterly, and amorous—all three. As he talks of his stars she watches him with luxurious contemplative interest : " Say some more of it to me ", she coaxes. As they travel together in the absolute isolation of space, she is thinking of him all the time, he only of his theories. For Swithin, though delighted and flattered by the companionship of this beautiful woman, so much above him in station, is emotionally untouched. He tells her that astronomy covers the whole circumference of his thoughts, and it is all too obvious to her that he looks at her with eyes full of speculative purity. His utter inability to conceive that there might be anything exceptionable in his relationship with her, an unhappily married woman, is quite beautiful : and it is saddening to think how impossible such a state of mind would be to our cinema-bred youth. The Venus and Adonis situation is not a pleasant one to contemplate, but there is something to be said for the temperate Victorian version that succeeded the frank paganism of Ovid and Shakespeare and has given place to the deeper spiritual brutality of the twentieth century. Viviette mooned and sentimentalised over her beautiful young scientist—a modern woman of her type would go swiftly and ruthlessly to work to ' seduce ' him ; Viviette made praiseworthy efforts to enter into his astronomical schemes—in a novel of to-day he would be torn bodily from them.

A crisis, both in science and in love, is brought about by one of the neatest of the Hardian freaks of fortune. Swithin has made an astronomical discovery, based on two years of watching and thinking. He sends off his manuscript to the authorities through whom he is to reach fame, but as he walks back from the post he buys an astronomical periodical in which he finds an article that shows him that his discovery has just been forestalled by an American. A serious illness follows the blow, and anxiety for Swithin's life brings Viviette's love to a point when it can be concealed no longer, at least from herself. In a short chapter that is a finished work of art in itself, she is shown, at the cost of great pain, just deciding to end the improper condition of affairs, when the Vicar comes to break the news of Sir Blount's death, nearly two years previously, in the secret depths of Africa. She makes some attempt to get Swithin to see the difference that this makes in the possibilities, but it takes Haymoss Fry and the rest of the chorus, talking together outside the tower, while Swithin, unbeknown, is inside, to open his eyes, like Benedict's before him, fully to the state of Viviette's heart. Hardy's comment is that a promising young physicist was thus spoilt to produce a commonplace inamorato, but Viviette's reaction is different—she seems to see, on his next visit to her, that Swithin has suddenly become a man, with fire in his eyes.

It does not seem necessary that the spoiling of the physicist should have been very drastic, but Swithin does find that love, under these rather exceptional conditions, keeps his mind from the concentration his work demands, and he lights upon the remedy of a secret marriage. It seems an extraordinary sort of remedy, but one that might have suggested itself to a very young man, and Viviette's yielding under the threat of his leaving England is probable enough. Its real *raison d'être* in the novel is Hardy's own predilection for this device. A secret marriage was almost as irresistible to Hardy as a girl masquerading as a man was to Shakespeare. Besides the present case, there are secret marriages in *Far from the Madding Crowd*, *The Mayor of Casterbridge* and *The Well-Beloved*, while Smith and Elfride only just stop short of one, and the marital experiments of Jude and Sue bear this construction at various periods. Viviette's consent to the marriage is called a " passionate decision ", but the loves of this book do not require that epithet. The " glow of enchantment shed by the idea of a private union with her beautiful young lover " is romantic rather than passionate. There is room in Hardy's fiction for these graceful loves, taking no deep or tragic hold on the nature of the lovers.

Before the marriage can be effected a remarkable letter arrives from Swithin's great-uncle Jocelyn, offering him a small fortune, for the purpose of research, on condition that he does not marry before he is twenty-five, and specifically warning him against continuing his relations with Lady Constantine. It is a good letter, well argued, on the assumption that " passion and thought " (Browning bracketed them) are mutually antagonistic ; and the irony is that if it had come a few months earlier it would have spared the whole tragedy, for it would have put the thought of this rather foolish marriage out of Swithin's head. However, he allows it to have no effect on him whatever, does not tell Viviette, and goes forward with the marriage, the scene of which is pictured with great skill—the trembling pair hovering on the verge of discovery or disaster, and surrounded by obstacles, omens, and premonitions.

The marriage has the desired result of restoring Swithin's scientific calm, but it has another and surely unintended effect : for a matter of a hundred pages it quite spoils the book, turning it from a fascinating work of art into an ordinary comedy of misunderstandings. However, the affair of the bishop, the brother and the bracelet (that " wanton object ", as the bishop calls it) is worked out with great skill, and culminates in the discovery that Viviette's marriage with Swithin is invalid, since Sir Blount's death had not, in fact, occurred until six weeks after their union had been solemnised. From this point the power of the earlier part of the book recovers itself, and is maintained to the end, but on tragic lines instead of those of comedy.

Viviette's distress over the illegality of the marriage is very great, especially when she perceives Swithin's casual air and his absorption in his telescopes. Then she not only discovers how she has been depriving Swithin of a fortune, but reads old Jocelyn's letter, with its cruel aspersions on her own character and aims. Of course they might have rejoiced in the realisation that their having miraculously managed to keep the marriage a secret, together with the new fact of its illegality, gives them a chance to make the best of both worlds by deferring the renewal of the marriage until Swithin is twenty-five. They do indeed decide to do this, but only after a terrible inward struggle on Viviette's part, for it is made clear that by this time her love for Swithin has grown very strong indeed. So Swithin departs for South Africa. And no sooner has he gone than Viviette discovers herself to be in the first stage of pregnancy.

Apart from the irony and the tragedy of the situation, one wonders what these two people, who (in that pre-contraceptive era) were so anxious to keep their marriage secret, had been up to, and when they were up to it. They had agreed to live apart— " exactly as we are now ". But circumstances had forced them to live together in Swithin's hut at the tower for three days just after they were married. That, however, had been ten months before Viviette's startling discovery, which occurs at the end of August : they had met in the February of the previous year, and married at the end of October. All the evidence points to their having kept apart after those first three days. But the day on which it was decided that they would wait until Swithin was twenty-five before marrying again, Viviette spent the evening, till midnight, in the hut with Swithin, and, says Hardy, " she yielded to all the passion of her first union with him ". This is dated by a note Swithin had written to her that morning, headed July 7th. She discovered her condition on the morning Swithin was to sail, which her brother gives as—" the 25th, that is, to-day ". But in the interim Viviette has had a letter from the Bishop headed July 30th, so this " 25th " must be the 25th of August. (It cannot be of September or later because it is clear that only a very few weeks pass between the Bishop's letter and the discovery.) Hence, after being sensible for nearly a year, it is on that last night of all (for they do not meet again) that Viviette took the risk, and lost.

I have laboured this point chiefly in order to show how meticulously Hardy watched the progress of his stories, and how carefully though unostentatiously he left the dated clues about to be noted by those whom they might interest.

So Viviette hurriedly accepts the Bishop's second proposal of marriage—for Swithin's ship had left the dock a few minutes before her cab drove up. One is sorry for the Bishop : he was a pompous ass with Swithin, but it was his duty to be so, and he wrote two beautiful letters. Having stepped in so conveniently to tide over the difficult situation, with equal consideration he dies just before Swithin's twenty-fifth birthday. So Swithin comes home to marry his Viviette—and she dies in his arms—and

3

Swithin, looking up for help, sees—" Tabitha Lark, who was skirting the field with a bounding tread—the single bright spot of colour and animation within the wide horizon ".

We have, from the very beginning of the book, had a succession of glimpses, generally of the briefest, of Tabitha Lark, with her pretty name, but it was not for some time that it began to be apparent that she was there for a purpose, and it was not till we were past the middle of the book that we got our first full-length of her : a pleasant, sensible girl, the basis of the favourite Hardy type, the country girl of natural refinement and plain simple culture (Tabitha reads to Lady Constantine and plays the organ at church).   Towards the end of the book certain interested people are busy coupling her name, quite unjustly, with that of Swithin, and now here she is to show that the suggestions that Swithin and Tabitha were well-matched had a certain propriety, and something more.

It is a wonderful ending to a wonderful book, which falls short of greatness only because the main characters, though full of interest, make no claim to anything like heroic proportions.

§ 4

Two Masterpieces, Urban and Rural

The Mayor of Casterbridge ; The Woodlanders

Once more we have, in *The Mayor of Casterbridge*, a supremely good opening.   The description of Henchard and his wife approaching Weydon-Priors is like a picture mirrored in clear water, reminding us again of the opening of *Far from the Madding Crowd*.   But while that picture was bright with sunshine and the joy of life, this one is dark with silence, fear and tragic personality.   It is interesting to note that in order not to spoil this effect, Hardy defers to mention the lighter touches in Henchard's clothing : here he speaks only of his brown corduroy jacket, fustian waistcoat and breeches, and tanned leggings ; the colour details felt at this moment to be inappropriate, are given long afterwards—" leggings yellow as marigolds, corduroys immaculate as new flax, and a neckerchief like a flower-garden ".

So much is landscape subject to mood : at the moment when the
first picture was painted these cheerful colours were obscured
by the artist's sense of the " dogged and cynical indifference "
of the central figure.

Immediately there follows the episode, told with all the power
of which Hardy was by now easy master, of Henchard's selling
of his wife (and baby daughter) to the sailor. No other novel
opens so dramatically as this. The incident epitomises Henchard's character—his recklessness, the effect of drink on him,
his hard inflexibility with a touch of softness in the afterthought.
Then, after one of Hardy's unforgettable early morning pictures
we have the almost equally dramatic taking of the oath to avoid
strong drink for twenty years, after which and some fruitless
searching for his wife, Henchard makes for Casterbridge. The
two chapters have been a prologue to the real story, which opens
seventeen years later. The prologue has laid down the broad
lines of Henchard's character, and has narrated an incident of his
very early manhood, one which he might well consider to be
lost in the past by this time, but which lies there germinating, a
seed of fate.

After the excitement of the prologue the story itself begins
quietly, with Susan, Henchard's one-time wife, and her daughter,
Elizabeth-Jane, searching for Henchard. Newson, the sailor
who had bought Susan for five pounds long ago, is supposed
dead—and Hardy very cleverly evades saying he actually was
dead without raising any suspicions that he wasn't. Slowly, by
means of hints and scraps of information, they draw near to
their ' relative ' ; Henchard gradually comes back into the
picture, and at last, to their astonishment, and ours, he is discovered presiding over a banquet, Mayor of Casterbridge.
Hardy's description of him at this point shows that he himself
does not feel for the Mayor the admiration he arouses in the
reader. Elizabeth-Jane's first impression is one of " generosity " :
a quality which, in its present significance of rich emotional nature,
can exist side by side with many faults of character and go near
to atone for them all.

The book is sub-titled, ' the story of a man of character ' :
it might have been called the story of two men of character.
For Farfrae, who comes into Henchard's life at this moment, and

whom Henchard compels into his service, is a man of character too. Character enables its possessor to make those who have less of it do things they would rather not do, but it has no power over circumstance. Henchard's character is stronger than Farfrae's, though Farfrae has in addition those two subtler qualities, personality and ' chairm '. In the story, Henchard, for all his great bull-like force of character, goes down, bludgeoned to death by circumstances, while Farfrae rides home an easy winner. This is not due to his degree of character, nor to his personality or charm, but to his luck. It is annoying to see everything turning out well for Farfrae and badly for Henchard, whose lovable qualities get a deep hold on our sympathies ; but Farfrae is a thoroughly good fellow : a little over-conscious of his merit, but not too unworthy of Elizabeth-Jane when his time comes.

Elizabeth-Jane is perhaps the subtlest of all Hardy's pictures of women. She is drawn in such pale tones that there is some danger of the exquisite beauty of the picture being lost under the fierce colouring of the two male portraits. She has to suffer for the ambiguity of her paternity, and Henchard's treatment of her when he finds she is Newson's daughter is cruel and hateful : but it is Elizabeth-Jane's one fault that she never appreciates the splendid irrationality of Henchard's character—perhaps it is not easy for a daughter, or even a quasi-daughter, to do this, especially if her mother has suffered more from the irrationality than she has profited by the splendour.

The other woman in the story (besides poor wind-tossed Susan, who fades quietly away in the middle of the book and leaves no gap) is Lucetta, Henchard's partner in an entanglement which happened some time in those lost seventeen years, and which we never really get to the bottom of. She is colourless in a completely unattractive way, in distinction to Elizabeth-Jane, whose lack of colour is the basis of her extraordinary attractiveness. Farfrae's turning to Lucetta in preference to Elizabeth-Jane is the one damning action of his life, and balances Bathsheba's folly over Troy. The situation which has Henchard, Farfrae, Lucetta, and Elizabeth-Jane as its four corners is, however, an interesting one, and provides not only a secret marriage between Farfrae and Lucetta, but a most remarkable scene in which

Henchard reads to Farfrae Lucetta's letters to him without divulging the name of the writer, Lucetta meanwhile listening on the stairs in mortal dread that this doubtful episode in her past is about to be exposed to her newly married husband.

Save in the matter of the Mayor's character, which burns like a flame throughout, the early part of the book (after the prologue) is almost pedestrian—plainly and sturdily wrought but with little of the art that transmutes. Life in a town, even a country town like Casterbridge, gives scope for whatever smallness there is in human nature, and there is a good deal of triviality here and there —as in the rival shows that Henchard and Farfrae get up to win popularity. (From one of Hardy's own notes, quoted in the *Early Life*, we see that Hardy felt he had made this book less good than it might have been by introducing incidents to fulfil the requirements of serial publication.) After the death of Susan, which coincides with the beginning of Henchard's downfall, the distant approach of tragedy drives out triviality, and the book begins to be that sombre thing *The Mayor of Casterbridge*. The coming of Lucetta seems to set it back again, but as Henchard's fortunes blacken, the thread of noble narrative resumes. His stoicism under the blows of fate is finely recorded, as is his smouldering hatred of Farfrae. His deliberate explosion into wild drunkenness the moment his religiously kept vow has expired shows ' character ' of the most elemental kind, like that of the boy on the burning deck. Seriousness loses itself again in the string of little incidents that chafe Henchard's hate to murder point, especially that in which the late Mayor, now a down-and-out, insists on welcoming the Royal Personage who is passing through Casterbridge : there is no disputing the humour of the passage in which Henchard, wearing his oldest clothes, and waving the Union Jack (tacked to a calico-roller) in his left hand, steps forward and blandly holds out his right hand to the illustrious Personage (he is said to have removed his hat as he went, but one is left to conjecture in which hand he held this). After the crisis —Henchard's attempt to kill Farfrae—Hardy's tragic genius takes complete hold of the story, which is from then onward of the deepest psychological veracity welded by art into supreme form.

The murder attempt itself, where Henchard wrestles with Farfrae and tries to throw him out of a granary door forty feet above the ground, is a thing few writers could have described without falling into either bathos or false-heroic, but Hardy avoids both, making the contest grim but not protracted. The struggle and its ending provide a remarkable instance of the simple emotional rhythm of Henchard's mind. Most men have a secondary movement of reason and interest which curbs and complicates the emotional curve ; Henchard acts just as he feels.

All these vicissitudes have their course within the town of Casterbridge, and Hardy takes evident satisfaction in the portrayal of the fine old capital of ' South Wessex '. (R. L. S. hit off *The Mayor* very well when he wrote to Hardy : " Henchard is a great fellow, and Dorchester is touched in with the hand of a master ".) He gives us an outline of the place as Susan and Elizabeth-Jane enter it at evening : its encircling ditch and bank planted with gnarled trees, its houses of timber or of brick-nogging, the shops fulfilling agricultural and pastoral needs. Later in the book we have a more detailed description of the High Street on market-day, and of the inhabitants of the ancient borough, done with all the tender humour of a lover ; and later still the picture is completed by a magnificent description of the great Roman amphitheatre outside the town. Moreover, everything as it happens receives its comment from a more varied ' chorus ' than we have seen before. They are a little more urban in habit than the usual rustic group, and so a little more worldly-wise ; they comprise not only people whose chorus-function is their sole one—Solomon Longways, Christopher Coney, Buzzford—but men from the corn-yard—Abel Whittle, Stubberd and Jopp ; not only men but women—Mother Cuxsom, Nance Mockridge and the furmity woman ; they congregate at the town-pump, on the two bridges, and at the low-class inn called Peter's Finger ; and through their agency scandal spreads " like a miasmatic fog " through the back streets of Casterbridge.

Henchard's material ruin being complete, his spiritual desolation is effected by the return of Newson. Seeing despair coming down upon him, he has tried to save himself by turning to Elizabeth-Jane : he knows by this time she is Newson's daughter, but he sees her loving nature and feels he must, for life's sake, have a link with pure affection somewhere. Within ten lines Newson is announced ; but Henchard gets rid of him

by the desperate lie that Elizabeth-Jane is dead, thus driving
another nail in his own coffin, because he is fated to be judged
by such unpremeditated acts of violence. Farfrae finds it
difficult to forgive him for the attack in the corn-loft, and now
Henchard knows that Elizabeth-Jane will not understand the
motive of his lie. A beaten man, he attempts suicide, but is
saved by what appears to him to be a miracle, and by Elizabeth-
Jane's help shakes off his despair. " Then Henchard shaved
for the first time during many days, and put on clean linen, and
combed his hair : and was as a man resuscitated thenceforward."
He was heard saying to himself, " Who is such a reprobate as
I ? And yet it seems that even I be in Somebody's hand ! "

A kindlier, perhaps a less moral, novelist might have closed
the story here, with a new beginning for everybody, since
Elizabeth-Jane is to be married to Farfrae (Lucetta being
dead). But Hardy will not have this easy ethics. Henchard's
happiness could not have endured, because it was built on a lie.
Hardy calls the lie to Newson " the last defiant word of an irony
which took no thought of consequences "—the " dogged and
cynical indifference " shown by his walk as he entered the book.
It is as if Henchard had prayed, Let me get what I want by this
one last act of unjust violence, and then I'll settle down and
be good. But it won't work—in the moral world of Hardy.
Henchard's happiness rests on Elizabeth-Jane's love and regard,
which must be withdrawn when she discovers the lie. At
least, Henchard quickly comes to believe this, and decides to
go away before the disclosure comes. It is suggested that this
was unnecessary, because " when she knew what he had done
to keep her in ignorance she would refrain from hating him ".
But when Newson does come back again, and laughingly tells
how Henchard had got rid of him some months earlier, Elizabeth-
Jane says, " I said I would never forget him. But oh ! I think
I ought to forget him now." We, for our part, see all round the
action, and we know that Henchard is a better man than at any
time before : love has come into his life ; for the first time he
puts someone before himself. This is why the end of the book
leaves such a noble impression on the mind. And in the chapter
that describes Henchard's thoughts and feelings as he wanders
about working again as a hay-trusser, we see the Michael

Henchard that might have been if the petty obstructiveness of
life had not brought to the top the worse side of his nature.
The chapter is full of Hardy's philosophy, and of his finest
and most characteristic writing, and repays careful reading.
Its final pages describe Henchard's hopeful journey to his
daughter's wedding, carrying the goldfinch he intended as a
present, his cruel reception by Elizabeth-Jane, and his parting
words :

> . . . he did not sufficiently value himself to lessen his sufferings
> by strenuous appeal or elaborate argument. Waiving, therefore,
> his privilege of self-defence, he regarded only her discomposure.
> ' Don't ye distress yourself on my account,' he said, with proud
> superiority. ' I would not wish it—at such a time, too, as this.
> I have done wrong in coming to 'ee—I see my error. But it
> is only for once, so forgive it. I'll never trouble 'ee again,
> Elizabeth-Jane—no, not to my dying day ! Good-night.
> Good-bye ! '

Henchard always rises to the occasion when magnanimity is
called for : hence we can forgive him the rest. Elizabeth-Jane
fails miserably to answer the call here : and we find it hard to
forgive her in spite of the rest. Hardy says of her, " her gestures
beamed with mind ", and this is the keynote of her character :
but at this point an impulse of unreflecting emotion, of
Henchard's sort, would have saved her much grief to come.
Yet she is but an instrument : this act of hers is the last sword-
thrust of Fate the Matador ; the old bull is to be killed, and
she is the weapon chosen : no other would have served :
Henchard is killed with his own new-found redeeming virtue,
love.

So Henchard comes into his own, and sorry figures Farfrae
and Elizabeth-Jane cut beside him at the end. Farfrae has
just objected to continuing the search for Henchard because
to do so ' will make a hole in a sovereign ', when they come
upon Abel Whittle, and into that simplest of all mouths is put
the story of Henchard's death, which had occurred half-an-hour
previously. Farfrae's comment is, " Dear me—is that so ! "
As for Elizabeth, she said nothing. Henchard's will is there
to make her realise just what she has done. She takes it sensibly,
but one is glad she knows.

Henchard's profoundly tragic end is the artistic conclusion of the tale. But Elizabeth-Jane is left with the last word, to show how the reasonable person can see and achieve life's compensations. This last page, though a trifle to set against the harrowing bitterness of the tale itself, does leave us with a taste of something other than sheer hopelessness, and perhaps suggests a gentler philosophy of life.

From the streets of a considerable market-town we pass to a scene as remote from civilisation as was the life on Egdon, isolated not by space but by trees : a few houses and cottages, gardens and orchards, snipped out of the woodland, a sequestered spot outside the gates of the world. In Casterbridge life was complicated by business troubles and the need to make money ; in Little Hintock men are not idle, certainly, but their work consists for the most part in lending a helping hand to nature, and the curve of success or failure is so gradual as to be indistinguishable from the equability of a straight line. A Tempevale, with the lady at the Great House as the divinity who shapes the ends of the dwellers therein, and a prankish, faun-like being in the clever young doctor, said to be in league with the devil.

Of all who inhabit this incredibly lovely spot, the two who are most closely akin to its green loveliness are Giles Winterborne and Marty South, the only two unflawed characters in Hardy. Old Melbury is a true woodlander, but a trifle spoilt by social ambitions ; his daughter Grace he has made into a little snob, but she has not taken the infection badly, and when it passes off it leaves her one of the most delightful of heroines. The doctor and the lady at the Hall are exotics, but their machinations never approach the sordid. Even the Italianised American who descends twice into the vale with intent to disturb its peace is turned into the shadow of Satan with his hour-glass, and is heard to sigh three times before he finally goes away swearing. For in the woodland all life, it seems, has a dignity that precludes the pettiness of incident that at times lowered the tone of the last novel. The seasons pass visibly through the woods, and Hardy notes them as they go : it is a Winter evening when the story opens ; suddenly Spring is there, so that the rush of sap in the veins of the trees can almost be heard ; soon it is Summer, and the woodland seems to change from an open filigree to a solid opaque body of infinitely larger shape and importance ; then early Autumn, with orchards encrusted with scarlet and gold fruit under a luminous lavender mist, and late Autumn, with fallen leaves getting redder and hornier and rotting underfoot ; and so to Winter again, and March and May and June, and on to the wet cold second Autumn, the one that killed Giles Winterborne.

Marty South opens the book, as she ends it : a girl of twenty, splitting thatching-gads with unerring skill, but with a soft and well-shaped hand that might have guided the pencil or swept the string ; her face has a fulness of expression developed by a life of solitude, and its provisional curves have been forced into a premature finality by the early necessity for taking thought ; her chief claim to beauty is a head of abundant chestnut hair, which at the moment is being vainly coveted by the otherwise wealthy Mrs. Charmond at the House.

And soon we see through Marty's eyes, something of what Hardy calls the Sophoclean life of Little Hintock. She overhears a tale told at dead of night by Melbury, the timber merchant, to his wife, by the light of a candle that casts a moving thorn pattern of shade on Marty's unseen face : he is standing by a hoarded footprint, that of his daughter Grace, now away at school, and he tells his wife (she is the second Mrs. Melbury) how he had won his first wife, Grace's mother, by a trick from a friend who loved her ; how this friend afterwards became the father of Giles Winterborne ; and how he, Melbury, had promised to atone for his falsity by marrying his daughter to young Giles the son of his wronged friend. And Marty, who loves Giles herself, goes home and incontinently hacks off her beautiful hair for the rich woman.

When we meet Giles, who is in the apple and cider trade, we are at once attracted to him by his delightful habit of driving about with a specimen apple tree ; he stands in the market holding the apple tree like an ensign, and fixed to the spot by that fact, even when he sees Grace Melbury coming towards him. Our first impression of Grace, as a country girl who has forgotten the difference between bitter-sweets and John-apples but re-members that Giles would have addressed the parents of her late schoolfellows deferentially, is not a pleasant one. Hardy does not spare Giles's social shortcomings : there is a party which he gives in the hope of " hastening on things " with Grace ; it is a humorously horrible failure, so far as Grace and her father are concerned, what with the sticky furniture polish on the chairs, and the gravy that got splashed over Grace, and the slug she found in the winter-green, the greasy pack of playing-cards, and the country dances Grace has forgotten. Not that this kind of thing has much effect on Grace, who is, as Giles calls her, a stout-hearted girl ; but it troubles old Melbury greatly. Once, while he is walking with his daughter, Grace is addressed rudely by a ' gentleman-farmer ' excited at the loss of a fox ; and Melbury is roused to the sound generalisation that a woman takes her colour from the man she is walking with. It is this incident that decides Melbury that his prize piece is too good to be wasted on rough Giles, and he orders Grace to have as little to do with Giles as possible ; her agreement seems weak, but we must remember that she is not in love with Giles.

Giles meets the man who is presently to take Grace from him through one of the most remarkable of the lesser happenings in the novels. Among all the woodland there is one tree of more than arboreal importance. It stands in the garden of old John South, Marty's invalid father, who lies watching it swaying outside his window, in perpetual dread that it will fall and " squash the life out of him ". Dr. Fitzpiers is called in, and Giles explains : " The shape of it seems to haunt him like an evil spirit. He says that it is exactly his own age, that it has got human sense, and sprouted up when he was born on purpose to rule him, and keep him as its slave. Others have been like it afore in Hintock." Fitzpiers, with townsman's common-sense, says the obvious remedy is for the tree to be cut down, and orders this to be done before the patient wakes next morning. Accordingly next morning, in the presence of Fitzpiers, Giles draws back the curtains and exhibits the vacant patch of sky where the tall tree had been. The old man gasps and falls back dying. " Damned if my remedy hasn't killed him ! " says the doctor, with the perfect nonchalance of the young medico ; and asks Giles as they go down the stairs, " Who was that young lady we looked at over the hedge the other day ? "

The young lady in question was Grace, and as Giles goes out of the picture Fitzpiers comes in. He is a philanderer of more than usual interest : a versatile student, numbering among his subjects alchemy, astronomy, astrology, literature, metaphysics and anatomy, with a keenly appreciative, modern, unpractical mind and a real taste for abstract philosophy. His first conversation with Grace is beautifully recorded, and is unlike anything we have had before in the novels : the characters are unique, and the dialogue quite new ; Grace, educated but unsophisticated, Fitzpiers as irresponsible as only a young bachelor professional man can be. He employs, at this first meeting, the Frank Harris formula : he tells her how he had seen her first reflected in a mirror—" I thought, what a lovely creature ! The design is for once carried out. Nature has at last recovered her lost union with the Idea." Of course, given Fitzpiers at Little Hintock, an ' affair ' with the prettiest girl in the village could be foretold with certainty ; it is the existence of Giles and Marty that provides the real interest in what is to happen. At first Fitzpiers, having social ambitions, contemplates nothing more than a pleasant flirtation, but as the love-making proceeds his respect as well as his liking for Grace deepens, while she, though oddly affected by his proximity, maintains her solid regard for Giles. Fitzpiers is sufficiently attracted by the happy limitations of sylvan life—its smoke and its smells, its queer-shaped tools made from a horse's leg, its legends of exorcised spirits returning to the woodland at the rate of a cock's stride every New Year's Day, Old Style—to let the possibility of marriage with Grace at least enter his head. At the local Midsummer Eve incantations he manœuvres Grace into his arms, and a new, more passionate relationship has begun. Yet within a few minutes he is chasing Suke Damson, a hoydenish village maiden with bare arms, into a hayfield, where they spend the night under the midsummer moon.

Then begins an exhibition of the more unpleasant side of Fitzpiers. He is given to sneering at " yeoman Winterborne ", and is brusque with Grace over her desire for a church marriage. Grace sees Suke Damson coming out of Fitzpiers' house early one morning, with a long cloak insufficiently hiding her nightdress. Her ready acceptance of his clever explanation shows her goodness, but shows also that she is not yet infatuated with him, for she is able to make cool use of the incident to get him to agree to be married in church. Fitzpiers' love is little but physical desire, touched up with the bait of Melbury's money—the amount of which is so small as to make the thought of it a mean motive. And Fitzpiers is still uneasy at the social lapse. However, the marriage takes place, and Grace, now luxuriously circumstanced, is seen shrinking from the roughness of, and feeling superior to—of all things, Giles at his cider-making. A heavenly picture is given us of the process and its auxiliaries, with Giles as the apple-god. Her shallow complacency at this time shows Grace in a poor light.

At length Fitzpiers meets Mrs. Charmond, the much-talked-of lady at the Great House, who has been away till now. He finds in her not only a boyhood acquaintance, but a kindred soul, romantic, idle, daring. Mrs. Charmond hides strong passions under a frivolous archness ; she loves playing inconsequently on the dangerous edge of things. Hardy tells us she has little to be ashamed of in her past, and (apart from the fact that she is presently engaged deep with a married man) she is presented as a likeable person. The power with which Hardy enters into the personality of a character so far removed from his Wessex folk is remarkable. As for Fitzpiers, he is one of the few characters in Hardy who fit the theory that men's lives are dominated by sex (Jocelyn Pierston is another, and to some extent Jude and in a sense Boldwood are others, but there is a great array on the other side, of men with whom sex is a fascinating item in a long list of varied interests). Fitzpiers has sacrificed social ambition for Grace ; he now sacrifices professional ambition for the sake of flirting with Mrs. Charmond —he turns down a lucrative Budmouth practice in order to stay in Little Hintock.

Soon Grace finds out her husband's infatuation for Mrs. Charmond, and about the same time learns how he has lied to her over Suke Damson. She takes both discoveries quite calmly, but realises the ghastly mistake she has made. Just now Giles begins to come back to her life, and as he does so the tale breaks into lyric beauty. The antithesis of polished infidelity with homespun faith is pointed, and Grace learns a lesson that many a Hardy heroine is in need of learning but learns only, if at all, when the first blind choice is no longer there to delude.

She had made a discovery—one which to a girl of her nature
was almost appalling. She had looked into her heart, and
found that her early interest in Giles Winterborne had become
revitalised into luxuriant growth by her widening perceptions
of what was great and little in life. . . . Having discovered by
marriage how much that was humanly not great could co-exist
with attainments of an exceptional order, there was a revulsion
in her sentiments from all that she had formerly clung to in this
kind. Honesty, goodness, manliness, tenderness, devotion, for
her only existed in their purity now in the breasts of unvarnished
men ; and here was one who had manifested such towards her
from his youth up.

Certainly Giles grows chapter by chapter a finer and finer figure.
Melbury, too, is aware of the worthlessness of Grace's husband,
and his sorrow and care for his daughter are a little like those
of Soames Forsyte for Fleur, especially in his inability to get
angry with her when she turns upon him, not altogether unjustly, as one of the prime causes of her sorry situation.

So Melbury goes and pleads nobly but vainly with Mrs.
Charmond, though she does not come too badly out of the
interview. Then, in a powerful and astonishing scene, in which
Grace and Mrs. Charmond are lost in the wood, Grace learns
the full extent of her husband's amours. She is startled and
mortified, but not wounded, showing a passionless strength very
wonderful in so young a girl—she must still be under twenty.
This is shown still more clearly when Fitzpiers, having been
flung off his horse and badly hurt in the wood, fails to return
home, and Mrs. Charmond and Suke Damson come uninvited
to Grace's room to wait for news of their all-too-common
beloved ! Grace is at first ironic—" Wives all, let us enter his
bedroom together "—but presently philosophy comes to her
aid and " a tenderness spreads over her like a dew ". But
Fitzpiers does not come back : he has gone, wounded, to Mrs.
Charmond, has been devotedly cared for by her, and carried
off to the Continent.

So love begins again between Giles and Grace. They are
absurdly scrupulous, for though Melbury has roused in them
some vain hope of a divorce, they dare not even kiss for fear
of wrong-doing. It is vexatious to see them so *very* careful :

but doubtless it is all or nothing ! Giles shows almost super-human self-restraint : for Grace, thinking the divorce is as good as got, wants him to be loving to her, while he, having had information that it cannot be obtained, but not daring to shatter her hopes, must needs refrain. He did indeed yield to weakness at one point.

Since it was so—since it had come to this, that Grace, deeming herself free to do it, was virtually asking him to demonstrate that he loved her—since he could demonstrate it only too truly —since life was short and love was strong—he gave way to the temptation, notwithstanding that he perfectly well knew her to be wedded irrevocably to Fitzpiers. Indeed, he cared for nothing past or future, simply accepting the present and what it brought, deciding once in his life to clasp in his arms her he had watched over and loved so long.

And that was the only satisfaction Giles Winterborne ever got out of a love as deep as any in Hardy.

It is now that Grace appears at her weakest. She is, as she always has been, completely at the bidding of her father. At his command she would have married Giles, at his command she married Fitzpiers instead ; at his command she has again encouraged Giles and again left him. Now he tells her she is to take Fitzpiers back—for that worthy has written to say he is returning to England and wishes to meet Grace. We must remember that Grace has never hated Fitzpiers : apart from the ' other women ' he has treated her quite nicely, and as she does not love him she has never been bitterly jealous. She is miserable, almost hysterical, at her father's new instructions, but says she will ' try '. She shows no character, but when she suddenly hears Fitzpiers' voice she does the only thing open to her—she runs away, disappears into the woodland. There, after going on for some miles, she stumbles on a little hut, and finds it inhabited by Giles. And so we have the infinitely beautiful and tragic chapter in which Giles, in spite of an illness that he hides from Grace, sleeps outside in the rain to shield her name, and so comes to his death—killed, as Grace realises, by ' cruel propriety '.

The rewooing of Grace by Fitzpiers that occupies the conclud-ing chapters is made pleasant by the skill and patience displayed

by Fitzpiers, but is fiercely satirical in its picture of Grace faithless
to the memory of Giles.   It is perhaps because he realised this
that Hardy included the episode of the man-trap.   Just as we are
beginning to forget Fitzpiers' failings we are reminded that he
has spoilt another marriage, that of Tim Tangs and Suke Damson.
And we come in sight of tragedy in Tim's preparation of the man-
trap (the terrors of which are powerfully described), especially
when we find it is Grace who is in danger.   It is as if Hardy had
suddenly remembered there had been no cruelty in this book so
far !   But the trap serves a better purpose in causing a moment
of tense emotion which is necessary to get Fitzpiers and Grace
round the point.   It has the effect of rendering Grace's surrender
less displeasing than it would otherwise have been, and is a fine
example of Hardy's technique.   Nevertheless, the surrender wipes
Grace out of the picture, and leaves us only with Giles and
Marty South.   Of Marty we have seen little for many chapters
now, but she comes to pray with Grace over the dead body of
Giles.   Marty has a gift of penetration.   When Grace says,
" He died for me ", Marty replies, " He belongs to neither of us
now, and your beauty is no more powerful with him than my
plainness.   He never cared for me, and he cared much for you ;
but he cares for us both alike now."   And when Grace objects
that they must not pray for Giles's soul, Marty says, " Nobody
would know ", and Grace cannot resist the argument.   Grace is
abased when she realises she has never understood Giles as Marty
has done.   She has a wonderful vision of the woodland life as it
was seen and known and loved by these two woodlanders, and
declares they should have married.   It is not till Grace goes back
to Fitzpiers that Marty feels she at long last has Giles all to
herself.   That immortal passage in which she speaks her love
over his grave is too great to follow immediately on the trivialities
of Grace and Fitzpiers, so Hardy skilfully prepares for it by inter-
posing a grand piece of chorus work.   The chorus of timber
workers gives its shrewd comments on the doctor and his wife,
and on marriage in general, and as they pass the graveyard they
see Marty South standing motionless by the gate.   " 'A was ever
a lonely maid ", says the chorus.   She was indeed, and the only
character in the book fit to be put side by side with Giles.   She is
a superb sketch, but done in too few lines—we should have liked

more of Marty ; and Winterborne stands as the only figure in the front rank of Hardy's great presentations of character. For this reason *The Woodlanders*, though the most beautiful of the Wessex novels (Hardy said he liked it as a story best of all), has some difficulty in holding place with the greatest of them.

§ 5

THE CLIMAX

Tess of the D'Urbervilles

Again (but for the last time) we find Hardy putting all his strength into an opening chapter. The method of presenting the necessary facts about the D'Urberville descent, the racy humour of the dialogue, the picture of John Durbeyfield : all are beyond praise. The second chapter is an equally beautiful piece of work, and more varied. Beginning with a description of the secluded and languorous Vale of Blackmoor, in which lies Marlott, Tess's home village, it goes on to present a group of girls and women, dancing according to ancient custom ; their dancing is disturbed by the richly comic passing of John Durbeyfield, singing drunk, in the carriage he has hired to transport his new splendours. This provides an introduction to Tess, who is one of the dancing maidens. Not much is made of her yet, but attention is drawn to her freshness, her innocent eyes, the phases of childhood that yet linger over the " bouncing handsome womanliness " that is hers at the age of seventeen. Hardy's making Tess the offspring of the father we have seen and the mother we are shortly to see reminds us of Candida and the equally impossible Burgess. But whereas Shaw's point is that education and environment can obliterate heredity, Hardy's is that in the absence of such education and meliorative environment heredity is everything. But the wealth of this chapter is not exhausted : presently comes Angel Clare, ' hiking ' through the village, and pausing in the evening light to watch the dancing : and the two star-crossed ones have their premonitory wistful first sight of each other. The whole chapter is seasoned with quiet ironic comment.

Now comes ugliness. The next chapter passes to a depressing

picture of the Durbeyfield *ménage*, the immediate stock and surroundings from which Tess sprang. Nothing of the idyllic side of country life here ! No detail is spared of the depravity of Mrs. Durbeyfield—considered as a mother : she is likeable enough in other connections ; a happy child, Tess calls her. Ugliness deepens when Joan Durbeyfield and her husband are found soaking in the public-house, not a decent village inn but a fusty bedroom with furtive after-hours drinking going on. Here, of course, is a first explanation of what is to come. Tess has grown up in this household, with its slip-shod morality, has been brought up by these slack-twisted parents. She is pointedly said to take after her mother in physical build. She is pretty, ignorant, easily-moved. The result is arithmetical, as one of the elderly boozers hints.

And then, to lift us out of the squalor, comes the story of the death of Prince the horse, with its pathos and heroism, its beauty and humour, and that modern beauty-humour synthesis that we shall find again in the poems. Its practical result is to make it necessary for Tess to begin earning money, and she is persuaded to apply to her " rich relation ", Mrs. D'Urberville, who lives with her son Alec at the big house called The Slopes. Thus all that has gone before has been leading up to Alec D'Urberville. And we have had a hint of Angel Clare. So the whole tragedy is implicit in the first few chapters.

These D'Urbervilles are nothing but Stokes who have bought up the old mansion and adopted the old name. Alec is twenty-four, swarthy, with full lips and a bold rolling eye. Hardy speaks again of the attribute in Tess upon which the rolling eye at once fell, " a luxuriance of aspect inherited from her mother " ; and, moved by the impending tragedy, he is inspired to those wonderful paragraphs on the cruel irony of Tess's fate that will be quoted later as examples of Hardy's noblest style. The mere passage of events brings Tess nearer to D'Urberville's embrace. Tess herself feels this obscurely, but her mother has put into her mind the idea of marriage with D'Urberville as a very likely possibility, and though Tess is angry at the question being talked about, she is naturally not repelled by the idea. Her state of mind is marvellously shown, but she does not—obviously cannot—behave otherwise than any decent country girl would behave. An emotional crisis is brought on when D'Urberville woos her, not with Troy's broadsword or Manston's piano or Knight's chess-playing, but with a furiously-driven horse and trap.

So Tess looks after Mrs. D'Urberville's fowls and Alec D'Urberville follows her about. It is all rather sordid after *The Woodlanders*, and worse is yet to come. Tess joins—with it but not of it—a Saturday night drinking pilgrimage to Chase-borough. A vulgarly-comic squabble arises, in the course of which Car Darch, D'Urberville's last wench, attacks Tess as her supplanter. Tess is rescued by D'Urberville, who carries her off on horseback into the woods. She is tired out, so he puts her down on the leaves, wrapped in his great-coat. She falls asleep, and wakes to find herself, as the next ' phase ' says, " maiden no more ".

There was every possible excuse for Tess. She was badly parented, badly brought up, and had been told over and over again that D'Urberville would marry her (" if not afore, then after ", as Mrs. Durbeyfield said, though not in Tess's hearing). She was " a little dazed " by him, and half-believed he ' loved ' her. She was only seventeen, she was tired out, and asleep. All this Hardy shows, with great clearness—shows it inevitable that Tess should ' fall '—in other words should undergo a simple natural experience before she was married. He now goes on to show how, through ' ideas ' of one kind and another existing in the minds of her fellows, this simple natural experience brought appalling misery and tragedy into several lives.

That is the moral side of the matter. From the point of view of pure art this is what happens. Hardy, the creator, says : Here is something, a human soul, unpromising enough, though with promising features. Watch while I make something else, something greater, out of it. To do this I can add either a happy element or an unhappy one. Either, if of the required quality, will produce the effect I intend. And thus, like a dispassionate scientist, he holds up his pipette (or is it burette ?—anyway, his dropping-tube) containing the happy element—Angel Clare ; but after a moment decides no, and adds the other instead.

In the second ' phase ' squalor is put aside, and beauty and dignity begin ; out of the squalor rises the tragic tale of Tess. She is indeed—so swiftly, so miraculously—a greater Tess.

Her handling of D'Urberville is magnificent—as if she were a real D'Urberville princess, he says. She feels the vital truth, that it is because there is not love between them that what has happened is " loathsome ". At her mother's reproach she turns passionately upon her ; " O mother, my mother ! How could I be expected to know ? I was a child when I left this house four months ago." The remainder of this section is devoted to a showing of the period of suspended animation that Tess endured until the death of her baby a few months old ; this phase closes with the classic picture of the baptism and subsequent burial of Sorrow the Undesired. The section includes, however, a great deal of argument designed to palliate Tess's ' offence '. Hardy doubtless felt this to be necessary, since the ' offence ' was, at that time, of a furiously controversial nature, with the argument chiefly on one side ; otherwise the length to which he carries his defence is inartistic, though we would not miss one point of his wise and tender reasoning. The substance of his defence will be considered later. At the moment it is desirable to note the suggestion that Tess's experience was a liberal education. If Angel Clare could have felt that ! The suggestion is an answer to my picture of the scientist and his two dropping-tubes. Clare and happiness from the beginning would have been best for Tess, but suffering with Alec D'Urberville first, followed by happiness with Angel Clare, would have produced a truly wonderful result.

But life is irrepressible, and Tess makes a fresh start : hope, youth, spirit rise again and give us the beautiful ' phase ' called The Rally. We have some marvellous colour-photography of the two vales, the one she is leaving and the one she goes to— the Valley of the Great Dairies, watered by the River Froom. As she comes down from the heights on to Talbothays' Dairy she breaks into the sublime canticle : " O ye Sun and Moon . . . bless ye the Lord, praise him and magnify him for ever " !

And presently comes the discovery that Fate has sent her to the farm where Angel Clare is working as a pupil. Hardy gives us an adequate sketch of him—fixed abstracted eyes, sensitive and delicate but firm mouth, nebulous, vague, preoccupied. The hard logical deposit that runs through his mental constitution is described later : this is not to be confused with a logical habit of mind, which he evidently has not, for he has been through precisely the same experience as that through which Tess has gone : " in London he was carried off his head and nearly entrapped by a woman much older than himself, though luckily he escaped not greatly the worse for the experience ". In describing it to Tess later on he tells how he had " plunged into eight-and-forty hours' dissipation with a stranger ". And Tess exclaims, " 'tis just the same ". But Clare never sees this. I wonder if that " deposit " ought not to have been called ' *illogical* '.

All this is in the future. Clare's attention is soon drawn to Tess, but he of course has no recollection of having seen her before, though she remembers him at once. From Clare and from others, during this period we get constant reference, dramatically ironic, to Tess's virginity. " What a fresh and virginal daughter of Nature that milkmaid is ! " If these references are merely ironic they are very crude and tasteless. But it is highly probable they are full of meaning—of Hardy's view of Tess as still essentially maiden and pure. Helped by a June evening, they draw near to each other. Each is attractively puzzled by the other. Tess becomes very happy indeed, for she has been transplanted from the scene of her grief, life is strong within her, and she is in the early stages of love, when it is exciting but not disturbing. Clare is as yet only interested, but their work with the cows in the summer dawns leads him further in, for at these times Tess looks to him like " a visionary essence of woman ", with a strange and ethereal beauty. It is strange, perhaps fateful, that he should have seen her under this aspect in these first impressionable days, for Hardy does as a matter of fact, lay great stress throughout this time on the opposite quality in Tess. At one time—" there was nothing ethereal about her face ; all was real vitality, real warmth, real incarnation ". At another, when she was flushed with sleep—" the brimfulness of her nature breathed from her ". So that when at last he clasps her in his arms it is as " the desire of his eyes ".

All this time, side by side with the main theme, there has been developed the second subject of the loves of the other three milkmaids—Izz, Retty and Marian—for Clare. It is beautifully, pathetically done, and includes in its course the exquisite idyll

of Clare's carrying of all four girls, in their Sunday muslins, one
by one across the flooded road.[1] The three girls and their feelings, at this and other moments, are subtly differentiated. Their
love for Clare is almost as real, quite as intense, as Tess's. Apart
from verisimilitude, why did Hardy introduce this second subject ? Was it to make Tess's love less exceptional, and therefore
less important ?—one of a bed of flowers drawn up by the sun ?
But there *was* that premonitory meeting four years ago.

And all the time, too, the landscape background is being
painted in : an unrolling picture of the life of the farm so rich
and fascinating as to divide the interest even of so absorbing a
human story.

The fourth phase shows us, during that long, hot summer,
Clare's love intensifying and Tess steadily refusing to agree to
any sort of binding or engagement. We get more knowledge
about Clare, and find him intellectually admirable. We see
more of his family, especially of his father—a good, enthusiastic,
intolerant parson. Suddenly a half-forgotten line of story comes
swinging in to converge upon the new one : we hear that Alec
D'Urberville has met old Mr. Clare and, having first quarrelled
with him, has been converted to a new way of life. The new and
apparently irrelevant fact lies waiting till the time comes for its
effect to be felt. Tess's holding out against Clare's importunity
is kept up almost to the point of incredibility, but at last she
consents to be " his for ever and ever ". Five times she has
tried to tell him of the obstacle, and five times has been driven
to a subterfuge. Having at last said yes, she breaks into a " dry
hard sobbing ", but in the days that follow she " lived in
spiritual altitudes more nearly approaching ecstasy than any
other period of her life ". We remember Hardy said that her
early days at Talbothays were the " happiest " in her life, and
observe the careful distinction of the two states of mind. As
they wander about, enjoying the new freedom and openness of
their love, Hardy continually points over their shoulder at the
waiting shadows : sometimes the air is tense with terror, as in
some old Norse saga of doom. The omens thicken, but the

---

[1] It is amusing to remember that for the purpose of serial publication
Hardy was forced to make Clare carry them across, not in his arms, but
in a wheel-barrow.

quiet wedding takes place; still they continue—the legendary death-foreboding coach, the crowing cock, the fearsome D'Urberville portraits, and finally the news of Retty Priddle's attempt to kill herself. This last blow turns the scale for Tess: she will tell Clare there and then. Had he not, even before his marriage vows, sworn that he would never hurt or neglect her?

And so we come to the most lacerating scene in all Hardy. There is tragedy as dark, sorrow as great, in *Jude*, but it happens to people who have chosen their own way, offered themselves to the torment, understand the nature of their punishment. But this is different—how different need not be laboured. The scene is one of the 'inevitable' ones of Hardy. The "hard logical deposit" explains, but it does not excuse, Clare's behaviour. What is unforgivable in it is his refusal to make any allowance for her on account of his own similar 'fall' (he has told his story easily, asked forgiveness coolly, and receiving it, has dismissed the business lightly), but one has to remember the Victorian formulas—one for men and one for women—on the subject. The relation of Clare and Tess, that night and the next day, is imagined absolutely. Clare's mental workings are not admirable. He shifts his ground in an odd way for one so 'logical'. At different times he objects (*a*) that Tess is not "pure, innocent", (*b*) that she is "another man's wife by nature", (*c*) that it would be bad for his children if their mother were known to have been seduced before her marriage. These last two cruel irrelevances merely confuse the issue. Yet the astonishing sleep-walking incident shows that some sort of love has got a hold on his heart. If he could have remembered that 'great thoughts come from the heart!'

Tess goes home to the philosophic Joan and her most unphilosophic husband, and Clare leaves England. Before departing he visits his father's house. The choosing of King Samuel's words in praise of a virtuous woman as the reading for the evening is as natural as it is ironic; but the irony is distinctly overdone, and probability lacking, when Mrs. Clare concludes her sequent homily with the words, "Well, I wish I could have seen her, Angel. Since she is pure and chaste she would have been refined enough for me." Excellent, however, is her perception of her son's agitation, and her quiet visit and question to him : " Angel—is she a young woman whose history will bear investigation ? "

" ' She is spotless ! ' he replied ; and felt that if it had sent him to eternal hell there and then he would have told that lie." And one comments : True ; but why ? For whose sake is the lie told ?—for Tess's, or his own ? Tess cannot stay at home, and wanders from place to place " with some of the habitude of the wild animal ". A pretty piece of satire on ' sport '—the dying birds in the wood after the shooting-party—gives her another opportunity to show her lovely brave soul. She chooses to work under a slave-driving master, preferring tyranny to gallantry. At last, in despair at not hearing from Clare, and ground down by poverty and drudgery, she decides to go and see Clare's parents. Her fifteen-mile walk is finely described, but ill-luck dogs her still, symbolised by the piece of blood-stained butcher's paper which beats up and down by the gate as she rings vainly at the vicar's bell. For she misses the vicar, misses Clare's mother, and ' contacts ' instead his egregious brothers and Mercy Chant, Clare's otherwise intended. Hardy calls this " the greatest misfortune of her life " : it certainly robbed her of her chance to wipe out all the others, and led directly to the culminating one of all. For plodding desperately back to her toil, she meets the converted Alec D'Urberville again.

The white-hot glow of inspired narration that has made us live the story with Hardy cools off a little now, and one has some slight difficulty in believing in Alec D'Urberville : his enthusiasm at learning of the baby that was born, and died, is unconvincing, his amusingly villainous " morally you belong to me " more so. An extraordinary thing is Tess's handing on of sceptical arguments learnt from Clare, not understood by herself, but producing the unintended effect of undermining D'Urberville's new and shallow-rooted beliefs. Once again it is soul-destroying weariness that bends Tess a little to acknowledge kindness in D'Urberville's offers of help, and realising the danger of the feeling going further she writes an infinitely pitiful letter to Clare. Clare, in the larger climate of Brazil has already realised how much of purely insular convention has underlain his shocked feelings, and about this time his morality is thoroughly cleaned up by a clear-headed stranger (who dies as soon as he has done his beneficent work). Nobly enduring all things, Tess now has to go to the assistance of her parents, and the misery of the eviction of the family stirs a bitter sense of Clare's unjust cruelty. At the same time D'Urberville's kindness grows more urgent, and what with one thing and another Tess is brought to entertain the idea that " in a brute sense this man alone was her husband ".

And so comes the ' fulfilment '. Clare returns to England, but though he has had Tess's two letters and another wonderfully concocted by Izz and Marian, he still hesitates as to where truth, decency and love should take him : by the time he has decided to seek Tess it is too late, and he finds her as D'Urberville's mistress. This term is a shocking one to apply to our sweet Tess, but in the paragraph describing her as she appears before Clare, Hardy deliberately depicts her as now for the first time smirched : and this is the book's tragedy.

> Tess appeared on the threshold—not at all as he had expected to see her—bewilderingly otherwise, indeed. Her great natural beauty was, if not heightened, rendered more obvious by her attire. She was loosely wrapped in a cashmere dressing-gown of gray-white, embroidered in half-mourning tints, and she wore slippers of the same hue. Her neck rose out of a frill of down, and her well-remembered cable of dark-brown hair was partially coiled up in a mass at the back of her head and partly hanging on her shoulder—the evident result of haste.

Her killing of D'Urberville at least wipes out *this* stain, and we are relieved to find that Clare does not shrink from her when he hears what she has done. He ponders stupidly on " the extinction of her moral sense ", but he embraces her, says he loves her ; and Tess is content.

Something like happiness, a ghost of happiness, begins for them as they roam about the countryside. Tess's simple soul has entered into Clare, and he says, " When they have forgotten us we can make for some port ". They wander into the New Forest, and find lodging in a vacant furnished mansion. This part of the story, brief as it is, is like the fairy tale their whole life should have been. After a week they slip out to avoid discovery and make for the North. Some novelists would have let them get there !—but Hardy must be true to life, and gives us a marvellous picture of the coming of dawn on Stonehenge and the quiet arrest. Here again, a lesser writer would have stopped. But Hardy, in a very short chapter of purest art, brings his story to its dreadful end, and puts the pinnacle on the massive structure of his indictment of society : " ' Justice ' was done ", he says. And leaves us with that strange picture of Clare and 'Liza-'Lu—bent, weeping, praying—creeping on hand in hand : 'Liza-'Lu, a spiritualised image of Tess.

Tess of the D'Urbervilles seems to me beyond doubt the greatest of the Wessex novels. The material of *Jude the Obscure* is vaster and more varied, but it is not completely digested, whereas the development of this story moves with the rhythmic certainty of music to its predestined close. As beautiful as *Far from the Madding Crowd* or *The Woodlanders*, it plunges far deeper into the tragic heart of life, and it has none of the imperfections that mar *The Mayor of Casterbridge* and *The Return of the Native*. Tess herself is the most sublime figure in Hardy, combining supreme beauty with a nobility that elevates the whole conception of human nature. And yet she is not, like Marty South, flawless : she has the *hamartia*, the fatal weakness, necessary to give tragedy a rational if not a moral basis. From whatever aspect it is considered—subsidiary characters, landscape background, intellectual and moral content, adequacy of style—*Tess of the D'Urbervilles* has no superior among Hardy's novels, and it must take its place among the three or four greatest works of fiction the nineteenth century produced in England.

§ 6

A REST, AND A GRIM CONCLUDING MASTERPIECE

The Well-Beloved ; Jude the Obscure

I find it difficult to know whether to take *The Well-Beloved* seriously or not. If it is accepted as a satire on the artistic temperament (at one point it is quite definitely a satire on middle age) there is no difficulty in taking it as a successful work, seriously intended and humorously written. There is plenty of ground for this view of the book, notably its conclusion, where the artist, having lost the artistic temperament that had so long led him astray, settles down as an energetic member of committees whose purpose is to modernise the ancient Isle of Slingers. But the preface asks us to read the book as a frankly fantastic story, one embodying moreover a Platonic dream. In such a reading the numerous instances of the ridiculous into which the story falls appear in a different and less helpful light. In either case the book is thoroughly enjoyable, though possessing few of the features that delight us in the other novels.

Part I presents well enough Jocelyn Pierston, the rake with a theory, who, while hesitating over Avice Caro as a possible embodiment of his flitting ideal, runs away, farcically and in-effectively, with Marcia Bencomb. He is then twenty. In Part II, twenty years later, he returns to the Isle to find Avice dead, and her daughter, otherwise her mother's image, an un-educated laundress. His middle-aged attempt to rouse the girl to tenderness over the linen is distinctly funny, and funnier still is the moment when he is confronted with his own roving tem-perament in the person of this young girl, Avice the second. " I have loved fifteen a'ready ! " she tells him laughing. And when he asks with a sinking heart, " Am I—one of them ? " she ponders critically before she replies, " You was ; for a week ". However, undiscouraged, he takes her to London, where he be-haves perfectly in spite of the episode of the mouse-trap, and finally asks her to marry him, only to be met with the confession that she is already married to a quarryman at home.

Part III begins with an amusing account of the unromantic bufferism of Alfred Somers, another middle-aged painter, in contrast with Jocelyn, who, even at sixty, refuses to grow up. Harbouring still his " genealogical passion ", he proposes to and is accepted by Avice the third, granddaughter of the first Avice. He decides to be honest with her, and tells her how he had loved her mother before her and her grandmother before that.

" But . . . Mr. Pierston ! You are not old enough ? Why, how old are you ?—you have never told me."

" I am very old."

" My mother's [young man], and my grandmother's " said she, looking at him no longer as a possible husband, but as a strange fossilised relic in human form . . ., " and were you my great-grandmother's too ? " she asked with an expectant interest. . . .

And so, Jocelyn having left Avice the first for Marcia, Avice the third now runs away from him to marry Marcia's son. Jocelyn has an illness, and recovering, finds himself old indeed—bald, sciatic, with his artistic sense quite gone, and with it the Well-Beloved bee.

I suppose that, in spite of all the anticlimaxes, Hardy does stick to his idea with such persistence and skill that he compels us at last to take it seriously.

Although *Jude the Obscure* was published in 1895 and *Tess of the D'Urbervilles* in 1891, Hardy tells us the later book was begun, at least as to note-making, eight years earlier. Nevertheless it is impossible not to see in it an artistic (not of course a narrative) sequel, or parallel, to *Tess*. It looks as if Hardy, having shown the consequences of certain things happening to a young woman, decided to show the consequences of the same things happening to a young man. The extent, and the limits, of the parallelism we shall examine as we proceed.

For the seven mystic phases of the story of Tess, we have here a more commonplace six. ' Marygreen ', the first, opens quietly, as a book long brooded, but with a striking contrast in Jude, a boy of eleven, being patted on the head by schoolmaster Phillotson, afterwards his deadly rival for the soul of Sue. The humblest of all Hardy's heroes in his origins, Jude scares crows in a wide and lonely depression in the land, land that is harrowed to a meanly utilitarian appearance as of new corduroy. We get the accustomed sense of Hardy's feeling for the soil, every inch of it worked over or played on through countless generations. But little Jude has a sensitiveness like Tess's : he feels his life united to that of the rooks by a magic thread of fellow-feeling which makes him an inefficient rook-scarer, so he is beaten and dismissed in a scene of sad and satirical comedy. He reflects on his unwantedness and his growing responsibilities, and we get our first indication that this book is to differ from *Tess* in being a book of thinking more than of feeling. Showing courage for a child of eleven he crosses the field which the farmer had forbidden him to be seen in again (not that any human orders could keep Jude out of this field : its depressing flattened hollow is symbolic, and many a crisis in Jude's history finds him crossing it)—and, climbing a ladder by a rick, he looks towards Christminster, the University town to which the schoolmaster has gone. He is an imaginative boy, and inspiration comes into the book to show us his worship of the distant City of Light.

Here begins that passionate and pathetic longing of Jude's for academic distinction that follows him through life. There are those who deny that Hardy can have meant this when he spoke in the preface of " the fret and fever, derision and disaster, that may press in the wake of the strongest passion known to humanity ", but much rereading and consideration leaves unchanged my belief in this interpretation. Jude's love flickers like an ill-filled lamp ; his dream of scholarship gleams white and bright to the day of his death. After all, it is the dream that drew Faust to destruction, the passion that was sung by those who carried the Grammarian to his funeral, the desire for ' fame ' which Milton called the last infirmity of noble mind.

Certainly the desire for abstract learning is strong within him now. Surmounting all obstacles, he grinds up Latin and Greek as he goes his baker's rounds, and by the time he is sixteen (to-day he would be passing his School Certificate examination, with a smattering of five subjects !) he is able to hymn the rising moon with the Carmen Saeculare, though his religious leanings cause him shortly to forsake this pagan trend for the Greek Testament. He supposes he will have to keep himself when he gets to Christminster, so he learns stone-cutting and becomes a skilled mason. Here is character, surely, the character that is said to mould circumstances. But circumstances have, for some people, an adamantine quality, and character itself may have its flaws.

One Saturday, when he is about nineteen, he walks home across the country counting up what he has done and what is yet to do, seeing himself one day Doctor of Divinity, perhaps a bishop, but anyway a pure and wise man and the pride of Christminster. At this moment Arabella throws herself obscenely into his life, and Jude wakes up to that fourth dimension, sex. Arabella is sex incarnate, and Jude is described as experiencing, after his first few words with her, an ardour, a fresh and wild pleasure, a feeling that he has acquired a bright sensitive new skin.

As Clare with Tess, it should have been Sue who came first. But there is a difference between the cases : Tess was a victim, Jude is consenting to his own seduction ; he sees this " with his intellectual eye, as by the light of a falling lamp ". Even though he at once perceives there is nothing in Arabella that he can respect, he is definitely attracted by her ; after which, if the gods are wroth, who can complain ? Yet it is not this that keeps him from Christminster, perhaps it is not altogether this that disturbs his happiness with Sue. It is not our greatest sins that necessarily have the worst consequences. Arabella we need not dislike at this stage : she is " a complete and substantial female animal ", and hungers for female animal satisfactions. Jude was made for higher satisfactions. For the time being he has turned to the lower one, and Hardy shows powerfully the catastrophic overthrow of his intellectual position at the first call of sex : Christminster has quite passed out of his mind. Arabella sets herself to work Jude up to copulation point, and succeeds at the second attempt—managed cleverly if grotesquely by means of an egg she is supposed to be hatching in her bosom.

Two months later, just as Jude has come to his senses, is seeing Arabella for what she is, and is thinking again of his ' plans ', she announces that a baby is on the way, and Jude at once agrees to marry her. This seems to mean the final abandonment of Christminster dreams, and he does some self-communing—but not much : Hardy's people, even in Jude, are not very introspective. Three discoveries follow on the marriage : that Arabella has been a barmaid, that she has false hair (as well as false dimples), and that the coming baby was a myth. The shock of the last discovery is well and restrainedly shown, and Jude's reflections on his plight afford Hardy the first of many opportunities to suggest his view of the imperfections of the marriage law. When Jude makes his final discovery, that Arabella had deliberately led him on to copulation as a step to a forced marriage, he ventures (for he is a very mild and tolerant young man) to argue gently with her, implying himself " entrapped " into paying " a life-long penalty ". He assumes his own blamelessness in the affair rather too easily. The scenes of the pig-killing and of the Sunday morning scuffle are almost intolerably hideous, but perform their legitimate purpose of plumbing the depths to which Jude has been dragged. If I may venture on an irreverent suggestion, there are touches in the former episode that make it read like a burlesque of the murder of Duncan in ' Macbeth '. For instance, Arabella : " Well,—you must do the sticking—there's no help for it. I'll show you how. Or I'll do it myself—I think I could." Jude makes a cool attempt to commit suicide, and this failing, gets drunk. Fortunately, at this point Arabella leaves Jude, and shortly departs for Australia. Jude is free again, but he is not the same Jude. He has tasted evil. However, without hesitation he resumes the scholastic path ; his getting back on the old track is beautifully shown, the exalted mood being presented with Hardy's own ineffable quietness of style.

Comparison with *Tess* at this stage will be useful. Jude's touch on the pitch has been heavier, more defiling, than Tess's ; yet he too might have had his ' rally ', at Christminster as Tess had hers at Talbothays. As she met Clare, he is to meet Sue : each the perfect mate—with an inhibition. Jude had been made by his ' preliminary ' impossible for Sue in fact (having a wife) as well as in moral nature ; Tess is unfit for Clare only in a conventional sense. Nevertheless, the main disruptive factor in the relationship of Jude and Sue is not Jude's secondary mating but Sue's, with Phillotson.

' Christminster ' opens with Jude's, and our, first glimpse of Sue—in a photograph, wearing a hat like a halo. His first real sight of her, some days later, shows her engaged in " a sweet, saintly Christian business," of lettering texts in an ecclesiastical shop. Both glimpses afford a striking contrast to the first meeting with Arabella, but the second misleads Jude as to Sue's religious position ; we presently see her, as he does not, buying pagan deities to put in place of " those everlasting Church fal-lals ". She is, indeed, the first (and last) ' free-thinking ' woman in Hardy, and saw the light about the same time as the early Shaw heroines. Where Jude has had experience of ' life ', she has had adventures in thought, and is intellectually far in advance of him.

Jude has a marvellous introduction to Christminster—how different from that of the normal freshman : but Jude was older, twenty-two ; men go up to the universities, especially to-day, much too early to make the most of the almost limitless opportunities. He quickly realises it is something more than a wall that separates him from college life, but for the present he is more deeply engaged in getting to know Sue. We have some wonderful descriptions of her—Hardy had seen this girl, just as he had seen Tess. Jude finds her " a revelation of woman ". She has charm—naturalness, impulsiveness, sensitiveness—that moves both Jude and Phillotson. For Jude has looked up Phillotson (still a schoolmaster) and, by the usual irony, has introduced him to Sue—presently persuades him to take Sue as a pupil-teacher. It is not long before he sees that Sue and Phillotson are on some sort of terms, and being handicapped by Arabella, can only cry hopelessly, " O, he's too old for her—too old ! "

And now he awakes to a sudden realisation that Christminster is not for him. Having written to five carefully if naïvely selected Heads of Colleges, he receives a single tardy reply advising him to stick to his job. His own calculations have shown him that in the absence of sympathetic help from inside, the gates of the University will never open for him, and now, in a cold sweat of terror he sees his dream blown off on the wind. Sue also being unattainable, he is driven almost mad with suffering. He returns, beaten, to Marygreen, and falling asleep for weariness, awakens in hell. " If he had been a woman he must have screamed under the nervous tension which he was now undergoing. But that relief being denied to his virility, he clenched his teeth in misery, bringing lines about his mouth like those of the Laocoon, and corrugations between his brows."

Yet, so strong is his " passion " that within an hour he has set his foot on a new path that might lead to a height not too far removed from the one he had been aiming at : he has interviewed the curate and opened to him a plan for entering the Church.

' Melchester ' is the scene of the next phase. Sue has gone into a training college there, so Jude gets work on the Cathedral, takes lodgings that would not have disgraced a curate, studies theology, and plays chants on a harmonium : this is the nearest he ever came to achieving the cultured life. Sue is engaged to be married to Phillotson in two years' time, but being of the slow-developing type is not in love with either Phillotson or

Jude. She studies Jude with interest, believing she has got far past his stage. He on the other hand calls her conventional —he is thinking of her actions, she of his orthodox mind. But presently he has full proof of her unconventionality. She refuses to stay in the training college, wades through a river to escape, and comes to Jude wet to the skin. He walks the streets while she changes into his Sunday clothes, and presently finding her asleep with some brandy he has given her, he stands with his back to the fire regarding her, and seeing in her almost a divinity. Is it not refreshing reading in this year of grace ?— Then comes the wonderful chapter of talk through the night— self-revelation on the part of Sue and shock on Jude's part. This is not surprising, for Sue has lived a queerly ' modern ' life—going for walking-tours with a Cambridge undergraduate and sharing a sitting-room with him for fifteen months.

But Sue is to marry Phillotson. The schoolmaster has up till now been presented in a totally unsympathetic light. Now for a short time we see him in his new school-house at Shaston, dreaming a dream of great beauty, reading Sue's frank, straight-forward letters, and, after some hesitation, kissing her photograph with the passionate devotion of a young man of eighteen. Afterwards, at his marriage, he sinks back into the most uninspiring of Hardy's men ; but the time of his regeneration is to come.

It is apparently Jude's disclosure of his marriage to Arabella that decides Sue on her own marriage, and she takes a spiteful revenge by asking Jude to give her away. Before the marriage Jude and Sue live through a period that is well called a " curious interval ", while they are waiting for a step to be taken which both of them dislike and fear. Jude's longings are voiced in some paragraphs of sombrely beautiful prose : they include an assertion that is bitterly ironical in the light of his later apostasy : " Gladly would he have compounded for the denial of her as a sweetheart and wife by having her live there as a fellow-lodger and friend, even on the most distant terms ".

Grief drives him again to drink, and drink, with a series of nicely calculated accidents, leads him to Arabella, now barmaid again in a Christminster public-house. Though he has arranged to meet Sue that evening, he makes an arrangement to meet

5

Arabella instead, and spends the night with her. This conduct is quite unforgivable, and shows he is a cheap fool, worthy of Arabella. The breaking of the appointment with Sue was entirely unnecessary, and the whole business was disgustingly stupid. His shame next day atones but little for his folly. When he does see Sue she discloses her want of feeling for her husband, and Jude, feeling unhappiness closing round them, returns with feverish desperation to his study for the priesthood.

' Shaston ' sees the breakdown of the impossible marriage. Jude and Sue cannot keep away from each other, and the relation between them at this time is more beautiful than at any other. Each has a sensitive knowledge of the other's mind ; they are given to an impulsive clasping of hands. Some of their meetings at the school are described with exquisite delicacy. At one of them Sue has definitely confessed that it is torture to her to live with Phillotson as his wife. Her trouble almost breaks down Jude's self-control. She is speaking to him from a window, at night, and he, flinging off the bonds of his rigid morality, gasps, " I'll never care about my doctrines or my religion any more ! Let them go. Let me help you, even if I do love you, and even if you . . . ."—A less celestial Caponsacchi, perhaps. But matters are not yet at such a height as to demand forceful rescue, and she dismisses him. " In a moment of impulse she bent over the sill, and laid her face upon his hair, weeping, and then imprinting a scarcely perceptible little kiss upon the top of his head, withdrawing quickly, so that he could not put his arms round her, as he unquestionably would have otherwise done. She shut the casement, and he returned to his cottage." The Hardian restraint with which these incidents are related is in entire keeping with the fine passion of which they are the symbols. And presently this same passion breaks bonds in the first kiss—a kiss which is called the turning-point in Jude's career, and which he recognizes as the purest moment of his life.

Their relation at this time is afterwards analysed with remarkable insight by Phillotson, who overheard one of their meetings, and told Gillingham, months later : " I found from their manner that an extraordinary affinity, or sympathy, entered into their attachment, which somehow took away all flavour of grossness. Their supreme desire is to be together—to share each other's emotions, fancies, and dreams." It must be admitted that Jude failed to live up to this diagnosis. Indeed the hero of this fourth book is Phillotson. He is quite blameless in the growing estrangement of Sue. He loves her unselfishly, which accounts for the insight noted above. When he understands clearly what it is that Sue wants he makes no effort at forcible restraint. He is most generous and judicious in his statement of Sue's case to Gillingham, and when she has left him he tells his friend : " I would have died for her, but I wouldn't be cruel to her in the name of the law ". Phillotson is, at this period, a fine picture of what middle-age can be, the product of those " years that bring the philosophic mind ".

Jude, on the other hand, begins to show signs of his capability of the betrayal that is to come. Quite early he has used a mention of Arabella as a goad to Sue's feelings, but she, with her cool and complicated mind, is unresponsive. But when she has left Phillotson for him, Jude is much discomfited to find she wants a separate room at the hotel they are going to. However, he agrees, and (since they feel they cannot now go to the hotel at which a double room had been booked) chance takes them to the one at which, not long before, Jude had stayed with Arabella. Sue's distress at finding this out brings from Jude the following gracious comment : " I never knew such an unreasonable—such a dog-in-the-manger feeling. I am not to approach you, or anybody else ! " To which Sue : " O don't you *understand* my feeling ! Why are you so gross ? *I* jumped out of the window ! " Perhaps she had no right to assume that he was as fastidious as herself (though Phillotson, too, had deduced this from their conversation), but when Jude understood her feelings he should have acquiesced in a less grudging and temporary way. If he could get as far as he did he could have got further.

The parallelism with *Tess of the D'Urbervilles* is apparent here again. It was an element of fastidiousness in Clare that Tess came up against.

And so we come to the last two books, on which, I suppose, the monstrous hostility which the novel aroused was chiefly based. Certainly it is into these two books that the tragedy has been concentrated. Up to this point the tonic note of the story has been one of aspiration and a chequered sweetness, with only such sorrows as men and women may bear. From here to the end the tale is, for the most part, one of intensifying terror and agony, sordid misery and intolerable folly.

' Aldbrickham ' sees Jude and Sue living together—in sin, and yet not in sin. They are not even married, though the two marriages, with Phillotson and with Arabella, have been annulled. Sue not only prefers the lover-relation, but fears the marriage contract—" How the light, light love he has wings to fly at suspicion of a bond ! " Then, one night, Arabella calls, and Jude, with shocking brutality, makes use of the incident to force Sue to yield up her fortress of chastity. This is the third, the worst, and the last exhibition of Jude's lower self. Oddly enough, though the other question, that of marriage, comes up from time to time, and they make several attempts to settle it, they never do actually get married. Like Hamlet, they think (and talk) too precisely on the event.

Now the strange child, Father Time, son of Jude and Arabella, comes into their life. Children are rare in Hardy, but the few he has drawn are worth noting. The first is little Johnny Nonsuch, in *The Return of the Native*. Mrs. Yeobright came upon him as she walked wearily across the heath after being, as she thought, cast off by her son, and " with the tendency of a minute body to gravitate towards a greater, he began hovering round Mrs. Yeobright as soon as she appeared, and trotted on beside her without perceptible consciousness of his act ". How often has one seen that child—something between a human being and a small animal. He talks and questions and makes wise childish comments, till she sits down to rest.

> When she had seated herself he looked long in her face and said, ' How funny you draw your breath—like a lamb when you drive him till he's nearly done for. Do you always draw your breath like that ? '
> ' Not always.' Her voice was now so low as to be scarcely above a whisper.
> ' You will go to sleep there, I suppose, won't you ? You have shut your eyes already.'

In the same book is the boy Charley, not altogether a child, perhaps, but evidently very young and innocent. It is he who makes the pact of Eustacia's hand—that he may hold it for half an hour in exchange for helping her to be present at the Christmas mumming. When Eustacia gave him her hand he " took it in both his own with a tenderness beyond description, unless it was like that of a child holding a captured sparrow ". Then there are Tess's little brothers and sisters—Abraham, 'Liza-'Lu, Hope, Modesty, and others down to the last baby. It is they who cry round the grave of Prince the horse, and ask between their sobs, " Is he gone to Heaven ? " It is they whom Tess awakes to be her witnesses at the christening of Sorrow, her dying baby, making them kneel round, putting their hands together with fingers exactly vertical. They blink at the strange ceremony with wide but sleepy eyes, and lisp the Lord's prayer after her in a thin gnat-like wail.

But of all Hardy's children there is none so memorable as Father Time. He comes to Aldbrickham by a late evening train, a small pale-faced child with large frightened eyes, a key round his neck and his ticket in his hat-band. A kitten in the carriage makes everyone else laugh, but the boy regards it mutely with his saucer eyes. When all the others fall asleep he seems to be doubly awake, sitting passive and watchful " like an enslaved and dwarfed Divinity ".

He was Age masquerading as Juvenility, and doing it so badly that his real self showed through crevices. A ground swell from ancient years of night seemed now and then to lift the child in this his morning-life, when his face took a back view over some great Atlantic of time, and appeared not to care about what it saw.

When he is set on his way to walk to the house of Jude and Sue, " The child fell into a steady mechanical creep which had in it an impersonal quality—the movement of the wave, or of the breeze, or of the cloud ". He is a gnome-like person, rather disturbing. While Jude and Sue are discussing with Widow Edlin one of their many ' decisions ' to get married, " a small slow voice rose from the shade of the fire-side, as if out of the earth : ' If I was you, mother, I wouldn't marry father ! ' It came from little Time, and they started, for they had forgotten him." However, it is later that Father Time gets his big chance.—It is interesting to see Jude's dream of a classical education, lost now so far as he himself is concerned, waking again in his thoughts of what he will do for this strange little son of his.

Jude and Sue get very near to tying the legal knot, but cannot bring themselves to go through with it. Still, they enjoy a short respite of quiet happiness, with its climax at the Great Wessex Agricultural Show, where they wander about among the flowers, hand in hand, in a sort of Greek joyousness. Hardy emphasises again here their " complete mutual understanding, in which every glance and movement was as effectual as speech for conveying intelligence between them, making them almost the two parts of a single whole ". We see, too, their " tender attention " to each other, their deep absorption in their own love, and perceive that this is the sole study Hardy has made of love as it should exist between husband and wife.

And then immediately, in Hardy's way, sorrow begins to come down upon them. They have done that which was right in their own eyes ; and the cloud of ill-repute and open scorn and hostility thickens round them. Settled work in any Wessex town seems to be denied them. There is some forcing of facts to fit the theory and carry on the plot here : in any large and unfamiliar town they would have been unmolested, married or not. However, as the story goes, they enter upon a nomadic life which endures, not unhappily, for nearly three years, at the end of which Jude contracts a chill which never really leaves him. This almost external accident, as is proper, does not materially affect their lives, except to bring them lower in the social scale than they might otherwise have fallen ; its real purpose is to afford a means for Jude's death when his time comes.

But first are to come those blind wanderings in a mysterious night of sorrow and dreadful error that give to the close of *Jude the Obscure* the semblance of some hideous dream of a hell of wailing in outer darkness. Premonition and preparation have not been absent. We have heard Arabella, now widowed of her second husband, expressing a fierce hunger and necessity for the reacquisition of the first. We have seen her waking in Phillotson's mind doubts as to the propriety of his release of Sue. And we hear Sue herself, on sight of Phillotson, speaking of " a curious dread of him " ; something that comes over her " like a sort of creeping paralysis ", and makes her sad.—The last act of the tragedy takes place at Christminster, whither they have returned, for the fair and scornful city is still unalterably the centre of Jude's universe, for the sake of his early dream. He listens rapt to the snatches of Remembrance Day orations, and harangues the crowd as one having authority, though, as the crowd recognises in astonishment, only a working man—as it were a carpenter's son.

They find temporary rooms after a search of some difficulty, in the course of which Sue, by her ' impulsive ' confession to a suspicious landlady of all the sad story of their hesitating love and legally uncompleted union, demonstrates to us with astonishing clearness that she is assuredly not made for this world. Jude has been compelled to find separate lodgings for himself, and this fact, together with the rather squalid unhappiness of the general situation, preys on the mind of the weird child, Father Time. An extraordinary piece of dialogue occurs between Sue and the boy. With the diabolic unanswerableness of a child, the swift perspicacity of a trained logician, and the relentlessness of truth, he lays bare to Sue, in semi-Socratic fashion, all the cruel culpability of her case and Jude's. It was not well to be in the world, in their position, was it ? And himself and these other children (there are now two of Sue's own) had been brought into unhappiness unconsenting ? And they only made things worse for their parents, didn't they ? Yes, and why was that—why were they had at all ? Oh, it was a law of nature, was it ? And as the little inquisitor puzzles over the absurd inadequacy of the defence, Sue informs him she has decreed to increase difficulties and sorrows by the addition of yet another child. Then indeed the torrent bursts :

" What ! " The boy jumped up wildly. " O God, mother, you've never a-sent for another ; and such trouble with what you've got ! . . . O you don't care, you don't care ! . . . How *ever* could you, mother, be so wicked and cruel as this, when you needn't have done it till we was better off and Father well ! —To bring us all into *more* trouble ! . . . 'Tis done o' purpose

—'tis—'Tis ! . . . Nobody would interfere with us like that unless you agreed ! "

The pity is that these home-thrusts do not light upon the person to whom they more fairly belong—Jude. The practical outcome of the boy's reasonings is that scene of " strange and consummate horror " in which all three children are found hanging, dead, with Father Time's laconic pencilled note, " *Done because we are too menny* ". In the midst of Sue's grief the voice of the organ from a neighbouring chapel is heard rolling forth the anthem, " Truly God is loving unto Israel ", and the consolation and faith which this might suggest is felt here to be replaced by contemptuous irony. At the end of the woeful chapter Sue's last child is prematurely born, and is, like the others, a corpse—an occurrence which almost necessarily followed from preceding events. The whole chapter reads like a scene from some despairing Russian tragedy.

Some remarks by the doctor are worth noting. Jude tells Sue,

It was in his nature to do it. The doctor says there are such boys springing up amongst us—boys of a sort unknown in the last generation—the outcome of new views of life. They seem to see all its terrors before they are old enough to resist them. He says it is the beginning of the coming universal wish not to live.

It is amazing that Hardy should have foreseen a trend which has only shown itself to most of us in these post-war days, when the failure of the " wish to live " constitutes a social problem.

The event itself has been objected to as going beyond the limits of the legitimate in horror. The affliction that has come upon Jude and Sue is partly a retribution for their abandonment of the path of ' married chastity ', but is largely the product of causes outside themselves and their control—poverty, the conventions of society, the nature of the strange child. From the combination, with the situation as it was, something terrible was certain to happen, but I am inclined to agree that Hardy does not convince us that this particular ghastly catastrophe was inevitable. Something less awful would have satisfied more. It is Hardy's parallel to the gouging out of Gloucester's eyes. Nevertheless, whether the magnitude of the catastrophe is probable or not, it is justified by its results. Two things were quite sure, in the fulness of time, to follow Sue's surrender to Jude : madness for her, remorse for him. The death of the children did not cause these—it simply hastened them. It is as if Hardy has concentrated a more protracted series of sorrows into one dire catastrophe. And considered in this light, as a piece of art or symbolic truth rather than as realism, the episode finds full justification. To the results let us at once proceed.

The chapter which embodies these two consequences, or shows that they have definitely set in, is one of Hardy's greatest, and the last part, commencing with Jude's discovery of Sue in the Church of St. Silas, is one of those miraculous scenes that are scarcely to be paralleled anywhere. To deal first with the signs of Jude's remorse, it cannot be said that it has yet bitten very deeply into his heart. A realisation of the ruin he has wrought comes to him, but it comes vaguely and coldly to his reason, and without any agonised conviction. However, he states the case, twice, with admirable directness and precision :

" You were a distinct type—a refined creature, intended by Nature to be left intact."

That is the unquestionable truth. And later :

" My God, how selfish I was ! Perhaps—perhaps I spoilt one of the highest and purest loves that ever existed between man and woman ! "

That again is final, and had he realised it completely it would have driven him to suicide—as perhaps it does later.

Turning to Sue, we perceive her cowed under the savage blow that has struck her down. Presently she is speaking of a ' solemnity ' in their early marriages with Phillotson and Arabella. Rapidly she advances to the position that she is still Phillotson's wife, and Jude Arabella's husband, and that her life with Jude is wrong, sinful. She gets hopelessly confused over marriage according to ' Nature ', ' Heaven ', and ' the Church '. From her old free thought she moves to ritualistic religion (probably the only thing that could have saved Sue at this point would have been an utter collapse into the bosom of the Roman Catholic Church), and she becomes totally oblivious of her old sane (though unsteady) reasoning on the marriage question. The flame of her new purpose is desperately nourished, and finally she drives Jude from her side, though in a Hardian glance that drives like a knife into the inmost heart of woman's nature, she exclaims as he turns to go, " O but you shall kiss me ! . . . I can't bear— ! " Only a woman, and a rare woman, can endure passion such as this, and yet retain strength to deny its call.

This is not the worst that is to come, but the doom has already fallen—Sue is mad. Under the sudden appalling crash of misery and failure and ruined hope her clear brain has collapsed : her mind is now obsessed with a single thought, an uncontrollable terror, to the exclusion of every other conception and feeling— which state is madness. This is not to be wondered at. Hawthorne says well, " Crime is for the iron-nerved, who have their choice either to endure it, or, if it press too hard, to exert their fierce and savage strength . . . and fling it off at once ". So of free-action ; to do and live according to one's personal ideals in defiance of earth's opposition and the thunders of heaven— such a course, with its almost inevitable disaster of defeat, is only for vast Promethean natures ; perhaps only for male natures ; certainly not for fine and fragile natures such as Sue's.

In this connection it is interesting to note the suggestion of a reviewer of *Jude*, who, Hardy tells us, regretted that the story had not been written by a woman, in which case Sue, the feminist woman, the intellectual, emancipated bundle of nerves produced by modern conditions, would not have been allowed to break down at the end.

So Sue, voluntarily, she thinks, but in reality driven by the staring fiend, the wild storm that shrieks and eddies in her soul, goes back to Phillotson, shrinking from his touch, and is re-wedded to him, though he, grave and unimpassioned as ever, again respects her desire, unspoken but evident, that he shall not ' intrude upon her personal privacy '. Meanwhile Arabella lures Jude back to her by the simple expedient of making him drunk, and marries him by making him more drunk. Let it not be imagined, however, that Jude is in any degree in the same case as Sue. No slightest unhingement has taken place in his brain. On the contrary, he has achieved the summit of his outlook upon life. On those sides at least which we are shown in this last period of his life his vision is much stronger, calmer, clearer than in his early days. His attitude is not one of despair, but of indifference. When a man has lost what Jude has lost in the way Jude has lost it, what is left to him of life is, by comparison, not worth the trouble of despising. In such circumstances, Jude's remark to Arabella, " What the devil does it matter to me ? " is a complete expression of perfect sanity and truth. An irreligious view of things ? Oh, yes, I am speaking of man as a human being now, not as a saint. A saint would never get into Jude's position, because he would never allow his world to be filled by a woman and an ideal of earthly happiness.

Three more scenes, all terrible, make up the tale. Jude, down with inflammation of the lungs, determines, as he tells Arabella afterwards, to do the only two desired things that remain to him —to see Sue once more, and to end his life. So through sleet and north-east wind he goes, and meets her again in the church. In the passionate and tragic scene which follows, their respective positions, already indicated, are made very clear ; he, gazing down in impatient, incredulous, almost contemptuous wrath, at her, pulsing with passion, yet cowering and trembling in the throes of the strange madness that possesses her. But it is in the next scene, one of the most pitiful and painful in Hardy, that the most abject depths of mental and moral ruin are reached. It is the scene in which Sue performs her act of ' ultimate penance ' to Richard Phillotson. To paraphrase would be destructive, for it is one of the inevitable scenes, whereof every word is vital, but there are points here and there that call for reference—points that emphasise either Sue's agony or the unutterable woodenness to which Phillotson has now returned in a worse form then ever. The whole picture of woe and folly is framed in the homely humorous common-sense of the Widow Edlin.

Like so many of the great scenes of tremendous tragedy in literature and history—the crucifixion of Christ, the death of Cromwell, the eve of the slaying of Cæsar, the murder of Duncan, the madness of Lear—this last desperate act is set in the terror of tempestuous night. Amid the shrieking of the wind and rain that rage round the house, the snoring of Phillotson is almost drowned. For it is from snoring slumber that Sue—erstwhile dreamer of romantic love dreams—has to waken this man with a shuddering " Richard ! " At the temporary silence she gasps eagerly, " Perhaps he is dead—I shall be free ! " Then she remembers—God ! As if God, or anyone but the devil, desired this ' fanatic prostitution ' ! He wakes with " Hey—what ? " He argues as to the exact desirability of this act, demands to know the precise number of times she has kissed Jude, and makes her swear future fidelity on a little brown Testament. All this while she stands or crouches in her night-clothes. As he continues his dull repetitions and queries as to whether she has fully considered the matter, she at length ejaculates from her pent soul, " O God ! " And he categorically asks, " What did you say O God for ? " At last he approaches her, and although she shrinks from his first touch, drawing from him stern reproof and further inquisitions, he lifts and kisses her. " A look of wild aversion passed over her face, but clenching her teeth she uttered no cry."

There are perhaps people who regard this as the painful but righteous execution of a solemn duty, and who see Sue here exalted to her highest as a strong and noble woman. To me she appears like nothing so much as the indescribable creature that resulted from the second fire-baptism of Rider Haggard's *She*. Jude again describes her fall with great truth : " She was once a woman whose intellect was to mine like a star to a benzoline lamp : who saw all my superstitions as cobwebs that she could brush away with a word. Then bitter affliction came to us, and her intellect broke, and she veered round to darkness. Strange difference of sex, that time and circumstance, which enlarge the views of most men, narrow the views of women almost invariably." William James says the feminine mind ' sets hard ' sooner than that of the male.

So passes Sue, though the last words of the book, on Arabella's lips, show that her tragedy is yet unfinished : " She's never found peace since she left his (Jude's) arms, and never will again till she's as he is now ". That is, till she is dead. For Jude has been left sleeping by Arabella, and he wakes with the sound of revelry and music in his ears. It is once more Remembrance Day at the University, and organ-notes mingled with cheering roll faintly in through his window. " Ah—yes ! The Remembrance games ", he murmurs. " And I here. And Sue defiled." Thus he voices, with completeness and

precision, the twin tragedy of the book.   Then, while still sounds
the joyous shouting, he whispers upon his own birth the deliberate curse of Job, and when Arabella returns and listens at
his heart she finds that " the bumping of near thirty years "
has ceased.

Jude the Obscure is a tremendous book.   But as a work of art
it falls below *Tess of the D'Urbervilles.   Tess* is superior in the
marvellous simplicity of the means it employs to its tragic end :
the initiating situation, out of which all grows, is so usual as
to be commonplace.   It is greater art to get high tragedy from
such a situation than from the complicated problems of *Jude*.
One feels, too, that the desperate sorrows are a little artificial
—are not so inevitable as those of *Tess*.   The tense rhythm of
Tess is not here : this has a little of the character of a chronicle ;
it admits purely episodic events, such as the comedy scene of
Jude and the hymn-writer.   Lovely as Sue is she is not quite
so divinely lovely as Tess, and she breaks at the end, as Tess
did not—though Sue suffered more.   Jude is a grander figure
than Clare, but his tripled sin of grossness drags him lower
than Clare's hard egotism.   The parallelism noted must rob
the later book of a little of its originality.   The parallelism does
not go very far, but it can hardly be denied in—the initial error
of Tess and of Jude ; the meeting of the ideal mate after the
fall ; the spiritual, fastidious nature of Clare and Sue—both
described as ' Shelleyan ' (though of course their dissimilarity
immeasurably outweighs their nominal likeness) ; the return of
Alec and Arabella, both in a state of religious conversion.   But
to say all this is to remove a few tons of rock from a mountain.
There is no end to the meaning and inspiration of *Jude the Obscure*.
It has an infinite variety that age cannot wither nor custom stale.
The problem of Tess is more soluble : we may decide and leave
it, grieving or rejoicing.   But there is no solving *Jude*.   It
wakes dim enigmas ; it starts strange trains of unanswerable
question that carry us out into the illimitable spaces of thought,
till we lose ourselves in *O altitudines* of wondering, and come
back at last having learnt the riddle of life—which is its inviolable
incomprehensibility.

II. THE ART OF THE NOVELS

Chapter I

CHARACTER-DRAWING

THE novel has laws of its own, but, being a comparatively new species, it had not the benefit (or disadvantage) of having those laws laid down for it by that dictator among critics, Aristotle. Every play that was ever successfully produced (if we except an occasional debating-piece by Mr. Bernard Shaw) has been compelled to follow Aristotle's maxim, that plot, in a highly-wrought, ' dramatic ' form, is the first essential of successful drama, whereas character, though invariably accompanying the prime factor, is nevertheless of secondary importance as an aim. It is only necessary to read a few typical masterpieces of prose fiction to discover that the essentials of the novel are, in trite phrase, first, character, second, character, and third, character. The change is due to the differing aims of the drama and the novel respectively. It needs but an *Othello*, a *Duchess of Malfi*, an *Oedipus Rex* to demonstrate how integral a part of high dramatic practice is the *katharsis* of the Stagirite's theory, and that the purging is and must be effected not by the nature of the characters but by the fiery intensity of the action. Now, the novel has no such drastic end in view. It is a kind of compromise between epic and drama : epic in its mode of presentation, but tending towards the dramatic in its closer unity and exclusion of the episode. It is intended, not for the vivid stabbing representation of the stage, but for the thoughtful serenity of the fireside ; its purpose is not to bring about sudden earthquake upheavings of the moral nature, but rather to inspire processes of grave reflection ; meditative, not purgative ; less divine, but more human.

This being the aim, what is the method? The novelist places before us importantly typical or significant specimens of humanity passing through turbulent or otherwise revealing phases of life, and exhibits the swirl and surge of their souls under the stress of circumstance and before the problems of existence.

It is for these reasons that mastery of character is considered the first essential of the novelist's art. Hardy's greatness in this direction is seldom questioned. One's memory bears unimpeachable evidence of the extraordinary range, variety and significance of his characters: Jude Fawley, the stone-mason of infinite hopeless aspiring, like the lines of the Gothic that he chisels; whose head dreams on Olympus, while high things close at hand are discerned but dimly, uncomprehendingly, and his feet stumble in unclean ways: Gabriel Oak, the enduring, the strong, the proudly self-sacrificing; watching with pitiful eyes; protecting, waiting, rewarded: Angel Clare, a man like a statue of frozen air; pure spirit of intellect; a fiery essence, untouchable; who, at the first sound of the whisper of sin, grows colder and harder than stone, merciless as winter skies; scarce human: Michael Henchard, swift-striding, unfettered giant of impulse, yet with sublime powers of self-control; fierce, but sinless; most magnificent of Hardy's men: Henry Knight, calm and masterful, knowing life in wide abstractions, who cannot flatter a pretty woman; his ironic tongue silenced by the quietly superior irony of life: Clym Yeobright, strong as steel and more unbending; ruthless egoist shearing his way through living hearts to truth and right: Giles Winterborne, a homely Christ of the woodlands, without a message. The secondary characters are hardly less interesting—Boldwood, Farfrae, Phillotson, Troy, Alec D'Urberville, Jocelyn Pierston. . . . All these male names we might forgo, and still have a gallery of everlasting delight in Tess, Sue, Bathsheba, Elizabeth Jane, Elfride, Eustacia, Ethelberta, Viviette, Grace and Marty and Anne: their names a symphony and every note a song.

Hardy's command of human personality being thus extensive, to what depth does it go? What and how great elements in human nature has he been able to seize and portray? By what process does he lay bare the hidden depths of human nature?

The answer needs little searching—it is prompt and decided. If there is one feature that above all others distinguishes Hardy from all other ' modern ' writers whatsoever, it is the way in which he, the wizard, the alchemist, places the crystals of human souls in his crucibles and subjects them to the awful test of a white enduring heat. It is not without advantage to approach Hardy *via* Meredith. One has laid down the *Egoist*, say, with words of callow enthusiasm : " Surely this is the most marvellous of novels. What minute and unerring mental analysis ! What miraculous discernment and setting forth of motive and mental process ! " And one picks up *Tess*. The change is remarkable. One instinctively feels that the atmosphere, though less highly oxygenated, is permeated by a diviner effluence. Brilliant intellectuality has given place to a serene, almost arrogant comprehension of the highest, most secret and dreadful mysteries of the soul. The agony of Tess of the D'Urbervilles is a thing that could have been handled by but one other among men—by him through whom all pains the immortal spirit must endure find their voice.

It is a familiar observation that in certain of the greatest of Shakespeare's tragedies not only does the progress of the action bring doom upon the characters themselves, but it also works a mysterious and far more terrible ruin in their souls. Lear's soul is shattered by the recurrent thunderings of woe and the storms of his mighty passion ; Antony's soul is enervated, disintegrated by his amorous enslavement to Egypt. Each of these plays is a Soul's Tragedy. Now, not in the rest of Elizabethan Drama, not in the rest of English literature, will you find another Soul's Tragedy until you reach Hardy, and this supreme feature of Shakespeare's tragedy is born again in the novels of a pure modern.

Consider Tess of the D'Urbervilles : the tragedy lies not in her desertion, her struggle for bread, her frightful death ; but in her sin, her bewilderment of soul at Clare's behaviour, the intensifying agony of her despair, culminating in the awful wrecking of her nature in the foul shallows of D'Urberville's renewed amours. To be crushed to death by lead or grief is nothing ; for ' a pure woman ' to be crushed into impurity—*there* is a Soul's Tragedy that has no equal in horror. Again, the pure, strong and beautiful soul of Sue Bridehead is wasted away by the bitter processes of sorrow, fear, error, until God only knows what it becomes—a shrivelled, maniac thing, too pitiful to be thought upon. Only in these two greatest of the novels is the characteristic found (and observe that in each case the subject of this special catastrophe is a woman), but in these two it is undoubtedly present, and the fact is sufficient to set Hardy, on the side of tragedy, above all other novelists. If a great novel was ever written, surely *Esmond* is great. It is written with an intellectual brilliance to which Hardy does not aspire, and the characterisation of the chief figures is profound, perfect ; but is there anything in it to compare, to equate, to the psychic sorrow of the lives of Jude and Sue Fawley ? Or put *Adam Bede* side by side with *Tess of the D'Urbervilles*, the outward action of these two novels being of the same nature, or turning upon the same fulcrum. In George Eliot's masterpiece we are shown the agony of a man of ordinary heroic mould caused by the faithlessness of his sweetheart, a pretty, worthless girl who drops out of the story as naturally as a spoilt sheet of writing-paper goes into the waste-paper basket, leaving her betrayed lover to see the folly of his ways and recover his faith in woman on lines totally unconnected with his first love. But Hardy gives us the frightful, mysterious fall of a great and noble woman, complicated by the presence of an idealising ' angel ' lover, with the consequent havoc played by Fate and sorrow in the quivering, long-enduring soul of the woman who has sinned.

This feature of the Soul's Tragedy is only one, though the highest, side of Hardy's mastery of character-presentation. In all the great novels—in the sad antagonisms of Angel Clare and Tess ; in the strange, half-comprehended comradeship of Jude and Sue, and their despairs ; in the grim struggles and vicissitudes of the Mayor of Casterbridge ; in the Southern splendours of the love of Eustacia Vye ; in the lightning-riven glooms of Squire Boldwood and the magnanimity of Gabriel Oak—in all these we are concerned with something less transient, fussy and mundane than emotion, more spontaneous, illogical, almighty than reason : something, in short, beyond definition and measurement, but felt to be in its essence spiritual, pertaining to the conflict and high-manœuvring of souls.

6

The claim made here is not extended to the lesser novels ; few writers ever get beyond the many-coloured sphere of temperament that is Hardy's ground in *Two on a Tower*, *A Pair of Blue Eyes*, *The Trumpet-Major*, and the rest ; that he should have ascended to the white radiance of psychic personality in five of his novels is a very great achievement.

Although contemporary magazine publishers objected to some of Hardy's characters as being improperly plebeian, it would be foolish to claim that he initiated an interest that has since absorbed one-half of fiction : Tom Jones and Oliver Twist had preceded him.   But before Hardy, the practice of almost all character-creators, whether in novel or drama, had been in accordance with Aristotle's theory, following, in some modified form, the precept that the hero (at least the tragic hero) must be a man of high rank. But survey the protagonists of Hardy's stage : Tess, milkmaid and hard-driven general farmhand, daughter of a haggler and his vulgar thriftless wife ;   Jude Fawley, stone-mason, sometime baker's assistant ;   Oak, shepherd, heavy-booted and smocked ; Sue, elementary school-teacher ;   Henchard, tramping hay-trusser.   These five, the very greatest of the heroes and heroines, are all drawn from the most commonplace walks of life, from occupations as devoid of romance for other writers (and indeed for the world in general) as a bagpipe is of music for the ordinary listener.   The milkmaid and the shepherd, of a dainty china kind, are not unknown to poetry ; even the stone-mason has (in Jonson and Carlyle) points of contact with literature ; but few before dared to credit the school-teacher or the hay-trusser with the possession of a soul, much less dreamed of going to the trouble of dissecting it and showing its grandeur and beauty.

Yes, this in Hardy is the peculiar grace ; this is perhaps his supreme achievement : to have gone down among the unnoticed, forgotten myriads of dull, prosaic, average humanity, and discovered here and there among them lives as mysteriously interesting and as spiritually adventurous as were ever those of queens and emperors.   He has gone some way to disprove Bradley's assertion that Hamlet's emotions could not have happened to a plumber. He has verified and visualised over and over again Carlyle's dream of the infinite shoe-black.   Some of us know by happy experience that here and there in the world-encircling ranks of apparently commonplace humanity are men and women with souls like Gothic Cathedrals—places of endless wonder, mystery, beauty, that we explore for ever, finding ever new crypts and hidden chapels, silences and beckonings to prayer ; it is this type of dim unapprehended personality that Hardy, for the first time in literature, has definitely taken up and made his own. In a sense it is Hardy's special contribution to the Spirit of the Age— Democracy. He first declared Demos himself to be individually a person of fathomless subtlety, Olympian grandeur. And the declaration, the design itself, apart from the execution, gives Hardy a quite extraordinary position among the great creators of character.

Deferring for a moment the consideration of the execution, one may remember, on the side of the theory—the advisability of this deliberate choice of plebeian figures—the warning suggested in the dictum of Robert Louis Stevenson : " Beauty should at least have touched society ; then, in a moment, it becomes conscious of itself, it puts on an elegance, learns a gait, and a carriage of the head—and, in a moment, *patet dea* ". Well (expanding ' beauty ' and ' society ' into ' human nature ' and ' culture '), one can only point to Tess, with her natural refinement, Oak, with his natural dignity, Henchard, with his natural grandeur, and ask, Has beauty, has human nature, no elegance, no gait, no carriage, inherent within itself ? Otherwise, though these three are of the very soil of Wessex, most of Hardy's other chief figures have the supposed necessary touch of the pale-faced world of education or society. Meanwhile there is some suggestiveness (of a Wordsworthian kind, and anti-R.L.S.) in the fact that the Arcadian atmosphere of *The Woodlanders* (the sweetest of all the novels), with its simplicity of nature, its ' goodness ', is disturbed solely by discordant notes of *urbs in rure*—the presence of Fitzpiers, Mrs. Charmond and the Italianised American.

Up to this point we have been concerned with what I have distinguished as the theory of the subject—the several conceptions that seem to underlie Hardy's practice in that most important side of his art, character-drawing. During this part of the discussion I have considered it advisable for illustrative purposes to effect some comparisons with the Master of Drama.

This will be no longer possible in dealing with the practical aspect of the matter, the presentation of character, since the methods of the novelist and the dramatist must obviously differ so widely here. In the drama, the very nature of which is to be as vivid, simple and direct as lightning, success in character-presentation is a thing, if not more easily achieved, at least more easily discerned and judged than in the lengthier and more composite novel. The veriest tyro in histrionics can feel the palpitating life-blood of Macbeth or Lady Teazle and the unreality of Addison's Cato, but it is a nicer task to say whether the innumerable strokes of dialogue and description which constitute character-drawing in prose fiction have or have not built up a breathing human being.

Hardy's method is exemplified perhaps most completely in Michael Henchard. Of course (as in all genuine novel and drama, where the central action is the expression of the central characters), the essential substance of the man is manifested in the main currents of his career. But in addition to this there are a host of incidental touches of portraiture—vivid descriptive phrases, metaphoric illuminations and revealing comparisons, chance utterances of the man himself—that are Hardy's means of building up a personality of extraordinary consistency, probability, warmth and reality.[1] We see Henchard first tramping the Wessex roads, a dogged and cynical indifference showing itself in the turn and plant of each foot, and even in the regularly interchanging creases behind his knees. With stormy drunken violence he sells his wife for five guineas, and takes a mighty oath to drink no more for twenty years—a vow religiously kept. Scene second beholds him Mayor by virtue of turbulent energy, grasping young Farfrae into his deep friendship on sudden strong impulse and with fierce satisfaction, admiring the Scotsman's numerical dexterity with a half-contempt—as Thor might regard Hermes. Immoderate in all things ; asking advice, and sweeping it instantly aside when it fits not his desire ; tempests of destructiveness darkening his face at insult ; he yet does resolute penance for his early rashness. He will mortify the

---

[1] In the account of Henchard's character that follows I have made free and full use of Hardy's own epithets and phrases, and the same fact will be observed of similar passages throughout the book.

flesh of poor Abel Whittle for unpunctuality, even while he keeps the old mother in coals all through the winter. Alternately cloudy and warm to Farfrae, he dismisses him in jealousy of his popularity, and regrets his haste when too late. Under his stern self-control the unruly volcanic stuff of his nature constantly heaves and surges, and he loves and hates with buffalo wrong-headedness. The stress of emotion sways him physically, as the wind a great tree ; his soul is vehemently gloomy, his greeting dry and thunderous. Though grimly generous, impartial fairness of thought is as foreign to him as light to a coal-mine, and in his eyes his rising rival Farfrae is a jumped-up jackanapes of a fellow ; his personality beside that of the Scot is as the sun beside the moon. He digs his strong eyes into men's faces, his blazing regard makes them blink, there is a red spark in his dark pupils. His laugh, rarely heard, is frightening to strangers of the weaker sort, and bespeaks no mild and constant kindness. Conventional suppression of feeling is no part of him : anger and warmth are plain in his strong-lined face ; he quarrels as hotly with a woman as with a man. He is constructed on too large a scale to read the niceties of love-making between Farfrae and Lucetta. Of course superstition attracts him strongly, as all untutored, irrational natures, though his practical largeness of view generally resists its influence. His behaviour over his affianced Lucetta's marriage to Farfrae is very indicative of the man : on her confession of it he dismisses her with rough reproachful toleration and mastery ; later goes to Farfrae with the set determination—rather on the unreflecting impulse of the moment—to ruin her happiness, but stops short of the one last word which would bring the explosive doom upon her—his quality being such that he could have annihilated them both in the heat of action, but the wrecking of hearts in cold blood appals him and is beyond the nerve of his enmity ; finally he delivers up to her the whole of the damning evidence. Bankrupt and ruined, he curses the pity of his creditors, and hands over their gift to a man in straitened circumstances ; stoically takes service under his old servant Farfrae ; and, the term of his oath expiring, bursts into drink. He is strangely moved by old melodies, and a single word of reproach from Farfrae, when Henchard is on the point of killing him, turns his fury into repentance ; he is broken—his stern virility crouches woman-like. To keep his daughter he lies impulsively, yet determinedly, to Newson, and is amazed at his own action. Love for Elizabeth wakes him from his massive despair, but he is purged of his despotism—is almost her slave, out of his yearning to keep her love—schools himself to accept her will : so much is he changed from the Henchard of former days. To keep her he is tempted again to falsehood, but his firm *Retro Sathana* shows how entirely unpremeditated had been his earlier deception of Newson. Yet must he lose her, and sternly subduing his anguish he strides out, alone once more, into the solitudes of the world. He comes back to gaze on her, standing like a dark ruin ; accused of his falsehood, he shuts his lips like a vice on any attempt at palliation—with his old irony he feels himself unworthy of the trouble of argument, with his old greatness he calms his daughter's discomposure, and departs for ever with simple dignity. He is found dead, and the grim bitterness of his will is recognised as a piece of the same stuff that his whole life was made of :

> That Elizabeth-Jane Farfrae be not told of my death, or made to grieve on account of me.
> And that I be not bury'd in consecrated ground.
> And that no sexton be asked to toll the bell.
> And that nobody is wished to see my dead body.
> And that no mourners walk behind me at my funeral.
> And that no flowers be planted on my grave.
> And that no man remember me.
> To this I put my name.
>
> —MICHAEL HENCHARD.

This completeness of realisation, and this method of effecting it—by the varied and reiterated emphasis of prominent traits, and the disclosure of substrata by frequent flashlights from new aspects—constitute the groundwork of Hardy's power in character drawing. The nature of Henchard is elemental, like a granite mountain ; with more civilised and complex personalities the method, though remaining essentially the same, exhibits a subtlety not apparent or necessary in this case.

Set description is, generally speaking, the resource of the inferior artist in character. Nevertheless, on occasion, for special and definite reasons, Hardy introduces a figure with considerable pomp of circumstance. The most remarkable instance of this rarer method is the case of Eustacia Vye in *The Return of the Native*. Viewing her image as it lies in his own mind, Hardy comes to the conclusion that she is a creature so unique, and one whose nature extends to depths so superior to those measurable by casual glances, that she calls for more deliberate treatment than usual. He knows likewise that the story hangs upon her personality, as a lunar landscape upon the light of the enchantress moon, and that its procedure and events will appear interesting or trivial according as she is comprehended or not. For these reasons he determines upon a set description, and, having determined, makes no mistake about thoroughness. After a succession of the usual light touches that bring her gradually forward out of the unknown—a motionless figure far away against the darkening sky on the summit of a gloomy barrow on vast and gloomy Egdon ; on closer view, stature and straightness ; a profile against the clouds suggesting Sappho and Mrs. Siddons ; momentary irradiation, showing two matchless lips ; and a sigh that is no fragile maiden sigh, but shakes her like a shiver—after this he enters upon a full chapter of description as marvellously rich as if the splendour and romance of " Drink to me only with thine eyes " should be prolonged over eight pages. ' Queen of Night ! ' There is no summarising the chapter, nor even the selection of salient points ; every phrase is salient, and arresting. The chapter must be studied in its entirety.

Though I call this chapter a ' set description ', it must be observed that no slightest attempt is made to catalogue Eustacia's charms—hue, form and feature. One remembers how, when Mephistopheles has conjured up for Faustus (in Marlowe's play) " the fairest woman the world ever saw ", Helen of Troy, we are given no portrait, but see only the effect upon Faustus of her appearance. So here : Hardy tells us less what Eustacia is like than what she suggests and what she stands for. Her hair is not said to be black—but a whole winter does not contain darkness enough to form its shadow ; nor her eyes—but they are Pagan, full of nocturnal mysteries. She is not a handsome brunette—but her presence brings memories of Bourbon roses, rubies and tropical midnights. She is not languidly passionate, graceful, and sweet-spoken—but her moods recall lotus-eaters and the march in ' Athalie ', her motions the ebb and flow of the sea, her voice the viola. And so throughout the whole miraculous chapter. It is the same later in the book, when Clym Yeobright is accorded a lengthier introduction than most of Hardy's heroes, though in this case two or three pages suffice. We learn that his appearance is typically modern, and exactly in what way it is so ; how his face is less a picture than a page ; and the thoughts that his name rouses in the minds of his acquaintances. When Hardy describes a man or a woman he does it not like a photographer, not even like the general run of portrait-painters, but like a transcendental phrenologist. He himself, in the process of limning a vague, floating, inexplicit, tentative, suggestive portrait of Grace Melbury in *The Woodlanders*, touches incidentally on some of the implicit features of his general theory and practice. How impossible, he says, precisely to describe a human being. Grace herself is a *reductio ad absurdum* of attempts to appraise a woman by items of face and figure. To look at her was to see mainly something that was not she. " The woman herself was a conjectural creature who had little to do with the outlines presented to Sherton eyes ; a shape in the gloom, whose true quality could only be approximated by putting together a movement now and a glance then, in that patient attention which nothing but watchful loving kindness ever troubles to give."

As a rule, of course, the two methods are used to supplement each other. A few more of the characters that stand out from Hardy's pages will be studied here ; I have chosen male figures because the women are to come in for separate treatment in a later chapter.

Almost at the opposite pole of personality to Henchard is Clym Yeobright. He embodies a favourite idea of Hardy's, that of thought as a disease of the flesh, an idea that culminated in Jude's tragic little son, Father Time. Hardy is a student of the effects of time and circumstance upon the human form. Elsewhere, in introducing us to Elizabeth-Jane, he shows how poverty is beginning to make its impression on " the provisional lines of immaturity " in her face. But thought digs deeper. Clym Yeobright's age, as expressed in his face, is to be measured by the intensity of his experience ; its beauty begins to be overrun by its parasite, thought ; an inner strenuousness preys upon the outer symmetry. Whatever its physical disabilities, the trait makes him an admirable philosopher. Though he can rebel, in high Promethean fashion, against the gods, his mind is elastic enough to take in ill-fortune as well as good. When his sight almost goes, so that he has to give up his project of opening a school and perhaps reading for a degree, he nonchalantly turns to turf- and furze-cutting at half a crown a hundred, and finds a calm enjoyment in his work. He becomes a mere brown spot in the midst of the expanse of gorse ; his daily life is microscopic, his world limited to the insects within a circle of a few feet. But the quality here shown is less admirable in its application to human relationships. His mother warns Eustacia—" You will find that though he is as gentle as a child with you now, he can be as hard as steel ! " His effort to get Eustacia back is the act of an intellectual, and a proof of how blind a guide cold reason can be. It is not only that the letter he writes is the letter of a man intellectually constructed, with little place for heart, but he has no generous impulse to send it off at once. He is the strongest man in all Hardy. Others have an equal enduring power, but his is the smashing strength of a great machine, beside which Henchard's easily turned rush is almost pathetic. Yeobright's treatment of his mother and his wife is cruel in its unflinching hardness : Clare and Knight merely resist the unpleasant facts they come up against, Yeobright dominates facts. Clare and Knight are simple egotists ; Yeobright's attitude is based on the considered philosophy of life called egoism. Only once, to show himself human, does he give way to weakness, in his not inexcusable ravings after he found his mother, broken-hearted and dying, on the heath. The favouritisms of authors, like those of parents, among their children, are not always altogether reasonable : Hardy thought Clym Yeobright " the nicest among my characters ".

How different again is Giles Winterborne. He is Hardy's last and loveliest variation on the theme of the patient man. Without Gabriel Oak's unbending endurance, John Loveday's serene cheerfulness, or Diggory Venn's sense of humour, Winterborne has a divine beauty of disposition that transcends them all. Like that other exquisite figure, Elizabeth-Jane, he is introduced by his creator with a studied undemonstrativeness. Beyond his power of suspending both judgment and emotion, and a habit of speaking his mind, we learn only of his attachment to that specimen apple tree of his. This, however, is the very key to his personality. He has a way with trees. " He had a marvellous power of making trees grow. Although he would seem to shovel in the earth quite carelessly, there was a sort of sympathy between himself and the fir, oak or beech that he was operating on ; so that the roots took hold of the soil in a few days." There is a picture of him planting young trees, assisted by that kindred spirit Marty South :

> The holes were already dug, and they set to work. Winterborne's fingers were endowed with a gentle conjuror's touch in spreading the roots of each little tree, resulting in a sort of caress under which the delicate fibres all laid themselves out in their proper directions for growth. He put most of these roots towards the south-west ; for, he said, in forty years' time, when some great gale is blowing from that quarter, the trees will require the strongest holdfast on that side to stand against it and not fall.

Marty draws his attention to their sighing :

> She erected one of the young pines into its hole, and held up her finger ; the soft musical breathing instantly set in, which was not to cease night or day till the grown tree should be felled —probably long after the two planters had been felled themselves.

Grace Melbury has little comprehension of Giles, but she is, ineffectively, aware of this aspect of him :

> He rose upon her memory as the fruit-god and the wood-god in alternation : sometimes leafy and smeared with green lichen, as she had seen him amongst the sappy boughs of the plantations : sometimes cider-stained and starred with apple-pips, as she met him on his return from cider-making in Blackmoor Vale, with his vats and presses beside him.

It is doubtless this identification of his life with that of the trees that gives him his imperturbable poise, and a passivity that comes near to the peace which passes understanding. He is likened to Horatio, having borne himself

> As one, in suffering all, that suffers nothing ;

investing himself thereby with a touch of sublimity. There is a rare magnanimity in his behaviour not only to Grace but to her father. Old Melbury, having realised his mistake in taking Grace from Giles to give her to Fitzpiers, cruelly stirs old fires as he tells Giles of his regrets, but Giles preserves his calm under the torture, and hides his feelings under a dry unimpassioned voice—' Oh, she never cared much for me '. His last sacrifice for Grace is the uttermost expression not only of his love but of his whole personality, and his death, like Henchard's, but in how different a manner, is of a piece with his life. Gabriel Oak is his nearest parallel. But Giles keeps more in the background of his story, a shyer, more sensitive figure. Take him for all in all, there is no male character in Hardy who can hold a place by his side.

With Angel Clare we are back to intellect, with all its limitations. An amazing proof of this is his practice of putting before Tess merciless arguments from the repertoire of scepticism, arguments which not only destroy Tess's simple faith, but ricochet off to bring down Alec D'Urberville and himself. His failure of Tess at the crisis of her life is due to the same absence of all generous warmth of spirit ; his experiment on Izz Huett shows the temperament of the vivisector. Another instance of his cold, un-emotional habit of mind is seen when he returns to England. His eyes have been opened to his folly ; he has already had one letter, full of infinitely pathetic love and appeal, from Tess ; now he finds a second, equally pathetic in its reproach. He is " much disturbed ", but he has time and freedom of mind to give his parents a snobbish little lecture on the aristocratic origins of the Durbeyfield family, and he actually delays for more than a week before setting out in search of Tess. In explanation of his behaviour at the crisis of the story Hardy suggests that " with more animalism he might have been the nobler man ". It is not animalism but imagination that Clare lacks. Nor indeed is he free from the charge of animalism, to judge by an odd incident that occurs before Tess and he are betrothed. It is early morning at the farm, and Tess has knocked at Clare's door to awaken him and has then returned to her room to dress. When a few minutes later, he meets her on the landing, he says, peremptorily, " Now, Miss Flirt, before you

go down. It is a fortnight since I spoke and this won't do any
longer. You *must* tell me what you mean, or I shall have to
leave this house. My door was ajar just now, and I saw you.
For your own safety I must go. You don't know." This
would seem to show Clare little better than a better-bred Alec
D'Urberville. Even apart from this it is not clear that he merits
Hardy's own description of him as ' spiritual '. His fastidiousness and emotional self-control (which latter quality he shares
with most of the heroes of the novels) can be sufficiently explained by his reasoned way of life and his up-bringing at the
hands of those excellent people, the Vicar and his wife. Conscience is very much a matter of early training.

Nevertheless, Clare is no creature of abstractions. His mind
is full of a rich pagan life. Gather his family, Mercy Chant
among them, and put the fallen Angel in the midst, and it
becomes apparent how much nearer to the living truth he is
than they : he has discarded their doctrines, but his religion is
life. Yet he has not swallowed quite all the formulas. Sad for
Tess that the one fragment of the early teaching that has been
too strong for him has been that concerning a woman's virtue.

Jude Fawley, the last of Hardy's men, is the most complex
of them : he seems a solid, living, inscrutable person, no figure
artificially built up of lines and characteristics. From his adventures with Arabella we understand that his animal side is
strongly developed. This is evident not so much in his succumbing to the extremest lure of sex, but rather in the fact that he
was attracted at all, and attracted powerfully, by Arabella's
essentially animal personality. Even after he has gone to live
with Sue he cannot see—or will not admit—that Arabella is
' coarse '. The mere fact of this attraction would seem to
mark him out at once as an impossible mate for Sue. But it is
Jude's glory to be the very type of the complete (though not
necessarily the highest) man—half-earthly, half-divine. Giles
Winterborne is a spirit, Sergeant Troy is an animal ; Jude
Fawley is a man—the spiritual animal. Moreover, except when
maddened or desperate, he has his flesh well in hand under
the reins of reason and will. His dealings throughout with Sue
demonstrate this, and the ultimate crime is rendered thereby
all the more culpable. He himself affirms that his two besetting

sins are love of women and love of drink, but they make their appearance with singular infrequence for vices of this description. With strength to refrain, when he indulges it is with cynical recklessness and wilfulness.

The ethereal side of his nature appears as soon as he comes in contact with Sue, and for some time increases in importance. A responsive sort of man, rather than an initiatory one, it seems. Somebody said men are what women make them, and Jude exemplifies this judgment. His realisation of Sue's spirituality —imperfect though it was till too late—was clearer than it would have been with most men. Even here his instincts were cloudy and unsure. The strength which he exhibited in keeping pure their early relations was largely founded on his orthodoxy, which laid down certain conventional laws of morality. Afterwards, when he had thrown orthodoxy to the winds, he began to see—and eventually saw fully—that something special and unique in Sue herself rendered it sinful to approach or consider her carnally.

He is described as having delicate features ; he has a sensitiveness to suffering, human and animal, beyond all the other men in Hardy : even Giles Winterborne set gins for rabbits ! His origin was lowly, his star was an ' obscure ' one, his sin was dark and degrading ; yet he rose to strange heights of understanding and self-mastery. Of all the characteristics with which his creator has endued him, the steadiest, and the most pathetic, is that passionate aspiration towards the intellectual life which was denied him because he was born half a century too early. It is interesting to wonder what he would have become had he lived in these days of educational grants and State Scholarships —to wonder whether the University would have done as much for him as life with Sue did. Hardy tends the flame of academic desire sleeplessly through the book. At the beginning Jude had carved on the back of the milestone from which Christminster could be so dimly seen—" Thither. J. F." As he creeps back, shivering and ill from his last sight of Sue, he passes this milestone, and lying down in the rain, feels the moss-grown inscription lovingly with his fingers before he goes home to die with the joyous noises of Eights Week sounding ironically in his ears.

The question of the humanity or probability of the figures is to some extent wrapped up with the former one of vividness, and may be partly answered in the same way. Yet only to a small degree. Ariel is vivid enough—much more so than her actual form would have been ; but she is hardly probable (in the ordinary sense), and has but few human traits. And the matter of humanity is so complex and important that a complete discussion of the subject will find fitter place in later chapters. Here all that seems apposite is to point out that Hardy's *personae* are, in the usual (humble, hypocritical or self-excusing ?) phrase, very human. There are no Grandisons or Lovels or Greatest Glorianas. *Hamartia* everywhere ; flawed gems all ; no angels, but of the earth, earthy.

Here and there stands forth a creature less imperfect—Giles Winterborne, John Loveday, Gabriel Oak ; and Marty South, that plant and flower of light. It is only that to do so would be to lose the very idea of *hamartia* that prevents me from adding Tess and Sue themselves.

On the other side of this notion of man as a piebald animal, Hardy has no unredeemed villains : Manston, Troy, Wildeve, D'Urberville—each has his likeable side, however thin. But opinions of guilt vary much more than opinions of virtue (though these differ widely enough). *A Laodicean* is not psychologically serious enough to count importantly in character-study, otherwise Dare is a remarkable personage whose spark of virtue might be difficult of apprehension. There are some of us who could blame God for creating such things as Arabella Donn, yet Sue—Sue—" can't help liking her just a little bit. She's not an ungenerous nature " ; and who are we to contradict Sue in such a matter ?

The members of the Hardy world are, in short, just such compounds of evil with good as their prototypes on the wider stage of earth. There is, however, an even broader ground of judgment the exigences of which our novelist must be prepared to fulfil. It is not sufficient that his characters should be human ; they must be also what is called universal. All *dramatis personae* that are not unreal, impossible, are either realist, typical, or universal. The designer of realistic figures works from keen but superficial observation of men ; he has an eye like a camera, and produces vivid—though possibly composite—photographs ; he presents only an outside view of his creations, and his art needs no plumbing of human nature. Such are the soldiers of Kipling, the sailors of Jacobs, the shop-girls of Pett-Ridge, admirable as they all are. Such are Hardy's rustics, though truly wonderful again. Their collective function precludes all but individual realism. To have endowed them severally with souls would have distracted attention from the main action. On occasion, an individual rustic may be allowed to exhibit something deeper than gait, dialect and mother-wit : as in the altogether perfect episode of Charley and Eustacia's hand in *The Return of the Native ;* Jan Coggan, too, for a moment plays a man's part with Gabriel Oak.

And yet, although the rustics belong distinctly to the realistic school of portraiture, there is thrown over them a veil of romantic glamour that is wanting in the other characters. They are in a degree idealised ; the faintest atmosphere of poetry laps them round—one result being that they are saved from the vulgarity or grossness rarely absent from rusticity in real life.

The second order of character creators plunges farther into the verities of human nature, gets below the surface of idiosyncrasy, classifies individuals, and arrives at types. The result, as to particulars, is less real, but the generalisation is wider, and the criticism of life more profound. To this class belong the characters of Jonson's comedy, many of Dickens' conceptions, and even the immortal figures of Molière's stage.

But there is a greater than these. To have grasped types is much—nay, is necessary ; but types are multiple, distinct and exclusive ; the presentation of one reveals nothing of another, nothing of ultimate man, because comprehension of types does not rest upon the roots and base of human nature. Such comprehension belongs only to that divine sympathy which has been the sure property of but a few writers. By its aid are created characters in each of which every observer in all ages recognises something of himself, inasmuch as they are built of the uttermost underived elemental material that is common to all humanity— the primitive clay and breath of God out of which old Adam was fashioned, and from which have sprung all the incalculable types, genera, individualities which make up the increasingly complex world. It is of such stuff that nearly all Shakespeare's characters are made ; of just such stuff Hardy has shaped Tess, Jude, Henchard, Winterborne, Oak, Bathsheba, Clym Yeobright, and Elfride ; also, I think, Stephen Smith and Knight, Sue Bridehead, and Eustacia ; and perhaps one or two others. Angel Clare is perhaps a type, and in consequence he appeals to a limited number of readers : his " hard logical deposit " is (perhaps luckily) not a universal quality of human nature, not even of masculine human nature. Jocelyn Pierston of *The Well-Beloved* is likewise only a type, and a rare type. For this reason the satire—the very clever and pungent satire on the artistic temperament—is less convincing than, say, Meredith's satire on Egoism in Willoughby Patterne, which makes us aware of the inherent possibilities of the ridiculous in all Egoists, whereas after reading *The Well-Beloved* we only grant that this particular artist was an unfortunate fool.

But most of the great characters of Hardy's novels are neither types nor mere individuals, but ' universals ' : each comprehends within itself the whole of human nature, which is one and indivisible. They have their varied casings of the coloured glass of individuality, but the light at the centre of each is white. To call Hardy a " fearless realist " is to misunderstand him or to abuse the term. In the matter of incident he is certainly neither romancer nor prude ; but in character his eye and hand are those of the Idealist—the Idealist who rises above the accidents and distinctions of external show, and looks deep down into human nature itself—into that restless, unpredictable, fascinating, incurably good and desperately wicked thing, the heart of man.

Chapter II

PLOT, SCENE AND EVENT

I AM making in the course of this study occasional references to the drama, chiefly by way of contrasting that species with the novel. It is natural that the subject of the present chapter should invite a further comparison, and it will be immediately evident that in this case such comparison can only, as before, result in the discovery of difference, at least with regard to plot. Reference has already been made to the superior brevity of the dramatic form, and to the much greater intensity of its action partly consequent upon that feature. It is as impossible for a dramatic intensity of action to be sustained through the length of the average novel as for a whole life to be passed in the exaltation of passion. This fusion and concentration is a mark of all great drama ; more especially of tragedy, but also, though in less degree, of great comedy. In the drama, the action is close-knit into a swift and irresistible sequence that is known as Inevitability. But this inevitability is the fruit only of the intensity of motive which is impossible—and undesirable—in the novel. So that we must not expect to find even the most tragic issues in the novel bearing down upon their victims with the awful logic and certainty that belong to the doom of Othello or of Macbeth.

But while the novel is thus differentiated from the drama, it should be no less clearly and admittedly separated from the chronicle. The chronicle—and most modern novelists are chroniclers—is an entirely admirable form of fiction, but it is not a novel. The novel should have a ' plot '—that is to say, the action should be governed by a single idea ; an idea much less powerful and compelling than the ' motive ' of the drama, but nevertheless a visible idea, and one of which the essential story

7   97

is the result. Whatever the nature of the original *novellae*, it seems to me that, since the English novel in the hands of its great masters—Fielding, Scott, Thackeray—possessed this characteristic as a necessary feature, the trait should continue to be regarded as essential. A novel must have a plot. There must be a certain unity and purpose in the action. It must be possible to discern a line, or lines, of progress towards a consummation of some sort. In all great drama, and in most great novels, the action is the logical outcome of the central characters. But even when character is most tyrannical in its control the plot is also the expression of an idea. And although the domination of character is incomplete in Hardy, owing to the important part played by circumstance, he belongs to the old and genuine school of novel in that the plot is there, the creation of the idea, ready to be seized and assimilated.

Now, it is not essential that this governing idea should be of a definitely ' moral ' nature—that its effect upon the mind should be elevating. All that we demand from a work of art is that it should delight, and thus elevate, not the mind but the soul (or the imagination, or the æsthetic sensibilities). Nevertheless, if the moral tendency is also there we may count it for gain, provided always that it is merely latent in the material used, so that it does not hinder the all-important æsthetic function. Hardy is among those who have given us works of art wherein, having grasped the central idea of each, we find it to be not only a thing of beauty but a grand moral lesson also. This is not to make Hardy ' a novelist with a purpose '. The novelist with a purpose gets his more or less moral idea first, and writes a tale to embody it. Hardy's method is to grasp into his mind a certain complete ' piece of life ', after which, fathoming its inner meaning, he discerns, or we discern, that meaning to be of profound moral significance. Thus his procedure is entirely artistic ; only it happens that his nature is such that it causes his artist-eye to light and linger upon only such pieces of life whose artistic grace covers a soul of righteous ethic. We have allowed Browning to coin the oxymoron ' dramatic lyric ' to describe his most characteristic productions ; I believe it is not less correct, and not more incongruous in sound, to call Hardy's genius didactically artistic.

According to the original and to some extent accepted signification of the term, a novel is a love story.   This tradition has been, however, only partially followed by the English novelists.   Few novels do not involve a love affair of some kind, but the passion is by no means always powerfully central.   In Richardson, Fielding, and perhaps Smollett it is so, but not in Sterne, and only in a degree in Goldsmith ;   Scott and Jane Austen obey the rule, but Dickens and Thackeray frequently abandon it.   Of Hardy's contemporaries and successors, Meredith, Henry James, Galsworthy, and Mr. Charles Morgan practically always make the love interest central, but Stevenson, Conrad, Bennett, and Mr. H. G. Wells as often as not keep it subordinated, or even absent.   The Wessex novels are almost without exception built solidly round an erotic situation, generally of a highly complicated nature. *The Mayor of Casterbridge*, though incorporating a marriage or two, is not a love story in any important sense ;   *Two on a Tower* is the plain though not unvarnished tale of the love of Swithin St. Cleeve and Viviette Constantine.   But in all the other novels the plot takes its rise from the fact of two or more men loving one woman, or two or more women loving one man, or from a combination of the two varieties of complication.   In *Tess of the D'Urbervilles* we have a simple ' triangle ', but in most of the other novels the arrangement of the people who are united by love relations of one sort or another can only be represented by a figure more like a rhomboid.

Let us set out some of them graphically, italicising the names of the women.

A Pair of Blue Eyes

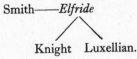

This might have been shown better as a triangle with the lady in the middle :

Far from the Madding Crowd—
takes this form too, with one additional element :

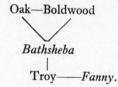

Oak—Boldwood

Bathsheba
|
Troy——*Fanny.*

The Hand of Ethelberta—
an abstruse figure, as befits a comedy :

Julian——*Picotee*
Ethelberta——Ladywell
Neigh
Mountclere.

The Return of the Native—
we are back at the rhomboid, which now has a tail :

Eustacia——Yeobright

Wildeve——*Tamsie*——Venn.

The Trumpet-Major—
another comedy, like *The Hand of Ethelberta* but simpler :

John
Anne——Bob——*Matilda*
Festus.

A Laodicean—
simple rhomboid :

Paula————Somerset

De Stancy   *Charlotte.*

The Woodlanders—
in spite of its seriousness can only be represented as a pursuit :

Marty → Giles → *Grace* → Fitzpiers → *Mrs. Charmond.*

Jude the Obscure—

a rhomboid, though of course the basis of the novel is the relationship shown in the top line (this was true also of *The Return of the Native*) :

Jude————————Sue
\ \
Arabella   Phillotson.

These diagrams will have brought out the marked simplicity of the typical Hardy plot. Concerning itself vitally with the lives of a few persons, the action proceeds in a few great movements, and in clean direct lines. Hardy felt that if a theme was to be treated profoundly it must of necessity be single, simple, unimpeded. In adopting this method of the broad simple outline Hardy departed from the practice of his immediate predecessors, Dickens and Thackeray, and established (with George Eliot) a method which held the field with most novelists of importance until quite modern times, when the crowded canvas of indistinguishable figures has become the fashion (with an occasional honourable nonconformer like Mr. Charles Morgan). This is perhaps the literary symbol of an age which appears to have lost the capacity to produce great men.

In *Jude the Obscure* the two principal figures, equal in interest, dwarf all the other characters, who exist only in relation to Jude and Sue : hand in hand these two take their solitary way down the grim descents of vicissitude. Scope is thus given for a profound study of their lives and souls. The study is effected through an action whose lines disentangle and become quite clear half-way through the story. The essential story lies about the companionship of Jude and Sue ; this is affected and brought to tragic issue by the confluence of four external factors—the earlier connection of Jude with Arabella, that of Sue with Phillotson, Jude's failure to comprehend and adapt himself to Sue's nature, and an outraged world. Winding through all which is the line of Jude's desire for academic acquirements. Here is an action, perhaps not simple—least simple of the great novels —yet single, central, clearly-visioned ; above all an action stern, slow-grinding, revealing, wherein the uttermost roots of being in the two protagonists can be sounded and searched forth and laid bare, as they indeed are. There is something of the method of the great surgeon, who with a few deep strong cuts gets down to the heart of the evil.

Tess of the D'Urbervilles is superbly simple. There is no second character. Clare is there, and of great interest, but he is rather portrayed definitely than studied and allowed to develop : his presence is chiefly necessary as part of Tess's environment. Nor is there any complexity in the action : Tess meets D'Urberville, and is seduced ; she meets Clare, and is wooed and won ; the two facts clash, with infinite ruin. Nothing could be more elementary. Yet what opportunity for psychology ! Not otherwise is it with *A Pair of Blue Eyes*, which is in three clear movements—the wooing of Elfride by Smith, her wooing by Knight, and the fruitless rivalry of the two men. The three characters, of equal importance, are merely placed in juxtaposition, and the rest follows. The plot here, as elsewhere, consists of a display of the souls of a few characters in a few tense and revealing situations. *The Return of the Native* may be regarded either as a story of Eustacia torn between Egdon and Clym Yeobright, or as one of Yeobright torn between Eustacia and his mother. *The Mayor of Casterbridge* is simple in another way : it is a one-figure story, and the dramatic conflict goes on in Henchard's soul. None of the major novels has a scheme which could not be stated in a few sentences, but some of the lesser comedies possess a mild degree of intricacy which shows that Hardy could have mastered this field had he so chosen.

The Woodlanders, being purely idyllic, possesses a plot much more loosely knit than usual. Things are quiet, and without intensity or strong coherence ; they move like a dreamer who wanders through sylvan shadows. The quiet love of Winterborne and Grace Melbury is broken by Fitzpiers, who, without tragedy or tears, steals the heart of Grace, and is presently wiled away by Mrs. Charmond in similar lightly-passionate wise. Then, after Fitzpiers' salutary rustic cure and the Socratically placid death of Winterborne, begins the quiet Indian-summer re-wooing of Grace by Fitzpiers, with happy ending. Strenuous plot would have destroyed the charm of the peaceful idyll ; this wayward ease of movement, as of the seasons, is in perfect keeping. *The Hand of Ethelberta* is as puzzling a tale as I ever read. In its less noble and tragic way it is a parallel to *The Mayor of Casterbridge*, in that it shows a single heroic figure battling with the press of life. But it leaves upon the mind an impression of many doubts. One cannot decide whether to like Ethelberta or not—whether her brave but calculating character is really attractive, repelling or indifferent. Then, ought one to be satisfied with the dénouement, both in itself and as a finale to the tale—a fitting end for Ethelberta ? Lord Mount-clere—how much sympathy does he move, and how much ought he to move ? Are Neigh and Ladywell contemptible or worthy ? —Neigh, blasé man of the world, yet with a certain strength ; Ladywell, brainless young dandy, yet with a certain generosity ; both with some sincerity. Is Julian's marriage with Picotee a disagreeable and farcical solution, or is it pleasing ? It is difficult to arrive at definite conclusions on these questions, perhaps because the story has too much plot, so that the underlying realities have not room for the clear presentation usually given by Hardy.

Generalising, it should be clear that for the most part Hardy's plots are self-supporting organic wholes. And however great the play of an external fate, the life or motive which is at the centre of each is essentially psychological. Every novel is an answer to the question, Given certain characters in certain situations, and allowing for the irony of fate, what will happen—what will become of them ?

I have said that only in the drama is it possible to convey the impression that what happens in the action is that which must inevitably have happened in the circumstances. Now, the total action, whether of novel or drama, is the product not only of the natures of the people concerned and the quality of their immediate environment, but of something larger than human nature and life—Nature itself, the vast law of the order of things in general. But the perfect and unconditioned test of psychologic truth is found, not in the plot or action, but in the scene or dialogue, which is fashioned by human nature alone before being seized and welded into the complete action by the larger order of things. And the scene is equally and similarly the province of both dramatist and novelist. In the hands of a master of psychology the scene would show not so much *what* must have happened (that is the work of the entire plot) but exactly *how* it must have happened—exactly how the various characters must inevitably have acted and spoken in each separate situation that goes to make up the entire sequence of events. Here inevitability is as possible to the novelist as to the dramatist. Nevertheless, of all our dramatists and all our novelists, I am aware of only one of each kind who shows himself so complete a master of the secrets of human nature as to be able to follow Shakespeare in this respect. Shakespeare himself, of course, has many such scenes—Macduff's reception of the news of his wife's murder, the Beatrice-Benedick dialogue after the charge brought by Claudio against Hero, the quarrel between Brutus and Cassius, Hamlet's dismissal of Ophelia, and others which will come to mind readily. In these scenes every thought, every sentence, every word, every gesture follows in its place with a precision and perfection of verisimilitude that is nothing less than terrible. Such scenes are to be found in two other English writers only—in Webster occasionally, and in Hardy with some frequence.[1]

It is impossible that scenes of this kind should appear with great frequence. They are struck out white-hot at moments when feeling and realisation have reached a point of intensity that must from its very nature be rare. There are only some half-dozen scenes that unconditionally satisfy the exigences of this kind : two in *Jude*, one each in *Tess*, *The Woodlanders*, *The Return of the Native*, and *A Pair of Blue Eyes*.

The first of the two in *Jude* is the conversation between Jude and Sue in Jude's rooms on the night when Sue escaped from the training college. It is pure dialogue, without action, and its inevitability depends on the absoluteness with which Hardy convinces the reader that the course it follows is literally, word for word, the course a conversation between these two at this point must have taken. And from the moment when Sue sets the ball rolling—" You called me a creature of civilisation, or some-

[1] Cf. Swinburne, *Age of Shakspere* : " There are only two (poets in the age of Shakspere) who make us feel that the words assigned to the creatures of their genius are the very words they must have said, the actual words they assuredly did say . . . Shakspere and Webster."

thing, didn't you ? " she said, breaking a silence. " It was very odd that you should have done that "—one is thus convinced. Sue discovers to him her lack of the more obstructive qualities of sex, telling of her life with the undergraduate. Of course, the man died—of consumption or broken-heart ; but what is consumption (or broken-heart) for but to carry off such weak and inappreciative fellows as this ? Her story evokes no such expressions of admiration from Jude. He asks, in a scared tone, " Good heavens !—what did you do then ? "—and presently has the condescending impudence to remark that " however she has lived, he believes she is as innocent as she is unconventional ". She herself denies that she is cold-natured and sexless ; she is merely " self-contained ". Certainly tenderness and an " emotional throat-note " are not lacking, at proper intervals, from this conversation, and something of this warmer sort is presently in requisition, for the two nearly quarrel over religious ideas. She is a free-thinker, but she is moreover, perhaps, definitely irreligious, and Jude strives to emphasise his religion in contrast to her irreligion. All he succeeds in doing is in demonstrating his unthinking orthodoxy. He looks pained, and calls her just animadversions on the ' explanations ' of the Song of Solomon " quite Voltairean ", meaning ' dreadfully wicked '. When she replies with spirit he is " surprised at her introducing personal feeling into mere argument ", the fact really being that he will admit no argument—he merely ' looks pained '. She on her part is intolerant in thinking high aims can go only with irreligion ; just as she is prejudiced in denying to students a knowledge of life and granting it to drunkards. Finally, with much reason, he finds her ' epicene tenderness ' too harrowing. He wishes he could get over the sense of her sex, realising what a comrade she would make,—if he could but accept her scepticism as part of her.

More wonderful, because containing a greater element of drama, is Jude's last meeting with Sue in the church of St. Giles. It has already received some description. How different is their relative position now ! He is great and sane, and she—poor Sue —is very small. At his " I *would* have died game ! " his tenderly contemptuous, " Sue, you are not worthy of a man's love ", she yields once more to his kisses, but she breaks away and stops her ears to the sound of his grave-yard coughing.

The scene from *Tess* is that of the disclosure to Clare. With the boldness of a great artist Hardy divides the scene into two, with the break between two ' phases ' in between : this multiplies the force and terror in a degree that would hardly have been supposed possible. Clare has told of *his* fault, and Tess, relieved, can tell of hers now.

Their hands were still joined. The ashes under the grate were lit by the fire vertically, like a torrid waste. Imagination might have beheld a Last Day luridness in this red-coaled glow, which fell on his face and hand, and on hers, peering into the loose hair about her brow, and firing the delicate skin underneath. A large shadow of her shape rose upon the wall and ceiling. She bent forward, at which each diamond on her neck gave a sinister wink like a toad's ; and pressing her forehead against his temple she entered on her story of her acquaintance with Alec D'Urberville and its results, murmuring the words without flinching, and with her eyelids drooping down.

And that is the ' end of phase the fourth '. Knowing that Hardy does not introduce images like that ' Last Day luridness ' and that ' sinister wink like a toad's ' without significance, one hardly dares to bring that dreadful pause to an end by turning the page. At last one does so, to find, sure enough, that hope and life have given place to death and despair. As she went quietly through her story, immaterial objects round her—the fire, the fender—had suffered transmutation, dissociating themselves unfeelingly from her plight. And now, ' the essence of things had changed '. Clare stirs the fire, presently begins to question her in an inadequate, commonplace voice, and after a while breaks out into horrible laughter. The scene progresses unerringly, inevitably, till at last Tess, worn out, sleeps, and Clare, with sterile face, sits wakeful—both surrounded by the indifferent night.

The Woodlanders gives us Grace's last night in Giles's cabin, when the storm comes on and she, unable to endure the thought of him in his exposed situation, calls to him, " Come to me ! I don't mind what they say or what they think any more ". But he thinks it better to remain.

The scene is one of those that fully and finally absolve Hardy from any charge of sensuality that may be preferred against him. I think I can hear Grace Melbury's voice as she utters that cry,

and the sound of it is that sound which is the mark of the most
beautiful thing in the world—a woman's flawless innocence and
purity of mind. No man who could conceive that innocence and
the frame of mind of Grace and Giles in that scene could ever be
a sensualist. The episode is comparable in purity and sweetness
with the ' Marine Duet ' in Meredith's *Lord Ormont*. But the
brilliant interplay of witty converse of the sea-scape is replaced
here by a naked simplicity of thought and utterance that makes
this the diviner of the two. It is among these elemental natures
that Hardy is most at home, and there is no one else at all who
has given us just such scenes as this.

In *The Return of the Native* I find one certain scene of this kind,
and perhaps a second. Unmistakable is that between Yeobright
and Eustacia in her bedroom after Yeobright has dragged the
whole truth out of Johnny Nonsuch : one of the greatest of all
scenes of combat between man and woman. In its agony, its
mutual misunderstanding, its passionate grief and regret, its
tremendous anger, it is profoundly reminiscent of some of the
scenes between Othello and Desdemona, especially of that in
Act IV, Scene 2. Such passages as this :

> " I shall no doubt be gratified by learning in good time what
> a well-finished and full-blown adept in a certain trade my lady is."
>
> " Do you say it to me—do you ? " she gasped.

—such passages appear to have been suggested by their Shake-
sperean parallels. But the battle is much more equal here :
Desdemona is no match for her terrible lord, while Yeobright
and Eustacia are of heroic mould both, though the man eventually
breaks the woman. And in this it recalls another magnificent
scene from Elizabethan drama—that between Melantius and
Evadne in Beaumont and Fletcher's ' Maid's Tragedy '. It is
no small tribute to Hardy's chapter that it bears the second comparison easily, and retains its greatness even beside the former,
far as it falls below it in terror and sheer poetry.

The scene repays examination line by line, but space forbids
that. One must just note, however, how much better, how much
crueller, than killing is the " scourging to the bone" that succeeds
Yeobright's earlier violence, and before which Eustacia at last
sinks down crushed. Yet, neither in this fierce shaming nor in

the rage that precedes it is there any sound of rant or noise. Nor is there anything but simple pathos in the bonnet-strings that he has to help her trembling hands to fasten, turning his eyes aside that he may not be tempted to softness.

The second possible scene for inclusion in this class immediately precedes the one just mentioned : it is that in which Clym questions little Johnny, and comes to the knowledge of evil through the lips of a child. It is a strange, breath-taking picture —the child, with his direct, uncoloured, impersonal statements, the child's mother, hating Eustacia and watching with fiendish pleasure the facts about her being brought to light, and Clym incredulously arriving piece by piece at the shocking truth. As Yeobright goes forth from the scene, meditating strange deeds, " there before him was the imperturbable countenance of the heath, which, having defied the cataclysmal onsets of centuries, reduced to insignificance by its seamed and antique features the wildest turmoil of a single man ".

The last of these ' inevitable ' scenes is the chess-playing between Knight and Elfride. There is an absolute verisimilitude about Knight's phlegmatic infallibility and Elfride's nervous anxiety, and the intense truth of the scene is visualised, as it were, by that keenly observant reference to the uncanny effect of a clock—especially an old clock—upon a highly charged atmosphere : " Nothing is now heard but the ticking of a quaint old timepiece on the summit of a bookcase ". It is perhaps unwise to class this lighter scene with the more tremendous ones previously cited, but the psychology is as unerring here as there. Missing the supreme quality of inevitability, but finely written with great fidelity to truth, are a number of other scenes which will readily be recalled. Such are the first passage of bitter dispute between Clym and his mother over his growing friendship with Eustacia ; and the double scene between Grace and Mrs. Charmond when they are lost in the wood. This latter gains in force from the rarity of dramatic encounters between two women. Grace has the woodland fibre, Mrs. Charmond is soft-bodied, and is brought to open confession under the stress of fear and cold. The picture of the two women, rivals, but one good and the other not too bad, afterwards clinging together for warmth and comfort, is of a piece with the book's quality. Another episode that lasts in the memory is that unbearably dreadful one already described of Sue going to Phillotson's bed. These three scenes stand very close to those in the first class of all. Others a little lower in the scale but well worth studying in detail are the cliff adventure in *A Pair of Blue Eyes*, the " gurgoyle " chapter from the *Madding Crowd*, the skimmity-ride in *The Mayor* (this made quite extraordinary by the method of its telling, by a maid-servant at an upper window in the hearing of Lucetta to whom, in her lower position, the procession is invisible), the incident of the fatal tree in *The Woodlanders*, the baptism of Sorrow the Undesired in *Tess*, the account of her frustrated visit to Clare's parents (a chapter of great creative force, showing how Hardy does not so much mould circumstances as draw them into his imagination with such intensity that they are compelled to develop upon certain strange and tragic lines), the swift night-piece of the arrest by Stonehenge, and the ghastly ending of the short life of Father Time. There are many other scenes, models of dialogue and characterisation, any of which would repay extraction and separate reading on its own brilliant merits.

One other striking fact is to be recorded here. There occur here and there in the pages of Hardy a phrase, a sentence, a thought —half a dozen of them again in all perhaps—which in their psychologic absoluteness are as far superior to the greatest of the scenes recently indicated as those were to the plots of the stories. They are instantaneous, dazzlingly vivid revelations of profoundest personality, ultimate truth of human nature.

In the prelude to that scene between Sue and Phillotson which has been already praised there occurs, for instance, this incident. She has gone to Phillotson's door ; she calls, and listens ; there is no sound. Then :

" Perhaps he's dead ! " she gasped. " And then—I should be *free*, and I could go to Jude ! "

I think there are no words needed to explain or demonstrate the miraculous nature of that brief passage. But as one reads, it arrests one like an unexpected flash of lightning, and the view it gives of Sue's feelings remains indelibly imprinted on the mind.

Again, in *The Woodlanders*, Winterborne is dead, and Fitzpiers stands in the cabin where Grace has lived, alone, for some days. He, thinking she has lived there with Giles, and having her admission that she loved the dead man, asks if he is to draw the obvious, the extremest inference.

" Yes ", she answered ; and there was that in her subtly compounded nature that made her feel a thrill of pride as she did so.

Now, forasmuch as we know that Grace has " more of Artemis than of Aphrodite in her constitution ", the delicacy and depth of that stroke of characterisation, with the illumination it affords of woman's nature in general, must be called nothing short of miraculous.

The last chapter of the same book, made up of varied elements woven with consummate art into a harmonious whole, achieves its climax of beauty in the conclusion : Marty South, solitary and silent girl, the " lost Aspatia " of the story, lays her flowers on Giles's grave :

> " Now, my own, own love," she whispered, " you are mine, and on'y mine, for she has forgot 'ee at last, although for her you died ! But I—whenever I get up I'll think of 'ee, and whenever I lie down I'll think of 'ee. Whenever I plant the young larches I'll think that none can plant as you planted ; and whenever I turn the cider-wring, I'll say none can do it like you. If ever I forget your name let me forget home and heaven !—But no, no, my love, I never can forget 'ee ; for you was a good man, and did good things ! "

It is well to speak with caution in cases of very great enthusiasm, but considering the passage as a finale to the chapter, one is constrained to ask where is the man who could have equalled the perfect and passionate beauty of that climax. And it is achieved as quietly and naturally as a child sinking to sleep.

In *The Return of the Native*, after the runaway couple have been found drowned, Clym takes Venn and Charley upstairs to gaze reverently on the cold Eustacia—*pallida mors* herself. Here occurs a sentence which, in a metaphoric flash that must be placed among the miracles of Hardy, presents completely his view of death, and incidentally of life :

> The expression of her finely carved mouth was pleasant, *as if a sense of dignity had just compelled her to leave off speaking*.

The italics are, of course, mine ; though it is hardly necessary to emphasise that astounding utterance. A dozen quiet words—

so perfectly quiet, with the hush of sublimity. Life—how this man scorns it! To die—it is to dismiss life with quiet contempt and superiority, a dignified closing of the lips.

Jude is so highly wrought in its details that these flashes of illumination occur several times. Towards the end of the chapter in which Sue, bewildered by the terrible death of her children, tells Jude she must leave him to go back to Phillotson, Jude, in agony, exclaims,

"Then let the veil of our temple be rent in two from this hour!"

He went to the bed, removed one of the pair of pillows thereon, and flung it on to the floor.

And when Jude, remarried to Arabella, ill, and so weak that he can scarcely move, asks her to send for Sue, Arabella unwisely replies:

". . . Have that strumpet in the house indeed!"

Almost before the words were spoken Jude had sprung from his chair, and before Arabella knew where she was he had her on her back upon a little couch which stood there, he kneeling above her.

"Say another word of that sort," he whispered, "and I'll kill you—here and now!"

And one might find one or two more of these, that I call the miracles of Hardy.

Such are some of the more interesting features in the constructional art of Hardy. Looking back over the subject, one may ask whether it has appeared that he is genuinely creative. That is to say, is his point of view so individual, and his insight into the nature of things so profound, that his presentments of life are both essentially new and—so far as we can judge—essentially true and worthy? And if this point of view, this insight, are his at all, how wide is the horizon that bounds his gaze?

Answering the last question first, one must admit that his outlook is restricted. So far as human nature goes, indeed, we have discovered—and we shall presently proceed much farther in our discovery—that the range of his comprehension and creation is extended beyond that of all but a very few great delineators of character. But in respect of the life that displays human nature,

Hardy has deliberately or involuntarily confined his attention largely to a single situation, which may be described as faithlessness, or indecision, or divisibility, in love. The plots noticed in the early part of this chapter were, with the exception of *The Mayor of Casterbridge*, all concerned to show us the strife of the soul under the stress of divided affections. They made clear, indeed, that such strife might take innumerable forms ; nevertheless the dramatic conflict was in each case set up by the same cause, the more or less bitter antagonism of love.

But within this sphere there can be no doubt of Hardy's creative power. The individuality of his position cannot be called in question : the fierce hostility with which his portrayals of life are met is sufficient proof that his attitude is no mere reflection of the mind of his time. Cultured critics, men of large practical common-sense, and untutored women are all found among the dissidents. The parallel between the different receptions accorded to Hardy and Meredith and those given in their day to Browning and Tennyson, though by no means complete, is not without instruction on this side. Concerning the veracity of the presentment of life one cannot be so dogmatic. To say that any given rendering of life is true is only to say that it falls in with one's own view of things. Still, as the psychologic consistency of Hardy's characters is seldom impugned, and as his stories arise with great naturalness and, in detail, even with necessity from the natures of the *dramatis personae*, it may be concluded that the greater Wessex novels, at all events, are true windows into the great world itself. Whether the view they afford is worthy or unworthy is a question that our discussion of Hardy's philosophy in subsequent chapters will attempt to decide.

CHAPTER III

HARDY'S USE OF THE MARVELLOUS

THE time has gone by when literature and the law took the supernatural seriously. Our ultra-civilised world, instructed by science and common-sense, looks down with impatient contempt on all our ancestors shuddered at. Even the peasantry—that most nearly changeless element of the community—no longer sets the nightly milk-bowl for Mab and Robin Goodfellow. The horns of elfland wind no more, howsoever faintly. The very children are sceptical of Grimm, thanks to careful parents and the rule of three. Yet some few of us refuse to yield our fairy-faith to logic, and look for a reconversion that would be but a belated effect of the Renascence of Wonder. Meanwhile, what is Hardy's attitude on the subject ? Has he anything to correspond to the ghost in ' Hamlet ' ?

(Reading that first paragraph, twenty years after it was written, I wonder if I do not now see signs of the ' reconversion ' there spoken of—in children, and in literature ?)

The word ' ghost ' has at least three definitions, of widening denotation. It answers first to the popular conception of the returning spirits of the departed in a more or less visible form ; ghosts of this type enliven the modern short story with some persistence, but it is highly exceptional to find one of them in the centre of a serious novel, such as Mr. de la Mare's *The Return*. More broadly, ghosts are bodiless presences of all kinds, real or imaginary, perceived not by the senses, but by their ' uncanny ' effect upon the consciousness of the observer. The huge despairing questioning of the grey sea is a ghost ; the nerve-shattering silence of a house after the departure of the Beloved ; the mocking things that creep from corners and cluster and push and jibe behind one's back in the firelight : these atmospheric effects and creatures of the wrought imagination are ghosts, and few things are more certain than the fact of their existence and power. Ghostly effects of this kind are quite characteristic of Hardy, though the practice of their introduction is not, as it so easily can be, overdone. The passage already quoted that gives the setting to Tess's disclosure to Clare of her past provides one powerful example. A vaguer suggestion of a similar nature occurs at the death-bed of Jude ; and Egdon Heath gives forth a ' ghost ' of tremendous power and continuity, which will receive further attention in a later chapter. Perhaps another instance is the de-materialising effect of certain highly charged atmospheres—noon, dawn, twilight ; a very wonderful and assured phenomenon which is excellently illustrated in the third phase of *Tess*. In that strange and solemn interval, the twilight of the morning, the spectral, half-compounded, aqueous light which pervaded the open mead impressed the lovers with a feeling of isolation, as if they were Adam and Eve. At this dim inceptive stage of the day, at that preternatural time, Tess looked ghostly, as if she were merely a soul at large—no longer a milkmaid but a visionary essence of woman. Hardy's own declaration of faith in this special kind of mysterious effluence from certain scenes and situations is made in the preface to *A Pair of Blue Eyes*, where he says, speaking of the shore and country about Castle Boterel : " The place is pre-eminently (for one person at least) the region of dream and mystery. The ghostly birds, the pall-like sea, the frothing wind, the eternal soliloquy of the waters, the bloom of dark purple cast that seems to exhale from the shoreward precipices, in themselves lend to the scene an atmosphere like the twilight of a night-vision." And indeed the whole ' Hardy atmosphere ', when it concentrates itself into his style, has something strange, weird, fateful about it.

But in its most comprehensive application the term ghosts is simply equivalent to ' more things than are dreamt of in your philosophy ', and this is Hardy's own use of the marvellous. His practice in this respect amounts to a denial of the Aristotelian doctrine that probable impossibilities are to be preferred to improbable possibilities. Only Mr. de la Mare, again (and that in an entirely different manner), approaches Hardy in the bold manipulation of natural events to produce a continuous and pervading impression of magic.

Outside deliberate tales of mystery and imagination, such as the *Romance of Wonder* exploited by the tribe of Walpole, Beckford and Monk Lewis, where shall we find in the novel a figure so exactly parallel in nature and action to the witches of *Macbeth* as the Reddleman in *The Return of the Native ?* Tall, silent, solitary, in close-fitting raiment, and lurid red from crown to heel, he is easily at one with the cryptic shades of Egdon. Across this vast abode of gloom he moves mysteriously ; omnipresent and all-watchful over the destinies of the other persons of the drama, he is ever ready with new moves, and interferes at all crises like the finger of a deity. He moves underground, rises unexpectedly from the earth, goes and comes none knows how ; and it is something more than startling to find him quietly married at the end of the story—he should have disappeared for ever like the ghost he is.

This, then, is one example of Hardy's method (reminiscent of Wordsworth's side of the " Lyrical Ballads " scheme) of using natural objects and occurrences in a perfectly natural way, and yet so as to invest them with an air of mystery. A case of a different type may be noted in the situation which gives rise to the title *Two on a Tower*. Consider that situation ; a tall, column-like tower, lone and wind-buffeted, rising from a group of sombre, sighing firs in the midst of untrodden fields ; at its summit, in a solitude more absolute than Crusoe's, a youth and a woman oscillating between the plumbless spaces of the night and the equally unfathomable depths of each other's souls : can a situation so unique, so wizard-like, so pregnant with delicate romance fail to render in some way remarkable the drama of which it is the stage ?

In one other novel a motif of marvellous nature has to be assumed. *The Well-Beloved* is ' frankly fantastic ', but the story is played out with real characters, though of an astonishingly passionless nature. And the presentation is equally calm : the fantastic consequence, the alarming inconsequence, of events are laid down in a manner as cool, as unsurprised as that of a datebook. The incredible incidents are presented with no more apology or comment than the adventures of Gulliver, and one

feels inclined to pay the book the Irish Bishop's compliment of
' hardly believing a word of it '.

But, on the whole, it is in respect of detail and accident that
Hardy's favourite and most characteristic employment of the
unaccountable is seen. The world of his Novel is by no means
a world in which all things can be reduced to obvious law and
explained by common-sense. The strange, the unforeseen, the
inexplicable occur everywhere and always. For instance, coincidence—that ubiquitous but lawless and unacknowledged
phenomenon—is as important a feature in the lives of Hardy's
people as it is in real life. It crops up everywhere, in crisis and
passing event.

That delightful satiric idealisation of the English girl, *A Pair
of Blue Eyes*, is built upon one large coincidence and riveted
together with many smaller ones. Young Stephen Smith, the
architect from town, is sent down into Wessex, where he learns
to love and be loved by his client's daughter, the blue-eyed
Elfride. But the stern father of the blue-eyed one remarries,
and as it happens, marries a lady whose cousin is one Knight,
erstwhile tutor and patron of the budding Smith, and already a
name of frantic interest to Elfride through having, by chance,
reviewed her first attempt at novel-writing. In the absence of
Smith comes Knight, is seen of the impressionable Elfride, and
makes only too complete conquest of her quivering self. The
essential conception of the story—the interplay and contrast of
these three characters—is thus given form by means of a situation
which is the result of a triple coincidence. But, more than this,
at every critical point in the story the same phenomenon appears
for good or evil. On the way back from the scandalous semi-
elopement, Elfride runs into the arms of her most interestedly
hostile acquaintance—the sinister Mrs. Jethway. Then there is
that ear-ring which she had lost while with Smith on the cliff :
it so happens that she rests afterwards with her second (or third)
lover in the same place ; the sun shines for a few minutes each
day into a certain cleft in the rock, and those few minutes coincide
with their presence, so that the jewel sends its incriminating gleam
into the mind of Knight ; whence arise jealousies and the tearing
asunder of lives. And perhaps Fate never drew together the
threads of separate lives in a grimmer mood than when she put

Knight and Smith into the very train in which lay the lifeless body of the woman whose hand they were once more about to seek in emulation.

Among events of less importance, Smith must choose, unwittingly, no other seat but the tomb of Elfride's first lover whereon to draw from her a confession relating to that unfortunate youth. At the very moment when, in the excitement of Knight's deliverance from his perilous position on the cliff-brow, their love breaks forth and they embrace for the first time—at that very moment Elfride observes that the boat that brings Smith home from abroad has reached the harbour below ; and Smith himself, as he walks up from the quay, sees far off a scudding white figure, that is his lost Elfride flying home with the new love in her heart. When Knight would have a keepsake, he must perforce choose the dwarf-myrtle that has been his predecessor's gift to Elfride. And again, as the two walk moodily home, troubled with mutual misunderstandings, they come in sight of the old church tower, and Elfride is inspired to quote—" Thou hast been my hope, and a strong tower for me against the enemy " ; whereat there is a rumbling and a swaying and the strong tower crashes to the ground, yielding at this moment to the efforts of the churchrestorers. Moreover, the dreaded widow Jethway was but then at her son's tomb, and is smitten to death in the ruins, seeming to free Elfride. But it is Knight who finds her, and he calls to his help a passing stranger who had seen the woman that afternoon posting a letter, which letter Knight receives, and the widow's vengeful tongue had spoken just in time.

In all these cases, had the one set of circumstances happened ever so little beyond the other, all life succeeding would have been different for those concerned (different in a more visible and vital way than that indicated by Carlyle's pebble). But it is Hardy's will that they should occur together, and the dual impact drives home the wedge of destiny.

The thoughtful and observant reader will have noticed that I was able to give a narrative commentary on *A Pair of Blue Eyes* without mentioning a single one of these coincidences. The inference is not that the coincidences are unimportant, but that they are specially important. An outline of the story (as of any of the others) tells what happens : the coincidences are why it happened (in so far as it is not an effect of character). Coincidence steps in at every point to give the action a push or a twist. We often see it doing so in life, and we may be sure there are many occasions when it acts without our seeing it : Hardy lets us see it every time.

Coincidence is so frequent in Hardy that there is some danger of its being regarded as a mannerism, or even as a pusillanimous device for bringing about crisis or dénouement. The method is, however, quite deliberately employed, and is well rooted in Hardy's philosophy. The vast web of existence that encompasses the world is hopelessly inextricable to the eyes of the bewildered beings who struggle along its threads. But it is the privilege of a few great readers of the Book of Life to be raised to a position whence the view is more comprehensive—whence the junctions and crossings and inter-weavings of the web become clear and explicable. The view once obtained, the artist must of necessity record it in his work, and if the result is marvellous in our eyes, it is because we are earth-folk—having never sat in the skies of life. Shakespeare's lines converge, giving the effect of inevitability ; Hardy's main lines converge, too, but they are constantly cut by other lines, with the result that we have at each such section a touch of that irony so dear to Hardy. His coincidences are not forced—they are always explicable, and sometimes explained ; nor are they so amazing as to be incredible, except in cases like the fall of the tower, when the action has reached a point of tragic intensity at which all things are possible, such wizard-like happenings being also entirely in consonance with that use of the marvellous and improbable which I have described as peculiarly Hardian.

Tess of the D'Urbervilles is more tragic than *A Pair of Blue Eyes*, and the coincidences are more sombre and ironic. I hardly know where to look for an effect so perfectly appalling obtained by such simple and natural means as that produced by the Scriptural admonitions that flame upon Tess so immediately after her sin. She has but that moment severed herself from her seducer, and as she walks on in the sad Sabbath morn of October, a stranger appears suddenly at her side, and paints out slowly, in letters of staring vermilion, the menacing declaration, ' Thy, damnation, slumbereth, not ',—placing a comma after each word, as if to give pause while that word was driven well home to the reader's heart ;

following it up presently with ' Thou, shalt, not, commit,——— ', at which poor Tess flees in terror. The overpowering dread of the inward intent, with the realistic and ironic humour of the setting, is only to be paralleled, I think, by the Porter-scene in Macbeth.

The not dissimilar power of an allusion, at the critical moment, to an event rendered already impressive—polarised, as Trench says—by connection with the Divine Tragedy, is recognised and used, I think, by Hardy in more cases than one. For instance, as Tess and Clare leave the farm after their marriage, the cock crows—thrice. To the superstitious country-folk the coincidence (of an afternoon crow with a marriage) is fraught with evil meaning ; it is explained by Mrs. Crick—and by subsequent events— as an indication of change of weather ; upon us who know how things stand, the combined effect of the superstitious and the Scriptural references is simply indescribable.

Some other instances in *Tess* of a specially ironic nature may be reserved for fuller treatment from that point of view. For Tess's accidental meeting, in the depths of her distress and estrangement from Clare, with Alec D'Urberville, it is one of the most probable of Hardy's coincidences (for the Wessex folk are home-birds), but withal a somewhat crude specimen. And the more so in that a precisely similar rencounter is introduced for a not unlike purpose in several other of the novels. Jude's discovery of Arabella behind the bar of the gin-palace, and the contretemps of Troy with Bathsheba in the circus-tent—the three situations smack too much of each other, and the triplicated device is an undoubted flaw in Hardy's art. (It would appear that the novelist realised the questionableness and danger of this third appearance of the mechanical god in *Jude*—the latest of the three novels—by the care with which the meeting is led up to : the gloomy wait for the train—the half-hour's depression, during which an old boon companion turns up—the adjournment to the drinking-saloon—the mirrored reflection of the barmaid in the next compartment—and Arabella.)

Perhaps sufficient instances have been adduced to illustrate the principle in question ; very many others have been passed over for the time being as containing the ironic element—which is, of course, present in all coincidence to which perceptible result attaches—in such degree as to merit special notice. The philosophy of the practice has been already suggested; it may be repeated as conclusion to this section, in Hardy's own words :

> Strange conjunctions of circumstances, particularly those of a trivial everyday kind, are so frequent in an ordinary life that we grow used to their unaccountableness, and forget the question whether the very long odds against such juxtaposition is not almost a disproof of it being a matter of chance at all.

Chance happenings of a not distinctly coincidental nature also play an important part on this stage. At two points in *Tess* a crisis is brought about by inadvertent interposition of an unfortunate Fate : the slaying of Prince the horse by the mail-van shaft is the immediate cause of Tess's introduction to Alec D'Urberville ; and her letter of confession to Clare, which she slips under his door, goes under the carpet and never reaches him, necessitating the *vis-a-vis* disclosure. The equally vital accident by which Sergeant Troy is spirited away on a seaward current has already been explained as an intervention of nature. These accidental occurrences might be manifolded among lesser events, but the feature will be familiar to all Hardy readers. The frequency of the fortuitous, while occupying its own place in Hardy's inexplicable world, may perhaps also be regarded as his contribution to the modern view of the overwhelming importance of little things, so well and wittily set forth by G. K. Chesterton in the chapter on " The Ring and the Book " in his *Browning*. A special series of these fortuitous events of a remarkably interesting and characteristic kind is exemplified in its most elementary form by Bathsheba's singing of *Allan Water* in her early unperturbed days before the coming of Troy.

> Subsequent events caused one of the verses to be remembered for many months and even years, by more than one of those who were gathered there :
>
> > For his bride a soldier sought her
> > And a winning tongue had he :
> > On the banks of Allan Water
> > None so gay as she !

This dim heralding of the future requires careful treatment, but in the hands of an artist it may produce impressive effects. In

grimmer wise it appears in *Tess* when Clare brings home his bride
to her ancestral mansion. She starts and shudders at two huge
portraits of her forebears, and well she may, at " The long,
pointed features, narrow eye, and smirk of the one, so suggestive
of merciless treachery ; the bill-hook nose, large teeth, and bold
eye of the other, suggesting arrogance to the point of ferocity ".
It is cruel, but the omen is powerful ; and flung up in glaring
contrast by the next lines, where Tess and Clare wash hands in
one basin, and their fingers get mixed—a pretty scene duplicated
from *Under the Greenwood Tree*.

Occasionally an important change pending is typified in the
concrete by a chance preceding event. Thus, at the moment
when Elfride is balanced with much nicety between the plain and
honest devotion of Smith and the dazzling fascination exercised
upon her by the more magnificent Knight, she receives a gift from
each. " There before her lay the deposit-receipt for the two
hundred pounds, and beside it the elegant present of Knight.
Elfride grew cold." Of a similar nature, but grander, with even
a touch of sublimity—not infrequent in *Jude*—is the place where
Sue, having brought home the statuettes of Venus and Apollo to
her room at the ecclesiastical repository, lies wakeful in the dark.
" Every time she opened her eyes there was enough diffused light
from the window to show her the white plaster figures . . . in
odd contrast to . . . the gothic-framed crucifix-picture, that
was only discernible now as a latin cross, the figure thereon being
obscured by the shades." The scene is a perfect type of the
swaying war of orthodoxy and heterodoxy that is to wage in
the story of her after-days, and suggests besides I know not
what dread premonitions of a lifting of the obscuring shades,
and consequent havoc in the soul unused to the light.

But the greatest of these prophetic occurrences is to be found,
also in *Jude*, in the respective means by which the hero is introduced to the two heroines of the tale. In Chapter VI of the
first part, one's dissatisfaction with Jude and disgust at Arabella
are so intense that one may easily overlook the marvellous allegory
of the event. But it is plain enough. The man, rapt in dreams
of a pure, wise, ascetic life, is awakened, and the lamp of his high
vision shattered (or at least overturned) by the sudden shock of an
obscenely suggestive fleshly thing flung by a light woman. No

comment could do more than dull the clearness of that masterly figuration. We turn on to his meeting with Sue. Having in earlier days seen her portrait, ' in a broad hat, with radiating folds under the brim like the rays of a halo ', he finds her in the ecclesiastical warehouse at Christminster.

> What was she doing ? Before her lay a piece of zinc, cut to the shape of a scroll. . . . Hereon she was designing or il-luminating, in characters of Church text, the single word
> ALLELUIA.
> " A sweet, saintly, Christian business, hers ! " thought he.

The contrast is stupendous ; and in Jude's attraction to both sides of it lies not only much of Jude's own history, but the type of half the woe and glory of mankind.

The fortuitous in its various kinds does not exhaust the realm of the marvellous as explored by Hardy. Life-histories are begun, crises are brought about, through the agency of events quite natural, yet strange, uncommon, fantastic. Recall, for instance, that scene in the hollow amid the ferns in which Sergeant Troy makes conquest of the heart of Bathsheba Everdene. Who but Hardy would have made him wage the battle of love with a broad-sword ? Yet such is the sole weapon used in the critical scene, and wondrously effective it is. Like a victim of some weird enchantment of old time, Bathsheba stands motionless while round her wheels and flames the great sword, making lightnings in the splendour of the setting sun, transforming the atmosphere into a panoply of restless gleams and whistlings, while through the luminous haze appears the form of Troy, the keen-eyed magician of the potent spell. She fears him, she sinks down overcome by a hundred tumultuous emotions, and the spell breaks (or reaches her heart) in a stream of tears as Troy kisses her unawares and disappears, " like a brand swiftly waved ".

It is magic, nothing less ; we are back in the days of charms and love-potions. Less fantastical and improbable but even more weird is the use of the precipice-adventure for the firing of love between Knight and Elfride. The scene itself is managed with a consummate art which, in its effects, differs from sensationalism only in its superior power, though, in the means taken to produce these powerful effects, widely enough by reason of the calmness, the cold-bloodedness, of the narration. But the scene, complete as it is, is not a mere episode ; an intensity of fear is skilfully wrought out and framed for the mind of the reader by Knight's solitary exploration into the infancy of the world—(It is not the least marvellous of Hardy's ' ghosts ', that panorama of Knight's thoughts as he hangs there 'in the presence of personalised loneliness ', almost in space itself, and on the veritable verge of death. Consider but that fossilised creature, that ghastly crustacean relic from a life infinite ages past, whose eyes, dead and turned to stone, stare into Knight's as he lies on the black rock !)—and the intense fear of the situation, and the excitement of the manner in which Elfride's woman-wit effects salvation, are the means by which the souls of the two lovers are charged to the sparking point.

Of a different order altogether, yet equally illustrative of Hardy's method of quaint or queer preliminaries, is the telegraph wire that takes George Somerset to Paula Power, and that afterwards plays so important a part in their ' story of to-day '. It leads him through the darkness ; it sings on overhead " with dying falls and melodious rises that invited him to follow ; while above the wire rode the stars in their courses, the low nocturn of the former seeming to be the voices of those stars, ' Still quiring to the young-eyed cherubim ' " ; it plunges over down, across road, through park, leaps over moat and wall, and vanishes through an arrow-slit into the ivy-mantled keep of a feudal castle. It is neither extraordinary like Troy's sword-play, nor tremendous like the cliff-adventure ; it is simply as exquisite a bit of fairyland as may well be found with the naked eye in the modern world.

The way in which Hardy's characters compel the powers of nature into their service is not the least uncanny of the marvels we are discussing. This is particularly noticeable in *The Return of the Native*. When Eustacia and Clym Yeobright meet on Egdon, the signal for their trysting-hour is nothing less than a lunar eclipse. The lesser glory of the relationship between Eustacia and Wildeve is measured by the fact that the signal for their meetings is the splash of a ' hop-frog ' in a pool, or a moth that flies into the flame of a candle. The Reddleman uses the secrecy and the weapons of the heath in his private war with Wildeve, and when he gambles him for the hundred pounds on Egdon at dead of night, it is by the light of a circle of glow-worms that they throw the dice, while the wild-eyed heath ponies steal up shadow-like to watch the game. A sprig of ivy helps Gabriel Oak to detect Troy in a falsehood, and in *A Pair of Blue Eyes* Knight uses the constellations as finger-posts to point out to Elfride the whereabouts of Smith and of different quarters of the globe. When Grace breaks away from Fitzpiers' arms on Midsummer Eve, the moon whitens her hot blush—reminding us by contrast of how when Eustacia laughed the sun shone into her mouth as into a tulip, lending it a similar scarlet fire.

In conclusion I may refer to a few casual unclassified instances of the strange. It is perhaps only a personal impression that renders an empty house peculiarly romantic and full of fairy possibilities ; certainly the introduction of the deserted mansion into the vicissitudes of Tess and Clare seems to me a very delightful and unworldly episode. Into their sphere of concentrating sorrow a tiny paradise falls from heaven and shuts them in safe for a brief spell of exquisite joy. Concerning the adequateness of the joy I say nothing here ; the magic of its coming and its nature seems unquestionable. The strange impressiveness of the christening of Sorrow the Undesired earlier in the same book is so great as to be saved from sensationalism only by the art, the humour, and the genuine feeling with which it is presented. Not altogether dissimilar in effect is the grim picture of midcentury superstition in *The Return of the Native*, where Susan Nonsuch, by means of a wax image pierced with innumerable pins, a hot fire, and the Lord's Prayer repeated backwards, seeks to work evil to Eustacia. In the same book, while Yeobright is proceeding to the talk with Johnny Nonsuch that was to produce such terrible results, he branches off into the track that leads to the spot where the child lives : " On inclining into the latter path Yeobright felt a creeping chilliness, familiar enough to most people, and probably caused by the unsunned morning air. In after days he thought of it as a thing of singular significance." The coincidence of Stephen Smith and the tomb of Elfride's first lover has already been referred to, but the case assumes an aspect almost startling when Knight stumbles on the grave and its already complicated history, though the humour of the thing is allowed to predominate over its weirdness. And the terror— almost amounting to horror—of the man-trap episode in *The*

Woodlanders derives an additional extrinsic power from the fact that we know how relentlessly cruel Hardy can be on occasion ; with any other novelist we should feel safe—no other novelist would dare to run the thing to its ghastly logical extremity, but Hardy knows no such qualms, and it is only because he is engaged in the charming idyllic *Woodlanders* that he is merciful for once. But up till the very moment when Grace is discovered unhurt save for a torn skirt one's flesh creeps.

Of all Hardy's suggestions of the natural-supernatural the most touching and beautiful is that describing Jude's first vision of Christminster, as a boy of eleven. Having climbed the ladder that he has been told may give him a view of what he thinks of as ' the heavenly Jerusalem ', he finds the distance shrouded in mist :

Perhaps if he prayed, the wish to see Christminster might be forwarded. . . . Turning on the ladder Jude knelt on the third rung, where, resting against those above it, he prayed that the mist might rise.

He then seated himself again, and waited. In the course of ten or fifteen minutes the thinning mist dissolved altogether from the northern horizon, as it had already done elsewhere, and about a quarter of an hour before the time of sunset the westward clouds parted, the sun's position being partially uncovered, and the beams streaming out in visible lines between two bars of slaty cloud. The boy immediately looked back in the old direction.

Some way within the limits of the stretch of landscape, points of light like the topaz gleamed. The air increased in transparency with the lapse of minutes, till the topaz points showed themselves to be the vanes, windows, wet roof slates, and other shining spots upon the spires, domes, freestone-work, and varied outlines that were faintly revealed. It was Christminster, unquestionably ; either directly seen, or miraged in the peculiar atmosphere.

The spectator gazed on and on till the windows and vanes lost their shine, going out almost suddenly like extinguished candles. The vague city became veiled in mist.

It would seem equally undesirable and unnecessary to prolong this chapter by the further accumulation of instances. Those already presented will surely bear out the claim made for Hardy as a master of mystery in a distinctly new and fascinating way. I find nothing else in the dynasty of the novel to parallel this feature. Suggestions of the sort here and there in other writers have quite different *raisons d'être*. When, for instance, the narrator of a famous story, rummaging in a garret, comes across a letter of scarlet cloth which, being accidentally held in front of him, appears to burn his breast, it is at once evident that Hawthorne is writing in a vein of high romance, as indeed the title-page confesses. Or again, that inward radiance which at mass-time shines from Véronique in Balzac's *Curé de Village*, effacing the marks of the smallpox, " brillant comme brille mystérieusement une fleur sous l'eau de la mer que le soleil pénètre ", is the merest commonplace among the miracles of the religion of mysticism and exaltation. But Hardy is neither romancer nor mystic, and it is eminently satisfactory and exhilarating to find in so acknowledged a master of the realities of life a belief so clear, so practical, in the immanence of the supernatural. The dismal materialism, the inculcation of which appears to be the aim and the necessary end of the mercenariness of modern life, finds no place in, and is utterly denied, attacked, and routed by, the proceedings of Hardy's world—a world which is full of shadows from another world less gross and limited, and of dim but undeniable indications of the endless miracle of existence ; a world, as I have said, pervaded by the profound faith that there are indeed more things in heaven and earth than are dreamt of in your philosophy. I think it is Mr. J. B. S. Haldane who has suggested that the world is not only a queer place, but queerer than we shall ever know. A delightful thought, of the truth of which experience makes one ever more convinced : and one is grateful to Hardy for bringing in the powerful support of his art to reinforce the natural magic of life.

CHAPTER IV

NATURE AND THE LOWER ANIMALS

WORDSWORTH, long acclaimed as the poet of nature, came to be recognised as equally the poet of man. Hardy, whose strength lies in the understanding and portrayal of humanity, can almost match this with his skill in the painting of nature. If word-pictures could be hung on walls, a great gallery could be filled with Hardy's nature pieces—large deliberate oil-paintings, delicate water-colours and etchings, whole portfolios of sketches and studies. There are circles in which this side of his art is still the only one accepted with unqualified approval. Certainly it is a source of satisfaction that the Hardian tragedy, like the human one, is set amid the all-consoling beauty of the most beautiful of possible worlds. To this age—with its one unconditionally admirable feature, a passion for getting afield—there should be something sympathetic in this nature-loving side of Hardy. Matthew Arnold said of Wordsworth that to read one of his longer poems was like a day spent in the country, and the assertion would apply closely to many of the Wessex novels. All the green life beneath the friendly sky of South England lives in their pages.

How exhilarating is it to scamper over the down with Elfride, ascare at her temerity in playing *La Belle Dame Sans Merci* ; to meet John Smith—brown as autumn, stalwart and healthy, Hercules-bearded, open at chest and arm ; or to lie with Knight and Elfride on the breeze-swept brow of the cliff without a name. The open-air principle, more intense and in much greater continuity, is present in the Chaucerian freshness of Tess Durbeyfield's life at the dairy-farm, the focus of the healthful influences of the vales of South Wessex. In the absorbing human interest of the story one is liable to turn its pages without immediate consciousness of the sky-roofed, unconfined, windy expansiveness of its stage. Robert Louis Stevenson has put upon record the fair and imperishable truth that " to live out of doors with the woman a man loves is of all lives the most complete and free " ; and no one may straitly say how much of beauty the love of Tess and Angel Clare gains from its environment of green pastures.

Such books as *The Woodlanders*, *Under the Greenwood Tree*, and *Far from the Madding Crowd*, bear the sign manual of Nature-loving Hardy in their titles, and the generous manner in which these novels fulfil the promise thus held out needs no demonstration. *The Return of the Native* demands separate treatment. It is the novel into which Nature enters more than into any other (save perhaps *The Woodlanders*). It is indeed the story of Egdon Heath. Egdon is not only the scene of the tale ; it dominates the plot and determines the characters. It is sentient : it feels, it speaks, it slays. The book opens with an impressive introduction to this, the protagonist of the drama. Egdon presents a face upon which time makes but little impression. Its sombre nature intensifies the sad hours of day and night, and is enigmatic, needing explanation. Exhaling darkness, it lies Titanic, in broodful anticipation of the crack of doom, and its haggard asceticism is friend only to the stormy visitations of the elements : it feels only as a light caress the tempest that wrenches its trees like bones in their sockets. It is changeless as the heavens or the sea, and moulded only by vast geologic fingers. The power of its infinite vegetable existence is hidden under the mask of an apparent death-like torpor. It barely heeds the changes of the seasons—only in mid-summer does it flame in crimson and scarlet ; and no absolute hour of the day is reckoned by the dwellers on its monotonous surface ; nor is it responsive to the pale beams of the watery moon.

Without doubt it lives ; Egdon has a colossal human existence. It is untamable, Ishmaelitish. At nightfall it wakes to a watchful intentness. It is vocal with a tone as weird as the sea's own : a worn whisper, dry and papery, the ruins of song ; a voice that varies with intelligent differentiation according to the character of the various parts of the heath—acoustic pictures are returned from the darkened scenery. It stubbornly asserts its privileges against cultivation, and drives back the despairing tillage from its barbaric soil. What response of awakening it gives to the on-coming of Spring is feline in its stealthiness. To its best-loved child it renders chilly premonition at the approach of evil ; and, the evil having fallen upon his soul, his anguish is met by " the imperturbable countenance of the heath, which, having defied the cataclysmal onsets of centuries, reduced to insignificance by its seamed and antique features the wildest turmoil of a single man ".

Clym Yeobright, the hero, is indeed the product of Egdon, and its shaggy hills are friendly and genial to him, exhilarating, streng-thening, soothing. In his prosperity its oppressive horizontality gives him a sense of bare equality with, and no superiority to, any living creature under the sun ; in his misfortune it swallows him up—absorbs him into its furze and its infinite winged and creeping things ; he becomes an indistinguishable part of Egdon. Eustacia, Queen of Night, would have seemed in some ways not unfit to reign as Proserpine or Hela to this abode of darkness, but the smouldering fire of her darkly-beautiful soul is intensified by a great—greater because impotent—hatred of this austere monster that holds her relentlessly back from the indulgence of her fierce passions. If Clym is the child of Egdon, the Reddleman is its spirit, and with him it is hand-in-glove—witness his constant use of it in his war with Wildeve. For pretty Tamsie alone has Egdon no ' ghost ' : to her it is impersonal open ground ; her fears of it are rational, her dislike of its worst moods reasonable.

Of its influence on the plot itself much has been implied in the foregoing remarks ; one other act of direct intervention may be pointed out : having suggested, early in the book, by reason of its intense blackness beside the incomplete darkness of the night atmosphere, the comparison of a mortal sin beside a venial one, it afterwards proves not unworthy of the simile, for, just as the tempest in *Lear* aided the ruin wrought by the ingratitude of the King's daughters, so Egdon here (perhaps the very same heath, as Hardy suggests) first wearies out the heart-torn wandering woman, and then kills her with a venomous creature from its own bosom. To Clym, its chosen son, it is kinder, and the story ends fittingly with a picture of him delivering the first of a series of moral Sermons on the Mount—on Rainbarrow, the culminating point of Egdon.

9

One might find much interest in the question of how great was the influence of Egdon on the shaping and colouring of Hardy's genius. For he was born on the edge of the heath, and " it was his playground when his genius was germinating ". The paragraph which says of Clym Yeobright that " he was permeated with its scenes, with its substance, and with its odours. He might be said to be its product. . . . His estimate of life had been coloured by it "—this is obviously autobiographical. Certainly the place, " perfectly accordant with man's nature—neither ghastly, hateful nor ugly ; neither commonplace, unmeaning nor tame ; but, like man, slighted and enduring ", is eminently symbolical of Hardy's philosophy.

Egdon is, after all, only the premier and most extended instance of Hardy's habitual and involuntary personification of nature. The practice and the feeling that compels it are of course not confined to Hardy. Your true nature lover can no more help seeing happiness on the face of a garden of flowers, hearing a shout of glory from the rising sun, perceiving a high contemplative dignity in the rooted masses of the hills, than he can or would disregard the Wordsworthian emotions that rise in his own heart in the presence of these things. Hardy nowhere expresses the extreme inference " that every flower enjoys the air it breathes ". For the definite formulation and acceptance of that faith perhaps the more transcendent vision of the poet is required (and we shall not find it in Hardy's poetry). From the very first, however, the implied, if not expressed, attribution of sentient qualities to nature, the perception in her of all possible moods and movements of the human consciousness, is discernible in Hardy. Even *Desperate Remedies* is capable of so fine a touch as this : " The water gurgled down from the old mill pond to a lower level, under the cloak of rank broad leaves—the sensuous natures of the vegetable world ". In the maturer novels one may open almost at random and find examples of this sympathetic interpretation. Thus of nature's encroachments upon the urban life of Casterbridge, in *The Mayor :* " In autumn innumerable tawny and yellow leaves skimmed along the pavements and stole through people's doorways into their passages, with a hesitating scratch on the floor, like the skirts of timid visitors ". The thought is worked out more extendedly in Kipling's story,

Letting in the Jungle, and very charmingly somewhere in *The Autocrat of the Breakfast Table*, but the tenderness of appreciation and sympathy that makes such conceptions possible is habitual with Hardy. He is constantly on the watch to find a human meaning in every part of the face of nature.

Pity for falling trees receives a new edge when, after describing the removal of the lower bark, Hardy says,

> If a fine product of vegetable nature could ever be said to look ridiculous, it was the case now, when the oak stood naked-legged, and as if ashamed, till the axe man came and cut a ring round it, and the two Timothys finished the work with a cross-cut saw.

A like sympathy prompts the following passage :

> The trees of the fields and plantations writhed like miserable men as the air wound its way swiftly among them : the lowest portions of their trunks, that had hardly ever been known to move, were visibly rocked by the fiercer gusts, distressing the mind by its painful unwontedness, as when a strong man is seen to shed tears.

But it is towards the animate section of lower nature that this tenderness is specially exhibited. A deep and real love for the brute-creation, a love worthy of comparison with that which man is capable of extending towards his own species, is rare ; probably even more rare than genuine philanthropy. It is in this high and exclusive sense that Hardy is a lover of animals.

I first realised this fact while reading *A Pair of Blue Eyes*. I came to the phrase, " a toad humbly labouring along ", and the word ' humbly ' opened my eyes to a new and delightful aspect of Hardy. No one but an animal lover in the most extreme sense of the term could have lighted on that word. An ordinary writer might have said heavily, clumsily, lumberingly, painfully ; any of which would have been more or less true. ' Humbly ' is an inspiration, and an inspiration of love. There are people who affect to be frightened of toads, even to hate them : but terror and hatred must vanish at that vision of the lowly creature's mind, filled with the humility of a sole desire—to pass unobservedly along into the peace and seclusion of its grassy corner. We rave (rightly enough) over the modesty of a violet, but what is that to the meek imploring self-effacement of the toad ? Be its beauty what it may, this despised and rejected reptile wears in its head a precious jewel that should inspire something other than fear and disgust.

Having become aware, through this expression (repeated, by the way, in *Far from the Madding Crowd*), of Hardy's love for animals, my delight received constant accretion as I proceeded. This man simply cannot mention an animal without showing his intense personal sympathy with and consequent understanding of its life and feelings. Frost comes suddenly down on Norcombe Hill, and his first thought is that " many a small bird went supperless to bed that night ". There is the ' young dog ' of Gabriel Oak's : he has no name in particular, but answers with perfect readiness to any pleasant interjection ; he is the ' son ' of old George (himself a dog of much character) ; he is learning the sheep-keeping business ; he is earnest but wrong-headed ; he is under the impression that since he is kept for running after sheep, the more he runs after them the better ; the results of his energy are disastrous, and the record ends with the following exquisite epitaph :

George's son had done his work so thoroughly that he was considered too good a workman to live, and was, in fact, taken and tragically shot at twelve o'clock that same day—another instance of the untoward fate which so often attends dogs and other philosophers who follow out a train of reasoning to its logical conclusion, and attempt perfectly consistent conduct in a world made up so largely of compromise.

The story is told with a most charming appreciation of doggy motives. And likewise (apart from the tragic aspect) with a very delightful and tender humour. You cannot laugh at a man's faults (laugh joyously, I mean, with friendly hands on shoulders) unless you love him passing well : the three most lovable men who ever wrote English, Chaucer and Shakespeare and Charles Lamb, laugh for ever at all mankind. And this same smile is often on Hardy's mouth when he speaks of his world of pets. Animals are the everlasting children of the world, and since children are (except for Wordsworth) infinitely comic, animals are exquisitely and always so. Hardy's keen eye invariably takes on a twinkle when it falls on one of God's own innocent creatures, as on those " sow pigs surprisingly large, with young ones surprisingly small ", in *The Trumpet-Major*.

Witness, again, Bathsheba's cat gazing from the lid of her travelling basket with half-closed eyes, and affectionately surveying the small birds round. The bull who chases Lucetta and Elizabeth-Jane in the *Mayor* is treated in like human and humorous manner : Hardy surmises that he " perhaps rather intended a practical joke than a murder ". When he speaks of " a bird singing a trite old evening song that might doubtless have been heard on the hill at the same hour . . . at any sunset of that season for centuries untold ", he is only expressing once more Keats's thought concerning the immortal nightingale, yet that word ' trite ' seems to me to pluck out the human heart of the mystery with a peculiarly happy touch. Just so the universally recognised ' perkiness ' of the sparrow receives its final interpretation when, as Henchard crosses the road in the steely light of dawn, the sparrows in his way scarcely fly up from the road-litter, " so little did they believe in human aggression at so early a time ". There is a thrush in *The Woodlanders* " who was repeating himself a good deal on a branch opposite Giles's hut " ; that sounds to me much more like what a thrush does than ' singing each song twice over '. I like that bee which got into Swithin's observatory on a sunny afternoon, and went singing round " inquiringly ". But for insects, we must go to Egdon, and work with Clym among the furze.

His familiars were creeping and winged things, and they seemed to enroll him in their band. Bees hummed around his ears with an intimate air, and tugged at the heath and furze-flowers at his side in such numbers as to weigh them down to the sod. The strange amber-coloured butterflies which Egdon produced, and which were never seen elsewhere, quivered in the breath of his lips, alighted upon his bowed back, and sported with the glittering point of his hook as he flourished it up and down. Tribes of emerald-green grasshoppers leaped over his feet, falling awkwardly on their backs, heads, or hips, like unskilful acrobats, as chance might rule ; or engaged themselves in noisy flirtations under the fern-fronds with silent ones of homely hue. Huge flies, ignorant of larders and wire-netting, and quite in a savage state, buzzed about him without knowing that he was a man.

The whole episode of the death of Prince the horse in *Tess* is comparable in charm and kindly humour with the dog incident quoted above. After his terrible wound he utters one groan, and then " stands firm and motionless as long as he can ; till he suddenly sinks down in a heap ". He is hoisted into the waggon he has formerly hauled and " with his hoofs in the air and his shoes shining in the setting sunlight he retraced the dozen miles to Marlott ". If anything could give a grace of poetry to a dead horse it is that touch of the shining shoes. John Durbeyfield rises splendidly to the occasion :

> " No," he said stoically, " I won't sell his old body. When we D'Urbervilles was knights in the land we didn't sell our chargers for cat's-meat. Let 'em keep their shillings ! He've served me well in his life-time, and I won't part with him now."

So Prince receives formal burial, and little Abraham sobbingly inquires, " Is he gone to heaven ? "

There are some other good horses, always treated with a respectful humour. Smart and Smiler in *Under the Greenwood Tree* are very nearly human. When Dick replied ' yes ' in a clinching manner, Smiler, thinking this the close of the conversation, prepared to move on ; and Smart, on another occasion, is said to have been lost in thought for some time, never dreaming that Dick could reach as far as his ear with the whip. When Mrs. Loveday and Anne and a maidservant drive together to see the manœuvres, the horse is fully conscious of being the master-mind and chief personage of the four : he goes at his own pace, and turns aside to drink whenever water comes in sight. When Anne, in the same book, unhooks Festus's horse and tries to frighten him away by flapping her muslin neckerchief in his eyes, the gallant steed does not move or flinch, and seems rather pleased than otherwise.

Hardy never insults his animals by treating them as neuters. The masculine pronoun and personality are particularly effective in the incident of the escaped porker in *Jude the Obscure*, where Hardy is as usual altogether on the side of the angels. Jude's own attitude is shown in the affairs of the rooks, the worms, the pig-killing, and the snared rabbit, which need no recalling, but which may be contrasted not only with the part taken by

Arabella in these episodes, but with the glimpse given of the opposite instinct in Sergeant Troy—one of the meanest of all Hardy's figures—" aiming light cuts at the horse's ear with the end of the whip as a recreation ". Indeed, Hardy often provides these little touchstones—indications as to their feeling for animals —for ascertaining the inmost quality of his characters. Oak's compassion for his sheep is shown on many occasions : notably when Bathsheba's sheep were blasted with wind, and after the massacre brought about by young George.

> Oak was an intensely humane man : indeed, his humanity
> often tore in pieces any politic intentions of his which bordered
> on strategy, and carried him on as by gravitation. A shadow
> in his life had always been that his flock ended in mutton—
> that a day came and found every shepherd an arrant traitor to
> his defenceless sheep. His first feeling now was one of pity
> for the untimely fate of these gentle ewes and their unborn lambs.

Both Jude and Sue are unable to rest until the trapped rabbit has been put out of its pain. (Giles Winterborne's habit, already mentioned, of setting gins for rabbits I simply do not understand —it must be a slip in the drawing !) We are not surprised to read that Paula Power evinced no quick sensitiveness in this direction : " Paula glanced down at the fire, and at the gnarled beech fuel, and at the woodlice which ran out from beneath the bark to the extremity of the logs as the heat approached them ". And it seems that Swithin St. Cleeve and Lady Constantine were not really nice people, for when they were staying in the hut, and found they had nothing to eat, Swithin offered to go out and. catch some of " those little rabbits, that the keepers call runners ". Fortunately he found this unpleasant project impracticable, but he returned with " four sparrows and a thrush ", explaining that he got them by knowing where they roosted. Humanitarianism apart, one cannot help wondering what sort of meal they made of four sparrows and a thrush !

A final and capital instance of the thoroughness and catholicity of Hardy's animal-sympathies is worth referring to from *The Return of the Native*. When Mrs. Yeobright is crossing the heath on the outward and happier half of her last fateful journey, we are told that—

All the shallower ponds had decreased to a vaporous mud, amid which the maggoty shapes of innumerable obscene creatures could be distinctly seen, heaving and wallowing with enjoyment. Being a woman not disinclined to philosophise she sometimes sat down under her umbrella to rest and watch their happiness, for a certain hopefulness as to the result of her visit gave ease to her mind.

See to what depths the love of this man pierces. Just as he found poetry in the soul of an elementary school-teacher, so he finds happiness and joy in watching the shapes and ways of creatures avowedly maggoty and obscene. One is reminded of how the sight of slimy things that crawled with legs upon the slimy sea awoke in the Ancient Mariner an unparalleled horror ; it was only the living things whose beauty no tongue might declare that drew from him an involuntary blessing. Even sweet and noble Shelley, whose gospel was universal Love, and whose practical benevolence extended to the ' restoration of fresh-caught fish to their native Thames ', allows an unfortunate restriction to creep into his invocation to the beloved brotherhood of earth, ocean, air, in *Alastor :*

> If no *bright* bird, insect, or *gentle* beast
> I consciously have injured, but still loved
> And cherished these my kindred.

But Hardy knows no such invidious distinctions as these. His attitude towards animals is like that of Joseph Paice towards women, of whom Elia records that " he reverenced and upheld, in every form in which it came before him, *womanhood* ". Just so the mere possession of brute-hood is an immediate and unimpeachable passport to Hardy's sympathy—to a sympathy warm, lively, full of complete and humorous understanding.

Returning to still life, we observe a form of nature that appears frequently and importantly in these novels, and evidently has peculiar interest for the novelist—namely, the tree. Of all species of inanimate existence, trees seem to be most akin to humanity. Their bulk, shape, attitude and general arrangement are easily consistent with our conceptions of sentient qualities. If in contemplative appearance they are inferior to the hills, they come nearer to man in their amenability to birth, to growth, and to death, and to many other of the ills that flesh is heir to. Above all, they have a voice, a multitudinous, infinitely variable, intelligible voice. In the eyes of poetry—and no unpoetic view of nature can be of permanent beauty or truth—the trees are veritably articulate with a large and special meaning ; are, as it were, the interpreters between nature and man. Hardy is fond of tree-voices. He has often listened to them—communed with them ; and there are many vocal forest-dwellers in his books. The fir plantation at the base of Lady Constantine's Tower will be remembered, with its sobbing and its steady stertorous breathing even in an apparently complete calm—" Nothing but an absolute vacuum could paralyse their utterance ". This thought of the tireless talking of the trees is put with powerful suggestiveness in a passage that has already been quoted from *The Woodlanders*. When in the mild stillness of an autumn fog, in *Far from the Madding Crowd*, there is a temporary silence, the trees stand " in an attitude of intentness, as if they waited longingly for a wind to come and rock them ". The tall elm whose sudden disappearance killed old John South has received some notice. Then there is the grim and ominous clump of firs beneath which Mrs. Yeobright sits down on her fatal journey across Egdon— splintered, lopped, distorted by fierce winds, blasted and blackened by lightning ; hight Devil's Bellows, and meriting the name in March and November ; at present making perpetual moan in the still afternoon air. And very picturesque is the account of the trees on Norcombe Hill, where—

> the instinctive act of human-kind was to stand and listen, and learn how the trees on the right and the trees on the left wailed and chaunted to each other in the regular antiphonies of a cathedral choir ; how hedges and other shapes to leeward then caught the note, lowering it to the tenderest sob ; and how the hurrying gust then plunged into the south, to be heard no more.

Hardy's ear for the sounds of nature is both sensitive and highly-trained. There is a passage in *The Return of the Native* which would seem to show him possessed of a sense of hearing as preter-human as an animal's sense of smell. It is the voice of Egdon that is being described :

The wind rose somewhat as the night advanced, and laid hold of the attention. . . . Gusts in innumerable series followed each other from the north-west, and when each one of them raced past, the sound of its progress resolved into three. Treble, tenor, and bass notes were to be found therein. The general ricochet of the whole over pits and prominences had the gravest pitch of the chime. Next there could be heard the baritone buzz of a holly tree. Below these in force, above them in pitch, a dwindled voice strove hard at a husky tune, which was the peculiar local sound alluded to. Thinner and less immediately traceable than the other two, it was far more impressive than either. In it lay what may be called the linguistic peculiarity of the heath ; and being audible nowhere on earth off a heath, it afforded a shadow of reason for the woman's tenseness, which continued as unbroken as ever.

Throughout the blowing of these plaintive November winds that note bore a great resemblance to the ruins of human song which remain in the throat of four-score and ten. It was a worn whisper, dry and papery, and it brushed so distinctly across the ear that, by the accustomed, the material minutiæ in which it originated could be realised as by touch. It was the united product of infinitesimal vegetable causes, and these were neither stems, leaves, fruit, blades, prickles, lichen, nor moss.

They were the mummied heath-bells of the past summer, originally tender and purple, now washed colourless by Michaelmas rains, and dried to dead skins by October suns. So low was an individual sound from these that a combination of hundreds only just emerged from silence, and the myriads of the whole declivity reached the ear but as a shrivelled and intermittent recitative. . . . Each of the tiny trumpets was seized on, entered, scoured and emerged from by the wind as thoroughly as if it were as vast as a crater.

So far we have seen Nature not so much described as allegorised or interpreted. The method of Thomson, however, is employed by Hardy with no less facility than that of Wordsworth. His landscapes have a " bare sheer penetrating power ", that results from a hand of unerring skill working in exact harmony with an incredibly observant eye. A few specimens may be quoted or referred to.

Oak raised his head and listlessly surveyed the scene. By the outer margin of the pit was an oval pond, and over it hung the

attenuated skeleton of a chrome-yellow moon, which had only
a few days to last—the morning star dogging her on the right
hand. The pool glittered like a dead man's eye, and as the
world awoke a breeze blew, shaking and elongating the reflection of the moon without breaking it, and turning the image
of the star to a phosphoric streak upon the water.

The strokes are few, but the picture is vivid, and essentially
descriptive, though touched and tinged by the almost inevitable
human emotion. Later in the same book there is a sweet
morning-piece wherein the dawn can be seen breaking with all
its scents and sounds, as clearly as in the opening bars of.
Mendelssohn's Overture to the *Midsummer Night's Dream*.
Bathsheba has passed the night in the woods :

> Whether she slept or not that night Bathsheba was not clearly
> aware. But it was with a freshened existence and a cooler
> brain that, a long time afterwards, she became conscious of
> some interesting proceedings which were going on in the trees
> above her head and around.
> A coarse throated chatter was the first sound.
> It was a sparrow just waking.
> Next : " Chee-weeze-weeze ! " from another retreat.
> It was a finch.
> Third : " Tink-tink-tink-tink-a-chink ! " from the hedge.
> It was a robin.
> " Chuck-chuck-chuck ! " overhead.
> A squirrel.
> Then, from the road, " With my ra-ta-ta, and my rum-
> tum-tum ! "
> It was a ploughboy.

There follows a team of horses, stopping to drink and flounce
in the silver water—the cool green of the dawn—the leaves that
have fluttered down upon her—the morning mist full of light
from the rising sun.

Henchard got such another morning picture as he emerged
from the fair-tent where he had slept :

> The freshness of the September morning inspired and braced
> him as he stood. . . . The whole scene lay under the rays of
> a newly risen sun, which had not as yet dried a single blade
> of the heavily dewed grass, whereon the shadows of the yellow

and red vans were projected far away, those thrown by the felloe of each wheel being elongated in shape to the orbit of a comet.

There is a powerful picture of evening in the rank-run garden of Talbothays dairy which catches the 'creepy-crawly' atmosphere as by magic. It finishes with a bit of 'truth of sky' that would have delighted Ruskin : " The light which still shone was derived entirely from a large hole in the western bank of cloud ; it was like a piece of day left behind by accident, dusk having closed in elsewhere ". There are some lovely valley views :

> Melbury mounted on the other side, and they drove on out of the grove, their wheels silently crushing delicately-patterned mosses, hyacinths, primroses, lords-and-ladies, and other strange and common plants [Hardy never forgets what is going on down below, beneath the feet and wheels of the humans], and cracking up little sticks that lay across the track. Their way homeward lay along the flank of Dogbury Hill, whence below them they beheld a wide valley. . . . It was the cider country, which met the woodland district on the sides of this hill. Over the vale the air was blue as sapphire—such a blue as outside that apple-valley was never seen. Under the blue the orchards were in a blaze of pink bloom, some of the richly-flowered trees running almost up to where they drove along.

The descriptions of Tess's two valleys, Blackmoor Vale and the Vale of the Var—where the waters were clear as the pure River of Life shown to the Evangelist, rapid as the shadow of a cloud, with pebbly shallows that prattled to the sky—are gloriously good, but too long to quote. A point worth noting is that Hardy's landscape, like Turner's, rests on geology :

> Soon he rose out of the valley, and skirted a high plateau of the chalk formation on his right, which rested abruptly upon the fruity district of deep loam, the character and herbage of the two formations being so distinct that the calcareous upland appeared but as a deposit of a few years' antiquity upon the level vale.

The Woodlanders sometimes breathes the very breath of the *Ode to Autumn* :

> Winterborne looked and smelt like Autumn's very brother, his face being sunburnt to wheat-colour, his eyes blue as corn-

flowers, his sleeves and leggings dyed with fruit-stains, his hands clammy with the sweet juice of apples, his hat sprinkled with pips, and everywhere about him that atmosphere of cider which at its first return each season has such an indescribable fascination for those who have been born and bred among the orchards.

But indeed *The Woodlanders*, as is fitting, is rich with natural description. It is built into the progress of the year, and is a complete ' Shepheardes Calendar '. The advance of the year is marked only less carefully in *The Madding Crowd* and *Tess*. The landscape background of the novels, and the working life, so faithfully painted in, of men and animals in the country, are of unique richness and importance, and constitute perhaps one-half of the permanent value of Hardy's work.

But Hardy's nature description seldom has the impersonalness of the camera. In a majority of cases the natural scenery shown to us at any point in a story will be found to have an emotional connection with the events happening at that moment. Some of the passages already quoted bear out this statement—the moaning firs on Egdon, and the dead pool that stared up at Oak after the death of his sheep. The daybreak from *The Madding Crowd* is more indirect in its human association. The tone of the picture is emphatically one of joy, but Bathsheba is intensely unhappy at the moment : however, the note may easily be one of hope, for the rather distant future. As a matter of fact Hardy's landscape is much more ready to show sympathy with people in distress than with the happy ones. Even the cheerful morning picture quoted is quickly followed by one of an astonishingly dismal swamp which suitably lowers the tone—almost to tragedy, but the innocent (and light-foot) Liddy trips across unharmed. The underlying principle of this emotional sympathy, and of the particular form it generally takes in Hardy, is suggested by the comment made on certain river noises—" sounds which a sad man would called moans and a happy man laughter ".

When Poorgrass is taking Fanny Robin's body in the waggon to the burial-ground, thick fog comes on, and the trees, after standing awhile " in an attitude of intentness ", begin to drop water hollowly upon Fanny's coffin—like Byron's trees before Quatre Bras, ' grieving, if aught inanimate e'er grieves '. Perhaps we see nature changing her mood in *Far from the Madding Crowd* (which is full of this nature-sympathy) : when Boldwood first emerges into the air after receiving the disturbing valentine he is nervous, excitable, vacant, and he finds the sunrise in keeping— the sun flameless and cold, light and shade preternaturally inverted, while " over the west hung the wasting moon, now dull and greenish-yellow, like tarnished brass ". But later he goes to seek Bathsheba, full of determination ; and now all nature is full of the joy and lushness of spring, with the notes of three cuckoos resounding through the air.

In *A Pair of Blue Eyes*, when Elfride, sick with apprehension, is creeping down the valley to implore mercy from Mrs. Jethway, there is fog again, and she hears an occasional shriek of a terror-stricken bird. At the last word of the miserable catechism by which Knight convinces himself that he cannot marry Elfride,— " the very land and sky seemed to suffer. . . . The scene was engraved for years on the retina of Knight's eye : the dead and brown stubble, the weeds among it, the distant belt of beeches shutting out the view of the house, the leaves of which were now red and sick to death."

It was again, perhaps, a proleptic sympathy that produced the sinister garden through which Tess made her way to Clare, drawn by the sound of his harp :

> The garden . . . was damp and rank with tall blooming weeds emitting offensive smells. She went stealthily as a cat through this profusion of growth, gathering cuckoo-spittle on her skirts, cracking snails that were underfoot, staining her hands with thistle-milk and slug-slime, and rubbing off upon her naked arms sticky blights which, though snow-white on the apple-tree trunks, made blood-red stains on her skin.

And when Grace is waiting at the hut, in great anxiety for Giles, who cannot come to her because he is dying, she looks out at the trees, ravaged by the wet autumn :

> Above stretched an old beech, with vast arm-pits, and great pocket-holes in its sides where branches had been removed in past times ; a black slug was trying to climb it. Dead boughs were scattered about like ichthyosauri in a museum, and beyond them were perishing woodbine stems resembling old ropes. . . . Next were more trees close together, wrestling for existence,

their branches disfigured with wounds resulting from their mutual rubbings and blows. . . . Beneath them were the rotting stumps of those of the group that had been vanquished long ago, rising from their mossy setting like black teeth from green gums.

There are other details, not all ugly, noted by Grace, and one compares her with the girl in Rossetti's poem, who, in a doubtless deeper condition of grief, observed but one thing in all the wood —that " the wood spurge has a cup of three ".

Whatever may be Hardy's opinions of life in general and human society in particular, there is no question about his feeling towards Nature. He knows that, however, the tyranny of existence may irk, there is always a sure retreat to a priceless treasure that worm nor rust may corrupt, and to which no thief can break through and steal—a Paradise so vast that even the grimy and plastered fingers of man can but soil it here and there.

Chapter V

HUMOUR

HARDY was not a humorist in any profound sense. He was quick to see the humour of things, and had an ear for a good story —his diaries are full of them, generally with a touch of the macabre. But his mind was not humorously built : humour did not enter into the substance or method of his thought. His genius was purely Teutonic, like that of Thackeray, George Eliot, Galsworthy ; he lacked that Celtic infusion that makes a different thing of the genius of Chaucer, Shakespeare, Lamb, Dickens, ' Erewhon ' Butler, Sir James Barrie, Mr. Bernard Shaw, Lord Dunsany, and G. K. Chesterton. Personally I have never been able to decide whether the extra lens thus added gives clarity or causes distortion : but it certainly turns the intellectual instrument into one of peculiarly English brand, even though it may sometimes be found in the hands of ' foreigners '.

Almost all the humour in the Wessex novels that is worth preserving is rustic humour—caught up with joy from the lips of the villagers themselves, redundances removed, the form perfected, but otherwise the pure unadulterated essence of the South English peasantry of the third quarter of the nineteenth century. Hardy makes Angel Clare discover, with a surprise he himself can never have known, the variety, interest and delight that lay behind " the pitiable dummy known as Hodge ".

The ground-work was laid down in *Under the Greenwood Tree*. There we find Grandfather William Dewy, with his face like the sunny side of a ripe ribstone-pippin ; Grandfather James, with little ditches of stone-dust all over his clothes ; Geoffrey Day, the keeper, with a wife whose ' doom ', said Geoffrey, " was to be nobody's wife at all in the wide universe. But she made

up her mind that she would, and did it twice over. Doom ?
Doom is nothing beside an elderly woman " ; we have Mrs. Day
herself, who insisted on doing her spring-cleaning on Fancy's
wedding-morning ; and Thomas Leaf of the ghastly looks, who
never had no head, but who knew a moment of passing glory
when he was allowed to tell his tale of how ten pounds became
a thousand : " Hear, hear ! " said the tranter. " Better than the
history of England, my sonnies." " Thank you for your story,
Thomas Leaf ", said Grandfather William ; and then Leaf sank
into nothingness again.

It is here that Hardy begins the use of those amusing locutions
implying motive or meaning of tones, with the effect of giving
a close-up of rustic character at certain moments :

> " Ay," said Mail, in the tone of a man who did not agree with
> everybody as a rule, though he did now.
> " Know it ! ah, I should think I did know it ! " Mr. Spinks
> was heard to observe at this moment, without reference to his
> fellow-creatures—shaking his head at some idea he seemed to
> see floating before him, and smiling as if he were attending a
> funeral at the time. " Ah, do I or don't I know it ! "
> No one said " Know what ? " because all were aware from
> experience that what he knew would declare itself in process
> of time.

All persons present put on a speaking countenance of admiration for the cleverness alluded to. . . .

But the quality of the rustic humour grew richer, if not finer,
as the novels went on. Quite perennially funny is the scene at
Stephen's homecoming in *A Pair of Blue Eyes*. John Smith's
account of his gradual and cautious recognition of his son ; the
steady vivisection of Stephen's changed appearance ; the tales
of idiosyncratic pigs—deaf, and melancholy, and insane, and
rheumatic ; the family joke that had been made at every pig-
killing for three generations, and had not yet lost its incomparable
flavour ; and the puzzle snuff-box whose secret was that it
wouldn't open at all ; the whole proceedings carried on with
epic seriousness by the hempen homespuns who are the actors :
it is all admirable, inimitable. Similarly rich is the example of
the rustic philosophy combined of covetousness and mother-wit
recorded by Mrs. Cuxsom after the death of Mrs. Henchard, the

Mayor's wife, who had requested that the four carefully saved
ounce pennies, having been used to weigh down her dead eyelids,
should be then buried :

> " Well, and Martha did it, and buried the ounce pennies in
> the garden. But if ye'll believe words, that man, Christopher
> Coney, went and dug 'em up and spent 'em at the Three
> Mariners. ' Faith,' he said, ' why should death rob life o'
> fourpence ? Death's not of such good report that we should
> respect 'en to that extent,' says he."
> " 'Twas a cannibal deed," deprecated his listeners.
> " Gad, then, I won't quite ha'e it," said Solomon Longways.
> " I say it to-day, and 'tis Sunday morning, and I wouldn't
> speak wrongfully for a zilver zixpence at such a time. To
> respect the dead is sound doxology ; and I wouldn't sell
> skellintons—leastwise respectable skellintons—to be varnished
> for 'natomies, except I were out o' work. But money is scarce,
> and throats get dry. Why *should* death rob life o' fourpence ?
> I say there was no treason in it."

Granfer Cantle in *The Return of the Native* is a new figure,
with his juvenility and his bounce :

> In the year four 'twas said there wasn't a finer figure in the
> whole South Wessex than I. . . . There was I, straight as a
> young poplar, wi' my firelock and my bagnet, and my spatter-
> dashes, and my stock sawing my jaws off, and my accoutrements
> sheening like the seven stars ! Yes, neighbours, I was a pretty
> sight in my soldiering days. . . . Faith, I was never afraid of
> nothing except Boney, or I shouldn't have been the soldier I
> was. 'Tis a thousand pities you didn't see me in four !

Christian, his youngest son, is a variation on Thomas Leaf,
but has oddities of his own—the man no woman would marry
because there was no moon when he was born : he asks,

> " Do you really think it serious, Mr. Fairway, that there
> was no moon ? "
> " Yes ; ' No moon, no man '. 'Tis one of the truest sayings
> ever spat out."

The Granfer used to stare at Christian as a hen does at a duck she
has hatched.

There is old Corporal Tullidge, who had had his left arm

" knocked to a pummy " in the French wars, and at Cripple-straw's suggestion exhibited the results to Anne Garland.

" Rattle yer arm, corpel, and show her," said Cripplestraw.

" Yes, sure," said the corporal, raising the limb slowly, as if the glory of exhibition had lost some of its novelty, though he was willing to oblige. Twisting it mercilessly about with his right hand he produced a crunching among the bones at every motion, Cripplestraw seeming to derive great satisfaction from the ghastly sound.

There is humour and wisdom in Sammy Blore's comments on Lady Constantine's loss of husband and fortune :

The curious thing is that my lady seems not to mind being a pore woman half as much as we do at seeing her so. 'Tis a wonderful gift, Mr. San Cleeve, wonderful, to be able to guide yerself, and not let loose yer soul in blasting at such a misfortune. I should go and drink neat regular, as soon as I had swallered my breakfast, till my innards was burnt out like a' old copper, if it had happened to me ; but my lady's plan is best. Though I only guess how one feels in such losses, to be sure, for I never had nothing to lose.

Later in the book there is a grand account of the walking of Sir Blount's ghost—recognised not only by shape but by smell,— " a high smell, a sort of gamey flavour, just as you'd expect of a great squire, not like a low man's 'natomy at all ". Hezzy Biles is moved to the memory of how he was confirmed at the same time as Sir Blount, and was prompted by that young gentleman to give " Women and wine " as the articles of his belief.

" Confirmation was a sight different at that time," mused Biles. " The Bishops didn't lay it on so strong then as they do now. Now-a-days, yer Bishop gies both hands to every Jack-rag and Tom-straw that drops the knee afore him ; but 'twas six chaps to one blessing when we was boys. The Bishop o' that time would stretch out his palms and run his fingers over our row of crowns as off-hand as a bank gentleman telling money. The great lords of the Church in them days wasn't particular to a soul or two more or less ; and, for my part, I think living was easier for 't."

A keen eye for the funny side of matrimony have these fellows. John Upjohn confides to the hollow-turner that

" When I went courting my wife that is now, the skilfulness
that she would show in keeping me on her pretty side as she
walked was beyond all belief. Perhaps you've noticed that
she's got a pretty side to her face as well as a plain one ? "

" I can't say I've noticed it particular much," said the hollow-
turner blandly.

" Well," continued Upjohn, not disconcerted, " she has. All
women under the sun be prettier one side than t'other."

As for Grammer Oliver and her head, which she sold to the doctor
for ten pounds, the full story of that, in *The Woodlanders*, must be
read to be believed. It is worth studying as a specimen of dialect.

Some non-rustic humour is to be found in Parson Swancourt,
in Neigh and Ladywell, and throughout *The Trumpet-Major*.
Hardy's satire is generally too bitter to be called humorous, but
here and there a gentler spirit of mockery raises a smile. A
drawing-room audience listening to Ethelberta singing is beautifully touched off :

Then she began, and the sweetness of her singing was such
that even the most unsympathetic honoured her by looking as
if they would be willing to listen to every note the song contained if it were not quite so much trouble to do so. Some
were so interested that, instead of continuing their conversation, they remained in silent consideration of how they would
continue it when she had finished ; while the particularly civil
people arranged their countenance into every attentive form
that the mind could devise. One emotional gentleman looked
at the corner of a chair as if, till that moment, such an object
had never crossed his vision before ; the movement of his
finger to the imagined tune was, for a deaf old clergyman, a
perfect mine of interest ; while a young man from the country
was powerless to put an end to an enchanted gaze at nothing at
all in the exact middle of the room before him. Neigh and the
general phalanx of celebrated club yawners were so much affected
that they raised their chronic look of great objection to things
to an expression of scarcely any objection at all.

There is an excellent piece of comedy that comes by way of
relief among the sorrows of *Jude the Obscure :* Jude has enthusias-
tically called on the composer of a " supremely beautiful " and
emotional hymn that he has just heard ; the composer turns out
to be a most commonplace individual who regards music from

a purely commercial standpoint, and is about to abandon it for the more lucrative wine-business.

But the profoundest humour of Hardy is to be found in those scenes where the rustic-groups exercise that chorus-function of which I have spoken. The quality of their commentary has already been characterised—its wit and humour, shrewdness and cynicism, its impartial advisory capacity, its fund of information, especially of the family history of the main characters. Some illustrations will be offered here.

The malt-house scene in *Far from the Madding Crowd* is crammed with humour—the ash-encrusted God-forgive-me, the bacon that was not to be " chawed quite close " because it had been dropped on the way from the shop, Joseph Poorgrass with his blushes and his reply to the owl, the malster whose age added up to one hundred and seventeen—but Shepherd Oak sees in the gathering an opportunity to get some information about Bathsheba, his new mistress : about her he gets little, but perhaps what he learns about her parents is not without its value :

" I knew them a little ", said Jacob Smallbury ; " but they were townsfolk, and didn't live here. They've been dead for years. Father, what sort of people were mis'ess' father and mother ? "

" Well ", said the maltster, " he wasn't much to look at ; but she was a lovely woman. He was fond enough of her as his sweetheart."

" Used to kiss her in scores and long-hundreds, so 'twas said here and there ", observed Coggan.

" He was very proud of her, too, when they were married, as I've been told ", said the maltster.

" Ay ", said Coggan. " He admired her so much that he used to light the candle three times a night to look at her."

" Boundless love ; I shouldn't have supposed it in the world's universe ! " murmured Joseph Poorgrass, who habitually spoke on a large scale in his moral reflections.

When Bathsheba decides to do without a bailiff there is old shaking of heads :

" A headstrong maid, that's what she is—and won't listen to no advice at all. Pride and vanity have ruined many a cobbler's dog. Dear, dear, when I think o' it, I sorrows like a man in travel ! "

When her sheep are in trouble through eating poisonous weeds, the chorus-function of the farm-hands is clearly marked : they stand round Bathsheba " with oriental indifference to the flight of time ", replying disinterestedly to her frantic questions, pointing out the desirability of sending for Oak, but not urging it, looking grave, but suppressing opinion, until, seeing her distress, one of them says compassionately, " I wouldn't cry about it, miss. Why not ask him softer like ?   I'm sure he'd come then. Gable is a true man in that way."   Just so, when Boldwood's hands gather round his house discussing the rumour that Troy has been seen alive, they hear all, see all, know all there is to be known, comment sympathetically, but take no action.

When Oak reproaches Joseph Poorgrass because he has loitered for drink while bringing Fanny's body to the churchyard, it is the rhythmic voice of innumerable life-worn generations that replies through Jan Coggan :

> " Nobody can hurt a dead woman ", at length said Coggan, with the precision of a machine.   " All that could be done for her is done—she is beyond us : and why should a man put himself in a tearing hurry for lifeless clay that can neither feel nor see, and don't know what you do with her at all ?   If she'd been alive, I would have been the first to help.   If she now wanted victuals and drink, I'd pay for it, money down.   But she's dead, and no speed of ours will bring her to life.   The woman's past us—time spent upon her is throwed away : why should we hurry to do what's not required ?   Drink shepherd, and be friends, for to-morrow we may be like her."

After the mysterious happenings of the first two chapters of *The Return of the Native*, it is from the conversation that goes on among a group of men and women standing round the great bonfire on Rainbarrow that we learn some of the necessary explanatory facts about Wildeve and Thomasin, and the coming return of Clym Yeobright.   Later on useful information is conveyed not only to us but to Eustacia, who listens up the chimney to some men working on a furze-stack close by.   She not only hears of the education and prospects of the returned Clym, but gets the first gleam of an idea that she presently developed : " I say, Sam, she and Clym Yeobright would make a very pretty pigeon pair—hey ? "   On the other hand, it is to a group of heath-workers (gathered for an *al fresco* hair-cutting) that Clym makes an inauspicious attempt to explain his motives for leaving Paris. He had once, he tells them, despised country-life :

> " I thought our life here was contemptible. To oil your boots instead of blacking them, to dust your coat with a switch instead of a brush : was there ever anything more ridiculous ? I said."
> " So 'tis ; so 'tis ! "
> " No, no—you are wrong ; it isn't."
> " Beg your pardon, we thought that was your maning."

Now he knew town life was not better—it was simply different :

> " True, a sight different ", said Fairway.
> " Yes, Paris must be a taking place ", said Humphrey. " Grand shop-winders, trumpets and drums ; and here be we out of doors in all winds and weathers——"

He tells them of his determination to give up the jewellery trade and open a school, and resumes his walk :

> " He'll never carry it out in the world ", said Fairway. " In a few weeks he'll learn to see things otherwise."
> " 'Tis good-hearted of the young man ", said another. " But, for my part, I think he'd better mind his business."

We have already seen that it was the chorus, gossiping outside the tower, that opened Swithin's eyes to Lady Constantine's feelings towards him : their actual words are too good to miss :

> " Is she meaning to enter upon a virgin life for the rest of her days ? " asked Sammy Blore.
> " I don't want to be unreverent to her ladyship ; but I really don't think she is meaning any such waste of a Christian carcase. I say she's rather meaning to commit flat matrimony wi' some-body or other, and one young gentleman in particular."
> " But the young man himself ? "
> " Planned, cut out, and finished for the delight of 'ooman ! "
> " Yet he must be willing."
> " That would soon come. If they get up this tower ruling plannards together much longer, their plannards will soon rule them together, in my way o' thinking. If she've a disposition towards the knot, she can soon teach him."

That passage might have been written by Shakespeare, and would have done him no discredit. The doings of Henchard, of

course, come in for ample discussion. Elizabeth-Jane hears a
little on her first night in Casterbridge :

" When did he lose his wife ? " she asked.

" I never knowed her. 'Twas afore he came to Casterbridge ", Solomon Longways replied, with terminative emphasis,
as if the fact of his ignorance of Mrs. Henchard were sufficient
to deprive her history of all interest. " But I know that 'a's a
banded teetotaller."

But he is forced to add—

" I've seen the sun rise over Durnover Moor these nine-
and-sixty year, and though Mr. Henchard has never cussed me
unfairly ever since I've worked for'n, seeing I be but a little
small man, I must say that I have never before tasted such rough
bread as has been made from Henchard's wheat lately."

Two excellent comments—profiting by the feminine element in
the chorus of this book—on Henchard's marriage to Susan deserve
quotation. (As Hardy says, Farfrae, who alone knew it was a re-
marriage, was unable to enter into the scene in its dramatic aspect
—in other words, he has no chorus-value):

" 'Tis five-and-forty years since I had my settlement in this
here town ", said Coney ; " but daze me if ever I see a man
wait so long before to take so little ! There's a chance even
for thee after this, Nance Mockridge."

But Nance sees things with her own eyes, and presently opines :

" Well—there's a difference between 'em, though he do call
himself a teetotaller ", said Nance Mockridge. " She'll wish
her cake dough afore she's done of him. There's a bluebeardy
look about 'en ; and 'twill out in time."

The attitude of Solomon Longways and Christopher Coney
towards the skimmity-ride is interesting. They send an anony-
mous letter (the chorus-equivalent of taking action) to Farfrae,
with a view to ensuring that he shall be away and not suffer the
indignity of seeing the procession ; but " for poor Lucetta they
took no protective measure, believing with the majority there was
some truth in the scandal, which she would have to bear as she
best might ". The chorus has a certain mild interest in seeing
justice done ; to its spirit of aloofness, mercy is a foreign sentiment.

But if the chorus can be hard, there is none like it for appreciating a woman's fineness. Hear the woodmen on Grace's mother, long since dead :

" I can mind her mother ", said the hollow-turner. " Always a teuny, delicate piece ; her touch upon your hand was as soft as wind. She was inoculated for the smallpox and had it beautiful fine, just about the time that I was out of my apprenticeship—ay, and a long apprenticeship 'twas. I served that master of mine six years and three hundred and fourteen days."

The hollow-turner pronounced the days with emphasis, as if, considering their number, they were a rather more remarkable fact than the years.

" Mr. Winterborne's father walked with her at one time ", said old Timothy Tangs ; " but Mr. Melbury won her. She was a child of a woman, and would cry like rain if so be he huffed her. Whenever she and her husband came to a puddle in their walks together he'd take her up like a halfpenny doll and put her over without dirting her a speck. And if he keeps the daughter so long at boarding-school he'll make her as nesh as her mother was."

It is all miraculous, too, in its own way. Hardy can't have taken it *all* down in shorthand, *verbatim !* And yet . . .! Consider, for a last example, the sheer prose force, the utter grace of style, of these remarks on Mrs. Charmond, which Fitzpiers hears out of his window towards the end of *The Woodlanders :*

" She is off to foreign lands again at last—hev made up her mind quite sudden-like—and it is thoughted she'll leave in a day or two. She's been all as if her mind were low for some days past—with a sort of fret in her face, as if she chid her own soul. She's the wrong sort of woman for Hintock—hardly knowing a beech from a woak. But I don't care who the man is, she's been a very kind friend to me."

" Well—the day after to-morrow is the Sabbath day, and without charity we be but tinkling simples ; but this I do say, that her going will be a blessed thing for a certain married couple who remain."

Fitzpiers repeats : " A sort of fret in her face, as if she chid her own soul ! " And we may leave it at that.

Chapter VI

STYLE

LET it be postulated that no man ought to take up pen to write unless he have something to say.   Something, that is, of his own ; somewhat of himself which, being of himself, no other man could possibly say.   Style —the style which is the man—then becomes a necessity, inevitable, involuntary.   Or perhaps here and there sufferance may be granted to a writer who has nothing individual to declare : one who is a mere reporter of the average utterance of the day.   To such a one style is not only unnecessary, but impossible.   At all events his style will be only that style which is the age ; the style that is seen in all its stupefying perfection in the *Times* first leader.   And it is an astonishing proof of the superiority of idiosyncrasy over the vast aggregate opinion of mankind that, while these average-striking world-utterances pass away like the hours they are born of, the personal proposal— so the personality proposing be sufficiently personal, sufficiently unlike the average—endures, and is worshipped of all time. Mankind is tiresome and ephemeral ; man himself is everlastingly interesting.   Only the work that has style can hope for immortality.

Style is as essential to a prose writer as passion to a poet.   To the endless controversy as to whether metre is or is not essential to poetry, a tolerably acceptable settlement is to the effect that the most intangible, and therefore the highest, part of poetry—the bloom on the fruit—is simultaneously cause and effect of the peculiar passion of the lift and fall of metrical rhythm.   In the same way style in prose not only depends on matter, it is a form of matter—the most ethereal, imponderable form.   It is the most personal, and therefore the most important, thing that the writer has to say.   That part of his meaning which is inexpressible in words he expresses in his style.   Hence, of course, the infinite variety of styles, since men—at least great men—are infinitely various, entirely non-recurring.

While style is thus unquestionably the man, it is probably not the whole man.   Nor does it always—not even in writers of equal genius—give us the man in the same degree.   It presents us with two separate aspects or facts concerning the man, and these two aspects or facts are combined in each man's style in a different ratio.   Pater's exquisite definition of style as rendering the writer's " sense of fact " fits all styles to some extent, and covers some completely.   In the case, however, of the greatest stylists— that is, of the greatest writers—the definition as it stands seems inadequate.   In these cases, where the writer's style is integral with, and an emanation from, the fundamental of his thought, it indicates rather his sense of *the* fact—the universe—life ; is the result and final expression of his prevailing outlook on the totality of existence.

This, then, is the first of these two determining factors that go to the formation of a writer's style.   Style is, however, modified importantly by another and very different thing : this is the writer's attitude towards his audience—or, to put the matter in its most comprehensive form, the special kind of delight the writer takes in the act of composition.   If you will project yourself into the mind of Sir Thomas Browne, for instance, as he wheels slowly forward, majestically, yet with delicate and beautiful care, his organ-pealing periods, you will perceive how greatly his peculiar joy in the fashioning of language influenced his style. In fact with Browne this egoistic trait is so dominant that his style is almost wholly due to it, the other factor, his bizarre outlook on life, making its influence felt sometimes with his humour. The two constituents, which may be called the philosophic and the artistic, are roughly measurable in the styles of various writers.   With Bacon, for instance, in contradistinction to Browne, the philosophic preponderates largely, and increasingly so as his grave mind matures.   Carlyle, chaotically splendid as a stormy sunset, exhibits all nameable style-factors : artistic and philosophic nearly balanced, the first strongly tinged with the ' attitude towards his audience ', the other not unaffected by the Paternal ' sense of fact ' (which I take to be more instant and limited than the wide grasp of things I intend by the ' philosophic ' element) ; the whole permeated through and through with ' the man '.

To come nearer to our own subject, Meredith and Hardy are antithetical in this respect (as in many others). Some critics have it that Meredith's delightfully strange style arises from his no less strange and delightful matter—the queer and recondite mental processes with which he is largely concerned. This explanation appears to me very incomplete. Doubtless Meredith's style could never have been (generally) as easy as Addison's or as translucent as Ruskin's, but surely it is his peculiar impressionistic joy in language that makes this writer's style what it is. Does it appear, for instance, that those fascinating allusions to " the last few poor pulmonary snips and shreds of leagues dancing on their toes for cold, explorers tell us, and catching breath by good luck, like dogs at bones about a table, on the edge of the Pole," or to those " luminous rings eruptive of the infinitesimal ", were *necessary* to deliver the subject-matter of the introductory chapter of *The Egoist?* No, Meredith is an artist, and in his style an artist purely for the sake of artistry.

Of later writers, Stevenson and George Moore are artists in style, Conrad and Mr. H. G. Wells not so : the style of these two (and both are masters of style) expresses the quality of their minds, and is not consciously formed ; Conrad's painful recasting of his paragraphs was motived by an earnest desire to make his style fit his meaning, not approximate to a sound-pattern. Henry James and Mr. Max Beerbohm are artists first and last—yet their style follows with minute accuracy the movements of their minds ; but their minds are works of art in themselves.

And Hardy's style is essentially of the philosophic type, an emanation of his mind. Hardy may or may not be a pessimist, but it is undeniable that his outlook on the visible world is grey. And his style is grey—grey as November skies or Odysseus' sullen seas. Beside Meredith or Carlyle it might seem that Hardy has no style. Certainly his variation from the style of ' the age ' is not outwardly obvious in the same sense with such writers as these. But judged by the more subtle indications of effect produced, transmitted impression, he is as individual and as unmistakable as either of them. Any five lines from one of the greater

novels would reveal him ' as the O revealed Giotto ', and inser-
tions in the same by another hand (unless it were that of the incomparable Max !) would be as readily detected as Fletcher's
lines in *Henry VIII*. The Hardy atmosphere is chiefly due to
his style ; it breathes in every paragraph, and is as recognisable
and characteristic as the scent of the salt ocean. It carries with
it an impression of stern, sad eyes, gazing steadily and unflinchingly out over the wilderness of the world's wrong. Whatever
there may be in it of bitterness is generally repressed. His great
masculine strength appears not least in his style. It is iron-cold
—cold with the stillness of dead passion. What opportunities
for raving, shrieking, moaning are offered by such scenes as
Yeobright's accusation of Eustacia, the christening of Sorrow the
Undesired, the finale of *The Woodlanders*, the death of the children
of Jude and Sue, and a dozen others. Yet nowhere is there a
suspicion of rant, of sensationalism, of noise of any sort. *Jude*
the most agonisingly, desperately tragic of all the novels, is the
coldest of all in its narration.

Hardy's style thus satisfies the first demand that all styles are
called upon to fill—it perfectly corresponds with and expresses
the profoundest intention of the writer. It is not conspicuously
beautiful ; it is not luxuriant or alluringly harmonious. It is,
in the main, a bare, significant narrative style, of easy but not
obtrusive balance. It is prose, pure prose : its movement has
nothing in it of passion, nothing of the passion which beats in the
Psalms, or in Ruskin's prose when he speaks of the mosses, the
grasses, the sea-foam ; passion akin to that of a Chopin nocturne
and the heaving of the human breast. The harmony is intellectual, but of its kind (the kind in which Bacon is the supreme
master) it is admirable. The fact can, of course, only be properly
judged by a consideration of large portions of Hardy's prose, but
a quotation not much above his average standard of excellence
will serve to exemplify these features of grey tone, coldness,
austerity, word-quality, and balanced progress :

> Having indulged in this wild hope he went upstairs, and
> looked out of the window, and pictured her through the evening
> journey to London . . . under the same sky of ribbed cloud as
> that he beheld, through which the moon showed its position
> rather than its shape, and one or two of the larger stars made

themselves visible as faint nebulæ only. It was a new beginning of Sue's history. He projected his mind into the future,
and saw her with children more or less in her own likeness
around her. But the consolation of regarding them as a continuation of her identity was denied to him, as to all such
dreamers, by the wilfulness of Nature in not allowing issue
from one parent alone. Every desired renewal of an existence
is debased by being half alloy. " If at the estrangement or
death of my lost love I could go and see her child—hers solely
—there would be comfort in it ! " said Jude. And then he
again uneasily saw, as he had latterly seen with more and more
frequency, the scorn of Nature for man's finer emotions, and
her lack of interest in his aspirations.

So much for the general level. Purple patches, however, are
legitimate objects of admiration, provided they are the outcome
of spontaneous rise in feeling. As might be expected, when
Hardy rises it is into passages of a sombre beauty. One occurs,
for instance, immediately before the extract last given from *Jude*.
Perhaps it can only be appreciated fully as the climax of the preceding pages, out of the feeling in which it rises naturally, but it
is intrinsically worth quoting :

He could not shake off the feeling that she would come back
and sleep in the little room adjoining his own, in which she
had slept so many previous days. Her actions were always
unpredictable : why should she not come ? Gladly would he
have compounded for the denial of her as a sweetheart and wife
by having her live thus as a fellow-lodger and friend, even on
the most distant terms. His supper still remained spread ;
and going to the front door, and softly setting it open, he returned
to the room and sat as watchers sit on old-Midsummer eves,
expecting the phantom of the Beloved. But she did not come.

A remarkable feature about these passages is the good English
commonplaceness of the words with which the effect is obtained.
Jude has many such outbreaks, and *Tess* still more, which will be
easily recognised. It is the same with all the novels in which the
theme and handling are of full Hardian solemnity. It may be
said of Hardy, as Dryden said of Shakespeare in a slightly different
connection, that ' he is always great when some great occasion is
presented to him '. The concluding paragraphs of chapters,

where the writer stays the progress of his narrative and shows us
the eddyings and disturbances that are being caused thereby in
the dark waters of his own soul, are very frequently in this more
noble kind. The chapter in *The Return of the Native* entitled
' Queen of Night ', already referred to for its subject-matter, is
no whit less glorious in the manner of the telling. The Hebraic
denunciatory note of Melbury's censure of his daughter in *The
Woodlanders*—" What has come upon you and us through your
giving yourself up to him is beyond reproach, beyond weeping
and beyond wailing. Perhaps I drove you to it. But I am hurt ;
I am scourged ; I am astonished " ; the storm-picture in *Far
from the Madding Crowd ;* the description of the amphitheatre
in *The Mayor of Casterbridge ;* these are examples that need no
multiplication. I shall quote but one other passage ; it occurs
towards the end of Chapter V of *Tess of the D'Urbervilles ;*
the second of the two paragraphs marks the culminating point of
Hardy's prose, and in its harmonious cadences, and its passionate
rhythmic rise to the mysterious sorrow of its close, seems to me
deserving of a place among the established *loci classici* in this
sort :

Thus the thing began. Had she perceived this meeting's
import she might have asked why she was doomed to be seen
and coveted that day by the wrong man, and not by some other
man, the right and desired one in all respects—as nearly as
humanity can supply the right and desired : yet to him who
amongst her acquaintances might have approximated to this
kind, she was but a transient impression, half-forgotten.

In the ill-judged execution of the well-judged plan of things
the call seldom produces the comer, the man to love rarely
coincides with the hour for loving. Nature does not often say
" See ! " to her poor creature at a time when seeing can lead to
happy doing ; or reply " Here " to a body's cry of " Where ? "
till the hide-and-seek has become an irksome, outworn game.
We may wonder whether at the acme and summit of the human
progress these anachronisms will become corrected by a finer
intuition, a closer interaction of the social machinery than that
which now jolts us round and along ; but such completeness is
not to be prophesied or even conceived as possible. Enough
that in the present case, as in millions, it was not the two halves
of a perfect whole that confronted each other at the perfect

moment ; a missing counterpart wandered independently about the earth waiting in crass obtuseness till the late time came. Out of which maladroit delay sprang anxieties, disappointments, shocks, catastrophes, and passing strange destinies.

The foregoing remarks have been based upon a consideration of what is doubtless the most characteristic of Hardy's three styles—that which expresses his sense of *Weltschmertz*. But he has two others. For the general progress of his narrative he employs a style that is undistinguished almost to baldness ; the statement about the revealing quality of short extracts must not be taken to cover this quite considerable portion of his writing. It is capable of taking on an almost shocking degree of banality at times :

The wondrous power of flattery in *passados* at woman is a perception so universal as to be remarked upon by many people almost as automatically as they repeat a proverb, or say that they are Christians and the like, without thinking much of the enormous corollaries which spring from the proposition. Still less is it acted upon for the good of the complemental being alluded to. With the majority such an opinion is shelved with all those trite aphorisms which require some catastrophe to bring their tremendous meanings thoroughly home. When expressed with some amount of reflectiveness it seems coordinate with a belief that this flattery must be reasonable to be effective . . . and so on——

His third variety is on a scarcely lower level than the first tragic kind : it is that used when Hardy gets thoroughly absorbed in the details of Wessex life. It is racy of the soil, humorous, perfect without self-consciousness, and dialect flows into and out of it without disturbance :

" We ought not to put her in a waggon ; we'll get a hearse."

" There will hardly be time, ma'am, will there ? "

" Perhaps not ", she said, musingly. " When did you say we must be at the door—three o'clock ? "

" Three o'clock this afternoon, ma'am, so to speak it."

" Very well—you go with it. A pretty waggon is better than an ugly hearse, after all. Joseph, have the new spring waggon with the blue body and the red wheels, and wash it very clean. And, Joseph——"

" Yes, ma'am."

" Carry with you some evergreens and flowers to put upon her coffin—indeed, gather a great many, and completely bury her in them. Get some boughs of laurustinus, and variegated box, and yew, and boy's-love ; ay, and some bunches of chrysanthemum. And let old Pleasant draw her, because she knew him so well."

Or that whole chapter from *Tess*, of her first morning among the cows at Talbothays. It begins with the milkers :

Each girl sat down on her three-legged stool, her face sideways, her right cheek resting against the cow ; and looked musingly along the animal's flank as she approached. The male milkers, with hat-brims turned down, resting on their foreheads and gazing on the ground, did not observe her.

It goes on to describe the master-dairyman, with his contempt for milk as a beverage, and ends with his story of the pious bull. It appeared that " a old aged man over at Mellstock, William Dewy by name ", had kept off a bull late one night by playing his fiddle to it till he was tired :

Well, then he called to mind how he'd seen cattle kneel o' Christmas Eves in the dead o' night. It was not Christmas Eve then, but it came into his head to play a trick upon the bull. So he broke into the 'Tivity Hymn, just as at Christmas carol-singing ; when, lo and behold, down went the bull on his bended knees in his ignorance, just as if 'twere the true 'Tivity night and hour. As soon as his horned friend were down, William turned, clinked off like a long dog, and jumped safe over hedge, before the praying bull had got on his feet again to take after him. William used to say that he'd seen a man look a fool a good many times, but never such a fool as that bull looked when he found his pious feelings had been played upon, and 'twas not Christmas Eve. . . . Yes, William Dewy, that was the man's name ; and I can tell you to a foot where he's a-lying in Mellstock Churchyard at this very moment—just between the second yew-tree and the north aisle.

To some extent the two styles are inspired by two different kinds of story, so that we find the pastoral style predominating in books like *Far from the Madding Crowd*, *The Woodlanders*, and *Tess*, the tragic style in *The Mayor* and in *Jude*. *The Return of the Native* is built equally of pastoral and tragic, while *Jude the*

Obscure which for a time goes in the very plain narrative manner, ultimately rises to the greatest heights of the tragic style. *The Hand of Ethelberta* stands apart in a well-balanced but otherwise undistinguished prose ; *The Well-Beloved* has a sort of undress ease.

Far from the Madding Crowd opens with a deceptive baldness, which serves to heighten the brilliance of the picture of Bathsheba and the cat that presently follows, the first of many passages of delightful writing. What expression of what observation there is in this of a sheep just shorn :

> The clean, sleek creature arose from its fleece—how perfectly like Aphrodite rising from the foam should have been seen to be realised—looking startled and shy at the loss of its garment, which lay on the floor in one soft cloud, united throughout, the portion visible being the inner surface only, which, never before exposed, was white as snow, and without flaw or blemish of the minutest kind.

The book is full of classical allusions, and sometimes a note of the antique enters into the style, as in this passage, which has the rhythm and shape of a Miltonic verse paragraph :

> (The ship's boat has just rescued the swimming Troy.) And now night drooped slowly upon the wide watery levels in front ; and at no great distance from them, where the shore-line curved round, and formed a long ribbon of shade upon the horizon, a series of points of yellow light began to start into existence, denoting the spot to be the site of Budmouth, where the lamps were being lighted along the parade. The cluck of their oars was the only sound of any distinctness upon the sea, and as they laboured amid the thickening shades the lamp-lights grew larger, each appearing to send a flaming sword deep down into the waves before it, until there arose, among other dim shapes of the kind, the form of the vessel for which they were bound.

The pastoral style is shown finely in a speech by Oak to Bathsheba :

> You know, mistress, that I love you, and shall love you always. I only mention this to bring to your mind that at any rate I would wish to do you no harm : beyond that I put it aside. I have lost in the race for money and good things, and I am not such a fool as to pretend to 'ee now I am poor, and you have got

altogether above me. But Bathsheba, dear mistress, this I beg you to consider—that, both to keep yourself well honoured among the work-folk, and in common generosity to an honourable man who loves you as well as I, you should be more discreet in your bearing towards this soldier.

Is there not a touch of the sublime here, where Bathsheba, in her desolation, goes to make it up with Oak ?—" She tapped nervously. . . . Gabriel opened the door, and the moon shone upon his forehead ".

The opening of *The Return of the Native* is, on the other hand, in a ponderous style not inappropriate to the vastness of Egdon. The allusions in this book have a tendency to Biblical origin. Clym's reproachful exposition of his mother's virtues at the end of the scene with Eustacia, beginning, " Call her to mind—think of her—what goodness there was in her "—is another specimen of that oratory to which all Hardy's people can rise when deeply moved. Here is a paragraph of a special Hardian timbre— wistfulness compounded of life and death, of earth and unearthliness :

During these operations he was constantly on the watch for Eustacia. That there should be no mistake about her knowing where to find him, he had ordered a notice-board to be affixed to the garden gate at Alderworth, signifying in white letters whither he had removed. When a leaf floated to the earth he turned his head, thinking it might be her footfall. A bird searching for worms in the mould of the flower-beds sounded like her hand on the latch of the gate ; and at dusk, when soft, strange ventriloquisms came from holes in the ground, hollow stalks, curled dead leaves, and other crannies wherein breezes, worms, and insects can work their will, he fancied that they were Eustacia, standing without and breathing wishes of reconciliation.

What I have called the pastoral style, in its more serious vein, is magnificently exemplified in the chapters describing Mrs. Yeobright's unhappy journey on Egdon.

The Trumpet-Major has a pleasant flat level of style that suits the quiet story, but every now and then it warms to the narrative and becomes rich and interesting, and once at least we have a patch of sombre prose, when John, on the night of his departure, sits by the mill-stream and watches the lights in the house—

till one appeared in Anne's bedroom, and she herself came forward to shut the casement, with the candle in her hand. The light shone out upon the broad and deep mill-head, illuminating to a distinct individuality every moth and gnat that entered the quivering chain of radiance stretching across the water towards him, and every bubble or atom of froth that floated into its width. She stood for some time looking out, little thinking what the darkness concealed on the other side of that wide stream ; till at length she closed the casement, drew the curtains, and retreated into the room. Presently the light went out, upon which John Loveday returned to camp and lay down in his tent.

Indeed, there is an intermittent stream of noble style running through this novel, all connected with the figure of the Trumpet-Major. Otherwise, the most noteworthy passage in the book is the set piece of the passing of the *Victory*. It is shown to us through the inexpert eye of Anne, who is at first describing to an old sailor what she can see through his telescope. The description is made even more remarkable by a succession of highly imaginative similes. Anne tells the sailor, " She is twisting round in a curious way, and her sails sink in like old cheeks, and she shivers like a leaf upon a tree " ; he interprets—" She is in stays, for the larboard tack ". Presently " the great silent ship, with her population of blue-jackets, marines, officers, captain, and the admiral who was not to return alive, passed like a phantom the meridian of the Bill. Sometimes her aspect was that of a large white bat, sometimes that of a grey one. In the course of time the watching girl saw that the ship had passed her nearest point ; the breadth of her sails diminished by foreshortening, till she assumed the form of an egg on end." And later, " she was now no more than a dead fly's wing on a sheet of spider's web ". The whole picture is as full of life, and of feeling, as if Hardy had himself been an eye-witness : he must have watched some tall ship thus pass, and his profound interest in the historic period enabled him to recapture the emotions attendant on the passing of this special ship.

The Mayor of Casterbridge gives us one of those interiors that Hardy does as vividly as he does his exteriors :

The accommodation of the Three Mariners was far from spacious, despite the fair area of ground it covered. The room demanded by intrusive beams and rafters, partitions, passages, stair-cases, disused ovens, settles, and four-posters, left comparatively small quarters for human beings. . . . The principle of the inn seemed to be to compensate for the antique awkwardness, crookedness, and obscurity of the passages, floors and windows, by quantities of clean linen spread about everywhere, and this had a dazzling effect upon the travellers.

He can touch in an old woman as well as an old man :

There was one case only, and the offender stood before him. She was an old woman of mottled countenance, attired in a shawl of that nameless tertiary hue which comes, but cannot be made—a hue neither tawny, russet, hazel nor ash ; a sticky black bonnet that seemed to have been worn in the country of the Psalmist where the clouds drop fatness ; and an apron that had been white in times so comparatively recent as still to contrast visibly with the rest of her clothes.

This book exemplifies over and over again how the Hardy tone tends to concentrate at chapter-ends :

She had learnt the lesson of renunciation, and was as familiar with the wreck of each day's wishes as with the diurnal setting of the sun. If her earthly career had taught her few book philosophies it had at least well practised her in this. Yet here experience had consisted less in a series of pure disappointments than in a series of substitutions. Continually it had happened that what she had desired had not been granted her, and that what had been granted her she had not desired. So that she viewed with an approach to equanimity the now cancelled days when Donald had been her undeclared lover, and wondered what unwished-for thing Heaven might send her in place of him.

In *The Woodlanders* there is a pretty example of Hardy's faculty of imaginative observation : " From this self-contained place (Little Hintock, seen at a distance of half a mile) rose in stealthy silence tall stems of smoke, which the eye of imagination could trace downward to their root on quiet hearthstones, festooned overhead with hams and flitches " ; and another of his power of imaginative vision : " Giles drove on ahead into the streets ; the churches, the abbey, and other mediæval buildings on this clear bright morning having the linear distinctness of architectural drawings, as if the original dream and vision of the conceiving master-mason were for a brief hour flashed down through the centuries to an unappreciative age ".

Although the whole Hardy world is founded in irony, irony as a figure is rare in his style ; I think the smoky flavour is here (of Grace meeting Giles under his apple tree) :

> The greeting in her looks and on her lips had a restrained shape, which perhaps was not unnatural. For true it was that Giles Winterborne, though well-attired and well-mannered for a yeoman, looked rough beside her. It had sometimes dimly occurred to him, in his ruminating silences at Little Hintock, that external phenomena—such as the lowness or height or colour of a hat, the fold of a coat, the make of a boot, or the chance attitude of a limb at the instant of view—may have a great influence upon feminine opinion, so frequently founded upon non-essentials ; but a certain causticity of mental tone towards himself and the world in general had prevented to-day, as always, any enthusiastic action on the strength of that reflection ; and her momentary instinct of reserve at first sight of him was the penalty paid for his laxness.

The book provides a marvellous example of Hardy's tragic style in its plainest manner :

> Everybody thought of Giles ; nobody thought of Marty. Had any of them looked in upon her during those moonlight nights which preceded the burial of her father they would have seen the girl absolutely alone in the house with the dead man. Her own chamber being nearest the stairs, the coffin had been placed there for convenience ; and at a certain hour of the night when the moon arrived opposite the window, its beams streamed across the still profile of South, sublimed by the august presence of death, and onward a few feet further upon the face of his daughter, lying in her little bed in the silence of a repose almost as dignified as that of her companion—the repose of a guileless soul that had nothing more left on earth to lose, except a life that she did not over-value ;

and an equally fine one of the pastoral style in Melbury's speech to Mrs. Charmond (the brief one to his daughter has already been mentioned). It begins, " I am an old man, that, somewhat late in life, God thought fit to bless with one child, and she a daughter ", and is too long to quote. The speech is (with Melbury's whole conduct of the interview) too good to be true ;

it is a perfect work of art, like an after-dinner speech by Sir
James Barrie ! In real life (and in Conrad) people flounder, and
get their thoughts out bit by bit if at all ; but it is a great joy
to see things done properly, like this.   This is Shakespeare's
method : with what unerring sense of form do his characters—
from Puck and the ' bleeding Sergeant ' in *Macbeth* to Fabian,
Oliver, Benvolio and Hamlet—sum up a long sequence of events
when called upon to do so.

Tess of the D'Urbervilles is rich in stylistic excellences.   As a
miniature (that goes deeper than blue eyes and a snub nose) of
Tess's newly-baptised baby, take this : " Poor Sorrow's cam-
paign against sin, the world, and the devil was doomed to be of
limited brilliancy—luckily perhaps for himself, considering his
beginnings.   In the blue of the morning that fragile soldier and
servant breathed his last, and when the other children awoke,
they cried bitterly, and begged Sissy to have another pretty baby."
All the developing relations of Tess and Clare in the ' Rally '
are done in a pastoral prose, incorporating much dialect, exactly
equal to its task.   There is a wonderful picture of the sleeping
farm, leading up to an even more wonderful one of Tess just
come down from her afternoon's rest :

> She had not heard him enter, and hardly realised his presence
> there.   She was yawning, and he saw the red interior of her
> mouth as if it had been a snake's.   She had stretched one arm
> so high above her coiled-up cable of hair that he could see its
> satin delicacy above the sunburn ; her face was flushed with
> sleep, and her eyelids hung heavy over their pupils.   The brim-
> fulness of her nature breathed from her.

A marvellous ' last paragraph ' has already been quoted in another
connection from the ' end of phase the fourth '.   The bleak and
terrible pictures of Tess and Retty working through autumn and
winter have that earth-contact which is a sixth sense with Hardy :

> Thus Tess walks on ; a figure which is part of the landscape ;
> a fieldwoman pure and simple, in winter guise ; a gray serge
> cape, a red woollen cravat, a stuff skirt covered by a whitey-
> brown rough wrapper, and buff-leather gloves.   Every thread
> of that old attire has become wire-drawn and thin under the
> stroke of rain-drops, the burn of sunbeams, and the stress of
> winds.

Of *Jude the Obscure* sufficient has been said, but it is worth noting how powerful is the aid given to the telling of the story by the quotations, chosen with genius and prefixed to the several books, those for the last book being from the Apocrypha : " And she humbled her body greatly, and all the places of her joy she filled with her torn hair "—and from Browning : " There are two who decline, a woman and I, and enjoy our death in the darkness here ". A very clever and imaginative person who had not read *Jude*, being given all the quotations in their proper arrangement, might reconstruct the story round them.

Hardy makes elsewhere considerable use of quotation. This is perhaps not an integral part of style, but an apt and unforced quotation may give great pleasure, partly intellectual and largely emotional, like that caused by a breath of floating perfume, waking sudden crowds of vague associative memories. And if the quotation is worked into the fabric of the narrative, becoming an organic part of it, the practice has distinct claims to be regarded as an element of style. This is Hardy's method. I do not recollect any novelist who makes such constant and admirable use of the treasures of precedent literature wherewith to enrich his own pages—taking either gems to stud the openings of his chapters, or warm dyestuffs and silken strands to weave into the tissue of his work.

The former procedure is, of course, by no means new. Scott's chapters and Victor Hugo's poems and Addison's essays all employ the artifice—none, I think, more daintily and happily than Hardy in the chapter-headings to *A Pair of Blue Eyes*. Only with the contents of the chapters full in mind can the perfection be recognised of such heraldings as—' A fair vestal throned by the west ', ' Allan-a-Dale is no baron or lord ', ' He set in order many proverbs ', ' Had I wist before I kist ', and the rest. A form of introductory quotation more frequent with modern authors, and well enough handled by Hardy, is the selection of a passage as the text for a whole book. *Jude* has a suggestion of ' purpose ' in " The letter killeth " ; the ironical note in " Vitae post-scenia celant " might have applied to *The Woodlanders* as well as to *The Hand of Ethelberta* ; and what pathetically vain compassion is in the motto of *Tess*—" Poor wounded name, my bosom as a bed shall lodge thee ! "

Yet, for all their aptness, these are but external illustrations, things stuck on from the outside and hence dispensable ; their omission would cause no wounds in the living substance of the tales. It is different when the excerpt is woven into the texture of the narration, as is done by Hardy very frequently, and always with faultless art. I am sure, for instance, that the hopelessly beautiful stanzas of *La Belle Dame* were never put to more exquisite use than by Elfride and Stephen Smith on their frolicsome May expedition. Or consider with what perfect skill the introduction of Newman's ever-beautiful hymn is managed in Chapter LVI of *Far from the Madding Crowd* : how the lines most peculiarly applicable are allowed to swell out to our hearing from the children's voices at precisely the right and natural intervals ; and the appropriateness of the tone and feeling of the hymn to the quietly-approaching autumn-fruition of the love of Gabriel and Bathsheba. Once again, listen to the immortal despairings of Job, whispered forth from the dying lips of Jude the Obscure, the abandoned. What fresh-formed words of lamentation could have had the effect of the syllables of that ancient sorrow ? And as with this, so with the others : besides their fitness for the use made of them, the wealth of intrinsic and associative beauty the quotations carry with them cannot fail to enrich the works into which they are introduced.

Less organic but very delightful in literary, historic and pictorial effect is the first chapter of the earlier Christminster book in *Jude*, where the ghosts of numberless Oxonians, from Jonson and Addison down to Newman and Arnold, move abroad in the streets of the beautiful and venerable city, making comrade of the youth importunate to join their company, with fragmentary passages of their life-works on their lifeless lips. Then, how integral a part of Michael Henchard's character and story are the comminatory verses of the Hundred-and-ninth Psalm that he forces the trembling Casterbridge choir to sing to Wiltshire tune over the unconscious Farfrae, repeating to himself the last fierce words,—

> And the next age his hated name
> Shall utterly deface !

And the nightingale's song that ends *Under the Greenwood Tree*, with " Tippiwit ! swe-e-et ! ki-ki-ki ! Come hither, come hither, come hither ! " is as pretty and apt an echo of the book's title and substance as might well be.

As for single quotations, their ubiquity is only exceeded by their standard of excellence and their catholicity, which embraces Horace and Catullus, Donne, Heine, William Barnes, and a host of others more commonly excerpted. Occasionally we are presented with a complete and most thankworthy poem, like the altogether admirable " ancient and time-worn hymn " sung by the Mellstock choir—

> Remember Adam's fall,
> O thou Man ;

or the very charming ' Point du jour ' that Clym Yeobright sings, so much to the distress of the rebellious Eustacia.

There are some other interesting minor matters of style in Hardy. The first is hardly a minor matter—rather a critical example of all that is best in his style : I mean the numerous places where he is obviously writing with his ' eye on the object '. When he describes an event he sees it happening ; and this is shown in small events better than in large ones. If a vehicle passes a window, Hardy is in the room and knows what effect its passing has on the light. " The sun fell so flat on the houses and pavement opposite Lucetta's residence that they poured their brightness into her rooms. Suddenly, after a rumbling of wheels, there were added to this steady light a fantastic series of circling irradiations upon the ceiling, and the companions turned to the window "—to see Farfrae's new seed-drill. On another occasion, " A yellow flood of reflected sunlight filled the room for a few instants. It was produced by the passing of a load of newly trussed hay from the country, in a waggon marked with Farfrae's name." Hardy is fond of these light effects. A striking bit of observation occurs in *Desperate Remedies*, where Cytherea, calling on Miss Aldclyffe for the first time, is shown into a rather dark room : " but underneath the door communicating with the next room of the suite, gleamed an infinitesimally small, yet very powerful, fraction of contrast—a very thin line of ruddy light, showing that the sun beamed into this room adjoining ". And keeping his eye on it, Hardy says presently that " the golden line vanished in parts like the phosphorescent streak caused by the striking of a match "—someone is approaching the door. How extraordinarily vivid that last image is. Most story-writers would think they had sufficiently entered into the situation when they said " Cytherea heard footsteps in the other room " : Hardy says this too, but he is watching the door with Cytherea, and fascinated by that bright streak. In the same book Cytherea and Springrove are sitting one on each side of a fire : " Its ruddy light shone on the underslopes of their faces, and spread out over the floor of the room with the low horizontality of the setting sun, giving to every grain of sand and tumour in the paving a long shadow towards the door ".

Several others among the instances of minute observation that I have noticed are connected with light-effects. The chiaroscuro of the great bonfire on Rainbarrow is deliberately watched and as faithfully set down—" nostrils were dark wells ; sinews in old necks were gilt mouldings "—and much more too long to quote. This careful elaboration of a scene at which Hardy had obviously been present is less remarkable than the more casual glimpses that show he is on the spot all the time, as it were ! A particularly charming instance is seen, also on Egdon, in those litters of young rabbits that " came out from their forms to sun themselves upon hillocks, the hot beams blazing through the delicate tissue of each thin-fleshed ear, and firing it to a blood-red transparency in which the veins could be seen ". In *The Woodlanders*, when Mrs. Melbury comes out into the night she carries a candle, " the light from which cast a moving thorn-pattern on Marty's face ". (This is even supererogatory observation, for the scene is being done from Marty's point of view, and Marty would hardly be aware of this pattern on her own face !) Melbury watches Giles out of sight under the boughs, " where cobwebs glistened in the now clearing air, lengthening and shortening their shine like elastic needles ". The ear, too, is keenly alert. As Giles sits alone in his house—taking a calm if dismal survey of affairs—" the pendulum of the clock bumped every now and then against the side of the case in which it swung, as the muffled drum to his worldly march ". Only those who have lived with an aged and eccentric grandfather-clock will appreciate the truth of that sound picture. The odd behaviour of another clock was perhaps excusable in the circumstances : when the Durbeyfields are moving Mrs.

Durbeyfield sits on the top of the waggon of furniture, " having in her lap, to prevent injury to its works, the head of the clock, which, at any exceptional lurch of the waggon, struck one, or one and a half, in thin tones ". Nose as well as ear is brought into play when Tess drowses in the midst of another girl's story, " the words of her informant coming to her along with the smell of the cheeses in the adjoining cheese-loft, and the measured dripping of the whey from the wrings downstairs ".

When the four muslin-frocked milkmaids are waiting on the bank for Clare to carry them through the flood, Hardy notes beautifully how " their gauzy skirts had brushed up from the grass innumerable flies and butterflies which, unable to escape remained caged in the transparent tissue as in an aviary ". When Jude looks down a well, Hardy looks with him, and sees the shining disk of water quivering below. And perhaps the most striking instance of all (spoilt for our day by the hideous creeping glycerine of the cinema close-up) is again in *Tess :* " she hardly observed (but her creator does not fail to do so) that a tear descended slowly upon Clare's cheek, a tear so large that it magnified the pores of the skin over which it rolled, like the object-lens of a microscope ".

Notable again is Hardy's skill in simile. It has been observed that metaphor appears to be more natural to poetry than simile : in Anglo-Saxon poetry, for instance, similes are rare, while metaphor is used boldly and profusely. Aristotle even has it that the power of metaphor is the characteristic of genius. In the light of the former observation I should limit this predication to that form of genius known as poetic ; and it appears probable that the simile takes the place in prose (though less character- istically) of the metaphor in poetry—in a word, that the simile is the prose form of the metaphor. A metaphor, like other poetic conceptions, is highly-wrought, instant, born in a flash ; it plucks out the heart of an analogy, but offers no detail. Your simile is of a different order ; it is quieter, it may have been thought out, it may be long and full of detail (even unessential detail, as some of Matthew Arnold's), which a metaphor cannot without changing its name and nature and becoming allegory. Hence the superior fitness of the simile for pure prose—the comparatively tranquil and thoughtful species. Of course, the simile is by no means alien to poetry, but there the figure is either endowed with a fine and far imaginative suggestiveness (as in Shelley) that quite distinguishes it from its more reasonable prose form, or, if deliberately elaborated (as in Arnold and Milton), it belongs, together with the bulk of verse, simply to a bold and beautiful prose.

I have said that Hardy's style is generally pure prose, and his similes are necessarily in the same kind—they seldom (though they sometimes) have the powerful imaginative penetration of the figure in its poetic form. But they arrest the attention and excite admiration by something as near this as prose can go—a very felicitous and original illuminating power, combined with a complete precision and appositeness in all parts of the comparison. (The latter element is perhaps as much a matter of careful choice as of happy instinct ; certainly not all good writers are so successfully exact.)

Observe (and it is worth study) the great simile that accompanies Jude Fawley's ensnarement by Arabella. He is faintly conscious of the woman's degraded nature. " He saw this with his intellectual eye, just for a short fleeting while, as by the light of a falling lamp one might momentarily see an inscription on a wall before being enshrouded in darkness." I think it is not necessary to demonstrate the beauty and perfectness of that image. The vistas of suggestion it opens up are almost poetically infinite ; the faint sound of ' Mene ! mene ! ' in that " inscription on the wall " is almost uncanny.

The stern solemnity of *Jude* seems generally to preclude figures : the only other noteworthy simile in the book is the one that describes with undue optimism Phillotson's position at Christminster, at the glow of which in the night sky the boy Jude is gazing : " in the glow he seemed to see the schoolmaster promenading at ease, like one of the forms in Nebuchadnezzar's furnace ". Nor have I remarked anything at all of the kind in *A Pair of Blue Eyes*, perhaps because the book is so largely composed of dialogue. There are few in *A Laodicean*, but this one makes amends : " Dare, finding himself rather in the way, took his leave as unostentatiously as a cat that has upset the family china ". An even better cat-simile is this, of cooking bacon in *Under the Greenwood Tree :* " The limp rasher hung down between the bars of the gridiron like a cat in a child's arms " : and there is humour again in the description of a rider passing cottages at night, " each cottage, as it revealed its half-buried position by its single light, appearing like a one-eyed night creature watching him from an ambush ".

Other than the first one quoted all these similes have been of the simple descriptive kind. Of a more imaginative order, and worthy to be set by the side of Jude's " falling lamp " is the famous one that was offered as an explanation of Clare's conduct to Tess : " Within the remote depths of his constitution, so gentle and affectionate as he was in general, there lay hidden a hard logical deposit, like a vein of metal in a soft loam, which turned the edge of everything that attempted to traverse it ". Similarly imaginative and revealing are several from *The Wood-landers*. Very powerful, and with something of Hardy's trick of vague premonition, is the one that occurs in the description of the wild night that brings death to Giles Winterborne while Grace lies sleepless in his cabin : " Sometimes a bough from an adjoining tree was swayed so low as to smite the roof in the manner of a gigantic hand smiting the mouth of an adversary, to be followed by a trickle of rain, as blood from the wound ". It is true, it is vivid, and it is fittingly ominous of dread things that may be happening. Then there are two fine astronomical images, both splendidly imaginative, and original : when Fitz-piers, having made the acquaintance of Mrs. Charmond, writes to decline a distant lucrative practice that he has been negotiating for, his motive is said to be " fantastic, glowing, shapeless as the fiery scenery about the western sky " ; and as Winterborne lies delirious his soul seems to be " passing through the universe of ideas like a comet—erratic, inapprehensible, untraceable ". This last has points of resemblance with one in *Far from the Madding Crowd :* " That night Gabriel Oak, beneath the screen of closed eyelids, was busy with fancies, and full of movement, like a river flowing rapidly under its ice ".

Another true and beautiful comparison which is perhaps not quite a simile is this : " In it stood Grace lighting several candles, her right hand elevating the taper, her left hand on her bosom, her face thoughtfully fixed on each wick as it kindled, as if she saw in every flame's growth the rise of a life to maturity ".

The Mayor has some finely imaginative similes. One follows

a simpler descriptive one : " More than once, in spite of her care, Lucetta had been unable to restrain her glance from flitting across into Farfrae's eyes like a bird to its nest. But Henchard was constructed on too large a scale to discern such minutiæ as these by an evening light, which to him were as the notes of an insect that lie above the compass of the human ear." There is something more than an embellishment of style here ! Or here : " Sneering at himself for his weakness, Henchard yet every hour conjectured her actions for the time being . . . till thought of Newson's and Farfrae's counter-influence would pass like a cold blast over a pool, and efface her image ". (Shelley has this simile, with the terms reversed, in *The Recollection*.) Or in this most sublime of all, of Henchard's return to find himself supplanted by Newson : " He rose to his feet, and stood like a dark ruin, obscured by ' the shade from his own soul upthrown ' ". It seems to me that it is a great mind in which the figure of a broken hay-trusser can inspire such an image as that. This of Eustacia on Egdon—" There she stood still, around her stretching the vast night atmosphere, whose incomplete darkness in comparison with the total darkness of the heath below it might have represented a venial beside a mortal sin "—is it somewhat forced, or is it symbolic of what is to happen to Eustacia ? Certainly the next one justifies itself : we have just had the simple but effective simile which tells how Bathsheba, hearing Boldwood approaching, feels that love is " encircling her like a perfume " ; and then, at the farmer's first low quiet words, Bathsheba trembles : " As the consciousness expands on learning that what was fancied to be the rumble of wheels is the reverberation of thunder, so did Bathsheba's at her intuitive conviction ".

Of the plain descriptive kind there are scores, frequently very original and illuminating. Poets have for centuries sought the perfect type of a woman's cheek. In one aspect they may cease their search. " She (Tess) turned her head in the same passive way, and he kissed the other side, his lips touching cheeks that were as damp and smoothly chill as the skin of the mushrooms in the fields around "—a slightly less beautiful but more exact image than Meredith's from *Love in the Valley*, " Her cheeks are cold as cold sea-shells ". A striking simile of a very different kind is that which describes the patch of blood that discoloured the

ceiling after Tess had stabbed D'Urberville : " The oblong white ceiling with this scarlet blot in the midst, had the appearance of a gigantic ace of hearts ". Few but Hardy would have seen the picture like that ! Amazingly beautiful again, and a revelation of truth that few can have discerned till Hardy showed it to them, is this of an opalescent evening sky : " Above, Jupiter hung like a full-blown jonquil, so bright as almost to throw a shade ". Another vivid one of stars seems almost incredible, but only actual observation would have prompted it : " the white stars twinkled so vehemently that their flickering seemed like the flapping of wings ". Not quite so original, but very telling is— " There was a gusty wind ; the sunlight would flap out like a quickly opened fan, throw the pattern of the window upon the floor, and withdraw as suddenly as it had appeared ".

Simple but useful is the simile which tells how the homely Melbury, seeking to protect Grace against the sophisticated Fitzpiers and Mrs. Charmond, " felt as inferior as a savage with his bow and arrows to the precise weapons of modern warfare ". A calculated comparison which succeeds in presenting the idea intended is this of Fitzpiers after he has told Melbury he wants to marry Grace : " When he was gone, Fitzpiers paused, silent, registering sensations, like a man who has made a plunge for a pearl into a medium of which he knows neither the density nor temperature ". And how else could this fact about a thought have been conveyed with equal brevity ?—" ' No wedden this mornen—that's my opinion. In fact, there can't be ', he said abruptly, as if the words were the mere torso of a many-membered thought that had existed complete in his head." On the other hand there is a quaint unexpectedness about the next that makes one suppose Hardy had just noticed the fact about the flower : " In short, beneath all that was charming and simple in this young woman there lurked a real firmness, unperceived at first, as the speck of colour lurks unperceived in the heart of the palest parsley flower ".

Not all Hardy's similes are beautiful. There is an ugly thing in *The Return of the Native*, where we are told of " oozing lumps of fleshy fungi, which at this season lay scattered about the heath like the rotten liver and lungs of some colossal animal "—a perpetration recalling the notorious blot on the loveliness of the

She had advanced to the secret recesses of sensuousness, yet had hardly crossed the threshold of conventionality." This metaphor of Tess illustrates rather than explains : " The sapling which had rooted down to a poisonous stratum on the spot of its sowing had been transplanted to a deeper soil ".

Much detached pleasure can be derived from the many letters that are scattered through the novels. The epistolary form has played an important part in the history of the novel, and, apart from those tales which have been told entirely by this means, many novelists have found it necessary or advisable to make their characters address one another by pen and paper. Not always, however, has the feature been quite successfully handled. The novelist has not always taken care to divest himself of his own corresponding style. There are, for instance, many excellent letters, from many classes of people, in *The Newcomes*, but through nearly all of them there is visible the fine and rich intellect of Thackeray himself. Hardy's letters are much less ambitious, but exhibit much greater differentiation. Their appropriateness is perfect and their variedness almost as great as that of his characters themselves. It is a special kind of dramatic self-repression or projection that is required here, and Hardy possesses the faculty in full degree. Some specimens may be mentioned to show the range and verisimilitude.

The noblest example is the letter written by Tess, abandoned and slaving at the farm-work, to Clare, far away in the New World. Having read it, one gasps, " Heavens ! what *would* a man do who received that letter ? "—a man in Clare's position, thinking and feeling about her as he does, and yet hearing that terrible cry, " Come to me—come to me, and save me from what threatens me ". The art of the composition is perfect—would seem too perfect, but that one knows that an untutored girl, pouring forth her heart unrestrainedly, can indeed attain an exquisiteness of art (including even an amazing perfection of literary form) that the most accomplished stylist may admire. It is a lyric in prose, and shows the brave but fainting soul of Tess as no other means could have done. If, bowing to modern convention, we debar soliloquy from the novel, only the letter can take its place—perform its function of allowing us to see the mind at work in solitude (though of course in letter-writing the solitude

is conditioned). Our thoughts, our very selves, are so different when we are alone from what they are in the most limited and intimate company. Hence, among other reasons, our gratitude for a letter of this sort.

It is, however, few of Hardy's letters that are thus profoundly revealing. They have other excellences. There is another letter in *Tess*, one from Mrs. Durbeyfield to her daughter, appreciation of which can only be expressed in the school-boy phrase, " A regular treat ! " Sentence formation and spelling are idealised, otherwise it is as perfectly natural and probable as it is endlessly comic. Equally humorous in a different way is the letter that contains the Bishop of Melchester's proposal of marriage to Lady Constantine. The episcopal dignity of tone, the logical, un-impassioned exposition of reason and inducement, touched here and there with hints of " varied agitation " and " ardent inward feelings ", the appreciative recognition of the lady's " steady adherence to church principles and interest in ecclesiastical polity ", the suggestion of calling upon her with " a few plain practical rules " which he has " drawn up for their future guid-ance "—all these things go together to hit off admirably the official-moulded personality of the bishop. (There is little at-tempt to invest the prelate in question with a distinct individuality —he is a type, and at that only broadly drawn, and from the outside.) In the same novel are two other good letters, one to Viviette from her brother, clearly differentiated, with its fraternal geniality, its worldly wisdom, and its coarseness of phrase, the other to Swithin from his uncle, which has already been praised for its Mephistophelian logic.

One of the most intensely humorous and satiric things in Hardy is the letter that comes in answer to Jude's enquiries made to certain of the Christminster Professors—he having written to a selected five " whose physiognomies seemed to say to him that they were appreciative and far-seeing men ". As part of the satire the epistle is so delightfully brief that I may quote it entire :

Biblioll College.

Sir,—I have read your letter with interest and judging from your description of yourself as a working-man, I venture to think you will have a much better chance in life by remaining

in your own sphere and sticking to your trade than by adopting any other course. That therefore is what I advise you to do.

Yours faithfully,
J. Tetuphenay.

To Mr. J. Fawley, Stone-mason.

That letter, I believe, needs no idle compliments—it is a gem of purest ray serene.

There are several other letters in *Jude*, among which great interest attaches only to the series of notes that passes between Sue and Phillotson before she leaves him. It is a most extraordinary scene in itself : husband and wife ostensibly teaching through the day in adjoining class-rooms, and amid the routine threshing out the problem of their position, embodying their conclusions at various stages in notes despatched by toddling youngsters. Once more the letters are very characteristic of the writers—Sue with her quotations from Humboldt and the primitive Christians, Phillotson with his insistence on ' respectability ' and the ' preposterousness ' of her notions. Cleverly managed, too, is the revised letter sent by Ethelberta to Christopher Julian—and then there is that wonderful letter to Ethelberta from her father, the old-time butler of genuine worth and solid though sententious sense, not unimproved by contact with his cultured daughter.

A very minor matter is the question of the names of Hardy's characters. Few novelists have cared to label their characters with names distinctive of the qualities the reader is to find in them. The comic dramatists have been less loth, and names like Morose and Millamant are almost too informing, while one like Tom Jones leaves the reader as free from predispositions as the author from the necessity of writing up to a name. Henry James seems to have chosen his names with care but without apparent relevance. Hardy sometimes goes farther. While Tess and Jude travel freely under designations that carry no element of descriptive meaning, their partners, Angel Clare and Sue Bridehead, are marvellously and subtly symbolised by their names. ' Fawley ' is geographical, being the ' real ' name of Jude's native village of Marygreen ; and ' Wessex ' is full of Winterbornes, though the name with its suggestion of bright stainlessness, is an exquisite choice for Giles. ' Phillotson ' is perhaps, and

certainly may fittingly be, a metathesis of 'Philistine'. 'Eustacia' again : no translation of the name is adequate for the rich physical and moral endowments of the Queen of Night, yet, if a word could compass and express her, it would be ' Eustacia '. ' Oak ' is something too obvious, but ' Gabriel ', ministrant, as contrasted with the ' Michael ', militant, of Henchard, is subtler. ' Farfrae ' is a light enough bond on the artist's hands, but ' Mrs. Menlove ', ' Dare ', and ' Paula Power ' are a trifle crude. Much better is ' Ethelberta '—the bright warrior-princess ; and the fairily-fair possessor of the Pair of Blue Eyes could not have been more happily christened than ' Elfride '.

It may seem unnecessary, and it will certainly appear ungracious, to point out in conclusion that Hardy's style is no model of grammatical accuracy. Nor did he ever trouble to acquire this minutest of all the tricks of the trade : *Jude the Obscure* is as full of errors as *Desperate Remedies*. It is not only that the calm of his pages is continually broken by the bickerings of misrelated participles, that his floors grate horribly with the fragments of split infinitives : after all, the second of these two solecisms was not clearly recognised for such in the nineteenth century, and weakness in the first is shared by most writers other than Milton. But Hardy indulges in more original lapses. " Looking altogether a different person from whom she had been hitherto " is an unsuccessful attempt to grapple with an undoubted difficulty. " Personal intercourse with such as her " is not only ugly but uncalled for, since the point of syntax was correctly dealt with fifty pages later in the same book. " Between each word " is illogical, and " Sue and Jude's private minds " again leaves an awkward corner unrounded. The following sentence limps, but can be mended by putting the ' of ' after ' unconscious ' : " They formed a pretty, suggestive, pathetic sight, of whose pathos and beauty they were themselves unconscious, and would not discover till . . . ". And there are errors of a less purely grammatical sort. Surely a quaint ambiguity attaches to this— " enlarged from the size of a man's hand to an area of many feet ". I think the word " kindling " should not have been used for Sue when " enkindling " had already been used of Arabella. There is some looseness in the use of the word " infinite ", and once " individuality " seems to stand for " identity ". It is sheer

slovenliness to write like this : " He thought he would write to Gillingham to inquire his views, and what he thought of his, Phillotson's, sending a letter to her ". And to talk about a crowd being " literally jammed " calls up a picture that even Hardy's penchant for gruesomeness cannot have intended.

All these, however, are mistakes that a schoolmaster could set right, and the same might be said about one or two odd little slips in matters of fact that are discoverable among the multitudinous doings of the novels. On page 165 of *The Mayor* Lucetta asks Elizabeth-Jane to meet her " the first fine day next week ", but on page 170 we read, of this meeting, " the day and the hour came, but a drizzling rain fell ". On page 324 of *The Woodlanders* it is said of Fitzpiers that he fell " and did not move, lying as Melbury afterwards found him "—but Melbury did not find him : he got up and went off to Mrs. Charmond. On page 198 of *Jude* Phillotson takes a boys' school in Shaston, but on page 252 it contains girls as well.

However, it may be that all these departures from rigidity are covered by Hardy's confession of faith : " The secret of a living style lies in not having too much style—in being a little careless, or seeming to be, here and there . . . ".

Hardy was not a born master of style like Thackeray, nor a made one like Stevenson. Like some good orators, he requires a stimulant before eloquence is forthcoming. But when his theme makes demands, as it does more than half the time he is writing, he is inspired by it to heights and splendours not easily excelled.

III. THE PHILOSOPHY OF THE NOVELS

Chapter I

THE IRONY OF FATE: HARDY'S VIEW OF GOD

Terminologically, the expression 'the irony of fate' has a serious defect, in that it personifies 'fate', and thus introduces an element of emotion into the way in which the fact symbolised by the term is received. The fact in question is that man, a recent arrival in the universe, is not yet at home in it. Before he can feel that he 'fits', he has to learn and understand the laws of the country of his (perhaps involuntary) adoption, and then either suit himself to these laws or alter them to suit himself. So far he has done none of these things, so that between desert, desire and endeavour on the one hand, and reward, attainment and achievement on the other, no sort of necessary connection is apparent. But the irony is not always a cruel irony—it is another defect of the phrase that it predisposes those who use it to overlook this. There is irony in Dogberry's watch being the instruments of the saving of Hero, as well as in Romeo's ill-timed arrival at Juliet's tomb. Hence, that aspect of existence on which Hardy lays so marked an emphasis is only half the truth. However, half a truth is better than sheer falsification, and if not all art is emphasis, at least the hyperbole is a legitimate figure of speech. Hardy does indeed invite the criticism that he over-indulges his delight in presenting 'the impishness of circumstance'. It is the only condition under which he allows his subject to carry him away. As an almost invariable rule he is complete, cold master of his material. Neither fear nor enthusiasm can make him swerve an inch from the iron course of the inevitable sequence of things which is his theme. Save only

that on occasion his passion for the Irony of Fate boils up in his heart and results in an event more gratuitously cruel than life itself.   In one sense he idealises his world—he makes it almost ideally cruel.   In another he introduces law, or at least simplifies the existing law : in life it is the unexpected that happens, in the world of Hardy's novel it is the undesirable-unexpected. There are grander conceptions and profounder teachings in Hardy than this of the bitter farce of life, but it is so constantly before him, his mind is so thoroughly impregnated with the idea, that it must be recognised as the most characteristic feature of his philosophy.   His whole novel is built, primarily, upon the doctrine of the Irony of Fate, as commonly understood.

It may appear sometimes that Hardy is manœuvring events with a special purpose, at those moments when his artistic handling of life fails quite to conceal itself.   Real life makes efforts— coincidences that are often neat but not seldom clumsy, ironic strokes that miss their aim as often as they go home.   But Hardy is no mere copyist, no superficial ' realist '.   With him coincidence is not only perfectly timed, but is never meaningless, as it often seems to be in life : once fate has loosed its arrow, there is no evading the barb.

We have already seen that coincidence, the fortuitous, the irony of fate, are part of an art that presents life as a tale of wonder. But the conceptions have a further *raison d'être*.   Most people are aware of the facts, but dismiss them as ' chance ' events, without significance : at most such happenings are held to resemble, say, ornamental studs on the surface of a box ; to Hardy they are the nails that hold the box together.   It is not mere blind casualness that brings it about that when Jude takes Arabella to an inn the picture on the wall is one of Samson and Delilah ; or that when, in the midst of his perturbation of soul, he wanders into church, the choir is singing the *In quo corriget*.

Tess of the D'Urbervilles, a novel of character if ever there was one, may yet stand as an example of the part played in human destiny by a capricious and (to all appearance) malign fate.   The tragedy is largely the outcome of two fatal incongruities.   If Clare could have come before D'Urberville (and he very nearly did) the book would never have been written—by Hardy ; and if, having come late, Clare's nature could have been almost anything

other than what it was, we should have been spared ' The Woman
Pays '.   But the thing goes deeper than this.   If Parson Tringham
had not said ' Good-night, Sir John ' to John Durbeyfield trudging
home that late-May evening, and then allowed himself to be persuaded to explain what he meant by the quaint greeting, the whole
tragic sequence of events would never have got started at all.
And when it had reached its climax, and desolation was about to
fall on Tess, what was there that alone could have saved her ?
That Clare should have been guilty of the same fault as hers.
The condition is fulfilled, but with unspeakable malignancy it
fails to operate : the life-buoy is there, and it sinks before her
eyes.   And of course at all points in the story things just happen
awry instead of just falling out right : her letter, slipped under
Clare's door, goes under the carpet ; the Vicar is out when she
calls—and so on.

And yet, so convincing is the narrator's art, so intensely conceived are the situations, that it is impossible to feel other than
that this is precisely how things would have happened.   Only in
some of the lighter books (particularly in *A Laodicean* and *Two
on a Tower*) does one get an impression of a hobby-horse ridden
too often and sometimes too far.

Generally the fictionist who is true to his trade puts his views
(' impressions ', as Hardy calls them) not into words but into
action.   They are implicit in the story ; but on occasion they
may become explicit, so that all may understand.   Thus, Jude
Fawley is struggling over the first steps in his dream-career of
learning.   " Somebody might have come along that way " and
helped him.   " But nobody did come, because nobody does."
There smacks the Hardy taste—the tone that pervades his whole
work.   Or again, less doctrinaire in form but equally essential
of Hardy is the last remark in the following dialogue, which occurs
when Fanny Robin of *Far from the Madding Crowd* has, by the
aid of a big stray dog (a grand animal), reached a harbour of refuge
in a dying state :

" How did she get here ? " said one of the women.
" The Lord knows ", said the other.
" There is a dog outside ", murmured the overcome traveller.
" Where is he gone ?   He helped me."
" I stoned him away ", said the man.

That is life. One can only hope the dog was a student of Hardy.
For there is no doubt about it—to have read Hardy is to be prepared to meet the injustices of existence with a shrug of contemptuous and unsurprised acceptance ; it is a better training
than average life itself, for it is more concentrated. (It is perhaps
worth remembering that there is no need to spend an exaggerated
sympathy on this dog, or on other animals coming in for treatment
that would cut a human being to the quick. To the dog the
whole episode would mean only that one human had induced
him to go into a strange enclosure and another had indicated that
he wasn't wanted there. The satire—the perfectly just satire—
is aimed at the man.)

Is it pity, is it *saeva indignatio*, or is it a kind of sadism that
leads Hardy to his wantonly cruel endings ?—wantonly cruel
because though the sequence of events is logical it is the author
that starts the sequence and foresees its inevitable end. No
Spanish inquisitor of old time was ever so merciless as the contriver of the conclusion of *Two on a Tower*. After all the sad
follies and vicissitudes of their love, after long despairing separa-
tion and years of sleepless waiting, Swithin St. Cleeve has returned
to find Viviette Constantine in her old place upon the Tower,
like Mariana in the Moated Grange. She is aged, by time and
sorrow, and she perceives his shocked recognition of the change.
With insistent humility she bids him go. " He was a scientist,
and took words literally. There is something in the inexorably
simple logic of such men which partakes of the cruelty of the laws
that are their study." He goes, but pauses to realise she could
not have meant what she said. He returns, clasps and kisses her,
and she dies. " Sudden joy after pain had touched an over-
strained heart too smartly."

I have already referred to the fiendish mockery of the coincidence in *A Pair of Blue Eyes* that sends Knight and Smith down
to Endelstow in the train that bears the body of Elfride. But
the whole burst of the ghastly satire comes upon them only when
they alight, and, after watching the disembarkation of the coffin,
are informed of the identity of the deceased. Nor is the mirthless
laughter of the game still yet. The two men half-quarrel, each
claiming that Elfride died true to him. And so they turn into
the church, and are shown the brass inscription that has been
prepared :

ELFRIDE
Wife of Spenser Hugo Luxellian
Fifteenth Baron Luxellian
Died Feb. 10, 18—.

After a silence :

" Elfride false ", whispered Knight.
" And dead "—

summarising the double irony.—It is almost needless to add that the inn they enter for further information is called the ' Welcome Home '.

It seems unnecessary to multiply examples of so notorious a characteristic, especially as many came naturally to light in the ' general survey '. An artist must present life as he sees it, and this conception of man's destiny here on earth is powerfully present in every novel from Hardy's hand. There are, however, two novels in particular whose tone and tang, bone, substance and soul are of the bitterness of death itself. *Tess* and *Jude* are bitter enough, but they have each another distinct and more important motive. *The Mayor of Casterbridge* and *The Return of the Native*, however, are pre-eminently the bitter novels ; the central purpose which inspired their composition seems to have been a fierce desire to lay bare the mocking cruelty of life. They might be regarded as studies in the Irony of Fate.

The Mayor of Casterbridge is, in name and in fact, ' a story of a man of character ' ; it is likewise a record of hopeless failure and defeat. The juxtaposition indicates the iconoclastic moral of the book. Dilettante dreamers of Utopian worlds are wont to propound the generalisation that ' character moulds circumstances '. Leaving us to remember that a previous circumstance may have already moulded character, Hardy replies with a picture, whose veracity it will be hard to impugn, of a man of surging, single, dominating character—no complex, hesitating Jude, no stricken woman, as Tess—a swift impetuous giant, going down among the walls and arrows of circumstance. You think a man is the author of his own salvation, the ruler of his temporal fate ? Consider the Life and Death of Michael Henchard.

An unusual interpretation of the above dictum brings us closer to the actual place of character in the manipulation of destiny, both in real life and in Hardy. Character is simply one of the

circumstances in a man's environment, but it is of a special and unique nature, inasmuch as it automatically modifies all the other circumstances, affects and changes them in a manner and degree peculiar to itself, so that two men whose outward circumstances were precisely similar would yet each enjoy an environment different in every detail from that of the other. It is in this sense that ' Character is Fate ', as Hardy quotes from Novalis in the book under discussion. It alone does not determine destiny, but it profoundly modifies all the other determining factors.

Thus, it is character that makes Henchard mayor and wealthiest citizen of Casterbridge. But it is his character also which, re-acting upon certain of his circumstances, has brought about several facts which are now part of his destiny, and which are to ensure his fall. The first group of facts are those connected with his drunken exploits at Weydon Priors nineteen years previously. The second are those concerning Lucetta Templeman. Lastly, he has, with impetuous affection, induced to stay in Casterbridge a young Scotsman who was passing through the town and whom Henchard meets and makes manager of his corn business. And it is this last action, the only entirely blameless one, that is the most direct and persistent cause of the Mayor's downfall.

Henchard's character has been delineated and his story out-lined in previous chapters, and it may be that those inadequate settings-forth do not appear to justify my judgment concerning the exceeding bitterness of *The Mayor of Casterbridge*. They probably conveyed the impression only of a man who suffered considerably, but on the whole deservedly, at the hands of fortune and his own errors. No such feeling can remain after reading the novel itself : no words but Hardy's can render the essential irony and agony of it all. It is no mere record of misfortune. It is simply the most hopeless book ever written. The tone of the telling, in the latter half of the story, is stony despair. The slow crushing into lifelessness by the weight of leaden gloom and the recurrent batterings of failure is expounded, in its consummated stage, in the following paragraph, the cold bitterness of which may be paralleled a score of times from the later chapters :

And thus Henchard found himself again on the precise standing which he had occupied five-and-twenty years before. Externally there was nothing to hinder his making another

start on the upward slope, and by his new lights achieving higher things than his soul in its half-formed state had been able to accomplish. But the ingenious machinery contrived by the Gods for reducing human possibilities of amelioration to a minimum—which arranges that wisdom to do shall come *pari passu* with the departure of zest for doing—stood in the way of all that.

The denouncement of fate has the deliberate clearness and steadiness of a concentrated hate so long reflected and so absolutely accepted as inevitable, as to have become a passive but fearless and unflinching scorn. With the conception (of the ingenious machinery) one may compare, in its own buoyant way, the passage in Browning's *Cleon*, where it is asserted that the increased faculties for spiritual joy that come with the development of man's nature are counter-balanced by what the poet calls the fatigue of the climb—the diminution of ' physical recipiency ' for gladness. And we know how Mr. Bernard Shaw proposes to put the ' ingenious machinery ' out of gear by pushing forward our ' prime of life ' by some hundreds of years.

But it is left for Elizabeth-Jane, a woman whose story, though full of vicissitude, is not prominently unhappy, to supply the medium for the most completely Hardian exposition of the grim philosophy of the book. I refer to the passage in which she is dismissed at the end of the novel :

Her position was, indeed, to a marked degree one that, in the common phrase, afforded much to be thankful for. That she was not demonstratively thankful was no fault of hers. Her experience had been of a kind to teach her, rightly or wrongly, that the doubtful honour of a brief transit through a sorry world hardly called for effusiveness, even when the path was suddenly irradiated at some half-way point by day-beams rich as hers. But her strong sense that neither she nor any human being deserved less than was given, did not blind her to the fact that there were others receiving less who had deserved much more. And in being forced to class herself among the fortunate she did not cease to wonder at the persistence of the unforeseen, when the one to whom such unbroken tranquillity had been accorded in the adult stage was she whose youth had seemed to teach that happiness was but the occasional episode in a great drama of pain.

Apart from the very insufficient retreat offered by the sarcastic
' rightly or wrongly ', there is perhaps in the last period a suggestion of a gentler philosophy. The ironic ' persistence of the
unforeseen ' is indeed insisted on, but the ' wonder ' that certain
anticipations of sorrow had been falsified seems to suggest
a possibility of error in the general outlook which the paragraph
demonstrates. That outlook is unquestionably so grey and
desperate that one would fain deny its truth. The mockery of
life in the face of man's hopes is only too often a fact ; but is it
indeed equally true that no human being deserves less than is
given ? Some of us get a good deal out of life, even though
but a fragment of what we aim at. But perhaps that question
will be more ready for consideration in a later chapter, when
we have examined some other components of the Hardian
equipment.

The Return of the Native is less emphatically a record of disappointment, though not less powerfully a picture of disillusion
and incongruity. It is no longer a study of a single mortal writhing on the toasting-fork of fate, but a wider puppet-stage with the
devil visibly at work on a greater complication of strings. There
is much irony of event, but the grand tragedy of this tale rises
out of incongruity of situation. On all sides we have greatness
bound in warring union with dissimilar greatness, virtue looking
on truth and failing to recognise it, splendour attracted by taw-
driness : we have Clym and Eustacia, Eustacia on Egdon, Mrs.
Yeobright and her son, Wildeve and Eustacia. Here is Egdon,
realm of night, and Eustacia, Queen of Night, born to reign on
Egdon like a rich jewel in an Ethiop's ear. And yet she hates
Egdon, hates Nature, and her fiery soul longs for the surface
brilliance, the shallow, hollow beauty and vanity of Paris, the
paltry excitements of promenade flirtations at a fashionable
watering-place ; an elegant summer suit eclipses for her the qualities of manhood clad in rougher raiment. Oh, the pity of it,
the cruel pity of it ! Might one not weep to see her go at last to
Wildeve—bemoaning her fate, yet going ; vehemently declaring
she has tried to be ' a splendid woman ' and exclaiming against
the cruelty of her situation in an ill-conceived world ? Grievous
the error, verily. Eustacia—married to Clym Yeobright, " her
perfect complement "—on Egdon : what more had the world

to give ? But she demands " life—music, poetry, passion ", and sees them, not here, but in Paris and Weymouth !

The leaven of Eustacia's sensuous passion pervades the book, and is the source or foundation of the dual incongruity that forms the tragedy of Eustacia's life—her seclusion upon Egdon, and her marriage to Clym Yeobright. I have pointed out in an earlier chapter the austere, celibate nature of the great Heath. It is a place which, to one whose love was akin to the cold sea, the pure stars, the windy sky, would be heaven upon earth, a perfect home, a constant inspiration. To Eustacia, seeking an outlet for her smouldering fires, it is a hell of mere voidness and solitude, oppression and restraint. Just so it is this side of her character that gives rise to the antagonisms between her and Clym. In other respects they are splendid mates, and each is worthy of the other. But with Yeobright, passion, as she knows it, is an incident, an interlude. He loves her, but his passion is high, " chaste as that of Petrarch for his Laura ". Passion to him is not all in all ; it is something that is to lift his being into a higher atmosphere where the rest of life is not forgotten but ennobled, apotheosized. Their conceptions of conjugal life are antithetical. She imagines, first, a world-oblivious rapture (with amazing self-projection she had read in his passing Good-night " the capacity for all emotional things "), and second—though hardly less important—an introduction to the whirl of fashion's delights. He regards her rather as a splendid help-meet in the great world-work he has set his heart upon, though when he tries to put his view of her into practical words (" she would make a good matron in a boarding school ") he speaks nothing but blatant bathos, and it is she who is right and reasonable when she declares " there is not that in Eustacia Vye which will make a good home-spun wife ". But provided he can raise his fellow-men, by whatever humble means, with her beside him, he is content. She catches a momentary glimpse of one side of this veritable love when she says, " I would rather live with you in a hermitage here (on Egdon) than not be yours at all ", but it is a fleeting phrase, half-meant, and Paris is the heaven she dreams of. Her fury at his enforced occupation of furze-cutting is almost ludicrous in its small-mindedness. He himself perceives that her tastes touch his own only at infrequent points. For him, he is

intellectually constructed, and though he " can rebel, in high Promethean fashion, against the gods and fate ", his mind is elastic enough to take in mishap as well as good fortune, while his outlook embraces with gladness the solitudes of Egdon and the simplicity of its dwellers, but passes contemptuously over the banalities of Paris. Hence, peers in grandeur of personality, Yeobright and Eustacia are not more alike than marble and molten gold, and their attempt at union is necessarily fraught with the tragedy of divergent aims.

An incongruity no less deep has already been shown existing between Yeobright and his mother, and he soon recognises the difficulties of his situation. " Three antagonistic growths had to be kept alive : his mother's trust in him, his plan for becoming a teacher, and Eustacia's happiness." Fate to some extent vetoes the second ; the other two break down from the difficulties inherent in the natures of the subjects. There is also Wildeve and his absurd unworthiness of Eustacia's condescension. As a matter of fact, once Yeobright has appeared on the scene Wildeve plays a very small part in determining Eustacia's destiny. It is her hatred of Egdon, her disappointment at the fall of her Paris schemes, her rage at her husband's lowly occupation, and the quarrel due to the death of Mrs. Yeobright, that drive her on to her fatal flight. Wildeve is used only as the somewhat despised instrument of escape. That he should have allured her at all, should have been allowed to approach and pay court to her, is one of the most painful unfitnesses of the story.

Thus much of the characters, and the pity of their multiple misunderstandings. The irony of events becomes prominent in the latter half of the book. It is just when Mrs. Yeobright has at last determined to take the great step that will put everything right that the demon of mischance begins his game, and plays it out to the death. We must guard against attributing the whole sorry sequence to fate. We are told of Eustacia that " instead of blaming herself for the issue she laid the fault upon the shoulders of some indistinct, colossal Prince of the World, who had framed her situation and ruled her lot ". This allotment of responsibility is not quite impartial. Indeed, though Mrs. Yeobright's death is the outcome of a series of ironic juxtapositions, these in themselves were not necessarily fatal but for human badness

or weakness—dilatoriness, fecklessness, obstinacy. Nevertheless the grand satire is in the fact that from whatever cause, certainly from no definite and deliberate human motive, at the very moment when the well-intentioned advance is made, events so fall out that the position is beaten back to a stage very much worse than before, and with appalling consequences.

For a time irony dies down, leaving us to watch the results of earlier fatalities, but soon after Clym has driven out Eustacia fate recommences its flippant jests. His wrath subsides, his love conquers his reason, and he writes to her to ask her to come back. The letter miscarries by a few minutes. Clym, unconscious of this, sits in his house, late, lone, like Browning's householder, awaiting the knock, call, cry. The night is of the worst—the heath is beaten by wind and rain. " The little gate in the palings before his dwelling continually opened and clicked together again, but when he looked out eagerly no one was there ; it was as if invisible shapes of the dead were passing in on their way to visit him." At length a woman's footstep ; he flushes hot—" Surely it is Eustacia ". He opens the door, and it is Thomasin come to tell him of Eustacia's flight with Wildeve, the flight that ends in drowning.

The Return of the Native is a less desperate book than *The Mayor ;* it is not so fiercely emphatic of ' the grimness of the general human situation '. The hero himself does not go down into utter darkness, and one may imagine there is yet before him much opportunity of finding a serener and more satisfactory world. But however that be, the doctrine is clear—that when circumstance so wills it the strife of man is unavailing, and that, on the whole, circumstance does so will it.

In the microcosm of Hardy's novels there is unquestionably a power—conscious or unconscious, personal or impersonal—that controls, influences, at least hampers and hinders the doings of man. The conception is so universally and consistently present that it is difficult not to see in it a main strain of Hardy's philosophy. He does indeed protest, over and over again, that that conception, like others, is to be regarded as the record of an impression not of a conviction, but the change of name alters nothing, for an artist's impressions are his convictions, and an impression that persists throughout a lifetime is likely to have

hardened into a belief.   Moreover, the outlook not infrequently,
as I have said, becomes explicit.   For instance, in that perhaps
minor matter of coincidence, Hardy's own deduction from observed facts is twice stated, once more casually in *A Laodicean*—
" . . . by a coincidence common enough in fact, though scarcely
credited in chronicles . . . " ; and with more deliberation in the
passage already quoted from *A Pair of Blue Eyes*.   On the
larger question he is no less definite.   It is Yeobright who
speaks, but he seems to speak for Hardy when he tells Eustacia,
" It is no use hating people.   If you hate anything you should
hate what produced them."   To which Eustacia, " Do you
mean Nature ? I hate her already."   As a matter of fact
Yeobright, if pressed, would doubtless have withdrawn the word
' hate ', with its implication of a personal ' producer ' : is it
possible to hate a wall that falls on you ?   This, too, is put suc-
cinctly in *The Hand of Ethelberta*, where it is said of Christopher
Julian—" Unable, like many other people, to enjoy being satirised
in words because of the irritation it caused him as aimed-at
victim, he sometimes had philosophy enough to appreciate a
satire of circumstance, because nobody intended it ".   Put again
with an effect even of finality towards the conclusion of *Jude
the Obscure*.   Poor Sue has been beaten from her intellectual
position :

> Affliction makes opposing forces loom anthropomorphous ; and
> those ideas were now exchanged for a sense of Jude and herself
> fleeing from a persecutor.
>   " We must conform ! " she said mournfully.   " All the
> ancient wrath of the Power above us has been vented upon us,
> His poor creatures, and we must submit.   There is no choice.
> We must.   It is no use fighting against God ! "
>   " It is only against man and senseless circumstance ", said
> Jude.

But these two passages are insufficiently corrective of the general
outlook conveyed by a multitude of others expressing a resentment so profound as to imply at least an ' impression ' of some
cause not quite impersonal.   Sometimes indeed the resentment
takes the form only of a too widely extended application of terms,
as in *Tess* :

And yet these harshnesses are tenderness itself when compared with the universal harshness out of which they grow ; the harshness of the position towards the temperament, of the means towards the aims, of to-day towards yesterday, of hereafter towards to-day.

More usually it looks through Hardy's constant personification of the Cause of Things : " Part of (Henchard's) wish to wash his hands of life arose from his perception of its contrarious inconsistencies—of Nature's jaunty readiness to support unorthodox social principles "—(which is rather like beating a walnut tree because it won't grow nut-crackers) ; or this of Jude—" And then he again uneasily saw, as he had latterly seen with more and more frequency, the scorn of Nature for man's finer emotions, and her lack of interest in his aspirations ".

Hardy has in the past come in for a great deal of condemnation for this relentless flogging of the gods. The novelist himself has told us of the ' gentleman who turned Christian for half an hour the better to express his grief that a disrespectful phrase about the Immortals (" The President of the Immortals had ended his sport with Tess ") should have been used '. It is protested that continual dissatisfaction with life is impious. Hardy, and those who think with him, are admonished to make the best of what is given them, and not to grumble. To make the best of things is a matter of policy, not of reverence or religion ; but that the second exhortation, not to complain, follows from the first, or is a necessary article in the creed of righteousness. appears in no wise to be true. A certain discontent with the world is as sure a piece of internal evidence as we have of the divine nature of the soul, as distinguished from the mass of sluggish and slavish existences which, so far as we know, accept their half-loaf without a murmur. No mere part of the order of things could thus recognise and rebel against its imperfections.

> Only, *for man*, how bitter not to grave
>   On his soul's hands' palms one fair good wise thing
> Just as he grasped it !

exclaims Browning the optimist. " Ah ! " sighs the careless epicure in life's present pleasures, rising for a moment to a

sublimer comprehension of a vaster panorama than his own
' predestined plot of dust,'

> Ah Love ! could thou and I with Fate conspire
> To grasp this sorry Scheme of Things entire,
>   Would we not shatter it to bits—and then
> Remould it nearer to the Heart's Desire !

And it is the exceeding fervour of his heart's desire, it is his
passionately vivid vision of ' the well-judged plan of things ',
that calls forth so untiringly the flash of Hardy's bitterness and
irony against the innumerable flaws in ' the ill-judged execution '.

If at this day there is any criticism to be brought against it,
it is that the indictment is too sweeping to be philosophical, too
impassioned to be directed against an impersonal Cause. For
its over-comprehensiveness we may perhaps find an explanation
when we come to deal with Hardy's pessimism. Its impassioned
quality, and the nature of its objective, will call for larger treatment under the poetry ; but while much may be accounted for
by the sensitiveness of Hardy's soul, there remains a large sur-
plus of bitter feeling that seems to me to be due to the transitional
place occupied by Hardy and the last quarter of the nineteenth
century generally. The Jewish and ' Christian ' God no longer
existed—for men like Hardy, but his place had not yet been ade-
quately filled. " I have been looking for God for fifty years ",
Hardy wrote, " and think that if he had existed I should have
discovered him. As an external personality, of course—the
only true meaning of the word ". But the negative proof was
not sufficient to wipe the conception out of the Victorian mind,
and there was still a sense that God *might* be there. The venom
of Hardy's satire seems wasted on an impersonal Cause of
Things. He seems to be trying to call God's attention to the
world : " If Law itself had consciousness, how the aspect of its
creatures would terrify it, fill it with remorse ". He still speaks
in terms of an anthropomorphic Creator : " Yes, man has done
more with his materials than God has done with his ". And
returning to the novels, there is at least a contingent Listener
implied in this complaint over the sorrows of Eustacia :

The gloomy corner into which accident as much as indiscretion
had brought this woman might have led even a moderate

partisan to feel that she had cogent reasons for asking the Supreme Power by what right a being of such exquisite finish had been placed in circumstances calculated to make of her charms a curse rather than a blessing.

And later in the same book there is a paragraph in which Hardy not only shows Clym Yeobright looking back on his life, but adds a comment of his own :

He did sometimes think he had been ill-used by fortune, so far as to say that to be born is a palpable dilemma, and that instead of men aiming to advance in life with glory they should calculate how to retreat out of it without shame. But that he and his had been sarcastically and pitilessly handled in having such irons thrust into their souls he did not maintain long. It is usually so, except with the sternest of men. Human beings, in their generous endeavour to construct a hypothesis that shall not degrade a First Cause, have always hesitated to conceive a dominant power of lower moral quality than their own ; and, even while they sit down and weep by the waters of Babylon, invent excuses for the oppression which prompts their tears.

Here is a suggestion, by implication, that the First Cause is a power of low moral quality that oppresses mankind. We know from Hardy's letters and journals that intellectually he occupied a position quite other than this, but throughout his creative work, both in prose and in verse, there is a latent philosophy of revolt and revenge. Just as Milton, while fully aware of the new Copernican theory of the universe, based his epic on an exploded but more picturesque cosmogony, so perhaps Hardy felt that the time had not yet come when a corpus of novels that claimed to be ' an impression ', if nothing more than an impression, ' of country life and passions ', could have behind it a conception of God that not one in twenty of his readers would understand—an Unconscious Will, unmoral, knowing neither good nor evil, and gradually becoming aware of itself. But God as Fate, as Providence, as something to be circumvented or endured —this was a belief, an instinct, as old as man himself, and likely to die only with him. This is the faith of Hardy's people, simple and sophisticated, and the metaphysical structure behind the Wessex novels is but this ancient code transmuted by its

passage through a strong, sensitive, brooding mind.   Hardy gave back to the common man his own religion artistically shaped, polished, and sharpened to a hard, fine cutting edge.

On the irony, as such, of fate, one word more. Let it not be dreamed that this outlook, this assertion that the fault is largely in our stars if we are underlings, is merely a feature of an unwholesome and decadent modern philosophy. You shall find it declared and accepted in the fresh and exhilarating dawn of literature. Consider but the warrings of the *Iliad*, how every fight is spoiled by those interminable, interfering, preposterous gods. Even the fight we have looked forward to throughout the epic— the Hector-Achilles duel—is a fraud : Athene ' blows aside ' the doomed Trojan's spear. But that word ' doomed ' gives the clue to all the annoying supernatural machinery. Homer, the first of the ancients, is at one with Hardy, the first of the moderns, in knowing and showing the relentlessness and hopelessness of Fate. The intermeddling of the gods is Homer's crude and vivid method of indicating how little avail man's prowess and will to effect aught in life on earth. The picturesque symbolism is, as I say, so crude as to make a fair-minded observer uncomfortable : the intervention is done with such indecent openness ! There are doubtless many who are even more disturbed by Hardy's less elementary but no less obvious and continual presentation of the same doctrine.

[*Note.*—Mr. W. H. Gardner, in his valuable study of *The Mayor of Casterbridge* (English Association Pamphlet No. 77), complains that I am " grossly misleading " on the part played by fate in Henchard's downfall. He says, " Mr. Duffin does not show that Henchard's fall was due much more directly to the rivalry of Farfrae "—than to the Weydon Priors folly. If Mr. Gardner will read my ' first ', ' second ' and ' *lastly* '—" the most direct and persistent cause ", on pages 113-114 of the first edition or pages 100-101 of the second (I am not sure which edition he was using), he will see that any misleading I have done was unintentional. The facts are reproduced, more briefly, in the foregoing chapter (page 188).—Mr. Gardner's essay includes an interesting parallel between Henchard and Lear.]

CHAPTER II

HUMAN NATURE : HARDY'S VIEW OF MAN

IN an earlier chapter we found much to admire in the skill with which Hardy presents the persons of his novel, and perhaps the skill is all that matters : perhaps the kind of person he has chosen to present is of little importance. This at all events seems to be the view taken by novelists. Writing to comment on a *Forsyte* essay, John Galsworthy expressed some impatience with discussion of the virtues and vices of his characters. " I suppose an author is incapable of liking or disliking his characters, and so can't understand how they affect other people. To me they are only badly or well made." So, too, it is to be supposed that a painter takes as much pleasure in depicting a dead rabbit as in depicting Psyche or an apple tree in bloom. It is the more illuminating that only in this latest war-diseased age has there been a general tendency among both novelists and painters to fill their books and pictures with ugly subjects and evil people. Something at least may be deduced about a writer, and about the age in which he lived, and about the view of human nature held by him and his age, by a consideration of the kind of people he chose to represent—their quality, their worth, their level in the scale of being. But how adjudge this level ? Tabulating their ' virtues and vices ' will not do, for there is no accepted order of merit in either virtues or vices ; moreover, one man's virtue is another man's vice, and from some not impossible angles some criminals may appear to stand higher than some saints.

There is a pleasant variation on the game of ' scandal ' in which you classify your friends according to their possession of Character, Intellect or Personality. This comes nearer to the kind of classification we want, but is useless in itself because the **three**

qualities named are approximately equal in value. Let me suggest a different analysis. The nature of man is fourfold : the
course and quality of his life are governed by four inward forces
or faculties. These are Passion, Reason, Emotion and Instinct ;
and they can be placed in an order of excellence, as they are here
—descending. Passion (an ambiguous term, but no other con-
notes the necessary intensity) is used with a spiritual signification,
denoting the senses of the soul, the ' unreasoning elements in the
higher nature of man ' (to misquote Jowett), and covering Love,
Religion, and Poetry—all three words being intended in a mys-
tical sense. Reason or Intellect needs no defining, but its second
place is assured. The Emotions are those urgings to action,
those promptings of the mind through the flesh, that are due to
our being a higher type of animal, while the Instincts—hunger,
sex, the will to live, so many others—arise from the fact that we
are just animals after all. This classification and valuation of
the elements of human nature may be taken as the gauge wherewith to measure any given presentment of mankind, whether in
life or in literature. It will be found that the scheme is recognised
by Hardy : the fourfold tabulation, with its falling rank, is implicit in his pages. My task, after illustrating this fact, will be
to conduct an investigation into Hardy's view of the relative
prevalence of the higher and lower kinds in human nature on the
whole. For it is clear that if he presents us with a world in
which Reason and the Passions play a prominent part we shall be
able to say that his conception of man is a lofty one ; whereas, if,
on the other hand, he shows us men and women ruled chiefly by
the less exalted senses it will be evident that his view of human
nature is not more complacent than we have seen his view of an
immanent God to be.

Conspicuous among the protagonists of Hardy's stage is the
pale, fine form of Angel Clare. I believe it will not be disputed
that the hold this man has on life, whether it be complete or
precarious, is essentially spiritual, ideal, free from grossness.
Indeed, the charge most frequently brought against him is that
his spirituality eclipses his humanity. His renunciation of Tess
is in direct contradiction of the tendencies of his emotional
desires, and is sanctioned by a voice that overrules even the
demands of reasonableness—the voice of the high passion which

has been vividly evident throughout the whole progress of his love. He is not guided solely by passion. Reason enters when he attempts to argue his position, and, forasmuch as Passion's methods proceed on a special logic, reason goes hopelessly astray —his defence of his course is on the whole mistaken. Passion's child, then, is Clare, and, be he lovable or not, there is surely no contesting the celestial beauty of his figure.

Clym Yeobright is again a man who yields little allegiance to emotion, and much to the nobler spirit sort. His love for Eustacia we have seen to be lofty and untainted by flesh. Nevertheless his general comprehension of truth is obtained rather through the medium of Reason than through that of Passion. His plan of life is closely considered and thought out, and from a nobly rational point of view. It is reason that brings him from Paris, formulates his didactic projects, gives him endurance under misfortune, and plays a considerable part, though a part shared by emotion, in his quarrel and attempted reconciliation with Eustacia. Hence, though his personality is great and strong, it has little of the supernatural brightness that illuminates Angel Clare.

In Farmer Boldwood, on the other hand, we find emotions of such fiery intensity as to partake of the transcendental nature of Passion. It is obviously unnatural and dangerous that the emotions, which have so great a hold on the physical being, should take upon themselves the fierce attributes of the movements of the soul, and the result in Boldwood's case is just what might be expected. His passionate emotions rend him like the possessing spirits of old, and hurl him to ruin, in contrast to the serene persistence of Gabriel Oak's life, in which emotion, hardly less strong than Boldwood's, is calmed, restrained and tempered by the reason which is the real ruling power of his being.

Giles Winterborne, of *The Woodlanders*, is the only male character besides Angel Clare that I should call definitely Passionate. All the essentials of high, pure passion will be readily recognised in the love of Winterborne for Grace Melbury. The portrait of him is too unsubstantial for close investigation ; only this aspect and the kindred one, his perfect affinity with Nature, are developed. Looking back on the story, indeed, one sees him as a woodland spirit, half-disappearing among the moving

tree-stems, half-indistinguishable from the motion and sound of breeze-lifted leaves and the elvish interweaving of the shadows.

If we turn now to Jude Fawley, we find a man in whom Passion is comparatively unimportant. His yearning for knowledge and academic distinction, though it has a passionate intensity, is a direct product of his strong brain, and Jude is primarily a creature of Intellect. His complex nature includes strong emotions and a noticeable dash of animalism, but these elements are well under the control of his mind. His mind retains its level throughout ; there are no storms or subsidings : and this is the mark of the reasonable nature. However, the only purely intellectual figure among Hardy's men is Henry Knight of *A Pair of Blue Eyes*. To him life appeals only in so far as it provides food for thought. His very love is mathematical, and when, on examination, it does not meet his requirements, it is rejected like an unsatisfactory solution to a problem. (Yet, with that inconsistency that is said to give ' roundness ' to a character, he once spent a whole day choosing ear-rings for Elfride.) Similarly, but in a less dignified way, the canny commercial faculties of Farfrae are the fruits of a reasoning nature, but his much more interested motives, and his business-like dabblings in amorous stock, indicate that at the bottom he is an alloy of reason and emotion, neither of a very high order. John Loveday is a nice balance of reason and emotion (unlike brother Bob, whose loose emotions run riot gaily uncontrolled). Swithin St. Cleeve is a young man of predominating intellect, and though the worm emotion bores away at his base it makes little effect on the hard bright substance of which he is made. Dare, of *A Laodicean*, I suppose is guided by reason, but it is a low type of reason in the service of emotions lower still.

Coming now to the third division in our classification, we find several men in whom Emotion predominates. Such is Stephen Smith, the contrasting rival of the intellectual Knight. Youthful sentiment and romance almost always spring solely from emotional flutterings, and Smith is the type of the attractively romantic blue-eyed youth. Even his praiseworthy control of his emotions is founded on the emotional basis of humility and good-feeling. Wildeve in *The Return of the Native* is not dissimilar, save that a dash of hot blood in him has turned his tendencies in an evil

' Sensitive Plant ', and Browning's less-known but even worse (because more uncalled-for and unerased) comparison of a sun-flecked cloud to a dead whale pecked by white birds ! Equally unpleasant is the description of the stone face carved over a Casterbridge archway, at which " generations of boys had thrown stones, aiming at its open mouth ; and the blows thereof had chipped off the lips and jaws as if they had been eaten away by disease ". One would imagine, too, that many a less painful, as well as more natural, simile might have been found for the setting sun than to say that it rested on the hill " like a drop of blood on an eyelid ".

I will call the closure upon this array of specimens by quoting one of the neatest and most characteristic of all Hardy's similes. Bathsheba has been lengthily and anxiously demonstrating to the sceptical mind of Gabriel Oak the worthiness of Sergeant Troy. She eagerly makes her last point—Troy's avowedly constant but secret and shy attendance at church. " This supreme instance of Troy's goodness fell upon Gabriel's ears like the thirteenth stroke of a crazy clock. It was not only received with utter in-credulity as regarded itself, but threw a doubt on all the assurances that had preceded it." The comparison is unexpected, almost grotesque, yet easy and natural, and of unimpeachable aptness. One may observe that Meredith, whose bold prose makes greater use of metaphor than of simile, sometimes forces the analogy of a fantastic comparison. Thus, " We may compare a lawyer to the rustic finger on a fiddle-string for the murdered notes that you get out of your practical instrument ". The likeness prob-ably occurred quite spontaneously to Meredith's recondite and humorous mind, but it has the appearance of having been sought for, an impression seldom caused by a simile of Hardy's.

It is interesting to note that Hardy felt compelled to call in the aid of metaphor in putting before us those two characters—unlike any others in the novels—Boldwood and Eustacia. Of Boldwood : " Nobody knew entirely (what Boldwood was) ; for though it was possible to form guesses concerning his wild capabilities from old floodmarks faintly visible, he had never been seen at the high tides which caused them ". And of Eustacia : " As far as social ethics were concerned Eustacia approached the savage state, though in emotion she was all the while an epicure.

12

direction, whereas Smith's were straight for the good. The vagaries of Fitzpiers show him emotionally built, with a strong tendency towards degeneration into instinctive animalism. His training has cultivated in him a strain of intellectual interests, but they are followed out with an epicurean and dilettante luxuriousness that is far enough from the austere delights of reason. Henchard, too, I think, falls under this division, though in his grim nature the emotions are so hard and permanent as to resemble the forces of intellect, while, as in the case of Boldwood, they are endowed with a grandeur more properly belonging to Passion.

On the lowest level there seem to be only two men whose lives are mainly motived by the instinct for animal gratification— Troy and Alec D'Urberville. Neither is unredeemed, both being capable of some degree of generous emotion.

I reserve the women for special treatment, but they will be found amenable to the same classification (with a line of deep and definite demarcation between the intellectual and non-intellectual types, not to be seen on the male side). I believe it to be a sound deduction from facts observed that human nature in Hardy, as in the world, is built of these four great groups of elements, and that each individual is characterised by being substantially of one group, more or less alloyed by admixture from one or more of the others. I do not doubt that to many this view will seem to be an absurdly rigid application of a very narrow formula to a subject far too complex to submit to such handling. I would point out, however, that the greatest conceivable complexity is ultimately reducible to order, and that the formula attempted here is elastic enough, and capable of infinite variation.

Now, it may be that ideal human nature would contain these four groups of elements in equal, or at least in carefully balanced proportions. Be that as it may, my purpose is to see which of them, if any, preponderates in human nature as portrayed by Hardy. Is Humanity, as he sees it, Passionate (that is spiritual), Reasonable, Emotional, or Animal, in the main ?

The question with regard to the last of the four factors may be quickly disposed of. Less than fifty years ago Hardy's novels were being publicly burnt by bishops and blushed over in private by many an anxious parent.   A reputable critic found it possible to describe *Tess of the D'Urbervilles* as ' sensational pornography '. What justification was there for all the puritanical fury ?   The story of *Tess* is (there is no hiding it) founded on a gross *faux pas*, renewed under the most outrageously vulgar circumstances later in the book.   In *Jude the Obscure*, the hero's *liaison* with Arabella Donn is motived by instincts almost entirely animal on both sides, and one of the tragedies of the book lies in the entering of Jude and Sue into sexual relations slowly led up to.   *The Return of the Native* was shown to be full of animalism in a less obvious sense : it is the tragedy of the revolt of human nature against close confinement within somewhat cold and rigid spiritual conditions. There is a betrayal and an illegitimate child in *Far from the Madding Crowd ;* there is also Troy, who should be (but, quaintly enough, is not) enough to put any book on the Philistine Index.   Fitzpiers' relations with Suke Damson in *The Woodlanders* are improper, and considerable influence is exerted over the action of *Two on a Tower* by the fact that St. Cleeve and his secretly married Lady Constantine found it impossible to limit their mutual interest to a sympathy of the spirit.   Truly, the gentle moralists had a case !

And yet, what a case it seems to be now !   Putting aside all question of comparison with the abnormal sex-obsession that floods the fiction of to-day, we find no explanation at all (other than a pathological one) for the incoherent vituperation.   Suppose one could put the facts given in the previous paragraph, among the bulk of the Hardy material, in the form of percentages ?   The earth is none the less a sphere, though Alps and Andes break the surface.   Hardy is avowedly dealing with ' country life and passions '.   And even were his subject the whole of society, could he truthfully reflect a smaller proportion of grossness ? Above all, let us get the Hardy world into perspective, and by broad and temperate observation, seek an estimate of love as it appears there, and of the whole relation between the sexes. From consideration of the great love affairs of his novels—those of Jude and Sue, Clare and Tess, Oak and Bathsheba, Clym and Eustacia, Winterborne and Grace Melbury—with corroboration and addition from the lesser cases, one arrives at some such conclusions as those that follow.

Love at first sight, as generally understood, is a myth.

Love is not so light
As straight to burn at first beholder's sight.

(Yet, since human nature is variable enough to spoil all generalisation, Picotee, whose love is as real as it is charming, is quite hopelessly caught in the toils at her first meeting with Christopher, one of the admirers of her sister Ethelberta, but Picotee's prize in the end.)   Nevertheless, when two people, destined for love (for Hardy constantly implies the prearranged nature of love), come for the first time within the range of each other's influence, there is set up in each a more or less unrecognised premonition in the form of a unique interest and attraction.   This, if circumstances permit, rapidly develops and very soon finds itself on a swift and irresistible course of increasing pace, which never thereafter turns back or ceases.   This attraction, now become ' love ', strengthens with intimacy, and induces an all-pervading union of sympathy and common interests ; or, failing this sympathy and interest, the love does not subsist and continue to grow, however, otherwise intense.   Love is not violently demonstrative, and provokes emotional outbursts only at intervals : on the whole, love is quietly content with the presence of the beloved.   Indeed, Hardy definitely asserts, " Of love it may be said, the less earthly the less demonstrative.   In its absolutely indestructible form it reaches a profundity in which all exhibition of itself is painful ". This may possibly be true : but somehow one would rather it were not !   After some continuation it gradually becomes a great and divine companionship, a grand camaraderie, which is the crystallised and permanent form of passion.   This must be achieved, for it alone is the impregnable basis of an eternal love. Sex instinct, in its primary form, seems to play a small and unessential part.   The flaming thing called love and passion by the eighteenth-century novelists is unrecognised, except in Arabella Donn and, in a totally different way, Eustacia Yeobright.   On the kind of ' love ' that has its origin almost entirely in primitive sex Hardy is pleasantly ironic :

Yet here Grace made a mistake, for the love of men like Fitzpiers is unquestionably of such quality as to bear division and transference.   He had indeed once declared, though not to her, that on one occasion he had noticed himself to be possessed by five distinct infatuations at the same time. If this were true, his differed from the highest affection as the lower orders of the animal world differ from advanced organisms, partition causing not death but a multiplied existence. He had loved her sincerely in his selfish way, and had by no means ceased to love her now. But such double and treble-barrelled hearts were naturally beyond her conception.

Shelley seems to have held Fitzpiers', not Hardy's, view :

> True love in this differs from gold and clay,
> That to divide is not to take away !

Love appears generally to be reciprocated, and in the same kind, in contradiction of Coleridge's assertion (which is perhaps correct) that " the man's desire is for the woman ; the woman's desire is seldom other than for the desire of the man ". Love is patient, and can wait, living for long years on little response or none, knowing that love for love must be the answer in the end. Only in one case did this result not come to pass : perhaps John Loveday went away because he knew that if he stayed it would. Parenthood is unimportant : indeed, it is a weakness of Hardy's presentation of love that he hardly ever allows his love stories to continue into the testing time of marriage at all. There was, too, a vital element missing from the conception—at least insufficiently stressed—till the defect was remedied in the last few novels. The quality of *tenderness* is not clearly present till we find it in Giles Winterborne's love for Grace—(there is a lovely touch in *The Woodlanders* that makes one remember the love-lyrics and exclaim, How this man knows love !—" . . . the discovery sent a scarlet pulsation through her for the moment. However, it was only Giles who stood there, of whom she had no fear ")—and is not present by name until we come to *Tess* and *Jude*. Angel Clare's love for Tess was imperfect enough, God knows, but it might have been very nearly perfect if it had not lacked this essential element : he was capable of it, but it came too late. After Tess has killed D'Urberville we read :

Tenderness was absolutely dominant in Clare at last. He kissed her endlessly with his white lips, and held her hand, and

said—" I will not desert you ! I will protect you by every
means in my power, dearest love, whatever you may have done
or not have done ! "

But it is the love of Jude and Sue which, with all its error and its
agony, most nearly approaches the ideal love : and this is the
one love that we are allowed to see persisting into years of married
life. Their perfect companionship has been already shown—
we know that " they had become such companions that they
could hardly do anything of importance except in each other's
company ", and that " they went along with that tender attention to each other which . . . " they took little trouble to disguise.
Did Hardy show just this one picture of a happy marriage because
he knew how rare such a relation is ?

Two quotations will help to complete the conception I have
been trying to build up of that love which plays its vital part
as a passion in the Wessex novels. One from *The Woodlanders* :

Her timid morality had, indeed, underrated his chivalry till now,
though she knew him so well. The purity of his nature, his
freedom from the grosser passions, his scrupulous delicacy,
had never been fully understood by Grace till this strange self-
sacrifice in lonely juxtaposition to her own person was revealed.
The perception of it added something that was little short of
reverence to her deep affection for him.

The other from the *Madding Crowd* :

This good-fellowship—*camaraderie*—usually occurring through
similarity of pursuits, is unfortunately seldom superadded to
love between the sexes, because men and women associate,
not in their labours, but in their pleasures merely. Where,
however, happy circumstance permits its development, the
compounded feeling proves itself to be the only love which is
strong as death—that love which many waters cannot quench,
nor the floods drown, beside which the passion usually called
by the name is evanescent as steam.

The part played by the flesh in the Wessex novels is not large,
but it is not noble. In this respect Hardy is perhaps Victorian,
and is opposed to the modern school that protests against the
doctrine of ' working out the beast ' in man. Assuredly to the
man or woman who is sane of mind and body the gift of racing

blood and springing sinew is one of inestimable grandeur.   Says
the Rabbi :

> As the bird wings and sings,
> Let us cry, " All good things
> Are ours, nor soul helps flesh more now than flesh helps soul ! "

Nor do I believe the conceiver of Tess's ' Rally ' is blind to the
splendour of our animal life.   Far less aware of it, indeed, than
Meredith or Richard Jefferies, say.   But, just before the exhortation quoted above, Ben Ezra had suggested,

> To man propose this test—
> Thy body *at its best*,
> How far can that project thy soul on its lone way !

And Meredith is concerned almost exclusively with man's body
' at its best ', whereas Hardy chooses rather to show how, at
its worst—perhaps at its normal, the flesh may be a drag and a
degradation.   Perhaps that is why the nobler loves of his world
know little of it.   Certainly there is far more in Hardy of the
love that is spirit than the love that is animal.   Of how many
novelists who have written since Hardy's death could that be
said ?

Other than Love, the passionate approach to experience is
not often allowed to play a central part in fiction.   Perhaps
Galsworthy sought to do this with religion in *Saint's Progress*,
Meredith and Mr. Charles Morgan with poetry in *Richard
Feverel* and *Sparkenbroke*.   Certainly religion and poetry are
capable of exercising distinct and powerful influence over the
lives of men, and should find a place in the mirror held up to
nature by the novelist.   An impression, not unfounded, prevails
that Hardy's attitude to religion is hostile.   This impression is
a natural consequence of his theory of Fate, which theory is,
however, by no means inconsistent with a religious outlook.   It
does not deny the existence of God, and even such denial would
be covered by Morley's aphorism that " it is as possible to dis-
believe religiously as to believe religiously ".   But whatever of
disbelief there may be in Hardy is not so obviously religious and
reverent as to afford no excuse for the orthodox man's complaint
that he treats great things scoffingly.   This is due to the fact that

what Hardy discredits (in the novels) is not so much the great faiths as their imperfect expoundings by their received professors. It is the stifling of religion by forms and creeds that he attacks : not God but the Church. When Jude looks back at the errors into which he and Sue have fallen he pronounces this verdict : " I was gin-drunk, you were creed-drunk : either form of intoxication takes away the nobler vision ".

As usual, and as is proper, his views are expressed in the concrete ; to know his attitude towards the churches and their teachings one must regard the clergy who find place among his *dramatis personae*. There are some half-dozen parson-portraits, and they are by no means all unsympathetically drawn, though it is sympathy of sorts. The one which will occur to mind most readily is that of the Rev. Mr. Swancourt, father of Elfride, in *A Pair of Blue Eyes*. He is a dignified if less generous reappearance of George Eliot's Rector Irwine, and as such is a standard representative of the genuine Anglican incumbent of a slightly bygone day, a type which still exists unchanged in great numbers in the country livings, but whose representativeness is now shared by the necessarily more strenuous and incidentally more sincere parson of the crowded city parishes. Thoroughly English in his conservatism and his faith in blue blood, he is classically educated, and most at home in his study ; lives over-well, and reads sermons written by his daughter ; is a good fellow, but ruled by narrow class prejudices ; swears mildly, and has a fund of good stories too bad to tell ; and is very strict on family prayers—when visitors are about. In a word, a jolly country gentleman slipped accidentally into a black coat, and carrying it with more grace than gravity and more gravity than godliness. The Rev. Mr. Torkingham, in *Two on a Tower*, inspires the definition of a parson as " a man who gets his living by discovering a bright side in things where it is not very perceptible to other people ". His superior, The Bishop of Melchester, who is greater in precisely the degree and way that a bishop should be greater than a parish priest, has already received some notice. Pa'son Maybold, in *Under the Greenwood Tree*, is a typical curate or youthful minister. He is sketched lightly, and we see little of his real religion ; he has no depth of character, but is earnest and well-meaning, the somewhat exotic friend and mentor of his simple hearty parishioners, and

14

necessarily content if he can get from their stolid souls conformity to the observances of his church.

The Anglican studies are not inspiring, but are not flagrantly hostile. They remind us of how Hardy said he was, by early association, by instinct and emotion, a Churchman. A more severe indictment against the Established Church (and modern Christianity in general) is brought in the chapter that tells of the death of Tess's baby. Her early schooling renders her miserable at the approaching death of the baby—unbaptised. " She thought of the child consigned to the nethermost corner of hell, as its double doom for lack of baptism and lack of legitimacy ; saw the arch-fiend tossing it with his three-pronged fork, like the one they used for heating the oven on baking days ; to which picture she added many other quaint and curious details of torment taught the young in this Christian country." Then Tess meets the parish clergyman, and demands to know if the simple ceremony of christening which she has performed will suffice for salvation. The paragraph that follows contains the two bitterest sneers uttered by Hardy against the Church :

> Having the natural feelings of a tradesman at finding that a job he should have been called in for had been unskilfully botched by his customers among themselves, he was disposed to say no. Yet the dignity of the girl, the strange tenderness in her voice, combined to affect his nobler impulses—or rather those that he had left in him after ten years of endeavour to graft technical belief on actual scepticism. The man and the ecclesiastic fought within him, and the victory fell to the man.

The somewhat vulgar insults of the ' tradesman ', ' job ', ' botched ', and ' customers ', reveal a definite hatred of the present Church constitution. The reference to the conflict is, I imagine, intended to be typical, and has, I believe, considerable ground for a wide application, though an application that is gradually narrowing. I have indeed known a minister of high-church principles concede that a free-thinker has as good a chance of heaven as an orthodox Anglican, though the fact that he was an impressionable young curate, and his interlocutor a charming woman (and something of a free-thinker herself), may have been to some extent influential in calling forth this concession.

But Tess's vicar refuses to apply his newly-framed liberalism

by giving the child a " Christian burial " : he fears the effect
upon his parishioners. In which fear one may sympathise with
him—conditions and congregations being what they are :

> First cut the Liquefaction—what comes last
> But Fichte's clever cut at God himself ?

However, moved to generosity once again, he declares the un-
consecrated burial will be as efficacious as if all ceremonies were
observed, with which second revolutionary judgment Tess is
content.

The picture is, apart from the jibes noted, not too unkind, but
the feeling behind is bitter and sarcastic enough. A psycho-
analyst might trace it back to an experience of Hardy's youth, when
he went to consult the vicar of his parish over the question of
infant baptism, and the bewildered man could do nothing but
lend him Hooker !

A very different feeling pervades the portrait of the Rev. Mr.
Clare, Angel's Evangelical father in *Tess*, a man of Apostolic
simplicity of life and thought, of great kindness of heart, with
a smile as candidly sweet as a child's. Even more narrow,
dogmatic, impatient of argument than the churchman last mentioned, his sincerity, enthusiasm, unselfishness and purity of
heart invoke from Hardy a thorough and ungrudged admiration.
His religious principles are no nearer Hardy's own than were
those of the other man, but his application of them, his essential
morality, has an unmistakable grandeur fully recognised by his
delineator. This character is, by itself, sufficient to absolve
Hardy from any charge of levity towards the ministry of God.
Not dissimilar, but with less austerity and more humanity—that
is, more frailty—is the Baptist minister who is so troubled at
Paula Power's Laodicean lukewarmness, a character again drawn
with great sympathy, and with some good humour.

On the whole, or at least on the side of doctrine, much of this,
as I have said, is bitterly hostile. But I find in it no enmity to
or disparagement of religion itself, but only of its present-day
substitute. A more serious charge might be made of the conspicuous lack of definite religion—by which I mean a powerful
and practical grasp of any spiritual ideal other than Love or
Poetry—that characterises his personages. His peasants may be

dismissed *en masse*. Hardy declares more than once and implies everywhere that the rustic faith of England is essentially naturalistic, pagan, animal. And it would seem that he conceives this state of things to extend to the more cultured classes. His men and women may have been painted over with orthodoxy, or have felt here and there the call of some philosophy or other, but at all critical moments the god they invoke and whose commandment guides them is their instinctive self. To this there are a very few exceptions : Jude Fawley is a fervid Anglican in his early days, but his outgrowing of orthodoxy is not intended as a compliment to orthodoxy. Gabriel Oak is in fact the sole representative of godliness : he reads the Bible with some regularity, and the sight of him at his habitual prayers induces Bathsheba, in her anguish of soul, to kneel beside Fanny's coffin, whence she arises with a quieted spirit—" whether from a purely mechanical, or from any other cause ". On the other hand, Giles Winterborne, as good a man as one may hope to meet in a day's march, keeps a prayer-book by him chiefly that he may whet his knife on its leather covers. It is not surprising to hear Fitzpiers confess that he dreams of a woman's ripe lips more frequently than he says his prayers, but the remark may be adapted and predicated of most of Hardy's *personae*. The converts, Alec D'Urberville and Arabella Donn, fling off with furious contempt their new and ill-fitting garments when the reappearance of former temptations excites their former desires. When Tess breaks into the *Benedicite*, Hardy says it was but a Fetichistic utterance in a Monotheistic setting. Sue Bridehead becomes religious only after she has lost her reason. It is very clear that Hardy knows how very small a part religion plays in the lives of English men and women of the nineteenth and twentieth centuries. Certainly amongst the characters of his stage it does not exercise the high spiritual functions of uplifting and restraint that belong to it as a Passion.

The familiar complaint might be made that simple hostility is not helpful, that destructive criticism should be accompanied by some suggestion of an approved substitute for what is being condemned. This, somehow, is never the way of the artist, whose function it is to show things as they are, so that faults and fallings-short can be seen, leaving it to the teachers—a Comte, a Huxley, a Tolstoy—to propound new ways. The only positive contribution offered by Hardy—and it is a valuable if not a new one—is spoken through the mouth of that most acceptable of prophets, Tess. To D'Urberville, who has abandoned his new-found attachment to Church principles, she says : " If you can't have—what do you call it—dogma, you can at least have the religion of loving-kindness and purity ".

Poetry holds more sovereign sway over the souls of Hardy's people. The unreasonable, almost violent and cruel ideal of womanhood that belongs to Angel Clare and that ruins the lives of Tess and himself is essentially poetic in appearance, nature, and power. Not otherwise are Jude Fawley's dream of scholarship and Sue's conception of the conjugal tie (in her early sane period). Here also must be classed the serene and nature-sweet chivalry of Giles Winterborne, and perhaps the philanthropy of Clym Yeobright. I find no other poets, but these four or five are assuredly of that Quixotic company. Are we to understand that Hardy sees this important proportion of poetry in the lives of modern men ? I fear he flatters us. Ideals—of beauty, truth, goodness,—seized with the up-straining hands of the soul, hugged to the bosom and desperately, triumphantly held in the teeth of self-interest, reason, and the terrors of hell—are these jewels to be discerned amid the gilded dust of our civilisation ? Yes, the stainless, quenchless ray leaps up here and there, just here, perhaps, and far away over there.

On the grand sum of the foregoing considerations it is evident that Hardy's conception of human nature is not by any means a low one. Taken in conjunction with his conception of Fate it leads us to a conclusion much like that so brilliantly extracted by Winifred Holtby from the work of a very different writer : " It is Virginia Woolf's particular philosophy to show that goodness in itself is what matters, but that it cannot alter human destiny ". To make the sentence fit Hardy, for the word 'goodness ' we must substitute greatness, quality, or—better—*virtue* in its old wider sense. Whether he pictures man as having made a sorry business of life we may discuss hereafter. It may be concluded at once that at least he does not believe Life to have made a specially sorry business of man. A piece of rich and complicated work indeed, and of infinite variety and faculty, he is not perhaps, in his normal form, very noble in reason, yet most express and admirable in mental and physical motion, and not far less than angelic in the multitude and wonder of his power and action, while at the high pinnacle of his apprehension his attributes are veritably those of a god. Thus he is indeed the beauty of the world, and still on one side merely the paragon of animals, his quintessential dust being of the earth, earthy, and stained with the foot of the ineradicable beast.

Now it is no business of an artist to do more than show things as they are : we do not ask of him that he should construct an ideal world, or an ideal man, and persuade us to live up to that ideal. There are teachers and preachers enough doing that, with noticeable lack of success. But we may be able to observe certain preferences and antipathies in our artist's choice of things to present, and in his way of presenting them, whence we may infer something of how he would have things be. In his presentation of men (the women we shall look at later) he has in three critical cases—those of Henry Knight, Clym Yeobright, and Angel Clare—shown men treating the women who love them with ruthless egotism (not quite so ruthless in Yeobright's case), and there is evident pity in his showing of the cruel results. I think we may take it that Hardy does not feel such egotism to be an admirable trait in men. On the other hand he chooses to depict a certain decent, self-controlled, considerate type of man so often, and handles him so lovingly in Gabriel and John, Diggory and Giles, that it is surely again a legitimate inference that here is a sort of man of whom Hardy very much approves.

*   *   *   *   *   *   *   *   *

An English magistrate once acquitted a lady who was brought before him on a well-proved charge of shoplifting. This exceptional act of leniency, much condemned by the democratic press, was explained by Mr. Chesterton on the ground that our well-born justices only comprehend the real nature of their cases when the accused is of the judge's own caste, the expressed inference being that for equitable treatment of the majority of cases, occurring as they do among the poorer classes, there is urgent necessity for ' Labour ' judges. In comment or corollary upon which proposition it was remarked to me, " What a good judge Hardy would make ! How he would understand ! "

Setting aside the question of whether it is good that a judge should understand his cases too well, the dictum concerning Hardy is of some interest. The major premise, that a great creator of character will necessarily possess peculiar insight into the motives of men other than those who inhabit his own private planet, appears to me in the light of a very reasonable assumption. I cannot, for instance, imagine Shakespeare ever being more than momentarily angry with one of his fellow-Elizabethans. I take it as demonstrated likewise that Hardy is a successful delineator of character—that he has a powerful, profound, consistent grasp of the fundamental bottom of human nature. It is not improbable that to have plumbed and comprehended absolutely a single specimen of mankind makes one free of the souls of all the world. However, there is some possibility that the soul of a peer or a professor differs almost essentially from that of a clodhopper or a clown, so that in order for our minor to be fully established it will be necessary to prove that Hardy is, like Shakespeare, equally successful, equally sympathetic, with all types of character.

Without instituting any impossible comparison with Shakespeare, it is at once apparent that Hardy has in some degree restricted his most interested and penetrating gaze to a certain portion of the community. He is, on the whole, concerned to seek life in the lower strata of society, leaving the more exalted classes to Meredith, Galsworthy, and Henry James. All the novels in Hardy's first division deal with ' country life and passions ', except that Angel Clare and Clym Yeobright come of clerical families, and even they belong by temperament and taste to the homely folk among whom they have cast in their lot. Some of the lesser novels touch ' high life ', only *A Pair of Blue Eyes* with any deliberateness. Of the only two society heroines in Hardy, one, Mrs. Petherwin, is the daughter of a butler, and the other, Lady Constantine, is much more of a woman than a *grande dame*. Of that peculiar reserve, coldness, artificiality, or whatever it may be called, that characterises the genuine English aristocracy and differentiates (or is it ' differentiated ' ?) it, for good or evil, from the middle and lower classes as distinctly as its accent, Hardy gives us nothing at all, save the faintest touch in *The Hand of Ethelberta* and *A Pair of Blue Eyes*.

Differentiates " for good or evil ? " One may judge that

Hardy accepts the latter alternative. At least in this—that whether the society tone be in itself a fault or a virtue, it obscures the nature behind, and as the novelist's study is before all things human nature, it is well that he should carry on his researches in the department where he can see it most clearly. To Meredith the veil was more readily penetrable, and in cases like those of Willoughby Patterne and Clara Middleton he provides studies almost as preternaturally perspicacious as Hardy's best. But Hardy goes to Nature undimmed, and finds it in the children of the people, like Tess, Jude Fawley, Sue Bridehead, Oak, Henchard, Giles Winterborne. Moreover by choosing his characters from the plebeian and labouring orders he places them under that primal curse of man, the necessity of working for a living. The gain is great. There is a certain grim satisfaction in finding here, as in life, the primary assumption of a relentless struggle for existence that binds its victims with inviolable bonds, so that when trouble comes there is no fairy-flight of escape.

However, the fact remains that Hardy is something of a specialist. He has in a large degree averted his ken from half of human existence—that half which is the consummated product of civilisation and culture. This is undoubtedly a limitation, but I cannot think it a vital one. For the half he has seized is the eternal, that which he avoids is the phase of the day, excellent perhaps and interesting certainly, but destined for the graveyard of Time. Since the world began there have been Tess Durbeyfields and Jude Fawleys, and however far ' progress ' may go there will (let us hope) always be men and women like them. But culture changes with the centuries : who can tell what the ' aristocrat ' of even a hundred years hence will be like ?

CHAPTER III

HARDY'S WOMEN : HARDY'S VIEW OF WOMAN

IT is one of Hardy's crusted characters who tells of a certain mathematical problem—' a mortal teaser '—that runs among the Wessex folk : A herring and a half for three-halfpence, how many can you get for 'levenpence ? He adds that " down in those parts, just as you try a man's soul by the Ten Commandments, you try his head by that there sum ". Not dissimilarly it may be said that the touchstone of a novelist's power, and the rock upon which he most frequently splits, is his handling of woman. The *Ewigweibliche* is a book written in a strange tongue. The " woman-country " may be " wooed, not wed " by " earth's male-lands ". It behoves even us, who do but map out Hardy's venturings on that perilous shore, to work warily.

It is a fascinating piece of investigation that we have before us. Think of the wealth of material !—run over the names of the women and girls who play their parts, great and small, in these tales. The chief names may be placed in three groups, according to their importance for the subject—each a handful of five. First group, full-length studies of women of a high order of personality—Tess, Sue, Eustacia, Bathsheba, and Elizabeth-Jane. Second group, full-length studies of women of less personal significance—Elfride, Ethelberta, Grace, Viviette, and Anne. Third group, a mixed one, of women who, though fully studied, are of much less significance, and of others who, though of deep significance, are not fully drawn—Paula and Fancy, Marty and Arabella, and, tying for the last place, Tamsie, Lucetta, and Picotee. And then, standing modestly in the background, but every one a figure of intense individual interest—Tabitha, Matilda, Fanny, Charlotte, the three Avices, and the three milk-maids, elder ladies like Mrs. Yeobright, Mrs. Goodman, the second Mrs. Swancourt, and the second Mrs. Melbury, poor Susan Henchard. . . . We shall begin by looking with some degree of closeness at a representative selection from this alluring array of names.

Among Hardy's women Tess Durbeyfield claims attention first, not only by reason of popularity, but more especially in that her creator distinguished her by the appellation of " a pure woman ". In a late preface (that to the Wessex edition), when some of the resulting foam and fury had died down, Hardy disclosed that he had appended the sub-title after reading the proofs of the novel, and had supposed it would be received without dispute. He now thought it would have been better not to put it— a regret that would never have occurred to Mr. Bernard Shaw, with his belief in the salutary nature of ' shocks '. Doubtless to the guardians of public morality in the 'nineties it must have appeared intolerable that to the injury of making a girl like Tess the heroine of a novel there should have been added the insult of calling her ' a pure woman '. Hardy had already taken the opportunity of a new edition to remind his critics that the very narrow and special meaning they were accustomed to attach to the word ' pure ' was " an artificial and derivative " one, resulting from " the ordinances of civilisation ". He might have quoted the epigrammatist who said that woman's virtue was man's greatest invention. Instead he reminded his readers that the controversial word had an æsthetic usage. This is a highly interesting suggestion. We speak of a pure curve, pure art, pure comedy (the Victorian moralists probably blushed to hear the plays of Wycherley, Congreve, and Etheredge described as ' pure comedy '). Let us adopt the suggestion and apply the word ' pure ' in this sense to Tess : unbroken, unspoilt, unadulterated, unflawed, perfect ! This is very satisfying indeed ; but we must remember that in the text of the novel another word is used—' standard ' : " an almost standard woman ", Hardy calls Tess. Now, ' standard ' means model, of a quality to be aimed at, by comparison with which inferior examples are tested and rejected. This is again an acceptable description of Tess, and confirms the meaning we have given to the word ' pure '. But Hardy's modification of the epithet ' standard ' must not be overlooked : ' *almost* standard ' is the expression. And he goes on to define the modification. What the modification was we shall see in a moment, but it had nothing to do with purity in the narrow moral sense. In that sense she was not almost but absolutely pure. "Purity is of the spirit, and with a spiritual (that is, non-physical) reference, the word ' pure ' may be unconditionally applied to her in the moral sense that the Puritans baulked at. Whether morality be of the mind, or of the heart (Ruskin's ' taste is the only morality '), or of both, there cannot be two respectable opinions about Tess's morals. She is as moral as any prude. Her behaviour, her thoughts, her desires, on all perilous occasions—with D'Urberville, early and late ; with Clare ; with her other admirers—are unimpeachable, considered from the most critical code and point of view. Moreover, her shame and remorse are infinite. She has a conscience that is quite amazing in view of the probability that conscience is almost entirely a matter of what one has been taught in very early childhood. Mentally and morally she is stainless, with strong intent to keep so, and probably continues so from first to last ; even during the later period of dissipation with D'Urberville her mind is drugged and dead with weariness, pain and despair, and so guiltless.

But it is man's privilege and problem to have a body as well as a mind, and in Tess the flesh was slightly at variance with her spirit. Early in the novel we read :

> She had an attribute which . . . caused D'Urberville's eyes to rivet themselves upon her. It was a luxuriousness of aspect, a fulness of growth, which made her appear more of a woman than she really was. She had inherited the feature from her mother without the quality it denoted.

Here Hardy clearly suggests an element in the flesh antagonistic to the mental purity emphasised above. He indeed denies the presence of the quality suggested. But this denial refers to the mental constitution. In several places Hardy emphasises the splendid animal nature of Tess. For instance :

> How very lovable her face was to him. Yet there was nothing ethereal about it ; all was vitality, real warmth, real incarnation. And it was in her mouth that this culminated.

Or again :

> Her face was flushed with sleep, and her eyelids hung heavy over their pupils. The brimfulness of her nature breathed from her.

Tess's sister, hand in hand with whom Clare makes his exit from the story, is described as " a spiritualised image of Tess, slighter than she. . . . " And the line of characterisation thus etched in is continued by Hardy with exquisite delicacy throughout the picture. Tess was, in her body, the daughter of her mother. What praise and wonder are sufficient for the purity of her soul that could keep her spotless, save for the momentary admission of D'Urberville's advances, for which in itself we have already found ample explanation.

Returning now to the ' almost ' with which Hardy modified his description of Tess as ' a standard woman ', we find in it a final explanation of her ' fall '. Hardy leaves us in no doubt as to what he means by his ' almost ', for he adds—" but for the slight incautiousness of character inherited from her race ". That is to say her mind had the touch of yieldingness that was just necessary to allow the touch of animalism in her flesh to respond to great external pressure.

Hardy's conception of Tess hangs thus on the two words we have been discussing. But this is to consider her in the abstract, as the embodiment of an idea—a thing which is plainly ridiculous. Tess lives in all her breathing beauty, with the touch of the imperfect upon the would-be perfect—as Clare perceived—that gave sweetness because it was that which gave humanity. Legend has it that Hardy drew Tess from a glimpse he got of a girl driving a cart in the West country, and certainly the picture has the warm reality of life—her long heavy clinging tresses of dark brown hair ; her deep dark eyes—Hardy loses himself in those " large tender eyes, neither black nor blue nor gray nor violet ; rather all those shades together, and a hundred others, which could be seen if one looked into their irises—shade behind shade —tint beyond tint—around pupils that had no bottom ! " Her grace and vitality constantly call up the likeness of a wild creature : " there was something of the habitude of the wild animal in the unreflecting instinct with which she wandered on from place to

place " in those hard days of Clare's desertion. As she slept on
the stone on the Great Plain, " her breathing now was quick and
small, like that of a lesser creature than a woman ". When
accosted by a man on the road her way of escape is to run like
the wind and bury herself deep among the trees. The life within
her is irrepressible—" she little recked the strength of her own
vitality ".

But her mental characteristics are no less rare and delightful.
She is high-strung, impressionable, poetic : her soul soars into
space when she gazes at the night heavens ; in the stress of her
emotions at the sound of Clare's harp the whole of the twilight
garden grows instinct with harmony and passion ; and at his
touch her accelerated pulse drives the blood flushing to her
finger-ends. She is heroic, for we hear of " her many months
of lonely self-chastisement, wrestlings, communings, schemes to
lead a future of austere isolation " ; and her long endurance of
retributive agonies is sublime. And she shows perfect nobility
and generosity of sentiment, in her attitude towards her simple
rivals at the farm and in her splendid faith in Clare, which
amounts indeed to a quite ineffable humility. Her knowledge
that she has never wronged Clare or any human being awakes in
her, just once, a passionate sense of cruel injustice. And as she
tells Clare her story in the firelight ; even more as she gets up
from her bed of stone and goes forward to the men who have
come to arrest her, saying quietly, " I am ready " : one feels
that she deserves that rarest of all the terms that can be applied
to man or woman—' great '.

Whatever else we call her, Tess remains the most lovable
of Hardy's heroines. All women adore her, and some men.
What she might have made of life, what life might have made
of her, had circumstances and Clare been kind, is beyond
dreaming.

Her most dangerous rival in supreme interest is Sue Bridehead.
Without so much claim to representativeness, she creates in the
minds of her beholders impressions that are far less generally
favourable. Indeed, many pople, inside and outside the story,
unhesitatingly declare that Sue is no better than she ought to be.
I shall hope to treat her more sympathetically, if not more
judiciously.

The most important, distinctive and interesting element in her nature is a certain sexlessness. And the concentrated essential perfume of this lily, the trait by which she is Sue Bridehead, is her desire for marriage without physical sex-union. This alone will be sufficient to damn her at the tribunal of half humanity. The conception is, of course, not put forth in *Jude* for the first time. The term ' Platonic affection ' has been often abused, but Sue's ideal of a sexless-union of spirits might claim some analogy with that which Socrates and his great pupil intended by Love. At the other end of time we have Mr. Bernard Shaw, in the introduction to *Man and Superman*, suggesting that spiritual and physical marriage should be distinguished and separated, the partnership of the soul being left to choice and spiritual affinity, while that of the flesh is arranged by the State on eugenic principles. One remembers also, perhaps with less relevance, how Pompilia won the disapproval of the Archbishop by refusing to surrender body as well as soul to her brutal husband.

There is, of course, the view that Sue is merely dabbling in one of the many subtleties of modern sex-relations. That may be the case. It would not necessarily be the worse for that. To subtilise is not always to degrade. But a more interesting possibility is suggested by Sue herself : Jude has declared her a phantasmal, bodiless creature, with very little animal passion in her ; to which she replies : " I am not so exceptional a woman as you think. Fewer women like marriage than you suppose, only they enter into it for the dignity it is assumed to confer ". This recalls Rossetti's sonnet :

> Lo ! they are one. With wifely breast to breast
> And circling arms, she welcomes all command
> Of love—her soul to answering ardours fanned ;
> Yet, as Moon springs or twilight sinks to rest,
> Ah, who shall say she deems not loveliest
> The hour of sisterly sweet hand-in-hand ?

Sue goes further—though as it is in that late period when affliction had wounded her mind we may discount her assertion if we wish—in a reply to Jude, who has asked, in pain and bewilderment at her apostasy, " But surely you loved me ? "

" Yes. But I wanted to let it stop there, and go on always as mere lovers ; until——"

" But people in love couldn't live for ever like that ! "

" Women could : men can't, because they—won't. An average woman is in this superior to an average man—that she never instigates, only responds. We ought to have lived in mental communion, and no more."

Of course, Mr. Havelock Ellis declares such ideas as this are of the usual man-made sort, and that there is practically no difference between the sexes in this respect. And there are others who apply to her whole attitude the crushing epithet ' schoolmistressy '. This last criticism has this to be said for it, that the attitude will doubtless have been strengthened by her reading, but it ignores the fact that women are not all made alike, any more than men are, and that it is evident that Hardy intended Sue to be a woman who stood out of the Havelock Ellis generalisation, whether this be sound or not. Moreover, there is no reason to suppose Hardy did not include this all-important element in Sue's nature when he spoke of her in a letter as " a type of woman which has always had an attraction for me ". She herself denies that the attribute goes deep enough to warrant her being called " cold and sexless", and here she seems to show the self-knowledge we should expect of her, for her relations with Jude exhibit no absence of any but the most primitive form of sex. She was certainly of the late-developing type, in direct contra-distinction to Tess. And one may pause to wonder at the creative insight that enabled Hardy to handle these two opposed types with equal sympathy, understanding and conviction.

Our classification in the previous chapter recognised love as a passion, spiritual in nature though generally bound up with the animal instinct of sex. What Hardy chose to do in his last novel was to show it existing, in a woman, with as little admixture of the second, lower, element as possible. He had already shown, though with much less explicitness, a degree of the same absence of sensuality in the love of Giles Winterborne.

But this fleshless love does not comprise the whole of Sue's epicene quality—it is either the consummation or the origin of it. A product or a less extreme form of the same quality is seen in her general attitude towards men. She can associate with men, live with them, talk with them on any subject under the sun, in an abstract, impersonal way that is no less admirable than rare. It gives her strange power. It permits her to indulge in dangerous experiments in emotion, like the undergraduate companionship and the marriage rehearsal ; it enables her, as Mrs. Richard Phillotson, to be so sweet to Jude that he cries in agony, Flirt ! Her behaviour is to some extent based on ignorance of human frailty and fire, but the strength and mastery are unquestionable, and are the fruit of her " curious unconsciousness of gender ".

> My strength is as the strength of ten
> Because my heart is pure.

She is described almost as vividly as Tess (indeed most of Hardy's heroines are ' seen ' in a way that is hardly true of any of the men). We even see her (through the eyes of her old aunt) as a child—a pert little thing with tight-strained nerves, often getting smacked for impertinence, celebrated for her tragic delivery of *The Raven* at the vicar's penny-readings, and given to sliding with the boys on the frozen pond. (Of Tess's childhood we were only told how she used to walk home from school on long stalky legs with little ladder-like holes at the knees, her hair hanging like pot-hooks and her waist embraced by the arms of two other little girls.) Now Sue has liquid untranslatable eyes, not large like Tess's, but full of mystery as well as of keenness and tenderness ; she is dark in colouring, light and slight in figure, mobile and living and all nervous motion ; she is " significantly light in touch "—indeed, when we get to know her better she is Ariel, all spirit and fire, incapable of being caught, held, pinned down. Her nervous constitution is more than once indicated, and towards the end she becomes " a mere cluster of nerves ".

Can we call Sue ' an intellectual woman ? ' Certainly she is, with Ethelberta and Elizabeth-Jane, on the one side of the line that separates the intellectual from the non-intellectual types, just as surely as Tess, Eustacia, and Elfride are on the other. But she is no hard-boiled logician, no self-regulating clockwork, no frigid unemotional robot. She is quiveringly sensitive, she is often perverse ; she is alive with emotions, and acts on lightning impulses. As she passes the shop of the poulterer who has bought her pigeons at the sale, " an emotion at sight of them, assisted by the growing dusk of evening, caused her to act on impulse, and first looking around her quickly, she pulled out the peg which fastened down the cover, and went on, trembling. The cover was lifted from within, and the pigeons flew away with a clatter that brought the chagrined poulterer cursing and swearing to the door." She tells Jude what " a wicked thing " she has done, and Jude has to go and repay the poulterer, of course. . . . She describes herself as " a woman tossed about, with aberrant passions and unaccountable antipathies". But she thinks as well as feels ; she is capable of estimating right and wrong by argument ; she could have met Clare and Henry Knight on their own ground. She is the less woman for it : argument is man's prerogative (or penalty) ; and we know what tragic part her reasoning plays in her destiny. One may observe further how excellently her reasoning power blends with her sexlessness to give her the faculty of speech. Sue is no un-expressive She, as Tess and Elfride : her position is at least as difficult of explanation as theirs, but she never fails to make herself perfectly clear to Jude and Phillotson. Her intellect combines with her under-sexed nature to give her that dangerous habit of playing with her emotions—Hardy calls her " an epicure in emotion ". Yet her intellectuality does not save her from falling, at the most critical moment of her life, a victim to the most unintellectual of human frailties—jealousy. Whatever may be thought of her yielding to Jude's demand that their marriage shall be brought to the ordinary consummation, there can be no two opinions as to the contemptible nature of the argument which eventually subdues her—a fear lest he should return to Arabella. But what a lovely queer disposition she shows in going to see Arabella next morning !

The one definite stigma she bears of being an " intellectual woman " is her unsatisfactory position with regard to religion. In the early period she uses reason alone to reach her conclusions, which are consequently not very profound. She declares she belongs not to the modern world with its railway stations, not to the middle ages with their churches, but to the world of the ancient pagan gods. She is, as a matter of cold fact, merely ir-religious. In the later stage she simply throws reason overboard, and of course is in no better case. Jude's summation, spoken to the Widow Edlin as he lay on the sick-bed from which he was never to rise, is worth noting :

> " Mrs. Edlin, she was once a woman whose intellect was to mine like a star to a benzoline lamp : who saw all *my* superstitions as cobwebs she could brush away with a word. Then bitter affliction came to us, and her intellect broke, and she veered round to darkness."

A woman of spiritual quality, born to live a life of fine passion, she made intellect her star : perhaps the ' complex ' that resulted is the explanation of her tragedy.

In the way of sheer greatness Eustacia Vye stands out with Sue and Tess. The contrast between Eustacia and Sue is so marked that it might seem that Hardy had in them sought to portray the two extremes of the splendid in woman—the one, in whom spirit governs, leaving flesh to play a purely ancillary part ; the other—who is to the first as a burning forest is to a star—whose flesh, glorious and exultant, has absorbed her soul, and has blood-red passions of its own. It is this second type that we have marvellously portrayed in Eustacia, and it is an astonishing thing that Hardy should have found one phrase which he thought appropriate both for her and for Sue. " As far as social ethics were concerned Eustacia approached the savage state, though in emotion she was all the while an epicure. She had advanced to the secret recesses of sensuousness, yet had hardly crossed the threshold of conventionality." An epicure in emotion, like Sue ! Well, perhaps. But how different are Eustacia's emotional feasts from Sue's cool experimental savourings. If epicures both, it was as *gourmand* and *gourmet* ! However, a rich sensuousness is undoubtedly her dominant characteristic, making her conspicuous among Hardy's women. She had " predetermined to nourish a passion for Yeobright ". She declares she once saw an officer of Hussars ride down the street, and though he was a total stranger and never spoke to her she loved him till she thought she should really die of love. It is not a pleasant thing, this nature in a woman ; it is only tolerable in Eustacia because her personality as a whole is heroic enough to glorify all its constituents. Her sensuous nature is incapable of thought. She is built entirely of highly-potentialised feeling. Her indolence covers, as Mrs. Yeobright perceives, very strong passions. Her every act is the instant product of impetuous desire. Her cry that she has tried to be a splendid woman is bitterest ignorance of self ; conscious and deliberate effort to be anything at all—to effect any change in her nature, to resist any impulse—is mere impossibility to her purely instinctive character. Such a woman must inevitably sin, according to all human notions of virtue : her soul dissolved in her hot blood, the restraint of reason absent, she has no guide but emotion and animal wants. As Hardy hints in the great chapter to which I must once more refer you, she belongs to that Southern type which is not well understood by the Teuton mind.

Purely Teutonic, and closer akin to our ordinary sympathies, is Elfride Swancourt. She is altogether lacking in that grandeur of personality that characterises the three women previously described, but she is an interesting study, and, despite her somewhat ironic finale, not unworthy. To call her fickle, and allured in turn by the young and romantic, the strong and intellectual, and the wealthy and aristocratic, is to take a superficial view of the matter. The third case is easily explicable—is indeed explained—and its irony is only intended to come home to Smith and Knight, between whom lies the essential struggle. The fact that each of these three absolutely different types of men found in her something deeply satisfying shows the wideness of her appeal. She is thoroughly feminine ; indeed, this side is marked almost to satire. Thus, she is incredibly foolish in her pettish obstinacy and reticence to Knight over the earlier affair with Smith. Yet there is the woman's truer instinct in her insistence on Knight continuing to love her whether satisfied or not as to her conduct, while he, proceeding on lines of mere intellect, demands satisfaction first. Again, she is high-strung in a much more nervous and unpoetic sense than Tess, as may be seen in the extraordinary scene of the chess-playing between her and Knight. Knight is, indeed, too massive and masterful to find fit place in her life. How telling—if Knight had but taken to heart the tale it told—is that passage in which Knight offers Elfride her choice of " a well-chosen little library of the best music " or a pair of pretty ear-rings ; and to his amused chagrin she chooses the ear-rings—because "music doesn't do any real good". By nature joyous, light-hearted, affectionate, she was Stephen Smith's queen and fairy; under the sterner influence of Knight she becomes love's vassal to a painful degree—her gay spirits are crushed, she is no longer Elfride.

The blot in her 'scutcheon—and a black one it is—is her desertion of Smith for Knight, which is done in a way that is nothing less than shocking. The change-over is made without a word of explanation: when Stephen comes home she agrees to meet him in the church porch—and simply fails to turn up; and when, after waiting for an hour, he goes to her house, he hears her talking and laughing with Knight inside. And when they do meet, in Knight's presence, she just treats Stephen as a stranger ! Stephen bore the mark to his grave; and if ever a woman deserved to 'pay' it was Elfride, though perhaps her punishment (like Tess's, though of course in far less degree) was out of proportion with her unreflecting offence.

Her sisters of real life see little in her; wonder 'if girls are really as silly as that'. She deserves more respect. Great she is not, but in her sphere she is decked with all the charm of Browning's *Pretty Woman*. She might have danced daintily through life; but Life came and tossed her down into the strife of harsher things, and she was not brave swimmer enough to beat her way up from the waves. Poor Elfride ! she goes down with the nebulous light on her hair, as when Stephen Smith saw her first, singing, with little instant understanding, but with some prophetic fervour, Shelley's dirge of Love.

Next in importance and interest comes Bathsheba Everdene. Some one has said you shall know a man by the sin he commits, and Bathsheba's character turns on her marriage with Troy. Viewed from a man's standpoint, this marriage would seem incredible. Here is Bathsheba, a sane, strong, successful woman; in her way comes Troy, whom any man knows to be a dirty scoundrel the moment he sets eyes on him : she is at once attracted, and with little difficulty wooed and won. The explanation lies in the personal attitude that a woman generally takes on questions of ethics. The man's behaviour is obviously offensive, but it apparently proceeds from admiration of Bathsheba's person; therefore it is praiseworthy. He gives evidence of no solid qualities—makes, indeed, little attempt to hide qualities of a very different order ; but women are capable of the most astonishing errors in the judging of men ; so although Oak and Boldwood wait in silent greatness, this tinsel and tin soldier carries the day. It is as distressing a picture of feminine folly as one may well desire, and the most distressing thing about it is that the picture is absolutely true to life. Never was the ruthless veracity of Hardy's character-drawing made more plainly manifest. Contrast the painfully truthful Chapter XXIV of *Far from the Madding Crowd*—where Troy meets, insults, and charms Bathsheba—with Chapter IV of Meredith's *Diana of the Crossways*. In this latter scene, how admirable is Diana—and how improbable ! Any good woman would have rebuffed Sir Lukin, but few even of the best of women would have been angry with him, or have thought worse of him for his treachery—inspired by love of her. Hardy is emphatic on the power of flattery over women ; it is well to remember that men are equally susceptible to flattery of a different kind—a kind which indeed to them seems less gross ; all men may have their price, but at least the price has to be adapted to their individual temperaments. Bathsheba, too, as Sue did afterwards, succumbed to the ultimate folly of jealousy. She confesses to Gabriel that she had married Troy because he told her " he had seen a woman more beautiful than I, and that his constancy could not be counted on unless I at once became his ". This particular frailty is surely woman's own speciality. Is it biological ?

There is nothing subtle or wonderful in Bathsheba's nature. She is more commonplace than any of the four women previously treated : even Elfride has the inexplicable charm of a dainty Caroline lyric ; Bathsheba is prose, and pedestrian at that. Yet she is a fine character, and Hardy certainly thought her worth studying ; indeed, he was enthusiastic enough about her to call her " an Elizabeth in brain and a Mary Stuart in spirit " ! She is a little overshadowed by some among her company, but she gains beauty from the tale of which she is the centre. One gathers, moreover, that the book shows her only in the workshop, undergoing the probation of pain that is to make her the woman she is meant to be—the worthy mate of Gabriel Oak. One fancies her, in an imaginary sequel, clothed in the sunset hues of a graver wisdom, a saner if sadder love, and a staunch comradeship that is foreshadowed in the scene of the saving of the corn-stacks.

Reference has already been made to the doubts raised by the character of Ethelberta Petherwin. She, with more exactness than in the case of Sue, may be called an intellectual woman. Sue was a marvellous blend—masculine in its complexity—of passion, intellect and emotion ; I find little in Ethelberta but cool, calculating reason. Of passion there is no hint, and her gleams of faint and colourless emotion are quickly extinguished in the cold douche of her argued scheme of life. One yields ready admiration for the woman's single-handed fight through the pressing seas of difficulty, but the feeling stops short at admiration : mere-cold-blooded strength in a woman is not lovable, and is not even noble unless the ideals striven for are high, which is not the case with Ethelberta, her aim being (perhaps necessarily) nothing more than her own maintenance. In love she is equally mathematical, and, as I have previously suggested, one cannot decide whether to regard her marriage with Lord Mountclere as a reward for her pluck or a punishment for her scheming.

Of almost supreme interest again is Elizabeth-Jane, the somewhat irrelevant daughter of sailor Newson and Susan Henchard. Her picture is drawn in the softest of half-tones, and does not at once catch the eye, but longer acquaintance with her story shows her full of fascination for the connoisseur in fine human pieces. She is another ' intellectual ' ; but how different from Sue or Ethelberta is Elizabeth-Jane's " grey-eyed reasonableness ". I believe she is the only girl in Hardy with eyes of grey— " aerial grey eyes ", he calls them, and they go well with her earnest and sober mien : perhaps even better with that inquiring aspect of her mind that leads her creator to describe her as " subtle-souled ". She is a single-hearted girl, with a marked " willingness to sacrifice personal comfort and dignity to the common weal ". Her personality is light and unemphatic, perhaps excessively modest in the earlier stages—she is almost too " impersonally human ". But her personality develops, first under suffering, when Henchard's discovery that she is Newson's daughter makes him treat her harshly—at this time she is " full

of dumb, deep feeling ", and is " construed not by a single con-
tiguous being " ; and later with her marriage to Farfrae.   Even
this, in its preliminaries, brings her more unhappiness, while
Farfrae is being led astray by his attraction for Lucetta, but
Elizabeth-Jane " bears up against the frosty ache of the treatment
as she had borne up under worse things ", and shows herself a
rare and special type of woman.   She was, or became, a little
philosopher, learning to accept life's habit of substituting for
the deeply-desired the not-desired-so-much.   Her secret lies
perhaps in her possession of a sense of humour : she is able to
note with amusement that " when Lucetta had pricked her finger
they were as deeply concerned as if she were dying ; when she
herself had been seriously sick or in danger they uttered a conventional word of sympathy at the news, and forgot all about
it immediately ".   (This sense of humour is an exceptional thing
among Hardy's women—only Anne Garland and the second
Avice share the quality.)   But her firm little character comes out
on numerous occasions, and includes a " craving for correctness
of procedure that was almost vicious ".   It is this, perhaps,
together with a certain deficiency of ' heart ' in her constitution,
that leads her to her one bad lapse from virtue—her unkind dismissal of the hopefully-returning Henchard.   But this does not
prevent her creator from regarding her as something approaching
the ideal—at least he calls her " this flower of Nature, Elizabeth-
Jane ".

By way of contrast, a dubious, unsatisfying character is that
of Grace Melbury.   She is indeed but a girl throughout the story,
and her strength at one point, when her rivals in love come
anxiously to her to inquire about her missing husband, is remarkable for one who must be still under twenty.   But her
half-digested ' superior ' education, and her childish subservience
to her adoring but over-bearing father, make it difficult for her
to have anything decided in the way of character.   Even with
Giles, of whom she " has no fear " she shows this weakness.
" You won't—go back to your husband ? " Giles suggested.
" No, no, no !   Don't make me ! " she cried piteously.   But, on
the whole, foolishly weak where her father's changing wishes are
concerned, she plays the tyrant with generous and non-insistent
men like Giles and Fitzpiers.

The most interesting feature in her character is that her emotions are set at a low temperature, and this fact is chiefly interesting because Grace shares the characteristic with two others among the heroines, Sue and Bathsheba. Hardy indicates the quality in each case (other than by the course of the action) by associating it with the name of a classical goddess. Sue we know : she herself demands the freedom of a relationship with men which she describes as " the wide field of strong attachment where desire plays, at least, only a secondary part—the part of—who is it ?—Venus Urania "—Aphrodite spiritual. Of Bathsheba we read, " Although she scarcely knew the divinity's name, Diana was the goddess she instinctively adored ". And now we are told that Grace had learned to understand, too late, the purity of Giles's nature and his freedom from the grosser passions, and that she reverenced him for it, since she herself " had more of Artemis than of Aphrodite in her constitution ". As Hardy took such beautiful care with the nomenclature of this triplicated quality we may assume that he had it in mind when he expressed a special liking for the ' Sue ' type, in whom it is so marked.

Apart from this, though Grace is a very charming girl, she excites less admiration than most of her fellow-heroines, and is perhaps worthy of her unheroic and not too auspicious ending. Her affection for Giles, uncomprehending as it was, was the one deep feeling of her life, and when that was withdrawn she underwent an obvious degeneration. She was not badly broken up by Giles's death, and her desire to be rid of the responsibility for it is only too characteristic. She had that kind of common-sense that takes the line of least resistance, and her chief claim to distinction is that she was the object of Giles Winterborne's chivalrous love.

But have we called Grace the heroine of *The Woodlanders?* Is there not Marty South, a figure of far greater beauty and interest ? There is, indeed ; and if it gives you any satisfaction to regard her as the principal female character of the book I shall not dispute her claim. She appears at infrequent intervals, and takes little direct part in the action. She quickly realises that Giles, whom she loves, is in love with Grace, and from that moment she becomes an almost silent but deeply interested

watcher of the passing show.   Only twice does she intervene.
Her writing of the rhyme in charcoal on the white-washed wall
of Giles's house is the action of the sprite she is (Giles thinks
the sound of her writing is the movement of a rose bush in the
wind).   The letter she sent to Fitzpiers about Mrs. Charmond's
fine head of hair (not her own but Marty's !) was an arrow loosed
at a very distant mark, but it does eventually fly home, and succeeds, where everything else has failed, in detaching Fitzpiers
from his charmer and bringing him back to his wife.   Most of
what little is shown of Marty we saw in the ' survey ' of the novel,
but Hardy's feeling for her is shown in this sentence :   " Giles
saw Marty standing in her doorway, a slim figure in meagre
black, almost without womanly contours as yet ".   When Hardy
loves one of his girl-characters, that is the way he describes her.
It carries a degree further the attribute so pleasantly noted in
Sue—" the small, tight, apple-like curves of her bodice, so different from Arabella's amplitudes ".   Marty is no inarticulate
country wench, and though her speech rises and falls—now crude,
now finely expressive—her thoughts are always lofty.   In her
plain, unpolished steadfastness she is a deliberate foil to Grace.
She had opened the book, and she closes it—with those words of
divine simplicity, mysterious beauty.   It is a great loss to literature
that Hardy did not make her the subject of a full-length study.

Of the lesser women, Arabella is a unique person, so different
from all the others that she would surely feel uncomfortable but
for her impudence.   Her coarseness and animal depravity are
emphasised in contrast not only to Sue's fineness and spirituality
but to the prevailing Hardy type.   Those who profess to like
her must take cognisance of the pig-killing and the Sunday
morning sequel.   Lady Constantine is weak and silly, but has
a good deal of charm and might have been more interesting if
Swithin had been ten years older.   At the opposite pole of personality is Mrs. Yeobright, an example of an excellent, noble-
hearted type of woman which disappoints because in it the mind
is so much less generous than the emotions.   Like her son, she
has great strength of character, and she is strongest, and least
admirable, in her dissension with Clym.   Her blind anger is due
to jealousy and to the frustration of the maternal instinctive expectation of obedience.   Sane and good, she can yet exclaim,

" O Thomasin, he was so good as a little boy—so tender and kind ! "—just because her grown son knows his own mind in his own affairs. Another elder woman, the second Mrs. Melbury, is a distinct individuality, with more shrewdness and humour than her husband. At the thought of Grace marrying Giles, Melbury exclaims : " Fancy her white hands getting redder every day . . . and her bounding walk becoming the regular Hintock shail-and-wamble ! " " She may shail ; but she'll never wamble ", replied his wife decisively. . . . Strong, again, and admirable throughout, is Izz Huett, one of Tess's rough-hewn friends. The pith of her character is seen in the episode of Clare's suggestion that she should accompany him to Brazil. She dwarfs him utterly—he, purely self-centred ; she, grand in her self-control and generosity :

> She burst into wild tears. . . . " O, Izz, don't spoil it by regret ! "
> She stilled herself by degrees. " Very well, sir . . .".

Under the Greenwood Tree is a light and charming summer's day story, in which one does not look for profound psychology. Yet there is one chapter in it, the first of part the fourth, in which the minds of a man and a maid are read and written with a success as perfect as anything of the sort I remember. And the reading is in no small degree cynical, so far as the girl is concerned. Miss Fancy Day is not among the great ones of her sex, of course, but her behaviour here and its effect upon Dick Dewy, with her consequent repentance and his necessary forgiveness—all of which are set forth too exquisitely to submit to summarising without injury—are easily paralleled in the lives of more heroic women, and are handled by Hardy with a light and playful but quite deliberate and deserved sarcasm.

What range and depth have we here ! All these women stand out as clear and distinct from each other as primary colours. If certain traits appear in more than one woman it is because Hardy was not a pure artist, but was a thinker and a dreamer as well : he was not content to paint the world just as he saw it, but must add a hint or so of what he would have it be. His power of differentiation is not a universal possession of great novelists : Ethel Newcome is in many ways only a lesser Beatrix Esmond, and Diana of the Crossways is declared sister with Clara Middleton and Lord Ormont's Aminta. His understanding of women goes deep, too. He is almost, like John Ford, a specialist in women. Profound as is his comprehension of human nature itself, it is in the female personality that he is most marvellously learned (unlike Mr. H. G. Wells, who knows his men thoroughly, but is barely on speaking terms with most of his women). Only at the end, in Clare and Jude Fawley, does Hardy show an insight into the depths of male character as preternaturally acute as he seems to have had into female nature almost from the beginning. I have already pointed out that it is only in the case of two women that he rises to that supreme pinnacle of psychologic revelation, the soul's tragedy.

At the same time, it could in no sense be said of Hardy (as Ruskin said of Shakespeare and Scott) that " he had no heroes, only heroines ", or even that his women put the men in the shade. A review of the men and the women, greater and lesser, of the Wessex novels, from the points of view of interest, significance, moral and general quality, shows an almost exact balance between the two sides. If there is a slight dipping of the scales toward the side of the women, this, I think, is how it works out in life. But it is very slight—almost imperceptible. Hardy was no feminist : was Shakespeare ? Perhaps it was easier to be a feminist under the Virgin Queen than under Victoria who worshipped and wept for Albert. On the other hand, Hardy has no really unlikeable women, whereas he has several very unlikeable men.

But now we must take note of an odd fact. Though Hardy's pictures of womanhood glow with love and admiration, the text of the novels is scattered freely with observations on ' the sex ' which seems to indicate a general attitude that can only be called cynical. Some of them are indeed dramatic, but they are uttered with a certain zest. . . . " When you've made up your mind to marry ", says Reuben Davy to his son Dick, " take the first respectable body that comes to hand—she's as good as any other ; they be all alike in the groundwork ; 'tis only in the flourishes there's a difference ". Perhaps there is a double edge to the Lylyan epigram propounded by the landlord of the Sleeping-Green inn, but one edge is sharper than the other : " 'Tis woman's

nature to be false except to a man, and man's nature to be true
except to a woman ". Jocelyn Pierston " was not disposed to
resent an inexplicability in womenkind, having found that it
usually arose independently of fact, reason, probability, or his
own deserts ". This last defect is indeed the stone from which
most of the sparks are struck—a woman's inability to appraise
a man. We have seen how insistent Hardy is on this in the action
of the stories, showing it in the blindness of Bathsheba, Anne,
Thomasin, and Grace with regard to Gabriel, John, Diggory, and
Giles. He seems to have felt with Donne that—

> A naked, thinking heart that makes no show,
> Is to a woman but a kind of ghost !

He himself made a private note—" I often think that women
. . . do not know how to manage an *honest* man ". And he
gives this nail a tap whenever he comes near it : " Women are
never tired of bewailing men's fickleness in love, but they only
seem to snub his constancy " ; " . . . feminine opinion of
men's worth, so frequently founded on non-essentials . . . " ;
" it is next to impossible for an appreciative woman to have a
positive repugnance towards an unusually handsome and gifted
man " ; and a longer passage in *A Pair of Blue Eyes* to the effect
that self-dispraise stirs a kindly response in a sensible man but
" inevitably leads the most sensible woman in the world to undervalue him who practises it. Directly domineering ceases in the
man, snubbing begins in the woman ; the trite but no less unfortunate fact being that the gentler creature rarely has the
capacity to appreciate fair treatment from her natural complement." Some other critical comments find a different target,
as that which declares that the brighter endurance of women in
life's dark hours " owes more of its origin to a narrower vision
. . . than to hopefulness ". Most sweeping of all is this full-
biological judgment enunciated in *The Well-Beloved :* " She was
another illustration of the rule that succeeding generations of
women are seldom marked by cumulative progress, their advance
as girls being lost in their recession as matrons ; so they move
up and down the stream of intellectual development like flotsam
in a tidal estuary. And this perhaps not by reason of their faults
as individuals, but of their misfortune as child-rearers." When

we add all these (and other) cynicisms to the satirical touches in the characters of women like Mrs. Yeobright, Paula Power, and Elfride, we find we have a body of adverse criticism of women as a sex, over against which we have only, as a counterbalancing criticism of men, those examples of unfeeling egotism that were noted in Knight, Yeobright, and Clare—though indeed there is nothing among all the actions of women in the novels that approaches the monstrous and gratuitous cruelty of Clare's proposal to Izz Huett.

A possible conclusion—I think the most tenable one—to be drawn from the foregoing facts is that Hardy saw the ordinary woman as inferior to the ordinary man, but regarded what Mr. Humbert Wolfe calls ' the uncommon woman ' as the flower of human kind.

His limitation of choice to the rural type is even more marked with his women than with his men. In *A Pair of Blue Eyes* and *A Laodicean*, which are ' society ' novels, the women are necessarily of more or less exalted birth, but outside these the only exception to the rule is Lady Constantine. But beyond this, I think we may say that Hardy's favourite heroine is a country girl with a dash of culture. The dash may vary in quantity, but it must not be too large ; part at least of the trouble with Grace Melbury is that to her sound rustic origin her father has added such a measure of education as to leave her neither fish nor fowl. But consider those girls and women on whom Hardy has lavished his loving artistry in greatest profusion : Sue, Tess, Bathsheba, Elizabeth-Jane, Marty, and—in lesser degree—Tabitha Lark. All are pure country, born and bred, and nearly all have some slight cultural background : Tabitha plays the organ and reads to Lady Constantine, Marty's soft hands ' might ', at least, have guided the pencil or swept the strings. Only poor Tess faces life in the full naked loveliness of ignorance absolute, with no shred of borrowed accomplishment to clothe her simple country mind, until Clare comes to take her in hand. . . .

In Sir James Barrie's copy of *Tess of the D'Urbervilles* a woman wrote, " How I *hate* Thomas Hardy ! " This expression of feeling, which would probably be subscribed by a majority of the women-readers of Hardy, is doubtless based primarily on his treatment of Tess, but need not be entirely so. Of the ten principal heroines, five are brought to tragic ends after great suffering, and several of the others endure much suffering though they escape the ultimate tragedy. But a just view will not ascribe these melancholy facts to a special pleasure Hardy got out of inflicting torment upon women. After all, he saw life as a very hard school, and if the women suffer more than the men it may be because woman is the weaker vessel. But surely some of the grimness may be due to a hurt idealism—to Hardy's sense of the gulf between woman's possible best and her actual achievement towards it. The pathetic deficiency seems to have come home to him with appalling force, and his ruthless pictures of woman's folly and suffering are the bitter cry wrung from him by grief. Shakespeare's cruel satire, in the *Troilus*, on all that the world esteemed noblest in human nature, was inspired not by hate, but by a wounded love, of mankind—the fierce dissatisfaction and disillusion that came between a joyous acceptance of the raptures of life and the large sad comprehending forgiveness of its baseness. It is in this intermediate stage that Hardy's view of woman seems to lie, and—if this explanation of his attitude has anything in it—he never got beyond it. However, no such explanation is in fact required. It is not Hardy who treats his women cruelly, but life—life as Hardy saw it. What Hardy could do for his women he did—he made them full of beauty, interest, fascinating and lovable qualities of all kinds, he gave them great parts to play, and let them (generally) play those parts well. His estimate of woman is high, but tempered and conditioned by keen observation of the realities around him. He has the necessary ideals of her as a creature nobly planned and bright with angelic radiance, but he knows also that it is only in rare cases that she is found free, undimmed, ideal. Is not this position the surest ? " Faith is something which survives a mood." And so Hardy, through all his dissatisfaction at the often sorry show that woman makes, manages to " hold fast, hope hard in the subtle thing " that is the spirit of woman. It is just so that we love : we are not blind to the imperfections of the Beloved, but through them all we keep our eyes fixed on the light of absolute loveliness that burns undyingly at the central shrine of her very self. Hardy is no misogynist, but true lover in very deed.

CHAPTER IV

CONVENTION : HARDY'S VIEW OF SOCIETY

ONE of the disadvantages of living in an imperfect world is that it makes the life of the pure artist a difficult one. The temptation to join in the hopeless labour of trying to bring reality up to the demands of the ideal must be considerable. Representationally, and in regard to material objects, including the human anatomy, the artist is permitted to indulge his longing. It is conceded that ' nature is a very second-rate thing ', and that it is the artist's business to hit the target that nature has missed. But in the sphere of human conduct to improve upon is to falsify, and it is only the inferior artist who does it. The other method of en-deavouring to raise ethical standards—by delivering lectures or sermons, whether concrete or cogitative—is still less within the province of the artist ; but there can have been few artists who have not at some time or other stepped outside their province in this way. Even Keats could not be content with the unblemished artistic presentation of his allegory in the original *Hyperion*, but must try to give his convictions more explicit form in the frag-mentary revision. And we have seen that Hardy made no attempt to hide the fact that he had ' views ' about women. On the whole, however, he tells his stories purely for the stories' sake, which is the novelist's art. Yet in the last two novels he stepped aside again to show, very emphatically, his views on two controversial questions. And somehow the two novels do not suffer through this aberration. That is to say, they remain the greatest of the Wessex novels, though whether they would not have been greater still if the ' views ' had had no place in them is not easily decided. Certain inartistic paragraphs might not have found place, but on the other hand the force behind the presentation of the stories might have suffered some diminution.

Tess of the D'Urbervilles and *Jude the Obscure* are great objective
stories, but they would be incomprehensible to a reader who did
not understand the social assumptions upon which their action
is based : the assumption that a girl who has been raped is thereby
rendered unfit for marriage with another man ; and the double
assumption that a man and a woman must not live together unless
they are married, and that once being married they must not
' come unmarried '. The two novels involve the larger questions
of chastity and monogamous marriage, which go deeper than
convention, but on the whole it is the Victorian conventions on
the subjects that provide the speculative substance of the books.

Individual human life is so complicated that a man on a desert
island has to make rules to govern his comings and goings, and after
a time, for a certain type of man, these rules will become sacro-
sanct.   Collective human life is enormously more complicated,
and the number of the rules increases, and with the number the
sanctity, as is seen in savage communities.   Civilised life is so
frightfully complex that the ordinary man would be scared out
of his wits if he were allowed to look directly at it and its problems,
so its course is run under the close-fitting blinkers of convention.
And again the said conventions, especially if countenanced by the
religious authority, tend to acquire the force of laws of nature or
of holy writ.   This means that they lose the elasticity that ought
to belong to them as mere arrangements of convenience, and that
infringements of them are treated with a seriousness not warranted
by their status as experiments in *modus vivendi*.   When this has
happened the convention becomes oppressive rather than helpful,
and brings upon itself the attacks of men of original mind and
rebellious temperament.

The two conventions whose oppressive working is exposed by
Hardy are neither of them simple arbitrary ordinances, like the
convention of clothes, for example.   Each has its roots in a profound spiritual reality of human nature, and I am not sure that
Hardy clearly distinguishes this from the artificial growth that
has been allowed and encouraged to develop from it.   The convention behind the *Tess* story, that a woman should remain virgin
before marriage, is a corollary drawn (logically or not) from the
conception of the human body as the temple of the holy spirit ;
but Hardy's arguments seem to be based indiscriminately on the

plain social rule and the mystic conception with their quite different degrees of permanence. (Clare himself works only on the tight social formula.) Thus, immediately after the incident of the rape, Hardy says it offends our sense of order that " upon this beautiful feminine tissue, sensitive as gossamer, and practically as blank as snow as yet, there should have been traced such a coarse pattern ". This is to use a different metaphor from that of the ' temple ', but one expressing the same feeling : it means that something no less fine than spirit has been desecrated. But a few chapters later—about a year and a half later in time— he speaks of her soul as that of " a woman whom the turbulent experiences of the last year or two had quite failed to demoralise ", adding, " but for the world's opinion those experiences would have been simply a liberal education ". This makes the event an infringement of an arbitrary social law, but otherwise rather a Good Thing, and does not square with the former more serious pronouncement. However, a combination of the two angles gives something like truth : what had happened to Tess was— as Tess well knew—cause for endless sorrow, but there was no need for the sorrow to be crushing and unendurable, had it not been for the false view taken of the matter by society.

There is another line of defence adopted by Hardy that seems not altogether sound. He tells of Tess's deep depression in the months before she escaped to Talbothays, and of how she used to go out at night-fall and, walking amid the creatures of the wild, feel herself out of harmony, " a figure of Guilt intruding into the haunts of Innocence ". All a mistake, says Hardy : she was not in antagonism but in accord. She had broken " no law known to the environment in which she fancied herself such an anomaly ". While this is true enough, it is surely a very poor defence, taking for its basis the animal origin and environment of man, and leaving out of account not only a (perhaps unproved) spiritual element but any substantial evolutionary progress. If the ' animal ' analogy is to justify Tess it justifies D'Urberville, it justifies promiscuous rutting, to say nothing of murder and theft, and altogether forgoes that ' moral law within ' that filled Kant with admiration and awe. Some conventions represent an endeavour to embody and fix a stage of man's progress upward *from* the animal, and such is the one that has for its aim the confining of copulation to love. Of course, the actual ' wording ' of the convention confines it to *marriage*, but this only means that another convention assumes—loosely and blindly, but with good intention —that ' marriage ' and ' love ' are interchangeable terms. It is the basic spiritual principle that lies behind the practical phrasing of the convention that gives meaning to Tess's ' fall '.

Hardy continues this line of reasoning presently, pointing out that it was " the thought of the world's concern at her situation that bowed her head so profoundly ", and suggesting that alone on a desert island she would not have been " greatly wretched " at what had happened to her. Not ' greatly ', certainly, for she herself was sinless. Yet the ' coarse pattern ' had been traced on her fine substance, and even if she was, as Hardy justly says, " not an existence, an experience, a passion, a structure of sensations to anybody but herself ", she herself, under all these aspects, must have felt—did unquestionably feel—the spiritual degradation of that.

Or was there no spiritual degradation ? Perhaps spiritual change, for good or evil, can only come from acts fully willed. This is where Hardy is completely convincing. He makes Tess ask herself, " Was once lost always lost really true of chastity ? " —implying a hopeful negative answer. And since she means physical chastity—for spiritually she is inviolate—we may eagerly accept the quiet cogency of Hardy's own reply—" The recuperative power which pervaded organic nature was surely not denied to maidenhood alone ". He shows this power beginning to make itself felt in Tess, " unexpended youth, surging up anew after its temporary check, and bringing with it hope, and the invincible instinct towards self-delight ". And so he gives us the beautiful ' phase ' of ' the rally '—the practical argument that clinches his thesis of regeneration. The splendour of the picture of Tess's new happy life carries conviction into the argument. We have already seen how Hardy underlines his attitude by frequent references, on the part of other characters, to Tess's conspicuous ' virginity '. He continues his dialectic palliation : it was impossible, he says, that any event should have left upon one so young an impression that was not in time capable of transmutation. He makes the general observation : " women do as a rule live through such humiliations, and regain their spirits, and again

look about them with an interested eye "—which tells us nothing
of importance on the moral question. On the mental one he is
quite convinced that Tess's experience had deepened her understanding of life : he shows Clare realising with astonishment that
this milkmaid knows the very " ache of modernism ", and Hardy
comments—" Tess's passing corporeal blight had been her mental
harvest ".

It is to be noticed that these arguments leave Tess herself
unconvinced. Even after her marriage we hear her whispering
to herself, " O my love, my love, why do I love you so ! for she
you love is not my real self, but one in my image ; the one I
might have been ! " But this does not justify Clare. Clare,
like Othello, is simply and unconditionally a fool. The arguments with which he supports his abandonment of Tess after her
disclosure are several and various, but all alike shallow. His main
line, more than once repeated, is that she has been one person but
now is another. This sounds impressive but means little : it
means nothing except that he had discovered a ' fact ' about her
that he had not known before ; it would have been equally true
if the new fact had been that she had been brought up on goat's
milk. The question is *in what way* different ? Here, of course,
he did not argue (that is, think) at all : he acted, as he says later,
on ' principle '—he allowed himself to be guided by the conventional instinct that had been bred into him, and which told
him that no virtuous woman had sex-experience before marriage,
although many virtuous men did. The two-fold convention,
though admittedly based on the property-sense (and property
vested solely in the male), had by the late nineteenth and early
twentieth centuries become so integral a part of the general
outlook that attempts were made to find in it a more permanent
necessity, founded in some inherent difference between man and
woman : " Dealing with the subject of sex-equality Sir John
Bigham (President of the Divorce Court, during the Royal Com-
mission on the Divorce Laws, 1912) said he did not think the
act of misconduct on the part of the man had anything like the
same significance as such an act on the part of a woman. . . . It
was not inconsistent with his continued esteem and love for his
wife . . . whereas an act of misconduct on the part of a woman,
was, in his opinion, quite inconsistent with her continued love

and esteem for her husband." And yet this difference between a wife's love and a husband's love has already lost acceptance—at least it does not seem to be recognised in the post-war novel and play : so short-lived are eternal verities produced to order !

Clare's other ' arguments ' are that D'Urberville is Tess's " husband in nature " (which is sheer clap-trap), and that any children he and Tess might have would suffer from their mother's ill-repute ; this, too, is very thin, for any children of Tess and D'Urberville would have been in little better case, and Clare is thinking of his own discomfort, not of that of the children ; besides which, as both he and Tess see at once, though neither mentions it, the disability, such as it was, had a purely local force.

In fact, the temporary and local nature of the whole social philosophy is apparent to Clare as soon as he gets free from the English climate. The very notion of leaving England loosens some joint in his mind and allows him to see it is mere convention that " makes life with Tess seem impracticable to him here ". And once under the wider skies of South America he is able to do some genuine thinking :

> Having long discredited the old systems of mysticism, he now began to discredit the old appraisements of morality. He thought they wanted readjusting. Who was the moral man ? Still more pertinently, who was the moral woman ? The beauty or ugliness of a character lay not only in its achievements, but in its aims and impulses ; its true history lay, not among things done, but among things willed.

His mental evolution is carried further by the cosmopolitan stranger, who (before being struck down by fever and the Hardian irony) adds to Clare's own discoveries the thought that " what Tess had been was of no importance beside what she would be ". And so at last Clare sweeps to a realisation of his grand inconsistency—that he, a determined Hellenist, had been condemning Tess for what only a narrow Christian morality regarded as sin. Hardy had probed to the very bottom of the convention, and put the truth about it with clearness and finality several chapters previously, when he defined Clare's ' limitations ' :

> With all his attempted independence of judgment this advanced and well-meaning young man, a sample product of the last five-and-twenty years, was yet the slave to custom and convention-

ality when surprised back into his early teachings. No prophet had told him, and he was not prophet enough to tell himself, that essentially this young wife of his was as deserving of the praise of King Lemuel as any other woman endowed with the same dislike of evil, her moral value having to be reckoned not by achievement but by tendency.

Clare has now seen all this as truth. That he sees it too late to help Tess only strengthens the force with which the ethical intention of the novel is thus doubly hammered home.

The marriage problem is a staple of fiction, and Hardy makes some use of it. He says in the preface to *The Woodlanders*, " In the present novel, as in one or two others of this series which involve the question of matrimonial divergence, the immortal puzzle—given the man and woman, how to find a basis for their sexual relation—is left where it stood ". The ' others ' are, I suppose, *Far from the Madding Crowd*, *The Hand of Ethelberta*, and *The Return of the Native*, as well as *Jude*. In all of them, and in *The Woodlanders*, some part (though generally a small part) of the story occupies itself with an unhappy marital relation, and in all of them, except *Jude*, the trouble is caused by an outside ' attachment ' on the part of either the wife or the husband. The situation is not, however, treated as a problem, it being tacitly assumed (as Hardy ironically says) that the looking aside is due to simple depravity. In *Jude* the trouble has a different origin, and the problem is worked out at length, in a way that leaves little doubt as to Hardy's own position. Indeed, he makes this plain in the preface to the Wessex edition of *Jude*, where he states his " opinion that marriage should be dissolvable as soon as it becomes a cruelty to either of the parties, being then essentially and morally no marriage ". This simplification, sound as far as it goes, is open to several objections (Phillotson being an illustration of one of them), and obviously offers nothing but a stop-gap remedy. Indeed, Hardy gives no evidence of having seen to the heart of this more complicated problem, as he certainly had in the case of the simpler question propounded in *Tess*.

Views given shape in the novel itself are, of course, not necessarily, or not always, the novelist's own, and at one point Hardy expressly warns us against reading them as such. Nevertheless there are many passages in which the author speaks with his own lips, and though it will be desirable to separate these out, they will be found to differ in no way from those voiced by Sue, Jude, and Phillotson.   Thus, we cannot be expected to overlook the ironic significance of Hardy's description of the ' wedding ' of Jude and Arabella :

> And so, standing before the aforesaid officiator, the two swore that at every other time of their lives they would assuredly believe, feel, and desire precisely as they had believed, felt, and desired during the few preceding weeks.   What was as remarkable as the undertaking itself was the fact that nobody seemed at all surprised at what they swore.

The satire perhaps misses the point of the ceremony, which is that, certain conditions being present (as indeed they seldom are) there is definite assurance that the ' contracting parties ' will actually perpetuate the beliefs, feelings and desires of the moment, so that there can be no objection to, though indeed no necessity for, their swearing the oath.   (The harm that has been done by the effort to screw impermanent feelings down on to a base of permanence *by means of* an oath is incalculable.)   Jude presently puts Hardy's ironically turned opinion in literal terms, when he realises that " their lives were ruined by the fundamental error of having based a permanent contract on a temporary feeling which had no necessary connection with affinities that alone render a life-long comradeship tolerable ".

Naturally it is the attached penalty that weighs most heavily on Jude—" their lives were ruined ".   Later we find him thinking—

> There seemed to him, vaguely and dimly, something wrong in a social ritual which made necessary a cancelling of well-formed schemes involving years of thought and labour . . . and of contributing his units of work to the general progress of his generation, because of a momentary surprise by a new and transitory instinct.

Undoubtedly the penalty is not only too severe but anti-social, like the penalty of poverty imposed on idleness.   Jude's sex-adventure with Arabella was a piece of criminal folly, but it did not deserve a life-sentence (as was the intention of the marriage-oath) and one which, moreover, would deprive society of a useful unit, replacing it with a double unit of misery.

So far the matrimonial problem has involved only Jude and

Arabella, but presently it draws Sue and Phillotson into its toils, so that further opinions become available. Sue, married by another mistake to Phillotson, is emphatic that " love's usual tragedy in civilised life is a tragedy artificially manufactured for people who in a natural state would find relief in parting ". She too, like Jude, has been guilty of culpable negligence, as she admits : " I had never fully thought out what marriage meant, even though I knew. It was idiotic of me—there was no excuse. I was old enough, and I thought I was very experienced." Indeed, the several indictments of the marriage law come a little too glibly from people who have abused rather than used the institution. They should at least have recognised that if the marriage law was pressing hardly upon them it was because of their obvious mad culpability in entering into false and impossible marriages. It is unreasonable to expect to escape from such follies without any penal consequences at all. Still, mistakes will happen, and *either* steps ought to be taken to make it less easy for people to enter into bad marriages, *or* the way out ought to be made simple and clean. Hardy joins in the indictment once more by showing his evident sympathy with one of the ' mistakes ' :

> Then the slim little wife of a husband whose person was dis-agreeable to her, the ethereal, fine-nerved, sensitive girl, quite unfitted by temperament and instinct to fulfil the conditions of the matrimonial relation with Phillotson, possibly with any man, walked fitfully along, and panted, and brought weariness into her eyes by gazing and worrying hopelessly.

Now a new angle is brought to bear by Phillotson, who is a victim of a painful marriage situation through no fault (or less fault) of his own. He comes to much the same conclusion as Jude, Sue, and Hardy, but not by argument, but through his decent humane instincts. He cannot or does not wish to argue the position : he admits to his friend Gillingham that his views on marriage are " old fashioned "—but " certain facts stared him in the face ", the facts of Sue's misery. So he makes this one particular marriage terminable on request. Gillingham voices the woodenly correct view—what will people say ? what would happen if everybody took this line ? at least don't let her go to her cavalier—and (privately) she ought to be smacked. The same standpoint is taken, with more effect, by the School

Managers, who dismiss Phillotson for ' condoning his wife's adultery '.

And having thus aroused our sympathy with his thesis of liberty, Hardy puts in a word for the policy of law and order by showing, in a passage of biting satire, the kind of people who came forward in support of Phillotson at the public meeting called by the schoolmaster to protest against his dismissal. His supporters belonged to a travelling fair that happened to be in the neighbourhood, and included " two cheap-jacks, a shooting-gallery proprietor and the ladies who loaded the guns, a pair of boxing-masters, a steam-roundabout manager, two travelling broom-makers, who called themselves widows, a gingerbread-stall keeper, a swing-boat owner, and a ' test-your-strength-man ' ". These champions of free thought upset the meeting, break the furniture, and set the venerable rector's nose bleeding. Phillotson is ashamed, but not of the line he has taken. The episode reminds us that freedom, though a ' noble thing ', is a dangerous possession. Like power, freedom is a thing few people are fit for. Certainly unlimited freedom, like unlimited power, demoralises almost everybody who possesses it. Moreover, good law is a means to freedom. This is no excuse for bad law, but it means we must not fall into one pit in avoiding the other.

When the question arises as to whether Jude and Sue shall get married, Sue is against the project, and Jude rather hesitatingly agrees with her. But he is inclined to think the ceremony would be bad in their particular case, while Sue insists that it is always bad. One remark of hers at this time cuts to the bone, and makes it necessary that we should point out just where she is wrong. For Sue, and Hardy, are not quite right in their negative attitude towards the institution of marriage.

Sue's remark is—" How hopelessly vulgar an institution legal marriage is ! " It has a special and quite sound reference at the moment, but as a general statement it comprehends much of her feeling on the matter—and it indicates the blind spot in her outlook. Marriage is not vulgar : it is poetic, romantic, a high adventure. Nor does the legal bond in any way detract from its romance. The Knights of the Round Table did not feel themselves hampered by their oath of fidelity to the King. The grip of the law may irk the conscript soldier, but we are not talking about conscripts. Honesty is no less a virtue, and the practice of it is no less satisfying, by reason of the laws against theft. The law doubtless seems oppressive to the thief, but we are not talking about thieves. Strange, incredible, paradoxical as it may seem, the marriage law, imperfect as it is, and intended chiefly to discourage the obvious evil of promiscuous unions, is yet, by some wild accident (and yet no accident, for it had its origin in the precept of Jesus), an expression of an ideal which has never been fully realised, from which we seem to be drifting further away at present, but to which the world must return some day, in the hope of its full general realisation : the ideal of monogamous marriage. Sue's impatience with the ghastly results of a woodenly-applied convention is only too well justified, but it needs a corrective : it needs to be reminded that it is not the last word on the matter : the last, or at least a later one, giving the necessary corrective, is supplied by some words of Studdert Kennedy : " Once we have got rid of the idea that Christian monogamy is primitive, natural or easy, and have realised that it is a supreme spiritual achievement toward which the race has been toiling and travailing down the ages, we begin to see things in their true perspective ".

Hardy saw convention mounting to a place in society to which it had no right : he saw it becoming master where it should have been a servant. Clare perceives, when his eyes are opened, that his mistake has been in " allowing himself to be influenced by general principles to the disregard of the particular instances ". The motto of *Jude the Obscure*, which applies as well to *Tess of the D'Urbervilles*, is " The letter killeth ". Rules there must be, but proportion must be kept among them. *The Woodlanders* is, as to Giles's death, a tragedy of propriety—Grace allowed the secondary laws of propriety to stand before the primary one of humanity. The misery of the two greater novels arises in both cases from narrow conventional views usurping the place of the one great law by which all others must be tested, the golden rule of love and happiness. The ordinances of society are administered with great neglect of this golden rule, in a rigid and unintelligent fashion. Laws—whether political or social—require to be framed with a view to order, but must be administered in the spirit of love, " on the broader ground of how to afford the greatest happiness to the units of human society in their brief passage through this sorry world ".

CHAPTER V

PESSIMISM: HARDY'S VIEW OF LIFE

YOUR pessimist is born, not made; and the optimist may have made himself: but either state of mind is capable of being accentuated by external happenings. Who shall say how much deeper and darker Hardy's birthright of pessimism became after the following incident, noted in his diary for January 7th, 1888? —" On New Year's Eve and day I sent off five copies of a magazine containing a story of mine, and three letters—all eight to friends by way of New Year's greeting and good wishes. *Not a single reply*. Mem: Never send New Year's letters, &c. again."

It turned out that two of the friends were dying (which cannot have helped much), and there was eventually one reply.

The foregoing apologue may seem to suggest that Hardy's pessimism is not to be taken too seriously. I do not see how pessimism can possibly be taken as anything but a symptom of a congenital mental condition, and to erect it into a philosophy is to confuse functions. A philosophy must be the outcome of a dispassionate survey of phenomena, and the pessimist, being born disgruntled, is incapacitated from making such a survey. The pessimist, wearing his irremovable dark glasses, sees everything a shade blacker than it really is. Hardy asserted in so many words that "tragedy *always* underlies comedy". Only born pessimism could account for that unphilosophical ' always ': could, when it had ' scratched deep enough ' to come to a tragic stratum, insist on stopping there instead of going deeper still. "Laughter", Hardy said, "can only come through forgetfulness." There is truth in that, but the predication can be made of tears with precisely the same degree and kind of truth. "I discovered several years ago that I was living in a world where nothing bears out its promise in practice." What! *nothing*,

Mr. Hardy ?   Not the promise of a Cox's Orange Pippin, or the promise of Beethoven and Shakespeare. or the promise of at least some early summer dawns ?

The same uncritical obsession makes itself felt in the novels. Not so much on the large scale of the narratives themselves : there, as we shall see, Hardy was compelled to show the balance of things that his undimmed artist's eye compelled him to see. But incidental observations are almost invariably made through those temperamental dark glasses.   When George Somerset turns his head to gaze at the evening glory that is lighting up with brilliant chromatic effects the moulded stonework he is measuring, Hardy comments : " There are few in whom the sight of a sunset does not beget as much meditative melancholy as contemplative pleasure, the human decline and death that it illustrates being too obvious to escape the notice of the simplest observer ".   This, as to its first part, is a very moderate generalisation compared with others we have quoted, but when it goes on to account for the ' melancholy ', it again clearly betrays the determined or involuntary distortion, for if a sunset is an illustration of human decline and death it should surely provide a joyful reaction, by reason of its peace, beauty, and promise of renewal.   Opening *The Return of the Native* we find Egdon described as " a place perfectly accordant with man's nature . . . like man, slighted and enduring ".   Few men who are reasonably treated by their fellow-men feel slighted and enduring ; it is impossible to think of such a feeling attaching, in any circumstances, to Michael Angelo or Einstein.

Provided it is accepted for what it is—as something that tells us a great deal about the writer but nothing about the world he writes of—there is, of course, no objection to pessimism as an artistic medium.   It has the eternal virtue of being much more interesting than many facile optimistic presentations of life, and is nearer to the truth than most of them.   Hardy did not disclaim the attribution of pessimism to his outlook.   He said it was his aim to present a view of things that harmonised with experience, but he admitted that his was a nature that became vocal in the presence of tragedy rather than comedy (though he was not, he thought, imperceptive of the latter).   He found, he said, a special interest in " the failure of things to be what they were meant to be ". So he gave us, in the Wessex novels, *La Tragédie Humaine*. He grew indeed a little tired of having the name pessimist hurled at him with opprobrious intent. Sometimes he would retort that to object to a writer being a pessimist was to wish him to close his eyes to human ills. Later, he rather inconsistently preferred the designation of ' meliorist '. " As a meliorist (not a pessimist, by the way), I think better of the world ", he wrote to some one who, soon after the Great War, had predicted that the next war would be worse still. Now, less than twenty years afterwards, this particular ' thinking better of the world ' looks like shutting the eyes indeed to human folly in a way worthy of none but the most pathetical optimist. But the toying with ' meliorism ' was a mere whim—a passing weakness. Generally Hardy was too deeply concerned with " the plight of being alive " to have time to notice whether life was climbing out of its plight. More often his tendency is to show things getting worse—especially to show a growing realisation of how bad they are. " The view of life as a thing to be put up with, replacing that zest for existence which was so intense in early civilisation, must ultimately enter so thoroughly into the constitution of the advanced races. . . . The old-fashioned revelling in the general situation grows less and less possible as we uncover the defects of natural laws, and see the quandary that man is in by their operation."

Sometimes the bias becomes an unconscionable warp. What end is served by propounding such a wild assertion as that " the planet does not supply the materials for happiness to the higher existences " ? It is so easy to give at least the first few items of a long list that might be made of the more readily accessible materials for such happiness. *Quot homines*—but, as a first contribution, say—love, friendship, and the ways of little children ; walking over the hills ; sleeping—and waking ; humour, and other sources of kindly laughter, ' irony itself ' as Charles Lamb would say ; food, wine and tobacco ; introspection and most thought processes, the higher mathematics ; poetry, prose, music ; natural scenery—particularly of lake and mountain ; the exercise and contemplation of kindness and other pleasant virtues ; good conversation, argument, chess ; truth, and beauty, and that intimate kind of beauty called loveliness ; ' the consolation of philosophy ', and of religion. . . .

And there is a point at which pessimism becomes cynicism : and as Hardy himself says in *Tess*, " No man can be a cynic and live ". Farmer Boldwood's kindness to Bathsheba was, it appears, no kindness, for " the rarest offerings of the purest loves are but a self-indulgence, and no generosity at all ". Logically there is no way out of this position (unless that found by Kant was a real way out), but a beautiful disposition is none the less beautiful, and none the less an object of delight and praise, because it cannot help its beauty bearing beautiful fruit. The disparagement of kindness is based on the bad old fallacy that virtue is not joyful but a matter of ' duty ', that only those actions can be called virtuous that are done against the grain. It is a dangerous ethic, and leads downwards not upwards. See again Hardy's materialistic comments on Swithin St. Cleeve's preparations for his wedding, at a spot which had probably seen the bridal ceremonies of prehistoric inhabitants :

> Little signified those ceremonies to-day, or the happiness or otherwise of the contracting parties. That his own rite, nevertheless, signified much, was the inconsequent reasoning of Swithin, as it is of many another bridegroom besides ; and he, like the rest, went on with his preparations in that mood which sees in his stale repetition the wondrous possibilities of an untried move.

What is this but to repeat what some other world-weary cynic intoned ?—" Nothing is new, nothing is true, and nothing matters : this is the first lesson that history teaches ". To which one can only reply, so much the worse for history, and the things that history deals with. Life and art teach no such lesson.

Pessimism need not be, and is not always with Hardy, so unreasonable. He attempted a justification of the outlook when he declared that " the highest flights of the pen are mostly the excursions and revelations of souls unreconciled to life ". This restatement of the proposition that our sweetest songs are those that tell of saddest thought (not quite fully demonstrated yet, for the joyous counterparts of Heine and Keats and Mr. Walter de la Mare may at any moment break through the silence) falls a good deals hort of the complete pessimist position, but is not unacceptable as far as it goes. A man may be dissatisfied with the laws of his native country without wishing to destroy it, or indeed to do anything but make it better. So, too, when Hardy described " some of these novels of Wessex life " as having been addressed " more especially to readers into whose souls the iron has entered ", he is putting in a right claim for the place of tragic literature in life. One has certainly known people who, in times of distress, have found the more sombre of the Wessex novels to possess qualities the very opposite of consolatory, but this was perhaps because the function of tragedy had by them not been properly grasped. No modern writer aims so deliberately and so effectively at the effect of the tragic *katharsis*, the purging by pity and terror (though it may well be that Hardy's prescription is too drastic to suit the modern constitution). Or again that recurring notion of his that the beauty of the human countenance is being eaten away by " the disease of thought ", so that the typical faces that will be chosen by the sculptors of the future will be but wrinkled copies of the serene types that served the Greeks —this, though bleakly turned, is an expression of a change that time and evolution may well bring.

We have already observed that once, at the end of *The Mayor of Casterbridge*, Hardy allowed himself to be betrayed into taking note of a fact which, if not joyful enough to be called optimistic, has at least an anti-pessimistic tinge about it. He made Elizabeth-Jane " wonder at the persistence of the unforeseen " which had brought her to " unbroken tranquillity ", although her youth " had seemed to teach that happiness was but the occasional episode in a general drama of pain ". Few enough of Hardy's characters find the ' unforeseen ' turning out in this way— Bathsheba and Gabriel Oak are perhaps the only others—but the possibility is recognised : darkness is not quite unrelieved. And if few find happiness, rather more learn wisdom from their protracted ordeal : not only Bathsheba and Gabriel and Elizabeth-Jane, but Clare and Yeobright, Tamsie and Paula Power. Measured by life's standards, this is a not ungenerous estimate of the proportion of people who win wisdom from suffering. Tess herself was not crushed into anything lower than herself by the cruelty of life that bore down so leadenly upon her, but against its pressure raised herself into something of infinite nobility. This is in some ways the most hopeful word Hardy has pronounced —if we can shut our ears to the discrepant word he said in Sue.

Indeed, no writer who presents human-kind so worthily can be a thorough-going pessimist. Your true pessimist is he who, like Swift, depicts man himself as degraded, contemptible. From Hardy's dark canvas there stand out the heroic forms of a mighty Adam and a beauteous Eve. With him man is far from god-like, but still a moral being, rich in interest and of high capacity. Negatively, Hardy has few low types among his people, and no scoundrels of the Dickens and Thackeray order. His Troy, his D'Urberville, his Arabella are angels of light compared with the freaks of depravity that crowd the pages of recent fiction. And twice he introduces a conception that makes nonsense of anything like deep-rooted pessimism : we have already heard him speak of Tess's youth surging up and bringing with it " the invincible instinct towards self-delight " ; and later in the same novel we read of " the appetite for joy which pervades all creation, that tremendous force which sways humanity to its purpose ". This endowing of the evolutionary urge with a name so full of eager meaning, so much more significant than an indeterminate ' life force ', ' *élan vital* ' or ' will to live ', seems to me a remarkable piece of evidence that Hardy was, as he said, " not imperceptive of the other side ".

But why not admit it more generously ? Even materialism may lay hold on life with both hands. Omar the tent-maker showed it can be done, and as a way of life based on one-half of the extant criteria I know nothing more satisfying than the way expounded in those melodious Rubáiyát. There is the wild hopeless wish to remould this sorry scheme of things nearer to the heart's desire ; there is grief that youth's sweet-scented manuscript should close ; there is wrath at the pitfalls and gins that beset the road ; there is ironic laughter at that which makes game of us in the magic-shadow show ; and there is calm acceptance of the unravellable knot of human destiny. But one is never allowed to lose sight of the compensating facts that still the Vine her ruby vintage yields, and still a garden by the water blows, and that with but a very few of the elemental sweets of life—ah, wilderness is paradise enow ! There is the constant call to fill the cup of life's wine, to drink of the well of life's rapture, even though it be but for a moment in a waste of annihilation, and though we and all things end in nothing.

I have suggested that the personal element in pessimism is so large as to disqualify it from the dignity of a philosophy. Yet pessimism claims, if not to explain, at least to be built upon an explanation of the universe, and though Hardy constantly denied that any such superstructure of belief could be formed of his ' impressions ', those impressions are so numerous and so consistent that it is difficult to suppose the considered philosophy was not at the bottom of them. His too-sweeping indictment of Fate must have been based on something more than observation and feeling : it must have had a metaphysic in a reasoned conception of nature, the non-human principle of the Universe, as antithetically opposed to man, definitely hostile to his aims, and thwarting him at every point. Censors of Hardy have been known to ask why the man did not commit suicide, and it is not impossible to deduce from his collected writings that he would have been willing to give in his adherence to the ultimate ethic of pessimism, the self-extinction of the race, that being the only way of correcting the primal mistake made by the Will in creating consciousness. I like to contrast with the cold logic of this epically base project the equally heroic and somehow more inspiring purpose of Olaf Stapledon's ' Last Men ' on Neptune, faced with the certain prospect of the total obliteration of the human race, but devoting the short age that remains to them to perfecting a method of disseminating the seeds of life through space, because though man fail, ' it must go on '.

It seems desirable to repeat that the pessimistic outlook is probably transitional. Though England did not take in the new facts till the end of the nineteenth century (after the word of our English scientist had come to corroborate that of the Scottish philosopher), the God of Christian orthodoxy had been destroyed in the eighteenth, and it was out of that negation that the Schopenhauer view of things was born. Hardy speaks in *Tess* of " the chronic melancholy which is taking hold of the civilised races with the decline of belief in a beneficent Power ". At the moment that ' melancholy ' appears to be in process of being replaced by a certain irresponsibility : this is an equivocal substitution, but is perhaps a necessary step towards the enthronement of a steadier joy and a wider hope that will come when the faith of the future takes hold upon human consciousness. That Hardy's ' meliorism ' included some conception of this new faith is apparent from his poetry, which we shall be considering presently.

CHAPTER VI

THE GIFT OF HARDY

IT has been pointed out more than once in the course of this study that Hardy was not, on the one hand, a pure artist, nor, on the other, what Mr. Bernard Shaw calls a philosopher-artist— a novelist with a purpose. Like most creative writers of the past hundred years he thought as well as felt and saw : and what he thought about things found its way into his work, but without disturbing its artistic shape. Matthew Arnold said no poet of his day could make much of his business unless he was intellectual. And so, for better or worse, we have the *Idylls of the King* for the *Morte* of Malory, *The Ring and the Book* and *The Testament of Beauty* for *Beowulf* and the Odyssey, the drama of Ibsen and Shaw for that of Sophocles and Shakespeare, and the novels of Hardy and Galsworthy for those of Scott and Jane Austen. The absolute equivalence of Truth and Beauty is accepted still by Mr. Walter de la Mare and Mr. W. H. Davies, but by few others. Hence these chapters on ' the philosophy of the novels '.

But what essentially do we get from the reading of Hardy ? What is it that he gives us ? This ' gift ', as I call it, of a writer, bears a direct relation to his art and to his philosophy (if he has any), but is seldom identical with either or both of them. To what extent is one better equipped for life by having read the Wessex novels ? It is a question that may be legitimately asked concerning any work of art, pure or adulterated. One is equipped for life by reading the most careless lyric of Sir John Suckling as certainly as by reading the ' Religio Medici ' or ' Sartor Resartus '.

We get from him first what we get from any good novelist, a knowledge of life. We go to school to life in our late teens and early twenties, but the lessons are badly presented, and few of us learn much. We can, if we choose, take in addition a kind of correspondence course, by reading with some care the works of a few great novelists. Here we shall find the lessons admirably arranged, artistically presented, with difficulties cleared up : experience at second-hand, certainly, but pre-digested and, if we will, easily assimilated. An ecclesiastical dignitary once advised any priest who was proposing to take a country living to read the Wessex novels as a preparation. The advice might be extended to all who are facing life in any form.

Another value that he shares with the great majority of writers of genius is that his essential morality is sound and healthy. He presents a state of society in which virtue is the natural order of things, not vice—as in the Restoration drama, and in many novels, plays and films of to-day. It cannot be said of him, as is sometimes said of Thackeray, that his honest folk are fools and his clever people rogues ; he excites sympathy with good and hatred of evil. I have referred to the difficulties I experience over *The Hand of Ethelberta* : they are probably due to obtuseness on my part. But in every other novel we are plainly compelled to take our stand beside the right, for its own sake—not, of course, for the sake of any material benefit that is likely to accrue thereby. Hardy holds out no false bait of happiness to ensue from the following of righteousness. But I believe that my contention as to the direction in which our sympathies are constantly moved by the affairs of his novel will be disproved with difficulty.

But when we come to Hardy's own peculiar ' gifts ', I find the first of them in a certain fortifying of one's faith in human nature, which springs from observation of the kind of person he chooses for sympathetic presentation. The kind can be briefly indicated by the word ' homely ', but the important thing is that in it we see human nature itself, unpolished, unadorned, with a minimum of education : the natural man. I have said enough about Gabriel Oak, John Loveday, and Giles Winterborne, but they are the three great exemplars of this homely type, this natural man, and they can stand against the world : I don't know which novelist will provide three to match them. And nearly all the best among the lesser figures are carved from this same good plain material : Reuben Dewy, John Smith, Diggory Venn, Miller Loveday, Marty South, Widow Edlin, Mrs. Melbury, Izz Huett.

. . If the stuff of human nature is as good as this, education, culture, civilisation ought to be able to make something of it.

And from the Wessex novels we learn again—what since the war we have been determined to forget—that there are ideals worth living up to. In the heart of Hardy's finest characters there burns a light, and that light is never allowed to grow dim. Remember Oak and his probity, Yeobright and his altruistic schemes, John Loveday and his self-renunciation, Giles Winterborne and his chivalrous consideration, Marty and her unchanging love, Tess and her fidelity, Jude and his undying dream, and Sue and her dream too. Of Hardy's treatment of love something has been said, but of its beauty as an ideal he speaks through the shining figures of the four faithful men, and of Marty, and of Tess, and of Jude and Sue.

Another result of reading the Wessex novels is that if one has a ' moral code ' one is compelled to reconstruct it. The reader is quickly driven to obey Dr. Johnson's precept and clear his mind of cant. Then, as he proceeds, there takes place a great rearrangement and reproportioning of ideas of morality. Narrow prejudices of right and wrong, hitherto unquestioned, begin to open out, to withdraw and disappear, and their place is taken by great principles of good and evil, differentiating and classifying not by surface name but by fundamental nature. There is little legislation, definite laying down of this to be blessed and that to be cursed. Rather, with regard to the central themes, he sets up a disturbing questioning among one's collection of moral judgments : the possibility of right behind the apparent wrong and of wrong behind the apparent right is made visible in the concrete, and tolerance, that divinely humane virtue, is born. We get a new insight into the possibilities of evil, especially the possibility of its unimportance in comparison with preponderating good. The idealist in morals—and he is the only moralist worth listening to—is apt incontinently to damn a man or a woman at sight of his or her sins. But it is in the highest degree necessary, when judging human beings, to remember, in the first place, that there are sides to a character. I have known men who, estimated on their appearance at certain moments, would seem to be utterly contemptible, and who were yet in other relations splendid to the hand-grip, nobly tender, heroic, even poetic. So that it seems to me that any book that can teach us at the same time a dread and a tolerance of sin is of divine efficacy. The theologians are not unanimous as to the desirability of complete tolerance, which is supposed to be antagonistic to zeal. But tolerance is charity, and intolerance means closing the mind. " The supreme ineptitude ", said Flaubert, " consists in wishing to conclude." Our aim is truth, not expediency, and toward the discovery of truth in the sphere of conduct Hardy performs the very useful office of clearing away the cobwebs of prejudice, making us aware of new points of view, new standards of right and wrong, and so enabling us to approach questions of morals with unbiassed mind and that sympathy which alone gives understanding.

But—if one may yield to the temptation to stray in conclusion a little from one's subject—perhaps Hardy gave us nothing quite so precious in his life and his work as he gave us in his death. How many men have felt the inspiration of the death of Socrates, with its tranquil discussion of the immortality of the soul. That famous scene now has its rival in the death of Thomas Hardy, as recorded in *The Later Years*. As he lay dying, during the last few days, he asked for three poems to be read to him. When I consider the significance of those poems, severally and in sequence, and associate them with the ' philosophy ' we have been discussing, I see a strange suggestiveness in this death-scene : if it lacks the sunlit spacious sublimity of the one recorded by Plato, it hovers over vaster depths of speculation, and perhaps speaks more nearly to the mind of that uneasy species, the modern man. On January 6th, five days before the end, in the middle of the night he asked his wife to read him *The Listeners* of Walter de la Mare :

' Is there anybody there ? ' said the Traveller. . . .

On the evening of January 10th he asked for *Rabbi Ben Ezra* (listening to it, Mrs. Hardy says, with a wistful intentness) :

> Grow old along with me !
> The best is yet to be,
> The last of life, for which the first was made :
> Our times are in His hand
> Who saith, A whole I planned. . . .

The next evening he asked Mrs. Hardy to repeat to him the stanza from the *Rubáiyát of Omar Khayyám* :

> Oh, Thou, who Man of baser Earth didst make,
> And ev'n with Eden didst devise the Snake :
>   For all the Sin wherewith the Face of Man
> Is blacken'd—Man's forgiveness give—and take !

A few hours later he died.

THE DYNASTS

LIKE Milton, Hardy projected an ' epic ' long before he settled down to write one, but unlike Milton he was never in doubt as to what his theme was going to be. From the *Early Years* and the *Later Life* we have evidence that the subject of the Napoleonic Wars was long considered ; seldom a year passed but some thought was given to the matter. The period had a personal attraction through the poet's ancestor, Nelson's Hardy, but active interest in the wars started with the boyhood discovery of a set of periodicals containing a contemporary history of the Revolutionary and Napoleonic campaigns, " with melodramatic prints ". He visited Brussels and Waterloo more than once, and tells us that a sight of Louis Napoleon in 1878 was of great value to him in imagining Bonaparte's appearance. The subject was likewise well suited to his philosophic views. In war, especially in a great war, man is more obviously the creature of fate : the individual has no power over his own fate because he is compelled, more than at other times, to render unquestioning obedience to his superiors, and the few who have no ' superiors ' are at the mercy of passions, ' dynastic ' and other, loyalties, interests, abstractions like diplomacy, the balance of power, national alignments and ' international relations ', as well as of the blind chance of events.

The Dynasts, as a conception, and apart from its form, stands unique in literature, certainly in English literature. The war epics, the *Iliad* and Morris's *Sigurd*, may be ruled out of the field of comparison by reason of their mythical subjects and their concern with the exploits of individual heroes. More reasonable parallels are to be found in Shakespeare and Scott. But though the historical plays of Shakespeare cover the period of the Wars of the Roses, there is very little active and deliberate unity of conception in the series ; and the same may be said of those half-dozen of the Waverley novels that have for their theme the misfortunes of the House of Stuart. In any case, the element of fiction in both Scott and Shakespeare is so large as to differentiate their historical work from that of Hardy. The nearest analogies to *The Dynasts* are to be found in Gibbon's *Decline and Fall* and, especially, Carlyle's *French Revolution*—works in which a period of history is imaginatively conceived and presented through the rich colouring medium of a great mind.

For *The Dynasts* is primarily a historical work. Its main purpose—or, let us say, its more obvious purpose—is to present in dramatic form the course of the Napoleonic struggle from 1805 to 1815, and this, of course, it does with all the faithfulness and accuracy of the modern scholar, and all the narrative power of the author of the Wessex novels. (The only omission of any importance seems to be the lack of notice taken of Napoleon's brilliant campaigns on French soil in the spring of 1814, between Leipzig and the abdication.) The opening date may appear to be chosen somewhat arbitrarily. The Peace of Amiens was a temporary lull in a war which was essentially continuous, and Napoleon had been in control of affairs since 1799. However, 1799 would have made an unsatisfactory starting-point ; and to have dramatised the Revolutionary Wars would have tasked the powers even of a Hardy. Issues were certainly much more clear-cut after the renewal of war in 1803 ; and 1805, with Napoleon fresh from the assumption of imperial rank, Pitt newly returned to power, and England at the climax of her expectation of invasion, certainly provides a dramatic moment for the rise of the curtain.

In one sense it is to be regretted that Hardy was impelled—by the reasons indicated above, as we should say, or, to use the language of the ' Intelligences ', by the ' Immanent Will '—to select this period of history as the subject of his epic-drama or dramatic-epic (he appears to have hesitated between the two descriptions, and the second seems at least as good as the one that was finally appended : the work is an epic in dramatic form rather than a drama in epic form). The modern epic should be something more than a tale of physical battle and material conquest. Even such magniloquent ideas, of statesmanship and of empire, as did inspire Napoleon's early, and to some extent his later, career, get but incidental attention, if any—are given no controlling part in the working out of his story. On the other side, however, there is this to be said : drum-and-trumpet history as this may be, it encourages no glorification of war. The aspect of war that is most emphatically stressed is its horror, waste and futility, and the foul obscenities of carnage. It would be of incalculable value to the cause of peace if imaginative writers of the calibre of Hardy could be asked to collaborate in the production of history text-books for schools. To turn the empty record of wars and battles into realistic pictures of their meaning in agony and bereavement would be but the first of many reforms needed in the teaching of history.

Even though the preface tells us that there has been no attempt to force the huge sequence of events into the organic structure proper to drama, the mighty conflict does, with the assistance of that foreknowledge which Hardy hoped would create a sense of artistic unity, appear to proceed in movements corresponding to the acts of a play. Even when the successive scenes do nothing but represent events going on in different parts of Europe at about the same time, a sense of unified action pervades them.

An examination of the three parts into which the whole great drama is divided shows the gain of having a struggle so vast and chaotic handled by an imagination of the quality of Hardy's. Part I is of Pitt, Austerlitz and Trafalgar : its action is plainly felt to be leading up to these two battles and to the statesman's death. It shows Napoleon starting (really continuing) on his career of conquest, and the source of his ultimate overthrow in British diplomacy and naval power. But the way is shown open for a new act in the drama, and is indicated in the words of the Parisian street-woman :

What shall hinder him ?

Spirit.   That which has hereto ; England, so to say.

Woman.   But she's in straits. She's lost her Nelson now,
(A worthy man : he loved a woman well !)
George drools and babbles in a darkened room ;
Her heaven-born Minister declines apace ;
All smooths the Emperor's sway.

The motif of Part II is the growing threat of Wellington. It shows Napoleon at the height of his power—Jena, Tilsit, Wagram, and the marriage with Marie Louise—but it shows French interference in Spain, resulting in the first of the Peninsular defeats. The vitality and dramatic interest of this part are more diffuse, have a less obvious unity, than those of Parts I and III. In the middle of it there is a dramatic suggestion of an end foreseen, though dimly. When Napoleon tells Soult he must leave the Spanish rebellion to him and Ney, while he himself turns back to what he thinks more important matters, the Spirit of the Years comments,

> More turning here may be than he designs.
> In this small, sudden, swift turn backward, he
> Suggests one turning from his apogee !

Indeed, one of the most admirably dramatic features of *The Dynasts* is the clear but unobtrusive sense of coming reversals of fortune, and especially of the gradual trend towards the great catastrophe. In the same way Napoleon, hearing of Wellington's successes in the Peninsula, exclaims, " Behoves it me Someday to face this Wellington myself ". Part III is of the Downfall— Moscow, Spain, Leipzig, and Waterloo. The achievements of Wellington are made to bulk rather large in Parts II and III, with great gain in dramatic effect : Wellington's star rises as Napoleon's sinks, so that when the two meet at Waterloo they appear of not unequal brilliancy.

The Dynasts succeeds in conveying an adequate impression of the war in its totality. Great power, dramatic or narrative, is also shown in individual scenes. Trafalgar, one of the two highlights of *The Dynasts*, is presented with absorbing vividness. It has been noted that Shakespeare must somehow have acquired a certain knowledge of seamanship to be able to give correctly the master's orders for manœuvring the King's ship in the first scene of *The Tempest*, but this was a toy affair compared with Trafalgar, and Hardy must have spent much time over maps and documents, making himself thoroughly familiar with the complicated movements that went to that classic masterpiece of naval warfare. Waterloo perhaps presented difficulties of a less unusual order, but they are surmounted with equal success, and the resulting impression of the battle is, in sum and in detail, marvellously clear. Our sense of the critical nature of the last stages of the battle is painful ; our nerves tear and grind with Wellington's as he stands there, issuing his orders with apparent calm— " the hour shaking him, unshakeable as he may seem "—swearing, by God, not to move from his position, and wishing for the Prussians as the shipwrecked Paul wished for the day.

Of lesser scenes some are in that homely vein in which Hardy was a supreme master. Such is the gathering of citizens outside the Guildhall after Trafalgar—the boy who didn't like Billy Pitt because (as the boy logically demonstrated) he had killed Uncle John's parrot, and the man who opened and shut his mouth when the crowd cheered, but uttered no sound, to save his breath, for somebody must save something these tax-ridden days. And a little later the burghers and boatmen round the fire at the Inn, with their tale of how the sailors on the ' Victory ', running short of grog, ' broached the admiral '. All the Wessex scenes are as racy and significant as one would expect, and the rustic humour is as rich as ever. The opening scene for the whole epic (after the ' Forescene ') is placed on a ridge in Wessex, and it is exhilaratingly good, the dialogue beautifully natural, with a dignity apt to the great occasion, and including a fine song from the marching soldiers—

> We be the King's men, hale and hearty,
> Marching to meet one Buonaparty. . . .

A later one of more humorous order concerns the burning in effigy of Napoleon, and the indignation of the rustic at discovering it was not Boney himself who was to undergo the fire : " There's no honesty left in Wessex folk nowadays at all !—making me lose a quarter who can ill afford it, and all for nothing ! " Some of Part II reads as a hash-up of rather dull history, but there are excellent scenes of a personal nature, such as that between Napoleon and the Queen of Prussia—the Emperor offering a rose with his hand on his heart, but turning frigid when the beautiful Louisa asks, " Let Magdeburg come with it, Sire ! " The picture of the cellar in Spain, just before Corunna, full of deserters, wounded men, and women, is worthy of Hogarth's brush : the Ironic Spirit calls it a " Quaint poesy, a real romance of war ". The pathos of Sir John Moore's death is made deeply moving, and the same can be said of the later scene of the death of

Josephine. In the hardly less pathetic scene of her casting off by Napoleon, her grief and Napoleon's brutality (perhaps one should call it inflexibility masked by rough good humour) come with some difficulty through the stilted verse. There is much dramatic irony in the various references to Napoleon made by Marie Louise before fate and Metternich make her the theme of that grim dynastic jest. There is character in the meeting of the magnificent procession bringing Marie Louise to Paris by the single carriage bearing Napoleon. Many telling contrasts are shown, the most notable occurring when the horrors of Talavera are immediately followed by—Brighton, the Royal Pavilion, and " the birthday dinner-party of the Prince of Wales ", this again being succeeded by a powerful impression of the dreadful fiasco of Walcheren. Some of the Parliamentary debates are dull, but the one that is seen through the eyes and comments of members in a London club-room is brilliantly rendered. All the battle pieces are excellently done (some, such as Albuera, harrowingly so), and the strength and vastness of the Lines of Torres Vedras are made most impressive, both objectively by description and subjectively through the effect produced on the astonished French officers. Another passage of pointed contrast with profound meaning in it is that one in which Napoleon calls up his legions to pass admiringly before the newly-arrived portrait of his infant son, and immediately afterwards expresses contempt for the Russian soldiers kneeling before the icon borne by the priests ; though indeed he shows his realistic mind when he points out the illogical nature of expectation of divine help in war, which, " defensive or aggressive either, Is in its essence Pagan, and opposed To the whole gist of Christianity ". Again, the hopes inspired by the sight of Moscow—

Napoleon.   Ha !   There she is at last. . . . Now what says
                              Alexander ! . . .
Soldiers.   Moscow !   Moscow !
                  This, this is Moscow city.   Rest at last !—

are swiftly followed by the ghastly anticlimax of the deserted and burning city, and the unparalleled horrors of the retreat, on which Hardy spends infinite pains with quite appalling success.

Napoleon is the great Antagonist of the Epic-Drama. It is

said that Milton made the mistake of drawing his Satan of too entirely heroic proportions for the part he had to fill. This is not altogether true, but at all events Hardy makes no such mistake with his Napoleon. Concerning itself only with his barren and bloody military feats, the record of Napoleon's achievements never approaches impressiveness, and the only marks of the sublime are contained in two or three references to the Emperor in his shabby great-coat and plain turned-up hat amidst his gorgeously uniformed marshals. Of ideas, with which Napoleon's brain was in reality seething, we get but a hint or two. He refers once or twice to his belief in himself as a man of destiny. When the Queen of Prussia asks him how he can refuse to yield the point that would win her life-long worship, he replies :

> Some force within me, baffling my intent,
> Harries me onward, whether I will or no.
> My star, my star, is what's to blame—not I.
> It is unswervable.

The Queen, feeling perhaps that this ' star ' is an evasion behind which Napoleon seeks to hide his native ruthlessness, says no more, but the Spirit of the Years commends the notion thus expressed :

> He spoke thus at the Bridge of Lodi. Strange,
> He's of the few in Europe who discern
> The working of the Will.

Near the end, when troubled by dreams of the murderous havoc he has caused, he asks (in his sleep)

> Why, why should this reproach be dealt me now ?
> Why hold me my own master, if I be
> Ruled by the pitiless Planet of Destiny ?

A poor remnant of revolutionary doctrine (again perhaps mere hypocrisy) is seen in Napoleon's accompanying his desire to conquer England with an expressed intention to set free

> From bondage to a cold manorial caste
> A people who await it.

What we see of the said ' people ' does not seem to show them awaiting the prospect with much enthusiasm ! As Mr. Belloc says, other nations are slow to recognise the essentially 'aristocratic' character of England.

As a soldier and military dictator Napoleon is, of course, shown as the matchless warrior he was. The first sight of him makes unmistakable his restless energy, his foresight, his demand of swift action from subordinates. At Wagram we have this wonderful picture of him : " From bridge to bridge and back again a gloomy-eyed figure stalks, as it has stalked the whole night long, with the restlessness of a wild animal. Plastered with mud, and dribbling with rain-water, it bears no resemblance to anything dignified or official. The figure is that of Napoleon, urging his multitudes over." He is a dictator of the old type, not dependent on popularity with the plebs—or perhaps feeling so sure of it that he can afford to ride rough-shod over it on occasion, as when he ordered pavilions and ceremonies at Soissons for the meeting with his new bride, and then ' dished the Soissons folk ' by meeting her elsewhere and driving through without stopping. His is the merciless egotism of the military imperialist :

> France shall wage
> Another fifty years of wasting war
> Before a Bourbon shall remount the throne
> Of restless Spain !

But for a time egotism pays, and at the height of his power the Ironic spirits exclaim—" The Will itself is slave to him ! "

Few of the human touches—elements of kindliness, even of weakness—which formed no small part of Napoleon's moral make-up are allowed to be seen. He is best in his early relations with Marie Louise, and his behaviour at the birth of her child is quite decent : he is nervous and anxious over his wife's ordeal, and on being told by the doctor that only mother or child can be saved, not both, he unhesitatingly says, " Then save the mother, pray ! Think but of her "—and this in spite of his desire for an heir. Moreover, when the doctor tells him, mistakenly, that the child is dead but Marie Louise safe, Napoleon exclaims—

> Praise Heaven for that !
> I'll not grieve over much about the child . . .
> Never shall she go through this strain again
> To lay down a dynastic line for me.

And when the President of the Senate brings congratulations on
" the advent of this New Messiah ", the Emperor replies—

> My thanks ; though, gentlemen, upon my soul,
> You might have drawn the line at the Messiah.

His susceptibility to women is also lined in faithfully.

That side of Napoleon which makes his overthrow at the end
of the story dramatically satisfying is kept before us from Part II
onwards. In Part II, apart from his treatment of Josephine and
the Prussian Queen, this is mainly seen on the physical side : at
Tilsit Napoleon " looks well but is growing fat ", and in Spain the
firelight flickers in " his unhealthy face and stoutening figure ".
These signs of physical deterioration multiply in Part III, and
culminate in the implication (which has some foundation in fact)
that Wellington won Waterloo because he was in better personal
condition than Napoleon. Attention is drawn to his puffed
calves and his continual cough ; after the first abdication, having
taken poison, he has to be shaken till he vomits ; as he rides into
Charleroi and reads the Allies' declaration of his outlawry, " his
flesh quivers, and he turns with a start, as if fancying that someone
may be about to stab him in the back " ; he is continually falling
asleep. Spiritual degeneration is seen in the incident of the
icon and the portrait ; when he finds his aims frustrated in Russia
he curses " the author of this war—that Russian minister " ;
whereat the marshals are silent with incredulous emphasis. On
his return to Paris he calls the loss of the Grand Army " quite
ridiculous which ever way you look at it "—at which even the
compliant Marie Louise utters a mild protest—and he will gild
the dome of the Invalides to make France forget her lost sons.
In disaster he is unscrupulous : at the first abdication he says,
" I'll mount the white cockade if they invite me " ; and at
Waterloo he gives orders that the troops shall be told that the
approaching Prussians are " Grouchy's three-and-thirty thousand,
come to clinch a victory " (but here he is only the good soldier :
all is fair in war—that is the horror of it). In the hour of his
downfall (at the first abdication) he insists on seeing infidelity in
Ney and others who have served him : one remembers how
Marcus Brutus, in a similar hour, joyed that yet in all his life he
had found no man that was not true to him. Before Ligny " a

vision passes before Napoleon as he lies, comprising hundreds
of thousands of skeletons and corpses in various stages of decay.
They rise from his various battlefields, the flesh dropping from
them, and gaze reproachfully at him.   His intimate officers who
have been slain he recognises among the crowd.   In front is the
Duke of Enghien as showman."   And in the midst of the Waterloo action he starts up from a momentary sleep exclaiming—

> A horrible dream has gripped me—horrible !
> I saw before me Lannes—just as he looked
> That day at Aspern : mutilated, bleeding !
> " What—blood again ? " he said to me.   " Still blood ? "—

but he disperses these thoughts by vehemently taking snuff.
His faith in his ' star ' grows dim : as Ney hurls himself in vain
against the English squares, Napoleon exclaims—

> All my star asks now
> Is to break some half-dozen of those blocks
> Of English yonder ;

and the request being ignored, adds despairingly, " Life's curse
begins, I see, with helplessness ! "

On the whole, Napoleon does not come through Hardy's
hands much better than Cæsar came through Shakespeare's,
though Hardy's iconoclasm is less violent (his idol being pulled
from a lower pedestal) and at the same time less subtle, especially
in what it leaves.   With his ancestry in the ' Victory's ' captain,
and being thus a true Nelsonian, Hardy could hardly avoid the
attitude he took.

The Protagonist is unmistakable England.   To this historic
truth Napoleon gives angry and emphatic adherence throughout
the course of the action.   In Part I the confusion and helplessness of Napoleon's military opponents in face of his bewildering
strategy are matched by Napoleon's own sense of England's encircling diplomacy, ubiquitous guineas and impassable sea-power.
In Part II, though direct action against England is out of the
question since Trafalgar, she is still the arch-enemy :

> England—Yea,
> Her he still holds the master mischief-mind,
> And marrer of the countries' quietude. . . .

An Austrian citizen compliments an English visitor to Vienna :

> I drink, sir, to your land's consistency.
> While we and all the kindred Europe States
> Alternately have wooed and warred with him,
> You have not bent to blowing hot and cold,
> But held you sturdily inimical !

Napoleon's joy at the birth of his son is damped by the news of England's stranglehold on his trade : the President of the Senate tells him many of their greatest merchant-houses are facing bankruptcy through this. And when Austria joins the Fourth Coalition, Francis's defection from his son-in-law is attributed to an enormous subsidy from Great Britain—" as Bonaparte says, English guineas are at the bottom of everything ". Ironically, the one thing Napoleon does not contemplate as even remotely possible is that his final overthrow will be due to defeat in battle by an English general.

Apart from the omnipresent subsidies and diplomatic activity of England, her spirit is incarnated in three men—Pitt, Nelson, and Wellington. Napoleon embodies England in Pitt :

> God, yes ! Even here Pitt's guineas are the foes :
> 'Tis all a duel 'twixt this Pitt and me.

Pitt we see only as an exhausted figure, with two intense desires— to get Napoleon broken, and to gain some measure of rest for himself from the intolerable strain of office. Death thwarts him of the one (he dies with his last thoughts on a new coalition), but grants him the other—the other that was denied him by the pathetic and futile but not ignobly drawn King George III. In the first glimpse we have of George he is violently protesting to Pitt, " Rather than Fox, why, give me civil war ! " In the other, technically mad, he is in some respects rather nearer sanity :

> I thought
> I was a poor afflicted captive here. . . .
> And yet he says
> That I have won a battle ! O God, curse, damn !
> When will the speech of the world accord with truth,
> And men's tongues roll sincerely !

18

Hardy's eye gleams with humorous contempt when it turns upon the Regent, with his swaggering, glittering functions (often shown immediately after some terrible picture of the battlefield), and his " Damn the peace, and damn the war, and damn Boney, and damn Wellington's victories !—the question is, how am I to get over this infernal woman ! " The portrait of ' Prinny ' is one of the best in the book—the last of the merry monarch tradition, a Charles II lacking the urbane wit and with a blusterous high-spirits instead, and with no brains to see through the adulation he wallowed in : a figure hardly less pathetic than that of his father. At the rumour that the king is dead he first exclaims, " Dead ! Then my fête is spoilt, by God ! " and then " provisionally throws a regal air into his countenance ". Whenever we see him he is the centre of his marital complications, upon which the Ironic Spirit composes an epigram that the Stuart libertine would have enjoyed :

> A wife of the body, a wife of the mind,
> A wife somewhat frowsy, a wife too refined :
> Could the twain but grow one, and no other dames be,
> No husband in Europe more steadfast than he !

Of Nelson we have the familiar picture. Wellington as the ultimate emblem of England's implacable resistance, is kept constantly before us in Parts II and III—a cool, strong, humorous, dignified, and skilful leader of armies—with the result that when the final conflict comes we are not surprised to find him the more impressive figure of the two commanders. Napoleon begins by mistrusting his friends and despising his foe, is shaken in the midst of the battle by thought of the multitudinous blood upon his hands, frets and curses his helplessness, and tries to inspire his soldiers with a false report with regard to the approaching Prussians. Wellington is unflinchingly grave and resolute amid the misgivings of his Staff, and holds his impatient regiments in until the very moment comes for the crushing blow.

The relative proportions of the two men thus set up are not, of course, historically true, but by restricting his field of vision, and by lightly emphasising these traits in the one man, and those in the other, Hardy secures an effect which is necessary for the artistic completeness of his epic-drama.

But *The Dynasts* is more than a transcript from history. It is a genuine work of literature in that it uses historical material for the purpose of giving expression to a personality—a philosophy—an artistic conception of life. This is effected by the normal epic device of a supernatural machinery. But the supernatural persons are employed in a unique manner : they take no part in the action, but we see the whole enormous drama through their eyes. The viewpoint is constantly high up—though at varying heights—above the earth. We are always aware of the watchful, criticising presence of these ' Phantom Intelligences ', flying above the scene like great birds ; how it strikes them is, in the main, what concerns us. Almost we feel that the action is played for them only : the conflict, the vast human tragedy, is but one brief scene in an infinite drama at which they are the first-night audience. It is this aspect of *The Dynasts* that most authentically displays the original genius of a great writer.

Some of the comments of the Intelligences are interesting. As the coronation rites in Milan Cathedral proceed, the Pities (the children in the party at the play) ask what the creed is that is being thus practised, and are told by the Spirit of the Years that it is " a local thing called Christianity ",

> Which the wild dramas of the wheeling spheres
> Include, with divers other such, in dim
> Pathetical and brief parentheses.

When the Austrian Archduke contemptuously compares his own royal lineage, " rooted on the primeval rocks of history ", with the low estate of the " upstart chief ", the Spirit Ironic drily points out that in five years they will be brothers-in-law. Similarly, after the Chorus of Ironic Spirits has celebrated the nuptials of Napoleon and Marie Louise in lively song—

> First 'twas a finished coquette,
> And now it's a raw ingenue—

the Spirit Sinister reminds its companions that the new bride is the grand-niece of Marie Antoinette—" the procession is, I see, appositely crossing the track of the tumbril which was the last coach of that respected lady ". At the Emperor's abdication the Pitiful Spirit makes the profound observation—

> Yet is it but Napoleon who has failed.
> The pale pathetic peoples still plod on
> Through hoodwinkings to light.

The same perspicacious Spirit, at Waterloo, warns us against being deluded by the glittering accoutrements of war into supposing it has any beauty in it.

The invulnerability of Homer's gods, so humorously copied by Milton, so wittily by Pope, is found here : at Waterloo the Spirit Sinister says—

> One needs must be a ghost
> To move here in the midst 'twixt host and host !
> Their balls scream brisk and breezy tunes through me
> As I were an organ-stop.

This looks like Milton, but coming from the Sinister Spirit is perhaps to be taken in the spirit of *The Rape*.

The merely physical side of this superhuman view of things is kept before us by frequent insistence, in the admirable ' stage-directions ', on the minute scale of things as seen from the presupposed lofty position of the onlooker. The peoples are discovered " writhing, crawling, heaving and vibrating in their various cities and nationalities ". Columns of men move with a " silent insect creep " ; a huge procession " looks like a file of ants crawling along a strip of garden matting " ; the French army retreating from Moscow is a " caterpillar shape " which " creeps laboriously nearer, but instead of increasing in size by the rules of perspective, it gets more attenuated, and there are left upon the ground beside it minute particles of itself " ; the Allied armies invading France " glide on as if by gravitation, in fluid figures, dictated by the conformation of the country, like water from a burst reservoir " ; those converging on Waterloo appear " like slow-worms crawling through grass " ; soldiers working on the Lisbon fortifications look like cheese-mites. Couriers " shoot shuttle-wise " between London and Paris, while at Waterloo aides-de-camp dart to and fro " like house-flies dancing their quadrilles ". " Moth-like " ships silently skim the sea, or are driven on " like preened duck-feathers across a pond ".

The view-point permits of a masterly exhibition of battle and other scenes, aided by a brilliantly contrived ' Dumb Show '.

Particularly successful are the presentations of the harbour of Boulogne while the preparations for the invasion of England are going on, and of the evacuation of Moscow. A place where the method might have been used to greater advantage is just before Waterloo, when the important and interesting strategic movements comprising Ligny, Quatre Bras, and the final great battle can hardly be understood without a map, the function of which might have been fulfilled by the aerial view-point. Occasionally, by way of change, a similar view-point is obtained for a battle from the position of Napoleon, Wellington, or (for Wagram) the Emperor Francis. Once, too, we get instead a concise account by the Spirit of Rumour.

It may be true that this notion of things, once conceived, is easily carried out ; but Hardy at least carries it out with marvellous continuity, consistency and variety. His mind moves as easily on the upper levels of the air as Milton's over the spaces of his even vaster field of action. A yet more strange series of glimpses afforded by this point of view, and one that emphasises the tremendous agony of the war, is that in which the land-forms below take on semblances of human-kind. At a certain moment in the Fore Scene, " the nether sky opens, and Europe is disclosed as a prone and emaciated figure, the Alps shaping like a backbone and the branching mountain chains like ribs, the Peninsular plateau of Spain forming a head ". From a much lower elevation the plain of Vittoria " looks like the palm of a monstrous right hand, a little hollowed . . . wherein the ball of the thumb is roughly represented by the heights to the East, on which the French centre has gathered ; the ' Mount of Mars ' and of ' the Moon ' by the position of the English on the West of the plain ; and the ' line of life ' by the river Zadorra running . . . toward the wrist of the said hand ". Lesser parallels occur : " the oval town of Mannheim, standing in a fork between the two rivers, has from here the look of a head in a cleft stick " ; and under the light of the flaming beacon the pits on Egdon Heath show " like the eye-sockets of a skull ". More in the nature of ordinary personification are the references to the swollen and troubled Danube which " seems wanly to sympathise " with the desolation of Ulm, and to the little Maceira stream which, close by the carnage of Vimiera, continues to trickle unconcernedly to the sea.

So, too, the sputtering greenwood fires, when the human tongues are still, seem to hold a conversation of their own ; while on the night before Waterloo, the hissing rain falls impartially on both the sleeping armies.

A less significant but artistically valuable consequence of the aerial view-point is that atmospheric phenomena and transitions are substituted for the usual fall of the curtain and change of scene. We have a " Curtain of Evening Shades ". At one place, " Clouds gather over the scene, and slowly open elsewhere " ; at another, " Dumb show concludes as the mountain mists close over ". As we watch the transports carrying Wellesley to Portugal, " A moving stratum of summer cloud beneath the point of view covers up the spectacle like an awning ". Terribly effective is our last glimpse of Walcheren—" The night-fog enwraps the isle and the dying English army " ; and a striking view is had of the Russian plains—" The clouds, opening and shutting fitfully to the wind, reveal the earth as a confused expanse merely ". Other notable ' curtains ' are—after a reception in London : " the confused tongues of the assembly waste away into distance, till they are heard but as the babblings of the sea from a high cliff, the scene becoming small and indistinct therewith. This passes into silence, and the whole disappears " ; after the coronation at Milan : " The scene changes. The exterior of the Cathedral takes the place of the interior, and the point of view recedes, the whole fabric smalling into distance and becoming like a rare, delicately carved alabaster ornament. The city itself sinks to miniature, the Alps show afar as a white corrugation, the Adriatic and the Gulf of Genoa appear on this and on that hand, with Italy between them, till clouds cover the panorama." For scene-shifting we may note how the change from London to Madrid is managed : " the reception chamber is shut over by the night without, and the point of view rapidly recedes south, London and its streets and lights diminishing till they are lost in the distance, and its noises being succeeded by the babble of the Channel and Biscay waves ". So the Spirits, hovering over Vauxhall Gardens, announce their intention of going to Leipzig, whereupon, " A chaotic gloom ensues, accompanied by a rushing like that of a mighty wind ". After Waterloo, in spite of the appalling horrors of the battlefield, " The night grows clear and beautiful, and the moon shines musingly down " ; presently we find it shining on the drawn and waxen face of Napoleon ; and at the end of all, " The moon sinks, and darkness blots out Napoleon and the scene ".

(A somewhat grotesque instance of the aerial view is the declaration of war between Austria and France as seen by the Intelligences—a letter as large as a mainsail floating across Europe like a cloud.)

But none of these varieties of vision, splendidly new and imaginative as they are, necessitates the presence of supernatural beings ; all could be obtained by a human observer, flying at very great altitudes, and endowed with increased powers of sight. But the spectators provided by Hardy, the Phantom Intelligences, have in addition a kind of second-sight—at least the Ancient Spirit of the Years has it, and can enable the other Spirits to share the results of its perspicacity. At certain moments in the action, the Spirit of the Pities finds the slaughter too much for its nerves, whereupon the Ancient Spirit—who is a sort of superior and snapping spinster aunt—chides the younger Phantom for its exhibition of feeling, and demonstrates the futility of such compassion, or of any kind of moral censure or praise, by presenting a vision which is the special privilege of the Spirit of the Years. Thus, in the Fore Scene, " A new and penetrating light descends on the spectacle, enduing men and things with a seeming transparency and exhibiting as one organism the anatomy of life and movement in all humanity and vitalised matter included in the display ". This is " the Anatomy of the Immanent Will ", and it is shown again at intervals throughout the action. At Napoleon's coronation at Milan, " There is again beheld as it were the interior of a brain which seems to manifest the volitions of a Universal Will, of whose tissues the personages of the Action form portion ". At Austerlitz, " The controlling Immanent Will appears as a brain-like network of currents and ejections, twitching, interpenetrating, entangling, and thrusting hither and thither the human forms ". On the road to Moscow, for answer to the Pitiful Spirit's question why the useless and cruel expedition must be undertaken, " the unnatural light before seen usurps that of the sun, bringing into view, like breezes made visible, the films or brain-tissues of the Immanent Will, that pervade all things, ramifying through the whole army, Napoleon included, and moving them to Its inexplicable artistries ". Here, and elsewhere, Hardy brings into line with his theory Napoleon's belief in his ' star ' : Napoleon alone is made to have some inkling of this working of an irresistible compulsion. Once again, at Vittoria, " There is shown visually the electric state of mind that animates (Wellington and his Staff on the one side, King Joseph and the French Staff on the other). This vision, resembling as a whole the interior of a beating brain lit by phosphorescence, in an instant fades again back to the normal." The thing is shown finally at the crisis of Waterloo, with a new and graphic suggestion that helps us to visua..ise this inconceivable state of affairs : " . . . By the lurid light (of the transparency) the faces of every row, square, group and column of men, French and English, wear the expression of people in a dream."

To these demonstrations of the Will in being, must be added, to arrive at a full understanding, the verbal expositions of the demonstrator. I quote the most significant of these—adequate paraphrase would occupy far greater space and add nothing to clarity :

> What of the Immanent Will and Its designs ?—
> It works unconsciously, as heretofore,
> Eternal artistries in circumstance,
> Whose patterns, wrought by rapt æsthetic rote,
> Seem in themselves Its single listless aim,
> And not their consequence. . . .
> . . . and ever will so weave.

> . . . of her the Travailler (the creative power of Nature),
>   herself a thrall
> To It (the Will).

> That immense unweeting Mind. . . .
> . . . far above forethinking ; purposive
> Yet superconscious (i.e. above consciousness).

> The cognisance ye mourn, Life's doom to feel,
> . . . came unmeant . . . by luckless, tragic Chance.

> Our readings Why and Whence
> Are but the flower of Man's intelligence ;
> And that but an unreckoned incident
> Of the all-urging Will, raptly magnipotent.
>
> So the Will heaves through space, and moulds the times,
> With mortals for Its fingers !   We shall see
> Again men's passions, virtues, visions, crimes,
>   Obey resistlessly
> The purposive, unmotived, dominant Thing
> Which sways in brooding dark their wayfaring !

It would appear that the doctrine of the Immanent Will thus built up conflicts with the political theory which informs *The Dynasts* : the title, reinforced by many passages in the course of the epic, indicates Hardy's satiric intention to expose war as forced upon reluctant and suffering peoples by their ambitious rulers ; but if both rulers and peoples are but unconscious elements of a universal organism, wherein lies the point of the otherwise just satire ?   Questions, too, suggest themselves.   Can an action be purposive and yet unmotived ?   Hardy would say yes, —with no motive beyond the immediate doing of the action, no regard for consequences.   Then can there be even this limited purpose without consciousness ?   It is doubtless found, practically, in the lowest forms of animal life ; but it is difficult to conceive of the universe being created out of, and controlled by, the mentality of a jelly-fish.   Again, morality is to some extent of the mind, and it is not easy to associate vast powers of mind with complete absence of morality.   How is it possible for a moral creation (man) to have come from a non-moral creator ? If you are obsessed by the *negative* results of creation, far easier to attribute them to mechanism.   But here we approach again the transitional aspect of Hardy's outlook.   His indignation with war and other sorrows of mankind is not satisfied by the limited objective offered by an impassive, irresponsible and unresponsive materialism.   So we find him, in *The Dynasts* as in the novels, saying bitter things about the Will, in the hope that It may hear :

> *Spirit of the Pities.*   But O, the intolerable antilogy
>   Of making figments feel !
> *Spirit Ironic.*   Logic's in that.
>   It does not, I must own, quite play the game.

And as poor King George trembles before his brutal doctors, the Pitiful Spirit exclaims that this is the work of no " unmaliced, unimpassioned, nescient Will ", but of " some mean, monstrous ironist ".

Hardy did claim to have emerged from this unsatisfactory position. In *The Dynasts* the advance is to be found only in certain observations of the Pities. At the end of Part II the Chorus of the Pities chants—

> Yet It may wake and understand
> Ere Earth unshape, know all things, and
> With knowledge use a painless hand.

And at the end of Part III the Spirit of the Pities asks—

> Shall blankness be for aye ?
> Men gained cognition with the flux of time,
> And wherefore not the Force informing them ?

while its Chorus sings—

> We hold that Thy unscanted scope
> Affords a food for final Hope
> That mild-eyed Prescience ponders nigh
> Life's loom, to lull it by-and-by.

And it is perhaps a general Chorus of the Intelligences that concludes the whole epic with the words—

> But—a stirring thrills the air
> Like to sounds of joyaunce there
> That the rages
> Of the ages
> Shall be cancelled, and deliverance offered from the darts that were,
> Consciousness the Will informing, till It fashion all things fair !

Hardy claimed that " the view of the unconscious force gradually *becoming* conscious, i.e. that consciousness is creeping further and further back towards the origin of force, had never been advanced before *The Dynasts* appeared ". We shall return to the point when it comes up for consideration in the poetry.

Like the plays of Shakespeare, *The Dynasts* is written in a mixture of blank verse and prose, with the two modes deliberately distributed, and with an occasional break into rhyme, chiefly for the purpose of song or other lyrical passage. The blank verse is, for the most part, flat and undistinguished, sinking here and there to something barely recognisable as verse. This, however, is partly explained by Hardy's statement that wherever the contemporary utterance was discoverable he had paraphrased it closely for the purpose of the verse dialogue. It makes some scenes hard reading, but at least prevents such illusions as those produced by Professor Gilbert Murray's beautiful ' translations ' of the Greek dramatists. At favourable moments the blank verse rises to varying degrees of excellence—in Nelson's last speech to Collingwood, in Napoleon's excited harangue to Decrès, in the first and last of the Josephine dialogues, in the Empress-Mother's side of the conversation with the Tzar Alexander, in Marie Louise's last speech, after hearing of the outlawry of her husband, and generally where no hampering ' paraphrase ' can have interposed, as in the Second Pedestrian's account of the embarcation at Boulogne—

> All yesterday the firing at Boulogne
> Was like the seven thunders heard in Heaven
> When the fierce angel spoke. So did he draw
> Men's eyes that way, the while his thousand boats
> Full-manned, flat-bottomed for the shallowest shore,
> Dropped down to west, and crossed our frontage here.
> Seen from above they specked the water-shine
> As will a flight of swallows towards dim eve,
> Descending on a smooth and loitering stream
> To seek some eyot's sedge.

The Phantom Intelligences are made to speak a different language : the versification of their speeches is harsh but dignified, their diction is weighty and compressed, often difficult and unusual, corresponding to the esoteric doctrines they enunciate. From their lips also proceed most of the admirable lyrics and lyrical forms that are scattered through the drama. The dirge of the hapless troops on Walcheren, the sombre chant of Albuera, the rondeau of the flaming skies before Salamanca, and the terza-rima that celebrates the destruction of the earth creatures by the trampling armies of Waterloo (Hardy said he thought this was the most original thing in *The Dynasts*)—these are the finest of the lyrics, and to them may be added the boatmen's deep-booming ballad of ' The Night of Trafalgar '. These five should take their place among our national poems of action.

The prose dialogue is always of the first order—terse, idiomatic, natural, significant. Hear the Second Spectator, gazing over the Channel :

> There's not a speck of an enemy upon that shiny water yet ; but the Brest fleet is said to have put to sea, to act in concert with the army crossing from Boulogne ; and if so the French will soon be here ; when God save us all ! I've took to drinking neat, for, says I, one may as well have his innerds burnt out as shot out, and 'tis a good deal pleasanter for the man that owns 'em. They say that a cannon-ball knocked poor Jim Popple's maw right up into the futtock-shrouds at the Nile, where 'a hung like a nightcap out to dry. Much good to him his obeying his old mother's wish and refusing his allowance o' rum !

Hear again those two old men who keep the beacons on Egdon—Hamlet's gravediggers returned, little rusted by their long withdrawal—when they espy a blaze in the west :

Second Old Man. He's come !
First Old Man. Come he is, though you do say it ! This, then, is the beginning of what England's waited for !

Hear finally those two servants, again quite Shakespearean, who enter to adjust the furniture after Josephine has been carried out in hysterics :

First Servant. So, poor old girl, she's wailed her *Miserere Mei*, as Mother Church says. I knew she was to get the sack ever since he came back.
Second Servant. Well, there will be a little civil huzzaing, a little crowing and cackling among the Bonapartes at the downfall of the Beauharnais family at last, mark me there will ! They've had their little hour, as the poets say, and now 'twill be somebody else's turn. O it is droll ! Well, Father Time is a great philosopher, if you take him right. Who is to be the new woman ?
First Servant. She that contains in her own corporation the necessary particulars.
Second Servant. And what may they be ?

First Servant.   She must be young.

Second Servant.   Good.   She must.   The country must see to
that.

First Servant.   And she must be strong.

Second Servant.   Good again.   She must be strong.   The doctors
will see to that.

First Servant.   And she must be fruitful as the vine.

Second Servant.   Ay, by God.   She must be fruitful as the vine.
That, Heaven help him, he must see to himself, like the meanest
multiplying man in Paris.

(Exeunt servants.)

THE POEMS

THE strength of a chain is reputed to be that of its weakest link, but a poet's quality is measured by his best. Hardy's finest achievement lies in his love-poems, and estimated by those he is a poet of rare if not exceptionally high quality, intense, sensitive, human. But it is possible to go further, and say that the keynote of his whole poetry is to be found in the love-poems. The differentiating essence of Hardy's love-poetry is that it shows, in a way no preceding love-poetry had done, the soul of a lover : a lover for whom the raptures of love are of less importance than that love for one woman remains quiveringly alive from eighteen to eighty and beyond. There is nothing of this :

> O, speak again, bright angel ! for thou art
> As glorious to this night, being o'er my head,
> As is a winged messenger of heaven
> Unto the white-upturned wondering eyes
> Of mortals that fall back to gaze on him,
> When he bestrides the lazy-pacing clouds
> And sails upon the bosom of the air.

Instead we have this :

> Woman much missed, how you call to me, call to me,
> Saying that now you are not as you were
> When you had changed from the one who was all to me,
> But as at first, when our day was fair.

> Can it be you that I hear ? Let me view you, then
> Standing as when I drew near to the town
> Where you would wait for me : yes, as I knew you then,
> Even to the original air-blue gown !

In the Shakespeare lines we are aware of a great poetic power that can build lyric beauty on a mere wisp of boyish passion ; in the others, passion is as deep as the world, and moves like lyric by its depth and sincerity, but lyric beauty itself is not there.

In Hardy's poetry we see—if we see little else—the soul of a poet, of one whose life was poetry. I think it is not a great soul ; not a great poetic soul ; not the soul of a great poet. It was too introspective, too broodingly concerned with little things—not unimportant things, but things of earth and this life here upon earth—to have the imaginative sweep of the great poets. Even when he reaches something like sublimity, as in the lines *At a Lunar Eclipse*, the centre of his mind is still occupied by " continents of moil and misery ". But this is not disparagement : it is but to state a difference. One of the things life teaches is that there are qualities not less precious than greatness. England is smaller than ' the Empire ', Borrowdale is a mere gutter to the Grand Cañon of the Colorado, and Keats was probably not such a great man as Napoleon. Is there any standard by which to compare human qualities and estimate their relative values ? Could it perhaps be done through their capacity for producing happiness ? If Hardy's poetry does not elevate like Wordsworth's, does it perhaps set up some inward disturbance no less vital ? If Hardy's poetic soul had not greatness, it had beauty, tenderness, pity—qualities almost as rare, and perhaps equally acceptable in the sight of the gods. And what he saw, felt, thought, he transcribed with a sincerity that is sometimes almost frightening.

Hardy's love-poetry has two divisions, the personal and the non-personal or dramatic. The preceding remarks apply to the personal love-poems, although the special qualities existing there cannot help occasionally making their way into the non-personal poems. The personal love-poems themselves fall into three subdivisions, those written before the death of Emma Lavinia Hardy in 1912 ; the poems of 1912-13 ; and later poems. Since the late volumes contain many poems written much earlier, the division cannot always be made with certainty, but many of the poems are dated, and all poems found in the first three volumes, published in 1898, 1902, and 1909, must belong to the first of our three subdivisions. As a matter of fact, most of the love-poems of the first three volumes are of the dramatic kind, but some of the most significant of these owe their force to a lyric interpenetration by Hardy's own sense of love, based on his own experience of it.

Of the love-poems published before 1912, only one is directly addressed to Emma Lavinia, the *Ditty* dated 1870. Through a pleasant verse form and a rather stiff diction there shines something real indeed, but pallid beside the white glow of poems on the same theme written half a century later, when the poet had seen seven decades. There is a supererogatory sounding of the melancholy note : he calculates the consequences of—what indeed " will not be "—his lapsing " to what I was ere we met " : how there would " spread a strange and withering change " round her dwelling ; he invites the pain of the unlover-like thought that he " might have kissed, loved as true, otherwhere " ; he is more logically sad to think how near he came to missing her altogether :

> And Devotion droops her glance
> To recall
> What bond-servants of Chance
> We are all.
> I but found her in that, going
> On my errant path unknowing,
> I did not out-skirt the spot
> That no spot on earth excels,
> —Where she dwells !

Strangely enough, it is among the love-poems of the second kind—where the poet is assuming a situation and a person not necessarily his own—that we get, in these early volumes, touches of what we afterwards come to recognise as the unique Hardy flavour. *Time's Laughing Stocks* includes a group called ' Love Lyrics ' ; in most cases these are plainly dramatic in intention, so that it would not be proper to assume that any of them are personal. Yet consider the first of them, that compact thing written in 1867 and called *1967*. The coming century, he says, will be different from the present one, probably better—but we, we two, shall be dead, and

> I would only ask thereof
> That thy worm should be my worm, Love.

19

How many readers to whom love is a word have been startled,
even revolted, by that violent figure ? But extreme feeling
requires extreme expression, and there is nothing but a great
tenderness in this ultimate image of the desire to lie side by side.
A not too dissimilar hyperbole occurs in some lines by that other
great lover, Robert Browning :

> There you stand,
> Warm too, and white too ; would this wine
> Had washed all over that body of yours,
> Ere I drank it, and you down with it, thus !

This is romantic love : the other is nearer home ; but the same
degree of passion is at the root of both.   I suppose wider acceptance will be found for the more normally beautiful expression of
the thought in the sad and lovely ' reverie ' called *In Death
Divided*.   The lover, more clearly not Hardy this time, laments
that he and she must be buried apart :

> No shade of pinnacle or tree or tower,
>   While earth endures,
> Will fall on my mound, and within the hour
>   Steal on to yours ;
> One robin never haunt our two green covertures.

Hardy's knowledge of love enabled him to enter, long before
it had become his own, into the situation of the poem *Bereft*.
Here, with the gaunt form to help him, he has created from the
simplest materials—a labouring man's wife and the incidents of
her everyday existence—a picture of grief, not bitter or cruel,
but mingled with lovely memories, killing and yet ennobling.
In narrative, too, we find him envisaging a lost love of such
intensity that the present and its gifts shrink into insignificance
beside it.   *The Supplanter* is such a tale :

> He bends his travel-tarnished feet
> To where she wastes in clay.

He is induced to step aside with another, but waking to reality,
spurns her : she kneels to him, imploring his kindness—this one
in the grave by which he stands knows not, cares not :

> He turns—unpitying, passion-tossed ;
> " I know you not ! " he cries ;

and the passion is for the one long dead, the pitiless scorn for the
new love offered.   And in lyric again, even in 1907 Hardy voiced,
through the lips of an imaginary lover, that sense which, after
1912, coloured his whole life.   This is in *The Phantom*, where
the lover declares he bears his lost love in his brain :

> Foremost in my vision
> Everywhere goes she ;
> Change dissolves the landscapes,
> She abides with me.

And so we come to the *Poems of* 1912-13-.   These again are
divided : there is the group of eighteen poems under that heading
in the *Satires of Circumstance* volume, published in 1914 (these
are stretched, not too happily, to twenty-one in " Collected
Poems ") ; and there are a number of others, mostly dated 1913,
scattered through the next three volumes (I think there are none
in *Winter Words*).   These poems are almost unique : I know
nothing of the same character except in the poems of Mr. Walter
de la Mare.   Of all preceding love-poetry in English, none
has the peculiar quality of intimacy that characterises these
poems.   The sense of loss would be unbearable, were it not for
the inspiration of the deathless devotion, the exquisite joy and
pain of living the past over again, of retracing these *veteris vestigia
flammae*.   The homeliness of their utterance permits an intensity
of quietness more shattering than any abandonment of grief.
We are admitted to the sovran shrine of the very temple of love.
There is tender reproach for that sudden unforewarned departure—

> Never to bid goodbye,
> Or give me the softest call !

There is pathetic recalling of her ways and traits : as the rain
falls on her grave he thinks how she would run to shelter her
delicate head even from a summer shower ; as life goes on he
thinks

> How she would have loved
> A party to-day !—
> Bright-hatted and gloved. . . .
>   . . . . But
> She is shut, she is shut
> From friendship's spell. . .

He feels a dead man himself, held somehow erect—

> O you could not know
> That such swift fleeing
> No soul foreseeing—
> Not even I—would undo me so !

She had the heart of a child : she is now part of the daisies she loved—

> Loved beyond measure
> With a child's pleasure
> All her life's round ;

he has buried her far from the home where he found her out by the hurricane-shaken ocean strand—

> Yet her shade, maybe,
> Will creep underground
> Till it catch the sound
> Of that western sea
> As it swells and sobs
> Where she once domiciled,
> And joy in its throbs
> With the heart of a child.

He re-enters their olden haunts, and finds her ghost leading him whimsically here and there—a ghost with " nut-coloured hair, and gray eyes, and rose-flush coming and going ". Certain places on that Cornish shore are drenched with memories. *Beeny Cliff* goes in melodious fourteeners—

O the opal and the sapphire of that wandering western sea,
And the woman riding high above with bright hair flapping free—
The woman whom I loved so, and who loyally loved me. . . .

—Still in all its chasmal beauty bulks old Beeny to the sky,
And shall she and I not go there once again now March is nigh,
And the sweet things said in that March say anew there by and by ?

Grander, if more rugged in form, with something of love's hyperbole, is *At Castle Boterel*. He drives through the lanes, and sees " distinctly yet "

> Myself and a girlish form benighted
> In dry March weather.

What they did and talked of matters little, but he feels that it gave the ancient hill a new quality :

> Primeval rocks form the road's steep border,
>   And much have they faced there, first and last,
> Of the transitory in Earth's long order ;
>   But what they recall in colour and cast
>   Is—that we two passed.

The series reaches its climax in *The Phantom Horsewoman*, of which I speak later.

With such insistent beauty is the chord of poignant memory and haunting loss played on—giving us an intenser and more lyric *In Memoriam*. And form and theme being fused by passion, the art of these poems is more satisfying than is always the case with Hardy. It was doubtless this that led to the choice of the particular selection printed in the 1914 volume, for others, written at the time but not published till later (together with a few on the same theme written later), are generally less finished in form though not much less moving in their appeal. Something taps on his window—only a moth, but he sees his Belovéd's face, weary with waiting in her lonely bed. This is the thought to which Mr. de la Mare gave supreme expression in *The Ghost* (the poem in the *Motley* volume)—and these later books of Hardy are full of the ghosts of dead women. At another time he stands by the Druid stone in the garden, and there falls on it a shadow like

> the shade that a well-known head and shoulders
> Threw there when she was gardening.

He speaks to her, getting " but the fall of a leaf as a sad response ", but he will not turn his head lest his dream should fade. Or again, in *A Night in November*—

> Dead leaves blew into my room,
>   And alighted upon my bed. . . .
> One leaf of them touched my hand,
>   And I thought that it was you.

What, he asks, is the good of going now to Yell'ham Hill and other places round their home ; but her shade reproaches him for losing interest, so he will continue to go—

> Since her phasm may flit out there
> And may greet me anywhere
> In those haunts we knew.

There is a lovely tenderness of remembrance in the lines *On a Discovered Curl of Hair*—all its fellows " gone into a caverned ark, Ever unopened, always dark ".   Once, " before the duller loomings of life defined them ", he had seen her standing in a green-slate quarry, and so now he never sees green slates on roof or wagon but they speak to him of her.   There is a piercing pathos in the short lines of *The Frozen Greenhouse* : one morning she had stood blank-faced at the thought that she had left the green-house plants to die during the frosty night, but now, though the greenhouse is warm,

> She who grieved
> At the sad lot
> Of her pretty plants
> Herself is colder,
> And knows it not.

He is proud to think she opened the doors of the West, of Romance, of Love to him, and now opens the door of the Past—

> Its magic lights,
> Its heavenly heights,
> When forward is little to see !

He remembers how his loneliness in an obscure lodging was consoled by dreams of her, and wonders if it is the same with lovers now.   So intimately pathetic are the verses on *Looking at a Picture on an Anniversary*—" But don't you know it, my dear . . . "—that it might seem sacrilege to have made such feelings public—except that it is thus that we others are taught to voice our own love.   He sees memory of the day they met vitalise the two deep eyes of the portrait—and if that is an empty fancy, then

> little I care
> To live myself, my dear,
> Lone-labouring here !

Indeed, in a wonderful poem among the *Late Lyrics and Earlier* he tells us he has two lives, one in the joyous past with her, the other in the lonely present : the one is as real to him as the other, and he asks which is the dream ?

It is a marvellous story we see through these star-holes. And the non-personal poems of these later volumes are not seldom tinctured with the same sweet essence. There is a clock-winder— a parish-clerk who clambers nightly up the dark church-turret to

> " wipe out one more,
> My Dear, of the sore
> Sad days that still be,
> Like a drying Dead sea,
> Between you and me ! "

And there is a carrier who never lets anyone sit in the vacant seat by his side—

> " They say you are in the grave, Jane,
> But still you ride with me ! "

The thought of true love always moves Hardy to a sympathy that thrills to music, and he knows that love has power to transmute ugly conditions to beauty : so he sings of a man and a girl who go to meet each other through mud and gale and streaming mist :

> But to their feet,
> Drawing nigh and nigher
> A hidden seat,
> The fog is sweet
> And the wind a lyre.

He can even conceive a life-long passion built on a single glimpse of a girl : in the strange poem called *The Glimpse* it is not even a living girl but the ghost of a girl long dead that passes through the door and sets the man who catches momentary sight of her searching for her vainly his whole life through.

Certainly these poems, besides constituting a priceless possession in themselves, help us to understand why love is so vitally central, so completely dominating, in all Hardy's novels. This is not to say that the novels altogether prepare us for the poems on this side. Great and noble as are the loves and lovers of some of the novels, there is something in their nature, and more in their circumstances, that generally cuts them off from the thought of lyric, with its abstraction, its loneliness, its impassioned serenity. The love of the poems brings Hardy closer and more endeared than even some other very human aspects we shall note.

It remains to observe that although this two-strung chord of exquisite happiness of immortal love and the exquisite pain of loss is the peculiar grace of Hardy's love-poetry, he knows as well love's infinite variety, and explores it in poems on the whole earlier than those we have been considering. In *Wessex Poems* we have something of that grim other side more marked in the novels. *Neutral Tones* is a *tour de force* in love turned to hate ; *Revulsion* shows the sophisticated lover, the wooer with his eyes open, calculating nicely that " Winning love we win the risk of losing " ; *At an Inn* passes strangely and suddenly from the appearance of beauty to the reality of horror. There is cruel satire in *At Waking*—" the vision appalling " of one who is scared to see in his love " but a sample of earth's poor average kind " ; the thought is repeated later in more horrid form in the lines called *In the Night She Came*. Irony of a less deadly nature appears in *Four Footprints* and *The End of the Episode*. Peculiarly pungent, again, is *Misconception*, a tragedy of the modern spirit, which decrees that not, as of yore, shall a woman sink her personality comfortably in that of her husband. *In the Crypted Way* gives an interesting situation, rendered in pure prose—perhaps necessarily, because the lover is hesitatingly feeling his way through a maze of thought. Of like nature is *The Dawn after the Dance :* the theme is prose and unpoetised ; its most significant lines bear out some of the teaching of the novels :

> Would that dancing were the worst thing from the latest to the
>   first thing
> That the faded year can charge us with ; but what avails a word !
> That which makes man's love the lighter and the woman's burn
>   no brighter
> Came to pass with us inevitably while slipped the shortening
>   year. . . .

The Sigh is an excellent example of the modern poet's—and the modern lover's—concern with little things ; its charming form is just spoilt by the ugly coinage ' up-eyed '. *The Conformers* is specially interesting. It is neatly turned and cleverly written, and the form is both original and beautiful. The thought is Hardian—the chilling effect upon love of a binding agreement —but goes further and drives home the point made in Browning's *Respectability*. (A comparison of the two poems—the cold precision of Hardy's against the warm life of Browning's—is interesting.) *He Abjures Love*, which concludes the *Love Lyrics* of *Time's Laughing Stocks*, is a great poem, gaunt and terrible in thought and movement. Both feeling and form are so integral and highly wrought that extraction is impossible : the poem should be read both for its intrinsic excellence, and as an example of Hardy's power to project himself into an alien personality and position. But the variety of these early love-poems does not fail to include the kindlier and more characteristic emotion. *The Division* is a true song, with the haunting pathos of Burns. *In a Cathedral City* is finer still—is, indeed, quite beyond praise. Its perfection of form, its calm beauty, its tranquil sunny dignity befit the title. And what daring juxtaposition of high romance and realism in the two lines—

> Nor have your faultless feet once thrown
> A pensive pit-pat on its floors !

The thought of faultless feet going pit-pat is delicious ! Prophetic of later developments are *The Re-enactment*, where a present substantial love is recognised as slight and tame beside the mere ghost of a dead romance, *Unknowing*, where faithfulness to a memory is the one sure thing in a world of uncertainties, and the very beautiful and tender *Thoughts of Phena*, which declares it best that only a phantom remains " fixed in my brain ", while *The Inconsistent* is a resolute expression of quenchless faith even to the memory of a faithless one.

§ 2

It should be apparent from the foregoing section that I do not undervalue Hardy's love-poetry ; and I hope presently to show my appreciation of the excellence of more than one other aspect of his achievement in verse. Before proceeding to a survey of those other aspects it seems desirable to suggest, nevertheless, that this verse achievement can never take its place with that of the great poets, because it lacks the vital element of poetic form.

In the last decade or so of Hardy's life it was not safe to suggest this : my doing so in 1921 set certain reviewers flaming with homicidal fury. To-day the atmosphere is calmer, and I have found critics of Hardy, not indeed in agreement with my opinion, but at least admitting that the question may be raised—that a doubt does exist, and may be discussed without blasphemy.

It is an established canon of ' romantic ' criticism that the æsthetic temperature of poetry is higher than that proper to prose, and that this higher temperature leads to a fusion, as it were, of language which turns it into a different medium—the difference being apparent mainly in the effect produced upon the reader : the poet's sense of his subject is, by means of poetic form, communicated to the reader's sensibility, creating in him a disturbance not only spiritual but physical. A beautiful and delicate instrument for the measuring, or detection, of this effect has lately been invented : we call it Housman's razor, and though some of Hardy's poetry answers the test, the proportion is small compared with what we find in any of the major, and some of the minor, poets. The instrument is an artistic not a scientific one, and is affected by the personality of the user, but with me it gives results when tested with *The Ballad-Singer*—

> Sing, Ballad-singer, raise a hearty tune ;
> Make me forget that there was ever a one
> I walked with in the meek light of the moon
>   When the day's work was done.
>
> Rhyme, Ballad-rhymer, start a country song ;
> Make me forget that she whom I loved well
> Swore she would love me dearly, love me long,
>   Then—what I cannot tell !
>
> Sing, Ballad-singer, from your little book ;
> Make me forget those heart-breaks, achings, fears ;
> Make me forget her name, her sweet, sweet look—
>   Make me forget her tears—

with that perfect lyric *Julie-Jane* and that perfect love-poem *The Phantom Horsewoman*—and with not many others.

This poetic form is, as to externals, partly a matter of rhythm and partly a matter of words and their use and their relation.

(Words by themselves can sometimes effect the miracle, but only in those rare lines that constitute what Arnold called touchstones of poetry : it is significant that Hardy's art does not produce these.) The poem *To Meet, or Otherwise* (no one but Hardy or Wordsworth would have appended such a title to such a poem) is as full of verse-melody as of deeply moving sentiment : but place beside it Yeats's simple poem on a kindred theme, *Down by the Salley Gardens*, and the difference between the thing and the absence of it is instantly felt. *Transformation—*

> Portion of this yew
> Is a man my grandsire knew
> Bosomed at its foot :
> This branch may be his wife . . .

expresses in the Hardy idiom Omar's thought " I sometimes think that never blows so red The rose. . . . " Hardy scores deep into the idea ; Fitzgerald merely touches it—but he touches it to music, and to a music that moves us to feel the thought as it moved Fitzgerald. Not that Hardy does not feel : sometimes his feeling is so profound as to make that of all but a few poets look shallow : but he remains rigid to his own feeling—he will not let it shake him. His Milton is deliberately mute !

Certain subjects—the fate of a girl or a woman, for instance— cut so deep into Hardy's imagination that a throb of poetic form results. *The Satin Shoes* is Hardy's *Lucy Gray*, having its plainly told narrative tipped at both ends with heart-stirring beauty :

> Yet she was fair as early day
> Shining on meads unmown,
> And her sweet syllables seemed to play
> Like flute-notes softly blown.

Or there are floating memories that knock poignantly on the bell of his heart and send out singing echoes most like poetry :

> I idly cut a parsley stalk
> And blew thereon towards the moon ;
> I had not thought what ghosts would walk
> With shivering footsteps to my tune. . . .

The song *Why Be at Pains ?* falters into the tenser medium. The deep pathos of *The Shadow on the Stone*, and some of the other love-poems, is given a plain conversational statement which convinces us that it is the perfect expression, and is at least the matrix of poetry.

I do not see how the fact I have asserted can be denied, and once the fact has been accepted it ceases to trouble and becomes even a matter for rejoicing. One comes to love this quiet thinking in verse—

> What are you doing outside my walls,
>   O Dawn of another day ?
> I have not called you . . .
>   So why do you come this way ?

—these deliberate precise statements, producing just the effect, emotional and mental, desired. Almost every poem is a finished conception : there is always form of this intellectual kind. Indeed Hardy's power of precise statement in verse places him among the great epigrammatists. The power is seen quite early in the eight lines of *Her Initials* or the three stanzas of *In a Eweleaze near Weatherbury*—for the power is shown not only in the cut agate of the genuine epigram, but in an exactness and economy of presentation that may extend over a poem of several stanzas. An admirable specimen is seen in *Shelley's Skylark*, a perfect summation of a moment's mood, that might well have taken sonnet form. Finer still is *A Broken Appointment* :

> You did not come,
> And marching Time drew on and wore me numb.—
> Yet less for loss of your dear presence there
> Than that I thus found lacking in your make
> That high compassion which can overbear
> Reluctance for pure loving kindness' sake
> Grieved I, when, as the hope-hour stroked its sum,
>   You did not come.
>
> You love not me,
> And love alone can lend you loyalty ;
> —I know and knew it. But, unto the store
> Of human deeds divine in all but name,
> Was it not worth a little hour or more
> To add yet this : Once, you, a woman, came
> To soothe a time-torn man ; even though it be
>   You love not me ?

The thought in the poet's mind was not a simple one, but it is expressed with absoluteness and economy, and yet without obvious effort at compression. The verse-form chosen here helps to produce an effect of satisfaction that is all but poetic.

It is a power that grows with experience. *The Convergence of the Twain* (lines on the loss of the ' Titanic ') : how could it be bettered ?—with its swift impression of the great jewelled ship, and of the " sinister mate " that had been prepared for her, and of their becoming " twin halves of one august event "—

> Till the Spinner of the Years
> Said " Now ! "   And each one hears,
> And consummation comes, and jars two hemispheres.

How neat and tight is the form of " *My spirit will not haunt the mound* ", how dry (and purely prose) its conclusion :

> And there you'll find me, if a jot
> You still should care
> For me, and for my curious air ;
> If otherwise, then I shall not,
> For you, be there.

There are great numbers of these lapidary lyrics—*A January Night*, *We Sat at the Window*, *Afternoon Service at Mellstock*. . . . Again and again the question puts itself, as it does over *A Thought in Two Moods*—how could that thought be expressed with greater brevity or exactness ? Perhaps sometimes in the later volumes one feels that though the epigrammatical force is still there the diamond-cut detail is less brilliant (in *When Dead*, from *Human Shows*, for instance)—but *Winter Words* gives us that masterpiece of brevity, *Boys Then and Now*, with its old-time little boy who was disappointed to be told that cuckoos were numerous, for he had supposed there was only one,

> Who came each year
> With the trees' new trim
> On purpose to please
> England and him.

Poetic form, the sense of which was largely lacking in Hardy, lies deeper than verse technique. In this latter sphere Hardy has again his supreme moments, has moreover a high level of skill at command, but great quantities of his verse show him either indifferent to accepted ideas, careless of results, or simply uncertain of ear. The ' indifference ' explanation, whether applied to metre or diction, is rendered doubtful by certain personal observations recorded by the poet ; he noted that there was a latent music in the sincere utterance of deep emotion ; he admitted that " poetic diction (of the real kind) is proper and even necessary in works of fancy (or imagination) " ; and he declared that the model he had set before himself was ' Drink to me only '. There is little of Hardy's poetry that we would willingly lose, yet it would seem that a more drastic principle of selection (much of his actual production is said to have been destroyed !) might have led to the exclusion of things like this—

> Be candid would I willingly, but dawn draws on so chillingly
> As to render further cheerlessness intolerable now,
> So I will not stand endeavouring to declare a day for severing
> But will clasp you just as always—just the olden love avow.

An appreciable proportion of the poetry is technically of this negligible order, and there are other poems in a harsh intractable jaw-breaking medium :

> O they were speechful faces, gazing insistent,
>   Some as with smiles,
> Some as with slow-born tears that brinily trundled
>   Over the wrecked
> Cheeks that were fair in their flush-time, ash now with anguish,
>   Harrowed by wiles.

The first stanza of *In the Servants' Quarters* defies recasting in verse form if presented without division, thus : " ' Man, you too, aren't you one of those rough followers of the criminal ?—all hanging hereabout to gather how he's going to bear examination in the hall.' She flung disdainful glances on the shabby figure standing at the fire with others there, who warmed them by its flare." There is a theory abroad that the poetry of to-day and to-morrow must needs be written in these uncouth measures, because all the obvious rhythms have been used up, and have become trite and meaningless. A survey of the greater poetic names of the last thirty years, however, relieves one of the necessity for entertaining any such apprehension. It is further maintained that a profound searching of the heart cannot issue forth in fluent and facile melody—that discord is necessary to truth-telling. There is some evidence, in literature and music, in support of this contention. Certainly the poetry which has least to say, says it most easily—*The Idylls of the King* as compared with *The Ring and the Book*, or Shakespeare's early blank verse as compared with that of his later tragedies. But there is not found in Hardy any strict correspondence between harshness of form and fullness of content, although the verse in the early books is smoother than that of the later ones, doubtless because packed content became increasingly general with time.

These lacunæ being set aside, Hardy's verse has many interesting features of a secondary order. His ponderous muse has a penchant for long lines, as in *The Lacking Sense*, sometimes disguised, as in *The Flirt's Tragedy*, which is printed in threes and twos, but is essentially written in anapæstic pentameters :

> Here alone by the logs in my chamber, deserted, decrepit,
> Spent flames limming ghosts on the wainscot of friends I once
>   knew,
> My drama and hers begins weirdly its dumb re-enactment,
> Each scene, sigh and circumstance passing in spectral review.

In *The Rash Bride* the sesquipedalian metre is not too successful, with its quasi-triple internal rhyme :

> And sweetly then she bowed her thanks, and smiled, and spoke
>   aloud her thanks—

though this is kept up with misapplied ingenuity for fifteen stanzas. *Wessex Heights* has a lilting long line full of a brooding melancholy. Where other poets gain an effect by an unexpected short line, Hardy gains his by an interposed long one, as in " *For Life I had never cared greatly* ", where the heavy amphibrachic verse is also characteristic :

> For Life I had never cared greatly,
>   As worth a man's while ;
>   Peradventures unsought,
>   Peradventures that finished in nought,
> Had kept me from youth and through manhood till lately
>   Unwon by its style.

But he can use a short line effectively :

> I need not go
> Through sleet and snow
> To where I know
> She waits for me ;

though he is more himself when able to lengthen his stride in a blend of short and long :

> As I lay awake at night-time
> In an ancient country barrack known to ancient cannoneers,
> And recalled the hopes that heralded each seeming brave and
> bright time
> Of my primal purple years. . . .

Hardy did little experimenting in metre and stanza form. Only once does he approach irregularity, in " *Not only I* " (*Human Shows*). On the other hand he often (like Browning) lets his theme call its own tune, which he then follows out in the stanza form thus evolved. *Fetching Her* obviously came this way :

> An hour before the dawn,
> My friend,
> You lit your waiting bedside-lamp,
> Your breakfast fire anon,
> And outing into the dark and damp
> You saddled, and set on.

The method produced an astonishingly powerful form in Corp'l Tullidge's story of *Valenciennes*. This grand piece of dialect narrative, with its dual stanza-form and its constant rhyme for the even stanzas, is worth careful attention : the difficult scheme is maintained with complete success to the end. The mingled trochaics and anapæsts of *The Vatican : Sala delle Muse* run to a sweet plain melody. (I am grateful to the *Times* critic who suggested that the One, the essence of all the Nine, who gleamed forth with " A pensive smile on her sweet, small, marvellous face ", must have been a distant cousin of Sue Bridehead's.)

Generally the verse is strongly individual, but on occasion we catch a hint of another poet. *The Ditty* already spoken of is in a Browning measure :

Beneath a knap where flown
　　Nestlings play,
Within walls of weathered stone,
　　Far away
From the files of formal houses,
By the bough the firstling browses,
Lives a Sweet : no merchants meet,
No man barters, no man sells
　　Where she dwells,

and though it begins well we feel before the end that Browning would have made more of it, as a song. *The Division* recalls Tennyson, till the third stanza goes out of his depth. That bitter and intense poem, *He Abjures Love*, might have been the work of one of the Elizabethan lyrists—Wyatt or Sidney—again till the conclusion turns pure Hardy.

Rhyme seldom inspires Hardy, as it does most poets : it certainly does here :

But next there came,
Like the eastern flame
Of some high altar, children. . . .

But he has complete mastery of its requirements—almost too complete in those poems where he cruelly compels every stanza to a single rhyme-sound, as in *My Cicely*, *A Sunday-morning Tragedy*, and others that have been noticed. He inclines to avoid the obvious in rhyme-formula : thus *At Rushy Pond* almost demands *a b a b*, but is given *a b b a* instead. Repetition he makes great play with. In *The Ghost of the Past* it is a simple device—

We two kept house, the Past and I,
　　The Past and I—

but in *The Change* (another of those ineffably beautiful love-lyrics left over from 1913) it is highly complicated, and carries passion with great power. It is charming in " *When I set out for Lyonnesse* ", but a little excessive in *Burning the Holly*. Alliteration, too, is characteristic.

Perhaps he does best with the simpler verse-forms, or those whose stuff is saturated with the music of long use. The ballad-stanza he uses (as we shall see) with success, and his sonnets are

20

invariably admirable. His strenuous and deliberate muse is appropriate to the sonnet. He uses the English and Petrarchan forms indifferently, sometimes mixing the two, but he shares the Italian objection to a final couplet, frequently ending the Shakespearean form without it. The sonnet to the Matterhorn has a sestet that is Miltonic both in form and in tone, but the majority are closely fashioned in the Shakespeare mould, especially the short sequence, *She to Him*, which will call for notice presently, with the finest of all the sonnets, *At a Lunar Eclipse*. Of the others the most Shakespearean is *The Minute before Meeting*, a noble poem of severe beauty, and as its name suggests, a perfect ' moment's monument ' of passion and pain. The imitation is extended to the familiar Shakespearean playing with words :

> And live in close expectance never closed
> In change for far expectance closed at last.

In *A Wet Night* he shows he can get a good sonnet out of a trifle. Of sonnets Shakespearean neither in form nor tone, *The Sleep-Worker* is powerful. The ' wave-movement ' is of the double-rising sort, but at the conclusion of the sestet, instead of a climax, we have a striking and beautiful anticlimax. In the other mode the best is perhaps *By the Barrows*, in subject-matter Milton in homely vein, and in form Miltonic except that, with characteristic freakishness, Hardy this time ends with the couplet (as of course Milton does once) :

> Nor far from Mellstock—so tradition saith—
> Where barrows, bulging as they bosoms were
> Of Multimammia stretched supinely there,
> Catch night and noon the tempest's wanton breath,
> A battle, desperate doubtless unto death,
> Was one time fought. The outlook, lone and bare,
> The towering hawk and passing raven share,
> And all the upland round is called " The he'th ".
> Here once a woman, in our modern age,
> Fought singlehandedly to shield a child—
> One not her own—from a man's senseless rage.
> And to my mind no patriots' bones there piled
> So consecrate the silence as her deed
> Of stoic and devoted self-unheed.

Specially delightful, even surprising, is Hardy's fondness for the song. Not merely the sinister jollity of the Hangman's Song—

> O my trade it is the rarest one,
> Simple Shepherds all—

or the rattling fine satirical song of the Sergeant—

> When Lawyers strive to heal a breach,
> And Parsons practise what they preach ;
> Then Boney he'll come pouncing down,
> And march his men on London town !
> Rollicum-rorum, . . .

but there are scores of simple tuneful things—about a lady seen from a train (this one a " radiant stranger ! "), or about singing lovers, or about the weather the cuckoo likes (" and so do I "), with refrains like " Death may come but loving is divine ". Particularly charming is the tit-like poem that gaily declares

> Any little old song
> Will do for me. . . .

Nevertheless it remains true that much of Hardy's verse has little but verse-stress and line-division to separate it from prose, and from a prose far less distinguished than that of the novels. Even that fine reflective poem, *Neutral Tones*, is expressed in bare if not bald prose ; even a spirited narrative like *San Sebastian* gains nothing but brevity from its verse-form—certainly in actual prose-form it would probably have lost by elaboration. It would be difficult to find a reason why this should have been cut up into lengths—

> A soldier and his young wife
> Were the couple ; his mother the third,
> Who had seen the seams of life.
> He was sailing for the East I later heard. . . .

Sometimes it is a neat and balanced prose, as in *Her Dilemma*, or the words may be hewn massively out of thought, as in *A Sign-Seeker*. *The Servants' Quarters* has already been quoted as indistinguishable from prose, yet there is this to be said—if the gospel story *is* to be re-told in a ' new version ' it should be in this utterly commonplace way. That excellent apologue *The Oxen* is in a fittingly colloquial medium, the pleasant melodious utterance native to such people as were sitting " in a flock " that Christmas Eve. Sometimes again one cannot help contrasting the masterly prose of the novels, and wishing some of those early narrative poems, for instance, had been cast in it. Once or twice comparison is invited—unwisely, in *Tess's Lament* and *Midnight on the Great Western*, which latter is forceful enough until it is placed beside the companion prose description in *Jude*. (These little self-rivalries remind one of Wordsworth and Dorothy's *Journal*.)

Prose, too, is the diction. Hardy is master of the exact word, especially of the right tragic word, but the inspired word seldom comes. Coleridge's inadequate definition of poetic style, the best word in the best place, to some extent covers Hardy. But there are occasions when the word chosen is anything but the best word. I refer to those coinages or idiosyncratic usages that are so well known a feature of Hardy's verse idiom. The practice is, like all others, to be judged by its success : Spenser (under relaxed rules) justified it, Doughty and Joyce and lesser moderns fail to do so. And I cannot persuade myself to like Hardy's neologisms. He has not the excuse of these others, who believe they have something to communicate that cannot be ' got over ' without new methods : Hardy can and generally does express himself with perfect clarity through the traditional instruments of language ; he does not really require the saxophone. Only petulance accounts for some of the departures from the normal. He says, " The sun ups it " instead of " The sun rises ", he says, " I backed on the highway ", meaning " I returned " (though a little later " He backed his tools " means " He slung them on his back "). He admits " went far to mend " as a phrase in poetry ; " Wish fixing when " as a line ; and " ail-stricken " as a word. We find " blanked by love " ; poor Liddell is made to confess to Scott that he has " belched many a moan " ; Time is called " the Fair's hard-hitter " ; even " darkled " occurs. At the same time, whatever one's feeling about these eccentricities, it is ridiculous to exaggerate their prevalence. In view of Hardy's evident liking for them they are remarkably rare, and in the great bulk of his work they appear (as Sir James Jeans would say) but a handful of hornets flying about in Piccadilly Circus.

§ 3

There is a thing that can be said about Hardy, as not about some greater poets, namely, that the content of his poetry is always interesting. His mind was rich, free, active, and all its wealth and freshness were poured into his poetry as it could not be into the severe scheme of the novels. His variety of observation and thought, if not infinite, was at least inexhaustible by a long life and a thousand verses. By the time you have got to the middle of *Winter Words* you might think you were prepared for anything he might choose to hand out—and then you get a totally new, bizarre, modern bit of portraiture, *A Countenance*, beginning, " Her laugh was not in the middle of her face quite ", and going on to say that her curls were like piled fir cones and that her lower lip cast a green shadow. He has innumerable girls and ghosts, and yet somehow *Louisa in the Lane* is different and unexpected : he asks her to " meet him again as at that time ", and then remembers that to do so she will have to come back to earth ; still, she will come, and say " with spectral frail alarm "—

> " Why am I still here found ?
>   —Ah, I remember !
> It is through him with blitheful brow
> Who did not love me then, but loves and draws me now ! "

The man Hardy, the man who is seen in the poems, is a most engaging person. He is almost incredibly sensitive. He is deeply disturbed by seeing a woman fall asleep while her friend plays to her, and hearing her murmur hypocritical appreciation afterwards ; the player died a week later, and now

> When I see the room it hurts me
> As with a pricking blade.

It was this sensitiveness that combined with his lively imagination to endow him with that profound pity that is one of the noblest of his attributes. What tenderness is beautifully expressed in the lines *To an Unborn Pauper Child :* " Fain would I, dear, find some shut plot of earth's wide wold for thee . . . " ; what divine sympathy with the *Dream of the City Shopwoman*. He cannot understand how anyone can miss an opportunity of being kind :

> But, unto the store
> Of human deeds divine in all but name,
> Was it not worth a little hour or more
> To add yet this : Once you, a woman, came
> To soothe a time-torn man ; even though it be
>   You love not me ?

The thought of a human being, born with capabilities of fine living, falling to evil and meeting doom, stirs the depths of his compassion in the poem *On the Portrait of a Woman about to be Hanged.* He grieves over young girls like Retty and *filles de joie* like Julie-Jane dying young, but feels a sad delight in seeing them pluck what joy of love they can from life before they go. With complete understanding he voices the common trouble of life in *After the Burial ;* and he does not fail to notice that the lodging-house fuchsias, of which the landlady had been so proud, are cut away at her death :

> She put up with their pushful ways,
> And made us tenderly lift their sprays,
>   Going to her door,
> But when her funeral had to pass
> They cut back all the flowery mass
>   In the morning.

Little things leave a memorable impress on his kindly nature. He has a thought to spare for the rejected member's wife, " smiling while hurt " ; in life's November he remembers (or makes a lover remember) how, just once in life's May, the beloved sighed—

> Sometimes I sit half-regretting
>   That she sighed ;

he says, " Good morning, my Dear ! " to a maiden on a hill, and though she passed him by (" And I did not try to make her understand ") the incident makes a charming poem. He enters ecstatically into a girl's happiness as she goes home with " news for her mother "—one of the most delightful of all the lyrics. He is clearly interested in women : he notes *A Woman Driving*—

> How she held up the horses' heads,
>   Firm-lipped, with steady rein ;

it is more to him that at a certain spot a woman fought to shield
a child than that it had once been the scene of a battle. Unpleasant women he can't abide (as Mr. de la Mare can't abide a
butcher), and in *Lady Vi* and *The Lady in the Furs* he scourges
two of them with Burns-like satire. Lady Vi is just a vain,
dancing, hunting, irreligious trifle; but the other woman is a
nastier type, and is displayed with some malice. (Not that
Hardy objected to dancing: *Reminiscences of a Dancing Man* and
other poems show him to have been a veritable addict in his
younger days.) Satire with a wider aim is seen in that bitter
epigram, *Christmas 1924*, in which the Church is roundly and
soundly indicted:

> " Peace upon earth ! " was said. We sing it,
> And pay a million priests to bring it.
> After two thousand years of mass
> We've got as far as poison-gas.

He can salute the old workman who was proud even of the work
that broke him, and there is a pathetic yet splendid pride in
An Ancient to Ancients :

> We who met sunrise sanguine-souled,
> > Gentlemen,
> Are wearing weary. We are old ;
> These younger press. . . .

But age did not dim his memories—he never forgot anything
worth remembering. During a wet August of 1920 he remembers
an August of long ago when " we lived out of doors ", and the
weather, whatever its kind, was " gilt over by the light I bore in
me " and by " the then golden chances seen in things ". A
poem published in 1925 describes the sun on Oxford Street " as
seen on July 4th, 1872 " ; another of the same period com-
memorates an hour " too satiate with soul, too ethereal " to be
caught in the net of words. *In Front of the Landscape*—that
sombre, funereal poem in its hollow pacing measure—affords an
insight into the strange double life he led—his body perambulating
in the present and the material world, his mind occupied by
visions and ghosts. For whether Hardy was a great poet or not,
he was always a poet : he saw and experienced everything *sub
specie poesis*.

Old things he loves : they move him not only to deep feeling but to a richer diction than usual.   The poem, *Old Furniture*, is one of the high-water marks :

> I see the hands of the generations
>   That owned each shining familiar thing. . . .
> Hands behind hands, growing paler and paler,
>   As in a mirror a candle-flame
> Shows images of itself. . . .
> On the clock's dull dial a foggy finger. . . .
> And I see a face by the box for tinder
>   Glowing forth in fits from the dark
> And fading again. . . .

Over his father's violin he broods most musically—

> Here alone I sadly con
> Your present dumbness, shape your olden story.

Winter Words does not contain much that is obviously beautiful, but the poem *Silences* is an exception : he meditates on " the rapt silence of an empty house Where oneself was born " :

> Past are remembered songs and music—strains
>   Once audible there :
>   Roof, rafters, panes
> Look absent-thoughted, tranced, or locked in prayer.

Since the love that played so great a part in Hardy's life and writings had its roots deep down in his nature, it included a love of animals that prompted some of his most delightful poems. The two greatest of these, *The Blinded Bird* and *Last Words to a Dumb Friend*, will receive notice presently, but there are many others.   Here we have Browning's ' wise thrush ' fallen on evil days, yet speaking still his lesson of the joy of earth :

> An aged thrush, frail, gaunt and small,
>   In blast-beruffled plume,
> Had chosen thus to fling his soul
>   Upon the growing gloom.

To Wordsworth's ' two-fold shout ' and Browning's ' minor third ', Hardy adds a third touch of interpretation—

> I hear not the contralto note
> Of cuckoos hid on either hand ;

and *Shelley's Skylark* is a beautiful pendant to the greater poem which inspired it, and has a note of concrete bird-love that Shelley, great lover of all things as he was, does not sound often in his poetry. *Wagtail and Baby* is a neat rendering of that regret for the broken ' social union ' of Nature which Burns stepped aside from his exquisite Scots to express in bald English prose. In *The Roman Gravemounds*, Hardy records with a tender irony the mood of a man who buried there " a little white furred thing, stiff of limb ", and who would have let die the records of Rome to have back his little friendly cat. When snow comes down in the suburbs Hardy first notices a sparrow bowled over by a falling snow-lump thrice his size, and then sees that

> The steps are a blanched slope,
> Up which, with feeble hope,
> A black cat comes, wide-eyed and thin ;
> And we take him in.

His reaction to the peace-peal (the church bells having been silent for four years) is to notice that the unaccustomed sound and vibration have driven the jackdaw out of the tower. He sees tragedy in the drowning of a mongrel, and in the eyes of the dog as he sinks " a wakening to the treachery he had loved with love so blind "—even " a loathing of mankind ". There is a charmingly pathetic set of verses on *Dead " Wessex " the Dog to the Household*, and a pitiful picture of a cattle-market, while *Compassion*, an ode composed for the centenary of the R.S.P.C.A., shows his earnest and unfailing enthusiasm for this cause.

Of great interest are those glimpses we get of Hardy's own view of himself, in a series of epitaph-like poems placed generally at the end of a volume. One that is not so placed, but which is entitled *Epitaph*, begins " I never cared for Life " (some of the poems that reflect the feelings of youth make one doubt that ' never '), and claims credit for not having asked too much from life. This thought is repeated in the poem morosely headed *He Never Expected Much*, written on his eighty-sixth birthday. Of a different and lovelier order are the poems that conclude *Satires of Circumstance* and *Moments of Vision*. In the former of the two, *A Poet*, he describes himself as observant, fantastic, critical, undesirous of fame and indifferent to society, and content with but one word of praise—" Two bright-souled women loved him well " (or " clave to him " as the Collected Edition emends). *Afterwards* is a greater poem—one of the most perfect and delightful of all the poems. It is written in one of the favourite long measures—sixes and fives, largely in anapæsts. He asks to be remembered as one " who used to notice such things " as the subtler signs of nature and the sound of passing-bells, and " had an eye for the mysteries " of the full-starred heavens. The loveliest stanza contains one of the two slight flaws that mar the poem's perfection, in the assonance of ' lawn ' and ' warm ' (more than the inexact rhymes) :

> If I pass during some nocturnal blackness, mothy and warm,
>   When the hedgehog travels furtively over the lawn,
> One may say, " He strove that such innocent creatures should
>   come to no harm,
> But he could do little for them ; and now he is gone."

The *Surview* that closes *Late Lyrics* is less complacent, and makes the poet's voice, crying to him from " the green-grained sticks of the fire ", accuse him of neglecting, in his younger days, the scriptural canons of truth, justice, purity, and charity. But in 1925 he wrote *A Placid Man's Epitaph* (Landor in the negative) :

> As for my life, I've led it
> With fair content and credit :
> It said : " Take this ". I took it.
> Said : " Leave " and I forsook it.

§ 4

That outlook on life—better, perhaps, that sense of life—which it is difficult not to call pessimism, permeates the poetry as it does the prose, but very much less thoroughly ; indeed, if we separate it (as we well may) from the semi-mechanistic philosophy also widely found in the poems, the proportion of ' pessimistic ' verse warrants Hardy's continued protests against what he felt to be the exaggeration of its prevalence. In the preface to *Winter Words* he complains that the critics had pronounced the previous volume " wholly gloomy and pessimistic ". This was certainly unreasonable of them, for not only *Human Shows* but the two volumes that preceded it, *Moments of Vision* and *Late Lyrics*, are remarkably free from the melancholy tone that is more prominent in the first four volumes, and that crept back into *Winter Words* notwithstanding the poet's belief that he had kept it out.

The impression of pessimism builds itself up partly (as in the novels) on the choice of narrative subjects—and narrative poems are very numerous. Hardy was a connoisseur in stories and situations of a cruel, ironic or otherwise tragic kind, and was continually adding to his grisly collection. Some of the choicest pieces may be mentioned. *The Flirt's Tragedy* is a story of cumulative misery, and concludes—

> But pass by, and leave unregarded
> A Cain to his suffering,
> For vengeance too dark on the woman
> Whose lover he slew ;

The Vampirine Fair is a revolting picture of depravity, without a spark of decent behaviour or feeling to lighten the gloom. These two early narratives are paralleled in the later books by the one called *Her Second Husband Hears her Story*, which reads like a cruel parody :

> Still, Dear, it is incredible to me
> That here, alone,
> You should have sewed him up until he died,
> And in this very bed. I do not see
> How you could do it . . .

and *The Brother*, a pretty tale of rape righted by murder, and murder mended by suicide. The title-poems of *Satires of Circumstance* comprise fifteen acrid little glimpses of life at bitterly ironic moments. Their only distinction of form lies in their brevity. The best are those of a man who accidentally overhears his beloved rating her mother, the poor lady who hawks books with the air of one doing it for a whim, the workman who stands gazing gaunt-eyed at the grave of the woman he had not loved, and—best of all—with its unusual but not improbable situation and its appropriately bald colloquial wording—the one called *In the Room of the Bride Elect* :

" Would it had been the man of our wish ! "
Sighs her mother. To whom with vehemence she
In the wedding-dress—the wife-to-be—
" Then why were you so mollyish
As not to insist on him for me ! "
The mother, amazed : " Why, dearest one,
Because you pleaded for this or none ! "

" But father and you should have stood out strong !
Since then, to my cost, I have lived to find
That you were right and I was wrong ;
This man is a dolt to the one declined. . . .
Ah !—here he comes with his button-hole rose.
Good God—I must marry him, I suppose ! "

And there are similar situations, briefly and bitterly touched,
like that of the lovers whose laughter by the canal-bank was in-
terrupted by the splash of a woman drowning herself for disappointed love, or the man who after years of hesitating bought
himself a fine pair of special waterproof boots to keep him dry
for life, and died next day.

But after all, this choice of narrative subject might be the
outcome of a macabre sense of humour. More authentic are
the lyric or reflective expressions of the same tendency. *A
Meeting with Despair* tells how the poet, passing over a bleak
moor " like a tract in pain ", feels it symbolises life, but, looking
up at the glory of the sunset, reproaches himself for having overlooked this sign of consolation, till Despair, meeting him, points
out that the glory has already disappeared. *To Life* shows not
only dissatisfaction with existence but that worst of all conditions,
boredom. " *I said to Love* " makes two depressing assertions—
that love is a sorrowful thing, and that the extinction of man is
a prospect that may be contemplated with apathy. The disillusion of *Shut out that Moon* is cruel : once midnight and the
moon were lovely with lingering scents, " living seemed a laugh,
and love all it was said to be ", but now—shut out the moon—

Within the common lamp-lit room
    Prison my eyes and thought ;
Let dingy details crudely loom,
    Mechanic speech be wrought :
Too fragrant was Life's early bloom,
    Too tart the fruit it brought !

In *Digging on my Grave* a queer pleasure is found in chasing a petty cynicism to its dingy death. That pretty thing, *The High School Lawn*, closes on a ' little victim's ' note :

> A bell : they flee :
> Silence then :—
> So will it be
> Some day again
> With them,—with me.

And once more it is declared, " Tragedy is true guise, Comedy lies ".

And yet, in support of Hardy's disclaimers, there is discoverable, running through the darkness, a slender thread of something brighter in hue. Twice in *Poems of the Past and Present* he allows himself to feel, and to record, that illogical and temporary but inevitable sense that we associate with Browning's " God's in his Heaven, All's right with the world ". *On a Fine Morning* declares he will " hold shadows but as lights unfolding " and see the glory of the moment as part of a benignant plan. And in that great poem *The Darkling Thrush* he is so impressed by the apparently baseless ecstasy of the carolling bird that—

> I could think there trembled through
> His happy good-night air
> Some blessed Hope, whereof he knew
> And I was unaware.

Again, in *To Meet, or Otherwise*, he goes a long way towards the optimistic position : still, for him, " things terrene groan in their bondage ", but " the one long-sweeping symphony of human tenderness " is there " as part of sick Life's antidote ". Once admit that there *is* an antidote, that there *are* compensations, and you are no thorough-going pessimist ! Even more definitely in the same direction points that exquisitely-cut epigram " *I travel as a Phantom Now* " : what he sees on his bodiless perambulations makes him " wonder if man's consciousness Was a mistake of God's " :

> And next I meet you, and I pause,
> And think that if mistake it were,
> As some have said, O then it was
> One that I well can bear ;

(and, one may add, *argal*, goodman delver, no mistake !). At another time the sight of " life laughing onward " in daisies and gambolling children causes his " too regretful mood " to die.

Not quite all the stories are gloomy ones. *The Husband's View* and *A Wife and Another* show how happily things can turn out if people will be sensible in their reactions to what fate sends them. So, too, the later sketch, *A Question of Marriage*, shows happiness coming at least to the deserving couple, the sculptor and his loving little wife.

Quite a large proportion of these sunnier moments have occurred in the later volumes, with dates that show them no product of " Troubadour youth ". When, however, we reach the final pages of *Winter Words* the signs are conflicting. The last poem but three indeed contains the far from desperate summation of the poet's life :

> I lived in quiet, unscreened, unknown,
> Pondering upon some stick or stone,
> Or news of some rare book or bird. . . .
> Tasting years of moderate gladness
> Mellowed by sundry days of sadness. . . .

But two pages later we are back to what must be regarded as normal—the sonnet of hopeless disillusion, asserting that " we are getting to the end " of the dream that better may follow worse, that man is a free agent, that the race may grow reasonable, that war may cease. And the poem on which Hardy closed his lips and died, darkly declares that what he discerns, what he has learnt, the truth by which he has been made free, is so awful, so deathly, that he will show it to no man—" he resolves to say no more ".

§ 5

Hardy must have felt that the Great War and its consequences went far to justify an even blacker pessimism than his own. He did indeed declare that it killed in him a certain belief in the gradual ennoblement of mankind. In 1902 he had written *The Sick Battle-God*, tracing a gradual decline through the ages of the worship of this deity, and concluding—

The lurid Deity of heretofore
Succumbs to one of saner nod ;
The Battle-god is god no more.

There were many who thought with him,—alas for human hopes !

Two of the best war poems Hardy wrote were on a distant war—*Valenciennes* and *San Sebastian*. Apart from their lyric and narrative excellence, they voice the deep melancholy of war, its bestiality, its remorse. To them may be added the glorious songs of *The Dynasts*. Some good poems of mild satire on war were written between 1902 and 1914, as in *Channel Firing*—

All nations striving strong to make
Red war yet redder. Mad as hatters. . . .

But when war actually came, in 1899 and in 1914, he wrote of it with little success. His war poetry has neither the large inspired patriotism of Wordsworth, nor the lyric fervour—whether of triumph or of sadness or of satire—of the young Soldier Poets. War is not congenial to Hardy : he could neither tranquilly ignore it, like Browne, nor fling his soul into it, like Milton. It is not that his feelings and thoughts on war are not true and deep ; but they do not call forth his greatest powers. War was a rough, harsh, brutal smashing in upon his preoccupation with nature and man, with God and Fate : his solitary muse comes to the new theme as to a task.

The second set of war poems is better than the earlier one, simply because the theme is greater. The first are poems of ordinary human pathos—the note of a ' little war ' ; the later ones have the tragic sound of a more dreadful catastrophe. *Men Who March Away* has the right note of sombre devotion to death ; *His Country* breathes Lowell's ' larger patriotism ' (but is dated 1913). In *The Dead and the Living One* he contrives to extract from the common incidents of war a situation after his own heart, and handles it with his own clarity and cruelty. *I Looked up from my Writing*, the last of this series, shows that by this time the horror and pity of it have made him feel the vanity of writing or living in such a world. And a later poem on the signing of the armistice expresses (in fittingly turgid verse) the utter bewilderment and misery that were incompletely ended by the armistice and the peace.

The case is different when we come to the small but famous lyric, *In Time of ' The Breaking of Nations '*, wherein even the cataclysmic insanity of the Great War seems but a passing mood to the everlasting unchanging ways of the labours of peasant man and maid.   It stands with A. E. Housman's *Epitaph on an Army of Mercenaries*—the two supreme epigrams that came out of the Great War.   Housman's poem has more poignancy for us, but Hardy's will have more meaning for posterity : his poem puts war itself into its place for all time ; Housman's lines have a limited reference, and their superb irony must have been lost even on many contemporaries.

§ 6

Hardy's genius for story found a second (or third) outlet in the very large number of narrative poems that he wrote.   He was a collector of odd, and generally tragic, incidents, situations, episodes, chiefly but not entirely connected with marriage or other relation of woman to man.   Some of these have been used in an earlier section, for the light they threw on Hardy's view of life. His narrative power exhibits continuous development.   In the *Wessex Poems* the stories are of a plain direct kind, frequently told by a soldier or a peasant.   Two of the best have been mentioned—*Valenciennes* and *San Sebastian*.   *The Fire at Tranter Sweatley's* is a good yarn told with sly humour.   More complex is *My Cicely*, a powerful story sufficiently well told, in spite of some stilted phrasing and the monotonous rhyme.   It continues that cynical tone with regard to women which was noticeable in the novels and recurs from time to time in the verse narratives. Hearing that his old love is dead, a man sets out to visit her grave ; arriving, he finds it is a woman of similar name who has died, but in the midst of his joyful surprise he learns that his Cicely is worse than dead—lives a life of besotted degradation ;   he returns in frenzied grief, but presently persuades himself that the one who had died was indeed his love :

> 'Tis better
> To dream than to own the debasement
> Of sweet Cicely.

> Moreover, I rate it unseemly
>   To hold that kind heaven
> Could work such device—to her ruin
>   And my misery.

The *Past and Present* volume works out this vein of complex and ironic tragedy. Sometimes, as with *The Dame of Athelhall* and *The Tree*, the verse-narration robs a powerful story of its effectiveness ; but the ghastly tale of *The Church Builder* could hardly have achieved the neatness of its concluding jest in prose : a man tells how he had ruined himself to build a church, which done, not only do disasters crowd upon him, but he finds his church unwanted in an age of unfaith, so he goes by night into the church and hangs himself to the rood-screen :

> Well : Here at morn they'll light on one
>   Dangling in mockery
> Of what he spent his substance on
>   Blindly and uselessly ! . . .
>   " He might," they'll say,
>   " Have built, some way,
> A cheaper gallows-tree ! "

So, the inhuman ending of *The Supplanter* would have been intolerable in prose. Of simpler stories *The Lost Pyx* is a most excellent ballad, and *A Man* is a fine record of an obscurely noble deed.

Time's Laughing Stocks is richer in narrative. *The Revisitation* is a finely told story, with the man this time making a very poor showing beside the woman : the back-sliding lover " cherished her reproach like physic wine ", but never saw her again—" love is lame at fifty years ". One of the finest of the shorter narratives is *A Tramp-Woman's Tragedy*, a vivid glimpse of jealousy and death flashing suddenly out of the easy comradeship of the road. The need for verse is felt here : its swift action and agonising sorrow would have been achieved with difficulty in prose, and the poetry of the story rises to rhythmic beauty in the stanza beginning " Lone inns we loved, my man and I ". *A Sunday Morning Tragedy*, too, is a great folk-poem, comparable with some of the best of the mediæval ballads. If it has one flaw it is that for the shorter alternate lines of the ballad-stanza Hardy has substituted a four-stressed line with a single rhyme-sound throughout ; but this is handled so well that it beats through the poem like the tolling of a funeral bell, or the insistent note in the Chopin Prelude in D Flat. In *The Rash Bride*, the three chief personages stand out as vividly as in a novel, but the queer jigging metre is more appropriate to the idyllic beginning than to the tragic ending. *The Dead Quire*—one of Hardy's own subjects— is a good story very well told, and has some finely poetic stanzas. *The Husband's View* and *A Wife and Another* form a companion pair with the same Hardian moral—in the one, a man hears with affectionate and approving interest that his wife is pregnant by another man ; in the other, a wife suddenly loses her jealousy on hearing that a child is about to be born of the illicit union of her husband and his mistress. These cold eugenist husbands and wives do not often get into literature, but they are as interesting as the jealous ones, and more original. Both stories are told with clarity and much economy of word. *The Curate's Kindness* shows again Hardy's command of dialect in verse. Indeed, by this time Hardy enjoys complete mastery of any form of verse he chooses to adopt. This is seen in the varied and pleasing measure of *The Noble Lady's Tale*, the story of which, intricately interest-ing, leaves one, like some of Browning's, guessing at possibilities, plumbing personalities, hunting for motives. Two other great narrative poems in the volume, *A Sunday Morning Tragedy* and *Panthera*, will be noticed later.

In the *Satires of Circumstance* volume are to be found a number of highly interesting narratives, but only one of out-standing merit as a poem—*The Elopement*, a fine story finely told. One perceives a racy, crusted personality behind the telling : there is ease, room, naturalness, inspiration. *A Con-versation at Dawn* is a powerful story—one shudders to think how real and cruel and dramatic it would have been in Hardian prose. In verse, though passing effective, the situation is seen rather than felt. *The Satin Shoes* is a cruel story, pitifully told, and the same, in less degree, may be said of *A Face at the Casement*, though the former goes exquisitely in ballad stanza, the latter awkwardly in a less seasoned measure. *The Sacrilege* is a good story told with more vital movement, and there are excellent satiric situations in *The Torn Letter*, *The Newcomer's Wife*, and *The Telegram*—with its one unusually beautiful line,

The yachts ride mute at anchor, and the fulling moon is fair.

The later books show an increase in the bizarre factor. *The Royal Sponsors* is a ghastly little Hardian story of a baby who died at an inopportune moment, but had to be christened, dead or alive, lest Personages should be put out. *The Contretemps*, told stickily in verse, would have made an excellent short story—of the man who rushed forward in the gloom to meet his sweetheart, kissed her, and then found she was the wrong woman—and he the wrong man, for at that moment the lover she had been waiting for appeared, together with her husband, the two of whom, washing their hands of this deeply-involved lady, abandoned her to the accidental last comer, who apparently accepted this gift of the gods—" One pairing is as good as another ". In *The Chapel Organist* verse justifies itself, and the story could hardly have been told so dramatically in prose. The long Tennysonian line helps the self-told story. Characterisation, too, is remarkably clear—we see the woman organist, the deacon, the people. *The Interloper* is a powerful and painful story, full of eeriness and dread. The form is most excellent and appropriate : it has the perfect ghost-story hollow tramp—tramp—tramp. The subject is obscure and mysterious : each stanza raises your shuddering curiosity, puts your half-formed question darkly aside, and passes on to the next alluring yet terrifying picture. It is as good as *The Twa Corbies*. *She Revisits alone the Church of her Marriage* shows again how fond Hardy was of analysing the feelings and thoughts of married people at the moment of marriage or after. *A Sound in the Night* presents with power another tragic marriage situation, and *The Inscription* is another queer story of a woman's complicated and uncertain love. *The Pedestrian* is interesting, if only as affording a measure of the difference between the poetry of the romantic revival and that of the other end of the century. Contrast the beginning of Wordsworth's poem—

" What, you are stepping westward ? "—" Yea "—

with the beginning of this—

" Sir, will you let me give you a ride ? "

Contrast also the two poems which follow these openings. The differences are too striking, and their significance too clear, to need enumerating. That Wordsworth's is the truer poem I do not doubt; whether Hardy's prosaically recorded incident does not open up larger mysteries is another question. *The Turnip Hoer*, on the other hand, might have found a place in *The Excursion*. *The Mock Wife* is a perfect ballad, with the stanza form disguised and a purely prose diction and rhythm : the story is a terrible one, but this is in the ballad tradition. And after the odd story of *The Wedding Clothes*, the narratives end on a dismal note in *The Ballad of Love's Skeleton*.

The name of Robert Browning has occurred more than once in the foregoing pages, in speaking about the narrative poems and in other connections. A closer analogy may indeed be drawn between Hardy and Browning than with any other among the poets. The supposed similarity between Hardy and A. E. Housman extends only to their common spirit of pessimism. The points of unlikeness are more numerous : Housman's exiguous output and limited range, his fastidious art and jewelled craftsmanship, his intenser lyric sense, his perhaps finer sensibility. Even Housman's disillusion is colder and more absolute than was possible to the older poet, with his roots in a pre-Darwinian age.

The reputation of Browning is a little in disregard at the moment, but no permanent judgment can pronounce him other than a very great poet indeed, though doubtless a ' giant ' rather than a ' god ', in which respect Hardy resembles him, without presuming to anything like his stature. Browning's genius was half narrative, and we have seen how much of Hardy's verse is of this kind. Some of the stories, moreover, have a distinct Browning flavour. *A Wife and Another* recalls the older poet both in matter and manner. The shorter poem, *Four Footprints*, might easily have been written by Browning :

> " But that I body and soul was yours
> Ere he'd possession, he'll never know.
> He's a confident man. ' The husband scores ',
> He says, ' in the long run '. . . . Now, Dear, go ! "

The Collector Cleans his Picture is Browning in spirit and form,—until the ending comes, when the picture-surgeon finds that the

Venus he has been laboriously uncovering is a diseased hag.
Others have been noted. *Thoughts of Phena*, a lyric, has a
Browning rhythm that Browning would have handled more
easily. '*You were the sort that men forget*' is a swift and penetrating character study strongly reminiscent of Browning. It
begins admirably—

> You were the sort that men forget ;
>   Though I—not yet !
> Perhaps not ever. Your slighted weakness
> Adds to the strength of my regret—

but does not quite sustain this level. Many of Hardy's poems
are of that ' dramatic lyric ' sort which Browning made his own.
It will not be forgotten that Browning is one of the few poets
whose love-poetry can claim kinship with Hardy's. And Oscar
Wilde's *mot* that " he used poetry as a medium for writing prose "
applies with greater force to Hardy than to Browning.

There is something superficially fantastic in drawing a parallel
between the most notorious pessimist and the most determined
optimist in English poetry, but there was nothing really negative
about Hardy's pessimism : both outlooks were the product of a
rich vitality of mind. This vitality and fertility, too, gave to the
poetry of Hardy, as to that of Browning, its wealth of varied
interest. It would not be too bold to take Landor's lines on
Browning and adapt them to the nearer case :

> Hardy ! Since Browning was alive and hale
> No man has walked along our roads with step
> So active, so inquiring eye, or tongue
> So varied in discourse.

§ 7

Almost all the humour of the novels is concentrated in the
rustic scenes, and as there is little in the poetry to correspond
with these there is little humour to be found in the poetry. On
the contrary, there is every sign that Hardy took life much more
seriously than a man with a pronounced sense of humour can
possibly take it.

Naturally most of the occasions when the comic side of things

does make an appeal to him are such as to result in a dry and
ironic humour. He remembers how he used to take part in
Afternoon Service at Mellstock—they sang without thought, looking out of the windows most of the time :

> So mindless were those outpourings !—
> Though I am not aware
> That I have gained by subtle thought on things
> Since we stood psalming there :

a sly dig at himself and other busy speculators. He has a
shrewdly-noted picture of *An East-end Curate :*

> He goes through his neighbours' houses as his own, and none
>   regards,
> And opens their back-doors off-hand, to look for them in their
>   yards :
> A man is threatening his wife on the other side of the wall,
> But the curate lets it pass as knowing the history of it all.

The satire is kindly—kindlier than in that " workhouse irony "
in which the well-meaning young pa'son got the rule about " the
men in one wing and their wives in another " set aside, to the
dismay of the old man who was looking for peace at last. There
is a sting here that is absent from the only half-laughable but
quite harmless bickerings between the newly-married couple in
The Homecoming. On the other hand it is with a slightly acid
pen that he records the thoughts of ' a beauty ' on her honeymoon
whom he observed in a London Hotel wondering why on earth
she had married this poor plain man, her husband. One can hear
the chuckle with which Hardy heard the story that he set down in
The Three Tall Men—of the tall man who made himself a long
coffin, let it be used for his tall brother, made himself another,
which was used for his tall son, made yet a third, and then died
at sea. The urbane enjoyment of a quaint incongruity expressed
in *A Gentleman's Epitaph on Himself and a Lady, who were Buried
Together* would have come well from Praed or Calverley. Either
of these poets, and quite a number of lesser humourists, would
have made something genuinely funny, as Hardy does not, out
of Liddell and Scott. And the sour humour of the second-
thoughts in *Middle-Age Enthusiasms*—

> We cried, " We'll often come :
> We'll come morn, noon, eve, everywhen ! "
> —We doubted we should come again—

reminds one of how this kind of thing was done perfectly (though
it is not fair to pit Hardy against Rostand on ground that is
peculiarly French) in the delicious *Souvenir Vague*—

> Nous étions, ce soir-là, sous un chêne superbe
> (Un chêne qui n'était peut-être qu'un tilleul). . . .

There is a new variety of humour, an intimate blend of humour
and beauty, discoverable here and there in modern poetry—
in Rupert Brooke, Sir Henry Newbolt, and Mr. de la Mare, for
instance—and illustrated once or twice in Hardy. The one
emphatic example is that philosophic epic in little, *An August
Midnight* :

> A shaded lamp and a waving blind,
> And the beat of a clock from a distant floor :
> On this scene enter—winged, horned, and spined—
> A long-legs, a moth, and a dumbledore ;
> While 'mid my page there idly stands
> A sleepy fly, that rubs its hands. . . .
>
> Thus meet we five, in this still place,
> At this point of time, at this point in space.
> —My guests besmear my new-penned line,
> Or bang at the lamp and fall supine.
> " God's humblest, they ! " I muse.   Yet why ?
> They know Earth-secrets that know not I.

Here, in addition to the earth-philosophy suggested in the last
couplet, and the divine Assisian charity of ' we five ', we have
the wonderful poetic vision of the chance meeting ' in this still
place, at this point of time, at this point in space '.   The moment
is seized and shown, big with eternity.   And yet the cosmic
conception is associated with ' a long-legs, a moth, and a dumble-
dore ', and that inimitably described ' sleepy fly, that rubs its
hands '.   This is a new thing, that a great poet should, even as
his soul reaches out into immensity, keep hold on the funny side
of life.   And I think there is a hint of this beauty-humour synthesis in the picture of the baby, with eyes blue and bright, its

cheeks like rose, pride of the human race, paragon of mortals, brought to christening by its shrinking unmarried mother

> Whose child is this they bring
>   Into the aisle ?
> At so superb a thing
> The congregation smile
> And turn their heads awhile—

especially in that inspired ' superb '.

§ 8

All Hardy's poetry is instinct with the breath of the English countryside, and yet, apart from his animal and bird poems, he has few poems about nature, either of natural description or directly drawing their inspiration from natural scenery. In view of the different state of affairs obtaining in the novels this seems strange. It may have been because all his poetry was the product of intense feeling : each poem was the emotional response to something he observed or imagined. The affairs of men and of animals provided these emotional stimuli, but he simply wasn't moved, or was seldom moved, to deep feeling by natural scenery. Not that he had no eye for it : *Afterwards* asks that he should be remembered as a man who " used to notice " natural phenomena, both animate and inanimate. But they did not often send him to his tablets.

A singularly illuminating contrast between Hardy and the true nature poet, Wordsworth, is provided in that charming poem, *In a Wood*. Full of delicate praise of " pale beech and pine so blue ", " brave hollies " and the rest, it yet expresses indignation that trees of different kinds cannot live side by side in amity ; so he " turns back to his kind ", finding there, now and then, life loyalties. The reversal of the *Lines Written in Early Spring* is almost deliberate, but the logic of the one poem seems no sounder than that of the other !

Satires of Circumstance includes a small group of nature-poems (*Before and After Summer*, *At Day-close in November*, *The Year's Awakening* and *Under the Waterfall*), all of which are delightful and contain memorable lines :

> Looking forward to the Spring
> One puts up with anything. . . .

The last named stands as Hardy's finest piece of natural description in verse, and one of the loveliest of all his poems. The situation, its details, its sensations, are beautifully and exactly described, diction and verse are sweet and easy, abstract nature is emotionalised by love :

> . . . the purl of a little valley fall
> About three spans wide and two spans tall
> Over a table of solid rock,
> And into a scoop of the self-same block ;
> The purl of a runlet that never ceases
> In stir of kingdoms, in wars, in peaces ;
> With a hollow boiling voice it speaks
> And has spoken since hills were turfless peaks.

Admirable again is *Voices from Things Growing in a Churchyard*. Form and tone are just right, keeping the balance between cheerful and eerie—the daisies that were a little girl, the dancing leaves, the yew-berries, the laurel, withwind, ivy—all the voices and green ghosts of buried folk. Slighter is *Weathers*, which has already been mentioned as a song. The late poem *Night-time in Mid-Fall* shows Hardy still in contact with earth, and still capable of a fine impression of nature worthy to be put with some of the prose :

> . . . The streams are muddy and swollen ; eels migrate
>   To a new abode ;
>   Even cross, 'tis said, the turnpike-road ;
> (Men's feet have felt their crawl, home-coming late) :
> The westward fronts of towers are saturate,
> Church-timbers crack, and witches ride abroad.

§ 9

More than one poem meriting the adjective ' great ' has been mentioned in the foregoing surveys, but I have reserved for separate treatment those, to the number of some half-score, which seem to me to be Hardy's outstanding achievements in verse. These are—the sonnet-group, *She to Him*, from *Wessex Poems ; At a Lunar Eclipse*, from *Poems of the Past and the Present ; Panthera*, from *Time's Laughing Stocks ; The Phantom Horsewoman*, from *Satires of Circumstance ; At the Word Farewell* and *The Blinded Bird*, from *Moments of Vision ; A Procession of Dead Days* and *Last Words to a Dumb Friend*, from *Late Lyrics and Earlier ; A Leader of Fashion*, from *Human Shows ;* and *Drinking Song*, from *Winter Words*.

The four sonnets constituting the series, *She to Him*, use the Shakespearean form, but avoid the concluding couplet in all but one case. The diction is as nearly Shakespearean as possible, lacking—for no man could catch it—the sensuous loveliness of Shakespeare's word-music, but retaining the more austere beauties. The movement of the verse is followed with great skill. Above all, the spirit of Shakespeare's sonnets, and the sonnet-structure that carries it, are caught to a miracle. A man who knew his sonnets pretty well, but had a poorish memory for poetry, would, if given the opening lines of these four sonnets, swear they belonged to the great originals :

> When you shall see me in the toils of Time. . . .
>
> Perhaps, long hence, when I have passed away. . . .
>
> I will be faithful to thee ; aye, I will. . . .
>
> This love puts all humanity from me. . . .

The progress of the single thought in the first sonnet, through its first two stages to the third and the conclusion, is perfectly imitated, and it was wanton of Hardy to refuse the couplet. The second, though the thought movement is again exquisitely true, is imperfect in that the rhyme of the second quatrain is carried on into the third, and the last two lines have no separateness. Number three, after the first quatrain, is a little less Shakespearean, but has the final couplet. The fourth, too, is marvellously copied in the opening quatrain but not quite so close afterwards. The figures and phraseology, too, are right jewels from the authentic mine—' my lauded beauties ', ' Sportsman Time ', ' Poor jade ! ', ' the tittle of a debt unpaid ', ' fleeting phantom-thought ', ' Death shall choose me with a wondering eye '. And the run and balance are exact :

Numb as a vane that cankers on its point,
True to the wind that kissed ere canker came. . . .

(I can but maledict her). . . .
For giving love and getting love of thee,
Feeding a heart that else mine own had fed.

And there are twenty other aspects of the brilliant transcription.
Nor is the result a mere literary exercise : the result is four
great sonnets—in which respect again Hardy was only following
the Elizabethan sonneteers, perhaps Shakespeare himself. The
spirit of the sonnets—a proud humility of love, a deification of
the beloved that ennobles while it abases the worshipper—
is even intensified : transferring the love and pleading to a
woman, Hardy makes them much more abject than anything in
the original.

At a Lunar Eclipse is probably the grandest of Hardy's sonnets :

Thy shadow, Earth, from Pole to Central Sea,
Now steals along upon the Moon's meek shine
In even monochrome and curving line
Of imperturbable serenity.
How shall I link such sun-cast symmetry
With the torn troubled form I know as thine,
That profile, placid as a brow divine, .
With continents of moil and misery ?

And can immense Mortality but throw
So small a shade, and Heaven's high human scheme
Be hemmed within the coasts yon arc implies ?
Is such the stellar gauge of earthly show,
Nation at war with nation, brains that teem,
Heroes, and women fairer than the skies ?

In form it is an almost perfect Miltonic sonnet, with an unorthodox shift in the thought at the fifth line. The immense
superiority of the Italian unrhymed ending is particularly apparent. It does not follow Milton or anyone else in any other
respect, but is pure Hardy. The thought is expressed with such
brilliant—as it were lunar—clearness that comment would only
be impertinent, but the poem invites comparison with two other

well-known sonnets wherein philosophic deductions are drawn
from nocturnal phenomena—Blanco White's *Night*, and Meredith's *Lucifer in Starlight*.   White's poem is easily the most perfect sonnet, from the point of view of form, as Meredith's is easily
the worst : Hardy's comparative inferiority in this respect lies
mainly in his inclusion of two distinct and separate ideas.   In
value of content, the two more modern poems leave the earlier
one far behind ; for profundity of insight and imaginative splendour of vision there is little to choose between Meredith and
Hardy—each of the two conceptions is characteristic of the writer.
In precision of term and nobility of poetic diction, Hardy's
sonnet undoubtedly bears the palm, and thus, all things considered, may be regarded as the greatest sonnet of the three.

Panthera is Hardy's nearest approach to a long poem.   The
story has a touch of epic, and is told with consummate art, in the
matter both of arrangement and of actual narration, which latter
exhibits a rare dramatic conciseness.   The events—of the crucifixion of Christ, and of his supposed parentage in a Roman
officer—are skilfully kept on a casual, unsignificant level.   Panthera, the Roman officer in question, is made to tell the story as
a warning to a younger colleague not to go getting illegitimate
children—he had seen *his* son die as a criminal :

> Fors Fortuna !   He who goes fathering
> Gives frightful hostages to hazardry !

The blank verse is admirable—far better than anything else
Hardy has done in this metre, its qualities being shared by the
rhymed portions of the poem.

The Phantom Horsewoman is the pinnacle of Hardy's love-
poetry, because here for once feeling is fused by æsthetic passion
to utter perfection of form.   The finely-original stanza-form is
made the vehicle for successive waves of rhythmic beauty and
passion.   Each stanza opens with a long line that holds out a
strange ' ghostly ' suggestion which, after a pause, runs swiftly
but rhythmically through seven short lines to another long one,
where the thought is held up again while we are left wondering
and recovering from the rhythmic sweep.   This goes on for three
stanzas, at the end of which the momentum leaps over, like an

electric spark, to the climax of the poem in the first words of the fourth stanza—" A ghost-girl-rider ". This is what we have been waiting for, what the heart has imaginatively felt coming ; and now, without pause or relaxing of tension, that poetic height is maintained through the last stanza, ending in the tranquil beauty of the loveliest of all Hardy's lines :

> A ghost-girl-rider. And tho', toil-tried,
>   He withers daily,
>   Time touches her not,
>   But she still rides gaily
>   In his rapt thought
>   On that shagged and shaly
>   Atlantic spot,
>   And as when first eyed
> Draws rein and sings to the swing of the tide.

At the Word ' Farewell ' is not stately among the 1913 poems, but is obviously based on a remotely early personal experience. It differs essentially from the poem last discussed, in that rhythmic ' form ' plays practically no part in the effect achieved. It hovers in the first stanza and the first two lines of the second, but is frightened off by the jolting line, " As of chances the chance furthermost ", and never returns. Yet the effect is parallel, and almost as profound. It is brought about by that special power of Hardy, cold precision of statement risen to inspiration. A poetic experience delineated with utter faithfulness must result in a great poem.

The Blinded Bird has a paradoxical greatness : it presents the spectacle of a mighty compassion evoked by a minute subject. Its concluding stanza deserves to be put with Blake's *Auguries*. Literal people, unimaginative people, people who have not grasped the unity of nature or the quality of the reactions of a great mind, have been known to express impatience with the assertion,—

> A robin red-breast in a cage
> Puts all heaven in a rage ;

and such dull people will doubtless be unaware of the monumental truth and beauty of Hardy's last stanza :

Who hath charity ?   This bird.
Who suffereth long and is kind,
Is not provoked, though blind,
And alive ensepulchred ?
Who hopeth, endureth all things ?
Who thinketh no evil, but sings ?
Who is divine ?   This bird.

A Procession of Dead Days is another love-poem, taking the form
of a backward survey of the poet's life, of the days, now dead,
that stood out like fire in the history of his love : the day that
sent him first down to the " spot strange and gray " where She
lived, the first meeting, the first kiss, the betrothal, the marriage,
her illness, and her death.   It is full of felicitous phrases.   Of
the first two magic ' days '—

Look at me, Day, and then pass on,
But come again : yes, come anon !

Adieu, O ghost-day of delight ;
But come and grace my dying sight.

The " day that brought the kiss "

lent new colour to the land,
And all the boy within me manned.

Then there was the " rainbow sign " of the promise, and the
" meteor act " of the marriage, leaving in its queue " a train of
sparks my life-time through ".   And the iron rod of the next
' day ', and the averted phantom-face of the last ' day ' with his
silent creep :

I shall not soon forget that day,
And what his third hour took away !

It is a unique and marvellous poem, with its intense, still expression of emotion remembered in anything but tranquillity.

In view of the fame of the dog Wessex, it is surprising that
Hardy's lament for his death, though most touching and beautiful,
lacks the touch of sublimity which the *Last Words to a Dumb
Friend*, addressed to a cat, undoubtedly possess.   The ineffable
tenderness of the first three stanzas is matched by the imaginative

power of the next two ; and the *L'Allegro* measure is perfectly handled and sustained. There are charming pictures of the white cat's personality—his wistful gaze, " while you humoured our queer ways ", his morning call up the stairs, " foot suspended in its fall "—

> Till your way you chose to wend
> Yonder, to your tragic end.

Better, says the poet, try to forget him—

> Selfishly escape distress
> By contrived forgetfulness
> Than preserve his prints to make
> Every morn and eve an ache.

So—most poignantly—

> From the chair whereon he sat
> Sweep his fur, nor wince thereat ;
> Rake his little pathways out
> Mid the bushes roundabout. . . .

Then feeling gets through to imagination. Strange, he says, that this speechless thing, our timid pensioner, should—

> By the merely taking hence
> Of his insignificance—
> Loom as largened to the sense,
> Shape a part, above man's will,
> Of the Imperturbable.

His bereaved owners must still retain the " mean estate by him forsaken ", but—

> this home, which scarcely took
> Impress from his little look,
> By his faring to the Dim
> Grows all eloquent of him.

So does a poet show us how we may " see a world in a grain of sand ".

Of all Hardy's satiric poems the greatest is the gentlest. There is no trace of bitterness in his treatment of *A Leader of Fashion*, yet, in a series of quiet statements, he shows her devoid of all reality. " Never has she known the way a robin will skip and come " ; she has not seen the dawn break on her as she walked, nor heard the sparrows rustling overhead at dusk,—

> Nor has she watched
> Amid a stormy eve's turmoil
> The pipkin slowly come to boil
> In readiness for one at toil ;

she has never waited for help to come to a dying man,—

> Nor has she ever
> Held the loved lost one on her arm,
> Attired with care his straightened form
> As if he were alive and warm.

It touches firmly, unerringly on those nodal points where experience meets truth, and in Hardy's special epigrammatic kind its form is perfect.

Finally, that astonishing *Drinking Song* from *Winter Words*. The most astonishing thing about it is that it is a real drinking song : it has no line that could not be sung without difficulty ; the whole thing goes with a grand swing ; the chorus is a good rolling one. And the subject-matter is worthy of the author ! One had heard (perhaps incorrectly) that the Book of Genesis had been turned into limericks, but to find the history of free-thought set as a student's song was beyond one's hopes. For complete success it needs, of course, a pit of philosophers—an audience of scientists—a college smoker. But there is no descent —no ' singing-down ' to the occasion : the wording of the song never loses touch with the demands of literary quality. It goes forward with a sort of serious good humour, and makes no pre-tensions to be uproarious, like its lusty progenitor, *The Grand Darwinian Theory*. Moreover, it ends on a solid moral note, neatly showing that a negative philosophy can go with a positive ethical code. For eight verses the chorus having rung out—

> Fill full your cups : feel no distress ;
> 'Tis only one great thought the less !

after the ninth and last it enlarges itself :

> Fill full your cups : feel no distress
> At all our great thoughts shrinking less :
> We'll do a good deed nevertheless !

This selection of poems is obviously a personal one, and might be extended by the addition of a number of others already mentioned, that almost, if not quite, reach the level of some of those in the first choice—*He Abjures Love*, *An August Midnight*, *In Time of ' the Breaking of Nations '*, *The Darkling Thrush*, *Under the Waterfall*, *Afterwards*,—and perhaps *In Front of the Landscape*, *Valenciennes*, and *A Tramp-woman's Tragedy*. Here is a round score of poems that any poet would be proud to have written, and all so strongly individual that none but Hardy could have written them.

§ 10

Those who turn to Hardy's poetry for a final and explicit enunciation of his philosophy will find ample materials for an answer to their question. We are not permitted to say they will find the answer itself, for Hardy never ceased to protest that he had no desire to propound a final solution to the great riddle. But then, who has ? In the preface to *The Dynasts* he issues a warning that had already become stereotyped, that the doctrines of the Intelligences " are but tentative, and are advanced with little eye to a systematised philosophy ". In the preface to *Poems of the Past and the Present* he says " the road to a true philosophy of life seems to lie in humbly recording diverse readings of its phenomena ". Elsewhere he maintains that his ' philosophy ', especially that discoverable in the poetry, is not intended as consistent or coherent, being made up of impressions of the moment, not of convictions or arguments. Such disclaimers are appended by implication to every ' philosophy ' emanating from a person over the age of eighteen and not a professional philosopher. We must, I think, be allowed to infer from impressions and opinions constantly and (in fact) consistently voiced something of the mind and outlook behind them. It is true, as Hardy said, that *The Dynasts*, like *Paradise Lost*, proves nothing, but *Paradise Lost* provides us with a tolerably accurate picture of Milton's religious position.

One difficulty arises. The poems were not published in the order in which they were written. All the later books contain many poems, dated and undated, written at earlier periods. Hence there is no possibility of tracing any progress in the poet's thought. All we can do is to note that poems expressing what appears to be the characteristic Hardy view-point are considerably rarer in the last four volumes than in the first four, while those few poems which, as we shall see, indicate the beginnings of an advance to a new position occur impartially from *Past and Present* to *Winter Words*.

The indictment of the order of the universe, begun indirectly in the novels, continued more systematically in *The Dynasts*, becomes, when distilled and concentrated in short poems written with that steely precision of which Hardy was a master, a thing of most effective and damaging potency. One of Hardy's reasons for preferring verse was that in it one can " say things (about God, etc.) without upsetting people ". By this he no doubt meant that the few people who read poetry are generally of the kind that is not easily upset. Yet some readers of poetry—readers perhaps for duty's sake—discovered an inadequate equanimity, for it was probably the pointed bitterness of some of the poems that led to condescending remarks being passed on " Hardy's special form of mental dyspepsia ". I shall be content to diagnose the complaint as a rather pronounced but not incurable astigmatism (caused perhaps by those faulty glasses that we found him wearing in a previous chapter).

The indictment has its basis and origin in the poet's conception of life as generally unsatisfactory, expressed in a number of poems to which we have already given some attention. Three other groups of poems offer explanations, increasingly complex, of the state of affairs thus indicated : in the first, ' Nature ' is arraigned as responsible ; in the second the indictment is transferred to ' God ' ; the ultimate charge is thrown upon an impersonal all-comprehending ' It '.

The first stanza of *To Life* is a succinct statement of outlook :

> O Life with the sad seared face,
>   I weary of seeing thee,
> And thy draggled cloak, and thy hobbling pace,
>   And thy too-forced pleasantry !

To one who should reproachfully suggest " There's solace everywhere ", Hardy replies with the allegory of the dismal moor,
with its eternal gloom, and the ray-lit clouds that swiftly fade into
night.   The process of making the complete pessimist is shown
in *The Dead Man Walking* :

> A troubadour-youth I rambled
>   With Life for lyre,
> The beats of being raging
>   In me like fire ;

but he begins to perceive " the goal of men " ; his friends die ;
his Love turns against him : and the successive shocks change
him to

> . . . the corpse thing
> I am to-day.

In *I Said to Love*—a piece of ebon melancholy marvellously
wrought—he accuses the age of joyless disillusion : Love was
once a bright boy, Love is now neither young nor fair, but goes
armed with " iron daggers of distress " ; Love shall be cast out—
and if this means extinction for man, the poet accepts extinction :

> " *Mankind shall cease.*—So let it be,"
> I said to Love.

In the later poem, again most deftly turned, *Before Life and
After*, he even yearns for such negation of life—

> Ere nescience shall be reaffirmed,
> How long, how long !

He desires personal unconsciousness—could be happy if he had
no more ' life ' than a tablet on a wall.   And the result of such
thought is shown in the icy apathy of *De Profundis*—

> Black is night's cope ;
> But death will not appal
> One who, past doubtings all,
> Waits in unhope.

Henley, with a difference ! Only does his appreciative sense of that part of life which is love sometimes make him admit that life may be worthy of man's living after all.

Life being thus bleakly delineated, blame for the state of affairs can be thrown upon ' Nature ' in nothing more than an oblique and figurative sense ; and it is only in a few poems in the *Past and Present* volume that Hardy does this. Mother Nature mourns (if she were less stupid she would rejoice) that Man, whom she had created, in a moment of " naughtiness ", for subtler praise, had instead turned her critic. Resentfully, but in beautiful verse, she declares she will go back to the earlier, less censorious forms of life :

> No more such ! . . . My species are dwindling
> My forests grow barren,
> My popinjays fail from their tappings,
> My larks from their strain.

> My leopardine beauties are rarer,
> My tusky ones vanish,
> My children have aped mine own slaughters
> To quicken my wane.

The Lacking Sense goes further, explaining that Mother Nature, though deft of finger and well-intentioned, is yet blind, and so evermore " wounds where she loves ". This monstrous vivid humanising of Nature is completed, rather horribly, in *Doom and She*, which represents the world as begotten by Fate, devoid of feeling, upon Nature, devoid of sight : she, mild, pitiful, helplessly creative—he, seeing all, but indifferent to results.

This is, after all, only an indirect continuation of the indictment of life. Nor does the next stage carry us much further, since it is designed only to show the consequences of orthodoxy. Thus in a mood of bitter satire, the poem *God-Forgotten :* God is reminded of the existence of Earth, and of its sufferings ; racking his brain, he recalls it to mind—' I thought it was dead long ago ; I lost interest in it from the first. However, now you draw my attention to its state, it shall be put right immediately, of course.' Similarly, *The Bedridden Peasant* reasons that God cannot know, or he would not permit : hence, praise him for the

mercies he would show if he but knew. And the next poem
shows God, after the world is really dead, grieving at the memory
of all the ancient wrongs it endured, and repenting that he had
ever created it. Another tries pointedly to ' educate God ' into
seeing the cruelty of his ways. In *A Dream Question*, God
impatiently dismisses the suggestion that he cares about the
criticism of his creatures ; but in *New Year's Eve*, he confesses
his inability to explain his logicless labours, and waxes querulous
over the severe ethic tests imposed by man. (It is noteworthy
that this calculated satire follows on the lovely opening stanza :

> " I have finished another year," said God,
>   " In grey, green, white and brown ;
> I have strewn the leaf upon the sod,
> Sealed up the worm within the clod,
>   And let the last sun down.")

And there are others more devastatingly bitter. The satire in
these poems is two-edged : the foremost edge is doubtless intended for those whose conception of the government of the universe is represented by the word ' God ' ; but the other is left
keen for that ' God ' himself, should he by any chance exist.
A Plaint to Man makes God himself recommend that anthropo-
morphism should be finally abandoned, and man's needs based
on his own best qualities alone.

The use of the word ' God ' by anyone but a Theist is dangerous, and invariably leads to misunderstanding. It led in Hardy's
case to Mr. Alfred Noyes charging him with having presented
God as an imbecile jester. Hardy replied that this was absurd,
because the Cause of Things (elsewhere he said this was the only
reasonable meaning of ' God ' nowadays, so that no modern
thinker could be an atheist) was *un*-moral, above love and hate,
knowing neither good nor evil. (When Mr. Noyes suggested
that this ' Cause of Things ' must be at least equal to the things
caused, Hardy made the odd but interesting retort that " the
assumption that intelligent beings arose from the combination
of unintelligent forces is sufficiently probable for imaginative
writing ".) And indeed behind all Hardy's thought on the
question of the Great Original one feels the presence of something vaster than ' Nature ', more impersonal than ' God '. In

The Subalterns, affliction, sickness and death are shown to be mere passive instruments in the hand of a power which is not named, but is clearly not ' God ' or ' Nature ' ; *The Wind Blew Words* gives a vaguely-terrifying impression of a pathetic " Me " in " huge distress " at the self-slaughter of natural laws ; and in *Nature's Questioning* it is asked whether what we see is the outcome of some Vast Imbecility, an Automaton, dying Godhead, or some High Plan passing over our heads. No answerer I, says Hardy. Yet he ever implies a cosmic It, which receives full expression in *The Dynasts*. In the later poem *An Inquiry*, ' It ' is, as ever, forethoughtless, and replies to the question why death had been given such power over life that the act was simply meaningless, without intent.

The Hardian metaphysic, then, accounts for the universe by presupposing a Prime Cause which is both transcendent and immanent. It is directive but not active : it uses as its active force the power that exists in the world of matter and energy ; it likewise controls, and causes, the activities of man. It is omniscient, for the whole of the future is known, and therefore necessitated ; at all events the future, whether known or not, exists ; and this future, together with the present and the past, forms a pattern that is being woven for its own sake, and bears no relation to the wants or welfare of the elements, human and other, of which it is composed. The Prime Cause has therefore an æsthetic faculty, and presumably an intellectual one, but has no moral faculty at all. It admits itself incapable of attaching any meaning to the terms right and wrong, and is indifferent to, because unaware of, the sufferings and happiness of the sentient beings it has indirectly created. This studied, at times even pointed, indifference gives its relations with human-kind an appearance of malignity ; the appearance is emphatically said to be an illusion, but the illusion is strengthened by the fact that the consequences of the Circumstantial Artistry to humanity are —according to the propounder of the metaphysic—much more unpleasant than pleasant : if the direction were motived by nothing but strict neutrality there would be, by the law of averages, a balance of good and bad among the results. However, the absence of malignity, as of benevolence, is fundamental, for the Cause is even unconscious, does not know what it is doing.

Sometimes its doings turn out badly for itself, causing it annoyance (it does know that degree of feeling !)—as when it made the mistake of giving man a critical mind. It is incapable of correcting the mistakes, and—if we put this with the fact that the whole pattern of eternity exists at once, though the Prime Cause is aware of, or concerned with, only that part immediately under its operation—we arrive at the conclusion that the Cause is the slave of the Pattern, which is the real ruler of things. Be that as it may, the Cause is growing conscious, with consequences unpredicted. In any case, before the Creator attains consciousness, consciousness may have departed from the Creation.

This scheme of things, this philosophy—amateur no doubt but not less interesting and valuable on that account—belongs to the phase of thought which I have called transitional. Though he had abandoned the conception of a personal and moral ' Cause of Things ', Hardy never acquired the impersonal attitude towards that Cause which should result from the abandonment. He could not quite stop resenting the blows of fate as if they were real blows. The poem called *The Blow*—the most concentrated expression of bitter resentment of all the poems—hopes that the foul stroke that has been dealt them came from no one of their own kind—

> Since it would augur works and ways
> Below the lowest that man assays
> To have hurled that stone
> Into the sunshine of our days ;

it recognises that the blow is the work of " the Inscrutable, the Hid ", " the Immanent Doer That doth not know ", and hopes It may repent its wickedness " in some age unguessed of us ". This is not the way one speaks and feels about an impersonal, unconscious Absolute. In the poem called *Hap* he wishes the cruelty of life *could* be attributed to a vengeful God instead of what he knows to be the cause, " Crass Casualty " (the phrase, and others like it, suggests that Hardy was a true Victorian in being a little too much under the influence of Darwinism) ; and it is plain that he does find it necessary to have some one or something on which to vent the satiric fury that flames out of his hurt pity.

The transitional stage in the progress of thought is, of course, a necessary one, but it is a little surprising that Hardy never fully got out of it into the next stage, that of conceiving the universe—life as we know it—as the present state of the Cause of Things itself, an elementary state, very incomplete, and therefore full of imperfections which are the ills of life ; so that life signifies not " a thwarted purposing " but an as yet unfulfilled purposing, the direction of which can be perceived to be upwards if the whole record of life be regarded, enabling us to have faith that the short length that lies under our immediate gaze, and appears to be going precipitously downhill, is in reality sharing in the general upward movement.   It is queer that Hardy seems to have considered himself a monist, to judge by the poem *Our Old Friend Dualism* :

> All hail to him, the Protean !   A tough old chap is he :
> Spinoza and the Monists cannot make him cease to be.
> We pound him with our " Truth, Sir, please ! " and quite appear
>   to still him :
> He laughs ; holds Bergson up, and James ; and swears we cannot
>   kill him.
> We argue them pragmatic cheats.   " Aye ", says he, " They're
>   deceiving :
> But I must live ; for flamens plead I am all that's worth
>   believing ! "

and he once said, " I would be a Bergsonian if I could ".   But surely this ' It ', this Doer, this Will implies dualism, a dualism symbolised in *Doom and She*, and by the blind giant of another poem, led by a mischievous dwarf—" the sorriest of pantomimes ".

We have seen, in *The Dynasts*, that Hardy did as a matter of fact take a step forward out of the difficulties involved in the conception of an evil-doing but not evil-intentioned, because unconscious, Will.   The ' hope ' expressed at the end of *The Dynasts* was, however, not only discounted beforehand by the passionless insight of the Spirit of the Years, but was a thing of no strong growth, for it was destroyed by the outbreak of the Great War.   Hardy said he would probably not have ended *The Dynasts* as he did had he foreseen that event.   He said the war gave the *coup de grâce* to any idea he may have entertained of a fundamental ultimate Wisdom at the back of things.   This, though a natural enough feeling that many of us shared, was parochial : even the Great War is an unnoticeable bump on the long road of evolution. But the advance in thought is more clearly marked in the Poems, and was not withdrawn, for it is found in poems published long after the war as well as in others published before it.

The last poem of the *Past and Present* volume suggests that with " ripening rule " of the " Willer masked and dumb ", " listless effort tends to grow percipient . . . and with percipience mends " ; he sees here and there a wrong getting righted : " whereat I would raise my voice in song ". This is going a long way for Hardy. In that remarkable poem, *God's Funeral*, written in the year immediately following *The Dynasts*, he says that in the blackness of the night occasioned by the death of God he saw, or seemed to see, " a pale yet positive gleam low down behind "— a small light, swelling somewhat, on the horizon. But he gives no indication as to the nature of the new light. In two poems that stand side by side in *Human Shows* he makes the dead creeds cry : " Out of us cometh an heir, that shall disclose new promise ", and that shall " make tolerable to sentient seers The melancholy marching of the years " ; and he makes a Voice declare that " the Great Adjustment is taking place " :

> " I set thick darkness over you,
> And fogged you all your years therein ;
>   At last I uncloud your view,
> Which I am weary of holding in.
>
> " Men have not heard, men have not seen
> Since the beginning of the world
>   What earth and heaven mean ;
> But now their curtains shall be furled."

All this is very general, after the first poem quoted, and is rendered largely abortive by *A Philosophical Fantasy*, definitely dated " 1920 and 1926 ", from *Winter Words*, wherein ' It ', ' the Causer ', speaks of

> that purposeless propension
> Which is mine, and not intention,
> Along lines of least resistance,
> Or, in brief, unsensed persistence.

And yet not quite abortive, for to this self-description there are appended (earlier in the poem) the words—

> Which state, though far from ending,
> May nevertheless be mending.

Thus, just as Hardy's pessimism is softened, ever so slightly, by the clamant good he found in love, so his frozen philosophy thaws into life at this peep-hole of vision. That he knew it had done so is evident from the claim of originality for the conception quoted with reference to *The Dynasts*. He put the claim forward again—" That the Unconscious Will of the Universe is growing aware of itself I believe I may claim as my own idea solely ". As to that, it may be suggested, as uncontroversially as possible, that the conception is to be found in the writings of more than one Lamarckian long before 1900—is indeed inherent in Lamarckism itself. The thing that matters is that Hardy's thought did take this minute but perceptible step in the direction of a live Creative Evolution.

It is of some interest that a similar progress (or perhaps merely disparity) is discernible in his references to the figures of Christian theology. In *Panthera*, and in *The Wood Fire* (blazing cheerfully, in a yard near Calvary, of logs sawn from the cross Jesus died on), we see a determination to treat the person and death of Christ with a commonplaceness that betrays not only the sceptic but the hostile sceptic. *In the Servants' Quarters* the incident of Peter's denial is transcribed in utterly commonplace terms, certainly, but yet with a certain sympathy (which may be just sympathy for a fellow-man in an awkward corner). *Thoughts at Midnight* concludes with an unusual lapse into an orthodox form of invocation—

> God, look he on you,
> Have mercy upon you !

More positive is *The Oxen*, with its pleasant picture of the folk round the fire on Christmas Eve, believing that at twelve o'clock the cattle in the byre fall on their knees in worship, and the poet " hoping it might be so ". That " hoping " reminds one of a very early poem, *The Impercipient*, where the poet, at a Cathedral

service, feels himself apart from the " bright believing band ",
but resents

> the charge that blessed things
> I'd leifer not have be.
> O, doth a bird deprived of wings
> Go earth-bound wilfully ?

He is, and laments that he is, blind and deaf to what they see
and hear ; his heart knows not the ease which they know. The
feeling is a strange one for so bold a spirit : the half-way position
is again indicated. A later poem, *In St. Paul's a While Ago*,
gives a very friendly picture of the second founder (or is it arch-
corrupter ?) of the Christian Church. And there is an important " Apology " prefixed to *Late Lyrics*, in which Hardy, having
first protested against the " disallowance of ' obstinate question-
ings ' and ' blank misgivings ' ", goes on to express his desire to
see " an alliance between religion, which must be retained unless
the world is to perish, and rationality . . . by means of the inter-
fusing effect of poetry " ; he proposes as a first agreed step that
" pain to all upon (the globe), tongued or dumb, shall be kept
down to a minimum ". All of which is in the highest degree
excellent, and completes the impression of one who was in no
true sense irreligious.

§ 11

From the point of view of literary value—and no other value
is ultimately worth considering in literature—it is probable that
no one of the eight volumes of Hardy's poetry is worth a single
chapter from one of his major novels. Nevertheless we have to
reckon with the fact that Hardy preferred his poetry to his prose.
He was a poet by nature, a novelist by genius. He found his
genius late, but he wrote (and read) poetry from the beginning.
He liked *Marmion* better than any of the Waverley novels, and
wished Scott had stuck to verse ! He felt he was nearer to life
in his poetry, and one of the things that make his novels so great
is that in them he tried to keep as close to poetry, that is, to life,
as possible. But in verse alone did he feel able to give concise
expression to that quint-essential experience that life was to him.

In writing verse he felt, he said, more " uninfluenced "—not interfered with or limited in scope by external pressure such as that of public opinion. He took serious objection to an American critic who called him " a realistic novelist with a grim determination to go down to posterity wearing the laurels of a poet ", and though the ' grim determination ' misses the mark, since Hardy was the kind of poet, if ever there was one, who sang because he must, Hardy did say, at the age of eighty-six, that his only ambition was to have some poem or poems included in a good anthology such as the Golden Treasury. This by no means modest ambition, which numerous editors have done their provisional best to see accomplished, was a worthy one ; yet only his lack of humour can have caused Hardy to see his poetry as greater than his prose, and certainly it was this that made him take criticism of his novels so badly that he gave up novel-writing at the height of his power. (A well-known contrarious critic has been known to deny that this was why the novels stopped, and there were doubtless other reasons, but we have Hardy's own words in the preface to the 1912 edition of *Jude the Obscure* that the reception given to *Jude* " completely cured him of further interest in novel-writing ".) However, wisely or not, with or without self-knowledge, Hardy felt his verse to be " the most individual part of (his) literary fruitage ".

Individual it certainly is. It is very Hardy. The almost complete absence of ' poetic diction ' helped here : with him (as, of course, not with a greater poet) poetic diction might have veiled somewhat of that utter sincerity, naked truth, which is the heart of his feeling and the essence of his poetry. What he felt he spoke, in verse ; and he felt all the time. He felt and thought mainly about the world of everyday life. His poetry keeps close to the surface of things, where most of us live ; it is well that we should be shown that, as Elizabeth Browning said, " Earth's crammed with heaven, and every bush and tree afire with God "— and not only bushes and trees but lesser things like cats and houses and prostitutes. Reading Shakespeare or Wordsworth or Shelley or de la Mare, one is lifted into a higher and truer world, the world of the poet's imagination, the world of poetry : one is oneself a poet. Reading Hardy one does not feel a poet : one feels—what a marvellous thing life is : how endlessly interesting is life, how incredibly beautiful and sad the world. For Hardy's poetry could be separated into two almost clean-cut and nearly equal divisions. The one would contain all the cruelty, the disillusion, the revolt ; the other would contain nothing that was not lovely and tender and true. And it seems likely to me that it is by this second half of his poetry that Hardy the poet will live.

INDEX

(*Novels, characters* in the novels, and individual *poems* will be found grouped under those headings.

Women and girls are given generally under their Christian names.

Very brief references to novels, characters and poems are not indexed.)